ABROAD

IN

AMERICA

ABROAD IN AMERICA

LITERARY DISCOVERERS OF THE
NEW WORLD FROM THE PAST
500 YEARS

EDITED BY ROBERT BLOW

Continuum · New York

1990

The Continuum Publishing Company
370 Lexington Avenue
New York, NY 10017

Copyright © 1989 by Robert Blow

First published in Great Britain by Lennard Publishing 1989

Printed in Great Britain

Library of Congress Cataloging-in-Publication Data

Abroad in America: literary discoverers of the New World from the
    past 500 years/edited by Robert Blow.
        p.   cm.
    ISBN 0-8264-0464-2
    1. United States—Description and travel.   2. United States—
Literary collections.   3. Travelers—United States—History.
I. Blow, Robert.
E161.A27   1990
973—dc20   89-28447
                                                                CIP

Contents

CONTENTS

CONTENTS

Introduction

America is the 'New World'. It is the New World even, and especially, to Americans themselves. The huge majority of Americans can trace their ancestry back – if not in much detail – to a particular country or district of the Old World. All Americans, apart from the Red Indians, know that five hundred years ago their ancestors were not in America.

No one who has thought, however briefly, about the relations between Europe and America can fail to be aware that they do not rest upon an equality. On both sides of the Atlantic the assumption is made, and instinctively felt, that America is 'discovered' territory. Even Red Indians ruefully accept this truth. But no European thinks the same of Europe. To him Europe has been in mind as long as history.

This prejudice is not, I think, the product of a Eurocentric view of the world. Africa and Asia are similarly immemorial presences in the European view. But America is the 'New World': it is the offspring of Europe. Europe discovered it, and Europe fashioned it. The children of Africa, who have added yet another ingredient to the whole boiling, are also Old World arrivals. Everything of America, except its geology and most of its landscape and a few of its people, is foreign implant. America is conquered territory.

In saying that the personality of America ultimately derives from Europe and Africa, I do not wish to deny the existence of a distinct American patriotism. America has in the twentieth century achieved a unique, exuberant identity. Any educated Englishman knows how much he owes to the Mediterranean countries in the formation of his culture. Those features of English life which we think of as uniquely English are often of very recent and dubious origin. The United States have likewise absorbed a bewildering variety of elements and moulded them into a coherent shape. No longer do visiting Europeans condemn America as a shoddy reproduction of themselves, as they did in the early nineteenth century: they evaluate it on its own terms. Americans clearly resented the old terms of reference by which European travellers judged them. Using the comparative method, travellers, the English in particular, wandered about the place with an impermeable sense of superiority, and complained. The English, of course, were still smarting from their defeat in the War of Independence, and they belittled the United States to compensate for it. After all, if America, were that low-grade, it was no great loss. The question of slavery added moral to cultural superiority. One senses that in the 1830s the United States had a position in world opinion somewhat akin to South Africa's today. Only after the Civil War, when slavery was abolished, did foreign attitudes to America become more complex. Robert Louis Stevenson in *Across the Plains* rehearsed the fashionable prejudices and refuted them. In his lecture-tour of 1882 Oscar Wilde stressed America's latent cultural potential and suggested that the way forward was not by imitation of the Old World but by harnessing the various indigenous elements. America's art should follow Whitman and celebrate its multitudes.

The cultural expansion of the late nineteenth century, and America's growing economic power, should have dispelled any suspicions that it was second-rate. Increasingly, though, America has come to be a place which foreign artists have visited simply to make money. Apart from continuing as a refuge for exiles, the United States has reverted, in European eyes, to its early role as a rich land for exploitation.

As the reader will see from the dust-jacket of this book, the New York skyline between the wars was one of the modern wonders of the world. No traveller who saw it failed to mention it. At night it looked like a fairground but the vulgarity was part of the attraction. Now this scene has almost been eliminated. Commerce triumphs. Manhattan cannot spread wider, so it must go higher. The taller the buildings the more money is made. Glass-plated stumps, devoid of decoration, planted regardless of space or site, everywhere fill the scene with hideous uniformity.

As late as the 1880s more sensitive Americans were beginning to see their own land as a place unfit for artists to live in. Henry James and James Whistler led the exodus. Eliot, Pound, Hemingway, Fitzgerald followed. The only way they could work was to get out. Henry James remarked on his dissatisfaction with America from the novelist's point of view in his biography of Hawthorne.

Old is not necessarily better. There are Americans who rejoice – most perhaps – in being bigger, livelier, and more modern. And there are Europeans who rejoice with them. But whatever is felt, all relations between Europe and America are spiced by judgements of superiority and inferiority on both sides; and the more ambiguous the foreign traveller in the United States is about his hosts, the greater the subtlety and discrimination of the writing.

On beginning work on this anthology I was immediately struck by how much material there was to choose from. I would have liked originally to have included some extracts of writers on America who have never been there, who have, as it were, gazed at the place through a telescope. But such are outside the scope of this book. My title limits me to those who have actually been there. This is in some ways a pity. A good reason for not wanting to go to a place can tell us as much about it as a first-hand description. Ruskin, for example, received many invitations to lecture in the United States but said that he could not endure living in a country even for three months that did not contain any castles.

I must confess that I, too, have never been to America. This does not seem to me to be a disadvantage in an anthologist. After all, the most famous anthology of all, *Palgrave's Golden Treasury*, was compiled by a man who never wrote a memorable line of poetry in his life. It is not always true that travel broadens the mind. I have a far more open mind about America than I would have done if I had been there. Often it is better to stay away. Some of the early nineteenth century English travel books about the United States simply fail to conjure up a spirit of place. Their writers have approached their subject, not with sympathetic curiosity, but with impenetrable smugness. They cannot view with detachment the place on its own merits but only as a low-grade imitation of what they have left behind. The bay of New York, which Mrs Trollope concedes to be one of the most beautiful sights she has ever seen, is allowed its primacy over all other bays with the rider that Mrs Trollope has never been to Naples. And Dickens's contorted whimsies, so apt for teasing out the hidden courtyards and crooked passage-ways of the City of London, seem inadequate to representing America's larger, less devious landscape.

Yet, despite their considerable limitations, Dickens's *American Notes* and Frances Trollope's *Domestic Manners of the Americans* oblige inclusion. I have not sought to avoid the obvious. Columbus's diaries: the Pilgrim Fathers: Stevenson's *Across the Plains*. Whether one likes these pieces or not – and Stevenson's I do very much – they earn their place because of their historical significance. Similarly I wanted to include representative examples of a particular type of traveller. I had to have at least one Jesuit missionary, Elizabethan sea-dog, a G.I. bride, and so on. Without them the selection would have been intolerably literary. Authentic impressions can survive an unsophisticated style; and all too often artful elegance works against vivid reportage. Ideally one hopes for a combination of both – Stevenson seems to me a model in this respect – but such talent is rare. I have, therefore, presumed that my readers want to be informed as much as entertained, and will want to find out something from the book about the history and topography of America and the manners of its peoples, as observed by foreigners, and the action of America and Americans upon the traveller himself.

Outside the classic territory the potential yield is enormous. There is material enough to make six or seven alternative anthologies all entirely different. Some rules of selection were, therefore, necessary.

From the start poetry, fiction, and drama were outside my brief.

I then limited my travellers to the mainland United States. So no Cossacks in Alaska, or Australian beach-bums in Honolulu. (I broke this rule in the cases of Columbus and Cabot for reasons too obvious to explain).

My third rule was more difficult. I was limited to 'foreigners': those 'abroad'. Now what exactly constitutes a foreigner? When Evelyn Waugh was travelling on the Pacific Railway he remarked to the Latin-looking waiter who was serving dinner, 'I am a foreigner here.' And the waiter said, 'We are all foreigners here.' This remark so impressed Waugh that he used the theme in the novel he wrote out of his American journey, *The Loved One*. 'There is no such thing as an American,' he explained. 'They are all exiles uprooted, transplanted and doomed to sterility.' However, the successful hero of *The Loved One* is one of the 'European raiders who come for the spoils and if they are lucky make for home with them.'

Certainly there have been many Americans who made no secret of feeling ill at ease in their native land. Few, however, went to the extent of renouncing their citizenship. T. S. Eliot became a subject of the British Crown at the time when he was received into the Church of England; both acts were a definite rejection of his Unitarian St Louis upbringing. Henry James's renunciation, made right at the end of his life, after he had lived forty years in England, was rather a political gesture: as a protest against the U.S. administration's pusillanimous response to the sinking of the *Lusitania* and as a gesture of solidarity with the English side in the Great War.

It was tempting to include both James and Eliot in this anthology, particu-larly James, who revisited America in 1904 after a long absence and wrote a book about it. The event of James's return is caught in a caricature by

Max Beerbohm. The expatriate is drawn confronted by a crowd of locals, including a negro boy dancing a cakewalk in celebration of his arrival and singing, 'We wants yer mighty badly – Yas, we *doo*!' Turning away from them we see James, his eyes shut, his face horrified by the noise, lifting a deprecating hand, and thinking (in an exquisite parody of his later style), '. . . So that in fine, let, without further beating about the bush, me make to myself amazed acknowledgement that, but for the certificate of birth which I have – so quite indubitably – *on* me, I might, in regarding, and, as it were, overseeing, *à l'oeil de voyagur*, these dear good people, find hard to swallow, or even to take by subconscious injection, the great idea that I am - oh, ever so indigenously! – one of them . . .'

But the temptation had to be resisted. Such a dispensation could get out of hand. There are in the United States second and third generation descendants of immigrants who feel a considerable attachment to the land of their parents' and grandparents' origin. To this observer at least many American Jews have during elections the foreign policy of Israel as much in their mind as the well-being of the United States. The romantic loyalty of Irish-Americans to Ireland is equally notorious. But though they do not often realize it their native spirit has been powerfully transformed by the customs of their adopted land. Irish-Americans, used to the lavish celebrations of St Patrick's Day in Boston or New York, visiting Dublin for the same event are appalled by the poverty of the display. I do not disparage these divided loyalties: they are, in the circumstances, natural. Perhaps it is impossible to make a blank distinction between natives and strangers: we are all exiles in differing degrees. For the convenience of this book I have made an arbitrary defintion of 'foreigner' as one who was born outside the mainland United States. This qualification lets in the Puerto Ricans. Puerto Rico has not been admitted to the Union; it is under colonial occupation. I thought it would be fascinating to include an account by a Puerto Rican, because their mass immigration to the mainland after the war has caused deep resentment amongst the longer established Italian and Negro communities.

The pieces in *Abroad in America* are first-hand accounts. All of them are to be found in book form. I have tried to avoid biographies wherever possible. Often it has not been. Not everybody I wanted to include has published their diaries and letters or an autobiography or a travel book. But I have been wary of secondary sources. I have preferred competent biographers, favouring those who were intimate with their subjects. And I have cut passages of comment and opinion and stuck to the facts.

As the reader will see for himself, the pieces have been arranged chrono-logically, not by date of writing or publication, but of when the event described took place. This reduces conscious arrangement to the minimum. But the proximity of certain pieces can arouse delicious, though unintended, associations. I have attempted to keep the gaps between the years small. Some decades are packed: the 1830s, when a great wave of British writers produced travel books; and the 1920s and 1930s, when ironically, America, which had retreated into isolation, and prohibition made the place repellent to the civilized visitor, received a huge influx of distinguished guests.

One final rule I made for myself was to avoid aphorisms. Readers who wish to stock up on one-liners are advised to buy a book of quotations. I think reading a collection full of short pieces is a bit like guzzling one's way through a box of soft-centred chocolates. I have therefore preferred writers who can sustain the long stretch. In most cases it has been possible only to include extracts from longer works. I hope that in some cases the reader will find these juicy enough to tempt him to go away and read the rest of the book. For just as recording bleeding chunks of Wagner in the days of 78s was never really satisfactory, so books can only be appreciated complete. Even the boring bits are part of the whole effect.

Abroad in America is divided into four historical sections. Preceding each is a short introduction. This does not anticipate what is to follow, but rather serves as a point of departure. Readers will notice that there is a preponderance of English writers in all but the first two sections. This insular preference is the result of my belief that translations do not travel well. *Abroad in America* aims at direct experience: however good a translation is it must inevitably lose this freshness. And I do not think that any translation can compensate for the loss of the author's individual voice.

The individual voice: this is what I hoped to hear in this book. For *Abroad in America* is not itself a history or a travel book; though in a sense it is both. Each man's America is different. All I have done is to choose a few morsels of experience.

Part One
The Forerunners of Columbus: Irish and Norse Legends of Discovery

Oscar Wilde said that America had often been discovered before Columbus, but it had always been hushed up. Funny, but not true. Already, in the late nineteenth century, scholars were beginning to lose their reticence on the subject and the shelves of the Royal Geographical Society in London contain once exciting, now forgotten, books with such provocative titles as *Columbus Did Not Discover America*.

It was never likely that Americans would accept 1492 as the starting-point of their history. Speculation on the subject has long been restless and the resulting theories have varied in plausibility. As Geoffrey Ashe puts it in his introduction to *The Quest for America*:

> On both sides of the Atlantic, the urge to believe – to believe in something before 1492 besides untenanted waters – has inspired not only memorable feats of imagination, but a harlequinade of grotesque theories which grab at the frailest props. One recent author, who at least realized that the 'case' for Theory A was as good as the 'case' for Theory B, accepted them wholesale and argued for a full dozen discoveries before Columbus. Another, convinced that South America was reached by Levantine traders centuries before Christ, published an ingenious interpretation of Edward Lear's *The Owl and the Pussycat* under the impression that it was an ancient ballad to which the key . . . had been lost.

Equally unverifiable theories, though not so charming, have gained more popular acceptance. *The Book of Mormon*, for example, is the culmination of a little tradition of prophecies which claim that the Red Indians are the successors of the Lost Tribes of Israel; who, uprooted from Palestine in 721 B.C., trekked through Asia, and crossed the Bering Strait on the ice. However, thanks to modern geographers and archeologists, it is almost certain that the Vikings had successfully discovered and colonized Iceland, Greenland, and North America in the tenth and eleventh centuries. The American colony was unsuccessful in face of the hostility of the natives, but for many years the inhabitants of Greenland and Iceland sailed west to Labrador to fish and to find timber. In the fifteenth century climatic changes brought ice and the Esquimaux south to threaten the Greenland settlement. The last ship sailed from Greenland to Iceland about 1410, and the colony, unable to support itself, died out.

What concerns us here, though, are the legends about the discovery of America which were current in the fifteenth century and which may have been known to Columbus. We are now inclined to dismiss 'legend' or 'myth' as synonyms for fiction: more imaginative ages were not so presumptuous. Less preoccupied by the notion that knowledge consists of the gathering of ascertainable, and preferably useful, facts, they could accept that poetic utterances could express instinctive truths, however imprecise in detail. If I may labour the point, the recurrent classical notion that there was land beyond the Oecumene, perhaps unsupported by solid evidence – just an inspired guess – turned out to be true. And the idea that runs through the classical and Celtic myths that this western land was 'Blest', 'Promised', 'Paradise', sole survivor of a past golden age: how many has this idea inspired to cross the Atlantic? Today immigrants to the United States may express their hopes in more sophisticated terms than their predecessors, but isn't the essence of their desires the same? To seek consolation in a land of riches and plenty where all may be happy and free.

Columbus may have known of two claims to have reached land by the western route; the earliest plausible claim is for discovery by the Irish.

The main source for this is the legend of the voyage of St Brendan, who was born at Tralee in 484. Despite his vocation to the monastic life he seems to have been a restless traveller, founding monasteries at Ardfert in Kerry and at Clanfert in Galway. He is said to have visited Wales and Brittany. In old age he visited St Columba on Iona. Tradition has it that at some point in his life he was absent from Ireland for a long time. Rumours grew that he had gone in search of 'the mysterious land far from human ken.' The seven year voyage was fruitless; but later he set sail again with sixty friends and at last reached 'that paradise amid the waves of the sea'; a vast, fabulous land a huge distance to the west of Erin, which some have interpreted to be Bermuda.

The voyage of St Brendan reaches its maturest form in the *Navigatio Sancti Brendani*, a Latin prose work written between 900 and 920 by an anonymous Irishman living in Ireland. As the title implies, this narrative is concerned solely with Brendan's voyage treated as a story in itself, rather than as an episode in the life of the saint. Although it is a work of 'fiction', and thus strictly outside the scope of this anthology, I have borrowed a passage from it which describes St Brendan sailing through an iceberg, possibly off the coast of Newfoundland. Of course no one knows whether St Brendan himself actually performed this exciting feat: he may have been a convenient prop on which to hang others' deeds. As Geoffrey Ashe says, the *Navigatio* is manifestly a fictional *Odyssey* with an established voyager as hero. It makes no claims to be biographical.

Columbus very probably knew the legend of St Brendan. During the twelfth century 'St Brendan's Isle' begins to be mentioned in geographical writings and to be drawn on maps. It was always located south-west of Europe, getting gradually further away, as progress in that direction was made. In 1448 a map by Bianco shows that one island has now become a group of 'Fortunate Isles' west of the Azores. In 1492, the year of Columbus's discovery, the globe-maker Martin Behain put a large St Brendan's isle near the actual location of the mouth of the Amazon.

The story's chief interest for us is that it implies geographical knowledge of the Atlantic Ocean long before the recorded Viking voyages took place; though there is, of course, no certainty that the source of this knowledge came from Ireland. However, the same texts which describe the Vikings' exploration of Iceland, Greenland, and beyond 'Vineland the Good', also recount the Vikings' own belief that Irishmen had gone before them. Possibly details from the Irish legends spilled over into the Norse sagas. The identification of 'Vineland' with America is not satisfactory. It sounds too far south to come within the Viking range, or else too warm for the lands they did reach. Perhaps having heard of St Brendan's 'Fortunate Isles' – a tropical island of grapes which has been identified with Jamaica – the Norse writers tacked it on to give an exotic flavour to their stories.

The Norse sagas may or may not have been known to Columbus, but they were of some use to the sailors of Bristol, with whom the Icelanders, disobeying the orders of their government in Norway, traded. The Bristolians also picked up from the Irish the tradition of the 'island of Brasylle'. (The name may come from the Irish breas-ail, meaning 'blessed' or 'very good'). In 1480 an expedition from Bristol failed to find it, having sailed for about nine months. These expeditions became an annual event. In 1498 the Spanish Ambassador, writing home, said that 'the people of Bristol have, for the past seven years, sent out every year two, three, or four light ships, in search of the island of Brasil'. As we shall see, the successful sailing from Bristol was that led by John Cabot in 1497.

As soon as we leave the Navigatio and turn our attention to medieval maps, we are transported from plausible surmise to the world of wishful thinking. The mapmakers of the age were simply slapping on names which they had heard of but could not understand. The Brendan tradition survived in this decadent form to influence and inspire Columbus. It served as an extra argument when he was trying to wheedle money and ships out of a succession of European monarchs. But for him ancient legends of discovery were only a means of wooing patronage; never a set of directions to follow.

A Note on Sagas

In Icelandic the word 'saga' is used to mean any kind of story, whether spoken or written down. In English the term is often restricted to tales of heroic exploits. Of these none is more vivid than the so-called 'Family Sagas', which recall the heroes who lived in Iceland in the tenth and eleventh centuries. Although none of these sagas were written down before the thirteenth century, many scholars maintain that they record authentic exploits. It is popularly believed that the sagas were composed shortly after the events in them took place, and handed down orally from generation to generation. Most modern specialists deny this, discerning in the sagas strong evidence of individual authorship. The accounts of the voyages of Bjarni Herjulfsson, Leiv Eriksson, and Thorvald Eriksson are taken from the Flateyarbok, that most beautiful of Icelandic manuscripts, which was composed in the post-classical style at the end of the fourteenth century. The account of the exploration of Thorfinn Karlsefni is from the Hauksbok, a collection of older sagas written early in the fourteenth century.

St. Brendan (539–551)

An extract from the tenth century Navigatio Sancti Brendani *relates how St. Brendan and his fellow monks sailed through an iceberg.*

At a certain time, when St. Brendan had celebrated the Feast of St. Peter the Apostle [June 29] on his ship, they discovered a clear sea [i.e. transparent] so much so that as a result they could see whatever was below the surface of the sea.

When they peered into the depths they saw various kinds of beasts lying over the sand. It also seemed to them that they could touch those beasts because of the wonderful clearness of the sea. There were flocks lying in pastures. Because of such a multitude they [i.e. the flocks] lay like a state in a circle by applying their heads to their posteriors.

The brothers asked St. Brendan to celebrate his Mass in silence lest the beasts hear him and raise themselves in order to pursue them. St. Brendan laughed and said to them: 'I wonder greatly at your foolishness. Why do you fear these beasts and you did not fear the devourer and master of all the beasts of the sea, while you were sitting and singing on its back [i.e. the back of the whale]. Furthermore, you cut wood and built a fire and cooked meat on its back. Therefore, why are you afraid of these beasts? Is not the God of all beasts our Lord Jesus Christ who can level all animals?'

When he had said this he began to sing as loud as he could. And the rest of the brothers kept peering at the beasts of the deep. However, when the monsters heard the sound of the singing they swam to the surface and began to circle the boat, so that as a result the brothers could not see into any part of the sea on account of the multitude of the different swimming beasts. Still they did not approach the ship but swam far and wide and thus they swam back and forth until St. Brendan had finished Mass and then they retreated. After this, as though they were fleeing, all the beasts swam through the different paths of the ocean out of sight of the servants of God. But St. Brendan, for eight days, even with a favourable wind and the sails extended could scarcely cross the clear sea.

On a certain day when they had celebrated their Masses there came into sight a column in the sea, and it did not seem far from them but it took three days to draw near it.

When St. Brendan had approached it he looked for its summit. Nevertheless he was unable to see the height of it, for it was higher than the air. Indeed it was covered with a strange curtain. It was so strange that the ship could pass through its openings. They did not know from what thing the curtain had been made, it had the colour of silver.

On the contrary, the column seemed to them to be harder than marble and was of a very bright crystal.

St. Brendan said to his brother: 'Bring in the oars and lower the mast and the sails and some of you may hold in the meantime the protrusions through the curtain.'

The aforementioned mystery occupied a large space into every direction away from the column as of a thousand paces and thus it extended onto the ocean. When they had done this St. Brendan said to them: 'Steer the ship within through some opening so that we may see the greatness of our Creator.'

When they had entered within and they had looked here and there, the sea appeared to them to be like glass so that they were able to see everything which was below. They were able to examine closely the foundations of the column and likewise the bottom of the mist lying on the surface of the column.

The sunlight was just as bright within as it was on the outside.

Then St. Brendan measured one opening between four curtains. It measured four cubits in every part. And so they navigated the entire day along one side of that column and in the shade they could feel the heat of the sun from without.

This they did until three o'clock. And St. Brendan kept measuring that one side. Fourteen hundred cubits was the measure through the four sides of that column.

Thus for four days St. Brendan worked between the four angles of the tower.

On the fourth day they found a chalice [cup] of the colour of the mist and a plate the colour of the mist and a plate the colour of the column, lying in a certain recess on the side of the iceberg facing south.

Immediately St. Brendan seized these vessels saying: 'Our Lord Jesus Christ has shown to us this miracle and it is revealed that it may be believed by many, He has given to me two gifts.' Immediately St. Brendan ordered his brethren to say the divine office and afterwards to refresh their bodies since they had had no rest since they had seen the column.

Bjarni Herjulfsson (970)

Learned men tell us that the same summer that Eirik the Red went to colonize Greenland, twenty-five ships set sail from Breidafjord and Borgafjord, but only fourteen arrived at their destination. This was fifteen winters before Christianity was legally established in Iceland [985].

[Herjulf] had a wife named Thorgerd and their son was Bjarni, a very promising man. He had taken to foreign voyages from his youth. This brought him both wealth and respect, and he used to spend his winters alternately abroad and with his parents. Bjarni soon had a trading ship of his own and the last winter that he was in Norway was when Herjulf undertook the voyage to Greenland with Eirik, and removed his home there. Herjulf settled at Herjulfsness.

Bjarni arrived in his ship at Eyrar [in Iceland] in the summer of the same year, in the spring of which his father had sailed away. Bjarni was much concerned at the news, and would not discharge his cargo. When his crew asked him what he meant to do, he replied that he meant to keep to his custom of passing the winter with his parents; 'I will,' said he, 'take my ship on to Greenland, if you will accompany me.' They all said that they would abide by his decision; upon which Bjarni remarked, 'Our voyage will be considered rash, since none of us have been in Greenland waters.' Notwithstanding this they put to sea as soon as they were ready, and they sailed for three days before they lost sight of land; but when the fair wind ceased, and north winds and fog came on, they did not know where they were going. This went on for many *doegr*.[1]

After this period they saw the sun, and so were able to get their bearings, whereupon they hoisted their sails, and after sailing that day they saw land, and they discussed among themselves what this land could be; Bjarni said he fancied that it could not be Greenland. They asked him whether he would sail to this land or not. 'I am for sailing in close to the land,' he said, and when they had done so, they soon saw that the land was not mountainous, and was covered with woods, and that there were small knolls on it, whereupon they left the land on the port side, and let the sheet turn toward it.

Then, after sailing two *doegr*, they saw another land. They asked Bjarni if he thought this was Greenland; he said that he did not think this was Greenland any more than the first place, for it is said that there are very large glaciers in Greenland. They soon neared this land, and saw that it was a flat country and covered with forest. At this point the fair wind dropped, and the crew suggested that they should land there, but Bjarni would not. They felt that they were short both of wood and water. 'You are in no want of either,' Bjarni said, and got some abuse from his crew for this remark. He ordered them to hoist sail; they did so, and turned the bows from the land, and sailed out to sea for three *doegr* before a southwesterly breeze; then they saw the third land.

This land was high and mountainous, with ice upon it. So they asked if Bjarni would put in there, but he refused, since, as he put it, this land appeared to him to be good for nothing. Then without lowering sail they kept on their course along the coast, and saw that it was an island; once more they turned the bows away from land, and held out to sea with the same breeze, but the wind increased, so that Bjarni told them to *svipt*[2] and not crowd more sail than their ship and rigging could stand. They now sailed for four *doegr* when they saw the fourth land.

The crew asked Bjarni if he thought this was Greenland. Bjarni replied, 'This is most like what was told me of Greenland, and here we will keep our course towards the land.' So they did, and that evening they came to land under a cape, which had a boat on it, and there on that cape lived Herjulf, Bjarni's father, and it is from him that the cape received its name, and has since been called Herjulfsness.

---

[1]   *doegr* = A measure of time equivalent to the passing of a night.
[2]   *Svipt* The meaning is ambiguous. It possibly means to hold the sails at mid-mast.

Leiv Eriksson (c. 1000)

There was now much talk of exploration. Leiv, Eirik the Red's son from Brattahlid, went to Bjarni Herjulfsson and bought a ship from him, and engaged a crew of thirty-five men. Leiv asked his father Eirik still to be leader of the exploration.

Now they prepared their ship, and when they were ready they put out to sea, and they found first the country which Bjarni found last. They sailed up to the land, and having cast anchor and lowered a boat went ashore, and saw no grass there. The background was all great glaciers, and all the intermediate land from the sea to the glaciers was like one flat rock, and the country seemed to them destitute of value. Then Leiv said, 'We have not failed to land, like Bjarni; now I will give this country a name, and call it Helluland [the land of the flat stone].' Thereupon they returned on board ship, after which they sailed to sea and discovered the second land. Again they sailed up to the land and cast anchor, then lowered the boat and went ashore.

This land was low-lying and wooded, and wherever they went there were wide stretches of white sand, and the slope from the sea was not abrupt. Then Leiv said, 'This land shall be given a name from its resources, and shall be called Markland [wooded-land],' after which they returned to the ship as quickly as possible. And they sailed after that in the open sea with a northeast wind, and were out two *doegr* before they saw land, toward which they sailed, and coming to an island which lay to the north of the mainland, they landed on it, the weather being fine, and looked around; and they perceived that there was a dew on the grass, and it came about that they put their hands in the dew, and carried it to their mouths, and thought that they never had known anything so sweet as that was. Then they went back to the ship, and sailing into the sound which lay between the island and the cape which ran north from the mainland, they steered a westerly course past the cape. It was very shallow there at low tide, so that their ship ran aground, and soon it was a long way from the ship to the sea. But they were so very eager to get to land that they would not wait for the tide to rise under their ship, but instead hurried ashore where a river came out of a lake; but when the sea had risen under their ship they took the boat and rowed to the ship, and took her up to the river and afterward into the lake, where they cast anchor, and carrying their leather kitbags ashore they put up shelters, but later, on deciding to pass the winter there, they made large houses.

There was no want of salmon, either in the river or in the lake, and bigger salmon than they had seen before; the amenities of the country were such, as it seemed to them, that no cattle would need fodder there in the winter; there came no frost in the winter, and the grass did not wither there much. Day and night were more equally divided there than in Greenland or Iceland: on the shortest day the sun was up over the Icelandic marks for both supper and breakfast time.

It happened one evening that a man of their party was missing, and this was Tyrker the southerner. Leiv was much distressed by this, for Tyrker had been long with his father and him, and had been very fond of Leiv as a child: so now Leiv, after finding great fault with his men, prepared to look for him, taking a dozen men with him. But when they had gone a little way from the camp Tyrker came towards them, and was received with joy. Leiv saw at once that his foster–father was in good spirits . . .

Tyrker had a projecting forehead and a very small face with roving eyes; he was a small and insignificant man, but handy at every kind of odd job.

Then Leiv said to him; 'Why are you so late, my foster-father, and why did you separate from your companions?' Tyrker at this spoke for a long time in Turkish, rolling his eyes and grimacing, but the others did not distinguish what he was saying. But a little later he said in Norse, 'I did not go much further than you, but I have found something fresh to report. I found vines and grapes.' 'Is that true, foster–father?' said Leiv. 'Certainly it is true,' he replied, 'for I was born where there was no lack of vines or grapes.'

Now they slept that night, but in the morning Leiv said to his crew, 'We will now do two things, keeping separate days for each; we will gather grapes and cut down vines, and fell wood, to make a cargo for my ship'; and this suggestion was adopted. The story goes that their pinnace was full of grapes. So a cargo was cut for the ship, and in spring they made ready and they sailed away, and Leiv gave the land a name according to its resources, and called it Vineland . . .

So after this they put to sea, and the breeze was fair till they sighted Greenland, and the mountains under the glaciers. Then a man spoke up and said to Leiv: 'Why are you steering the ship so much into the wind?' 'I am paying attention to my steering,' replied Leiv, 'but to something else as well: what do you see that is strange?' They said they could see nothing remarkable. 'I do not know,' said Leiv 'whether it is a ship or a reef that I see.' Then they saw it and said that it was a reef. But Leiv was longer sighted than they, so that he saw men on the reef. 'Now,' said Leiv, 'I wish that we should beat up-wind, so as to reach them if they need our help and it is necessary to assist them, and if they are not peaceably disposed we are masters of the situation and they are not.' So they came up to the reef, and lowered their sail and cast anchor: and they launched a second dinghy they had with them.

Then Tyrker asked who was the captain [of the shipwrecked party]. 'His name is Thori,' was the reply, 'and he is a Norseman, but what is your name?' Leiv told his name. 'Are you a son of Eirik the Red of Brattahlid?' said Thori. Leiv assented. 'Now,' said Leiv, 'I will take you all on board my ship, and as much of your stuff as the ship can hold.' They agreed to these terms, and afterward they sailed to Eiriksfjord with this freight, until they came to Brattahlid where they unloaded the ship. After that Leiv invited Thori and Gudrid his wife, and three other men to stay with him, and procured lodgings for the rest of the crews, both Thori's men and his own. Leiv took fifteen men from the reef; he was called Leiv the Lucky, from then on. So Leiv gained both wealth and honour.

Thorvald Eriksson (c. 1000)

Now there was much discussion of Leiv's expedition to Vineland, and Thorvald, his brother, thought that the exploration of the country had been confined to too narrow an area. So Leiv said to Thorvald, 'Now you, my brother, may, if you desire, make use of my ship for a trip to Vineland: but I wish the ship to go first for the wood which Thori had on the reef.' And this was done. Thereupon Thorvald prepared for this expedition, taking thirty men on the advice of Leiv, his brother. Afterward they made their ship ready and held out to sea, and there is no report of their voyage before they came to Vineland to Leiv's camp. There they laid up their ship, and remained quiet that winter, catching fish for their food.

In the spring Thorvald told them to make ready their ship, and ordered the ship's pinnace with some of the crew to go to the west of the country and explore there during the summer. It seemed to them a fine wooded country, the trees coming close down to the sea, and there were white sands. There were many islands, and many shoals. They found no traces of either men or beasts, except that on an island to the west they found a wooden barn. Finding no further human handiwork they returned, and came to Leiv's camp in the autumn.

The next summer Thorvald sailed to the east with his trading ship, and along the more northerly part of the country: then a sharp storm arose off a cape, so that they ran ashore, breaking the keel under their ship; so they made a long stay there to repair their vessel. Then Thorvald said to his companions, 'Now I wish that we should raise up the keel here on the cape, and call it *Kjalarnes*,' and so they did. Afterward they sailed away thence and eastward along the coast and into the nearest fjord mouths, and to a headland which ran out there: it was all covered with wood. Then they moored their ship, and put out the gangway to land, and there Thorvald went ashore with all of his crew. Then he remarked, 'This is a beautiful spot, where I should like to make my home.' After this they returned to the ship, and saw on the sands inside the headland three humps, and on approaching they saw three canoes of skin, with three men beneath each. Thereupon they divided their party, and laid hands on all of them, except one who escaped with his canoe. They killed the eight, and afterward went back to the headland, when they saw inside the fjord some mounds, which they took to be dwelling-places. After this there came over them so great a heaviness that they could not keep awake, and they all fell asleep. Then came a cry from above them, so that they all woke up, and the cry was, 'Awake, Thorvald, and all your company, if you value your life: and return to your ship with all your men, and leave the land with all speed.' At that there came from within the fjord countless skin canoes, which made toward them. So Thorvald said, 'We must set the war-shields over the side, and defend ourselves as well as we can, while assuming the offensive but little.' So they did, but the savages, after shooting at them for a while, afterward fled away, each as quickly as he could. Then Thorvald asked his men if they were wounded at all; they said there were no casualties.

'I have got a wound under my arm,' said he; 'an arrow flew between the gunwale and the shield under my arm and here it is, and it will be my death. Now my advice is that you prepare to go away as quickly as possible, after carrying me to that headland which I thought the best place to dwell in: maybe it was the truth that came into my mouth that I should stay there awhile. Bury me there with a cross at my head and at my feet, and call it Crossness hereafter forever.' Greenland was by then converted, though Eirik the Red died before conversion.

Now Thorvald died, but they carried out all his instructions, after which they went and met their companions, and told each other such tidings as they knew, and they stayed there that winter, gathering grapes and vines for their ships. Then in the spring they prepared to go back to Greenland, and arrived with their ship in Eiriksfjord, with great news to tell Leiv.

Thorfinn Karlsefni (c. 1002–1007)

At this time there was much discussion at Brattahlid during the winter about a search for Vineland the Good, and it was said that it would be a profitable country to visit; Karlsefni and Snori resolved to search for Vineland, and so the project was much talked about; so it came that Karlsefni and Snori made ready their ship to go and look for the country in the summer. The man named Bjarni, and Thorhall, who have already been mentioned, joined the expedition with their ship, and the crew which had accompanied them. There was a man named Thorvald [evidently Thorvard] who was connected by marriage with Eirik the Red. He also went with them, and Thorhall who was called the Hunter; he had been long engaged with Eirik as hunter in the summer, and had many things in his charge. Thorhall was big and strong and dark, and like a giant: he was rather old, of a temper hard to manage, taciturn and of few words as a rule, cunning but abusive, and he was always urging Eirik to the worse course. He had had little dealings with the faith since it came to Greenland. Thorhall was rather unpopular, yet for a long time Eirik had been in the habit of consulting him. He was on the ship with Thorvald's men, for he had a wide experience of wild countries. They had the ship which Thorbjorn had brought out there, and they joined themselves to Karlsefni's party for the expedition, and the majority of the men were Greenlanders. The total force on board their ships was 160 men ... [After this] they sailed away to the Western Settlement and the Bear Isles. They sailed away from the Bear Isles with a northerly wind. They were at sea two *doegr*. Then they found land, and rowing ashore in boats they examined the country, and found there a quantity of flat stones, which were so large that two men could easily have lain sole to sole on them: there were many arctic foxes there. They gave the place a name, calling it Helluland. Then they sailed for two *doegr* with a north wind, and changed their course from south to southeast, and then there was a land before them on which was much wood and many beasts. An island lay there offshore to the southeast, on which they found a bear, and they called it Bjarney [Bear Island], but the land where the wood was they called Markland [woodland].

Then when two *doegr* were passed they sighted land, up to which they sailed. There was a cape where they arrived. They beat along the coast and left the land to starboard. It was a desolate place, and there were long beaches and sands there. They rowed ashore, and found there on the cape the keel of a ship, so they called the place *Kjalarnes*: they gave the beaches also a name, calling them *Furdustrandir* [the Wonder Beaches] because the sail past them was long. Next the country became indented with bays, into one of which they steered the ships.

Now when Leiv was with King Olav Trygvason and he commissioned him to preach Christianity in Greenland, the king gave him two Scots, a man called Hake and a woman Hekja. The king told Leiv to make use of these people if he had need of speed, for they were swifter than deer: these people Leiv and Eirik provided to accompany Karlsefni. Now when they had coasted past *Furdustrandir* they set the Scots ashore, telling them to run southward along the land to explore the resources of the country and come back before three days were past . . . They cast anchor and lay there in the meantime. And when three days were past they came running down from the land, and one of them had in his hand a grape cluster while the other had a wild [lit: self-sown] ear of wheat. They told Karlsefni that they thought they had found that the resources of the country were good. They received them into their ships, and went their way, till the country was indented by a fjord. There was an island outside the fjord. They took the ships into the fjord. There was an island, and about it there were long sounds [*Straumar miklir*], so they called it *Straumsey*. There were so many birds on the island that a man's feet could hardly come down between the eggs. They held along the fjord, and called the place *Straumsfjord*, and there they carried up their goods from the ships and prepared to stay. They had with them all sorts of cattle; and they explored the resources of the country. There were mountains there, and the view was beautiful. They did nothing but explore the country. There was plenty of grass there. They remained there for the winter, and the winter was severe, but they had done nothing to provide for it, and victuals grew scarce, and hunting and fishing deteriorated. They went out to the island, in the hope that this place might yield something in the way of fishing or jetsam. But there was little food to be obtained on it, though their cattle throve there well. After this they cried to God to send them something to eat, and their prayers were not answered as soon as they desired . . .

Now they consulted about their expedition, and were divided. Thorhall the Hunter wished to go north by *Furdustrandir* and past *Kjalarnes*, and so look for Vineland, but Karlsefni wished to sail south (and off the east coast, considering that the region which lay more to the south was the larger), and it seemed to him the best plan to explore both ways. So then Thorhall made ready out by the island, and there were no more than nine men for his venture, the rest of the party going with Karlsefni.

Afterward they parted, and they sailed north past *Furdustrandir* and *Kjalarnes*, and tried to beat westward, but they were met by a storm and cast anchor ashore in Ireland, where they were much ill-treated and enslaved. There Thorhall died, according to the records of traders.

Karlsefni coasted south with Snori and Bjarni and the rest of their party. They sailed a long time, till they came to a river which flowed down the land and through a lake into the sea. There were great shoals of gravel there in front of the estuary and they could not enter the river except at high tide. Karlsefni and his party sailed into the estuary, and called it *Hop*.

'They found there wild [lit: self-sown] fields of wheat wherever the ground was low, but vines wherever they explored the hills. Every brook was full of fish. They made pits where the land met high-water mark, and then when the tide ebbed there were fish [flounder] in the pits. There was a great quantity of animals of all sorts in the wood. They were there a fortnight, enjoying themselves, without noticing anything further: they had their cattle with them.

And one morning early, as they looked about them, they saw nine skin canoes, on which staves were waved with a noise just like threshing, and they were waved with the sun. Then Karlsefni said, 'What is the meaning of this?' Snori answered him, 'Perhaps this is a sign of peace, so let us take a white shield and lift it in answer.' And they did so. Then these men rowed to meet them, and, astonished at what they saw, they landed. They were swarthy men and ugly, with unkempt hair on their heads. They had large eyes and broad cheeks. They stayed there some time, showing surprise. Then they rowed away south past the cape.

Karlsefni and his men had made their camp above the lake, and some of the huts were further inland while others were near the lake. So they remained there that winter. No snow fell, and their cattle remained in the open, finding their own pasture. But at the beginning of spring they saw one morning a fleet of skin canoes rowing from the south past the cape, so many that the sea was black with them, and on each boat there were staves tied. Karlsefni and his men raised their shields, and they began to trade: the strange people wanted particularly to buy red cloth, in exchange for which they offered skins and grey furs. They wished also to buy swords and spears, but Karlsefni and Snori forbade this. The savages got for a dark skin a span's length of red cloth, which they bound round their heads. Thus things continued for a while, but when the cloth began to give out they cut it into pieces so small that they were not more than a finger's breadth. The savages gave as much for it as before, or more.

It happened that a bull belonging to Karlsefni's party ran out of the woods, and bellowed loudly. This terrified the savages, and they ran out to their canoes, and rowed south along the coast, and there was nothing more seen of them for three consecutive weeks. But when that time had elapsed they saw a great number of the boats of the savages coming from the south like a rushing torrent, and this time all the staves were waved withershins, and all the savages yelled loudly. Upon this Karlsefni's men took a red shield and raised it in answer. The savages ran from their boats and thereupon they met and fought. There was a heavy rain of missiles; the savages had war-slings too. Karlsefni and Snori observed that the savages raised upon a pole a very large globe, closely resembling a sheep's paunch and dark in colour, and it flew from the pole up on land over the party, and made a terrible noise where it came from. Upon this a great fear came on Karlsefni and his party, so they wished for nothing but to get away up-stream, for they thought that the savages were setting upon them from all sides; nor did they halt till they came to some rocks where they made a determined resistance . . .

It now appeared to Karlsefni's party that though this country had good resources yet they would live in perpetual state of warfare and alarm on account of the aborigines. So they prepared to depart, intending to return to their own country. They coasted northward, and found five savages in skins sleeping by the sea; these had with them receptacles in which was beast's marrow mixed with blood. They concluded that these men must have been sent out from the country [outlawed], and they killed them. Later on they discovered a promontory and a quantity of beasts; the promontory had the appearance of a cake of dung, because the beasts lay there in the winter. Now they came to Straumsfjord, where there was plenty of everything.

Some men say that Bjarni and Gudrid stayed there with a hundred men and went no further, while Karlsefni and Snori went south with forty men, staying no longer at *Hop* than a scant two months, and returning the same summer.

They considered that those mountains which were at *Hop* and those which they now found were all one, and were therefore close opposite one another, and that the distance from *Straumsfjord* was the same in both directions. They were at *Straumsfjord* the third winter.

At this time the men were much divided into parties, which happened because of the women, the unmarried men claiming the wives of those who were married, which gave rise to the greatest disorder. There Karlsefni's son Snori was born the first autumn, and he was there three winters when they left.

On sailing from Vineland they got a south wind, and came to Markland . . .

Part Two
Braving the New World: Exploration and Colonization of America 1492–1776

In 1453 The Turks beseiged and captured Constantinople, immediately dislocating commerce between Europe and Asia. The chief casualty to Europe was the spice trade, as in pre-refrigeration days, spices were essential food preservatives.

The capture of Constantinople and the blockade of the Bosphorus created the problem of how to bypass the overland trade of spices and to transport them by sea. From 1416, expeditions sponsored by the Portuguese patron, Prince Henry the Navigator (1394–1460) had cherished the hope of a sea-route to India by way of Africa. Portuguese aspirations were never westward, but their enterprises led to westward exploration. The ship which Columbus used, the caravel, was developed by the Portuguese to meet the needs of long sea-journeys in difficult waters.

In Prince Henry's lifetime progress round Africa was slow: by 1460 Portuguese sailors had only reached Sierra Leone. In the meantime they sailed out into the Atlantic capturing Madeira in 1418, and re-discovering the Canary Islands in 1419. Influenced, it is said, by the legend of St Brendan, Henry sponsored a western expedition which reached the nearest of the Azores in 1427. It took another quarter of a century before the remoter islands of the group, Flores and Corvo, were reached by Diogo de Tieve. Always men wondered what lay beyond. Rumours spread amongst the Portuguese colonists of sighting the island of St Brendan, but it remained tantalizingly beyond their grasp. On Tenerife a legend telling of a visit by the Irish saint insensibly became part of the tradition of the native Guanches. In 1473 a search for St Brendan's isle was undertaken from the Canary Islands. But throughout the century the Portuguese crept further and further around the coast of Africa. They had still not achieved the Indian Ocean when Columbus began to urge that the best route to India was across the Atlantic.

Columbus's aim was not eccentric and it is wrong to think that most educated people in the fifteenth century believed the world to be flat. In the fourth century B.C. Aristotle, following Pythagoras, had watched the shape of the earth's shadow as it crossed the moon in an eclipse, and noted the difference in the stars as seen from different countries. From these observations he had concluded that the earth was a sphere and that 'there is but a narrow sea between the western points of Spain and the eastern border of India'. The revival of Aristotle in the twelfth century by Arab scholars would have made his geography familiar to the medieval schoolmen who adapted his ideas to Christian ends. Fired by the travels of Marco Polo, who had arrived at the court of Kublai Khan in 1275, men dreamt of a westward route to India and China with a few intervening islands. No one guessed that what lay between was an undiscovered continent. But neither did they believe that by hazarding this journey they were in imminent danger of sailing off the edge of the world.

Already doubts were being expressed as to the conventional layout of the continents. Evidence suggested that there was land closer to Europe than anyone had previously thought. Corpses with 'Mongolian' features and strange driftwood with tool marks had been carried by the Gulf Stream and washed up on the shores of the Azores. Hardwood, which we call Brazil, but which actually came from Mexico, was washed up on the west coast of Ireland in sufficient quantities to be traded. 'Irish wood', as it was called, was used in the 1460s to panel a library in the Louvre, although no one doubted that it originated from Asia.

In 1474 King Alfonso of Portugal commissioned a report from the Florentine astronomer Paolo Toscanelli on the business of getting to the Indies by sea. Toscanelli recommended the Atlantic route. He estimated that the difference between the Canary Islands and Japan was 3,000 nautical miles; it is in fact 10,600.

Local tradition claims that Toscanelli was confirming what Alfonso knew already. In Lisbon there stands a memorial to one João Vaz Corte Real, 'the discoverer of America'. Whether he actually made the trip in 1474, as is claimed, is doubtful as the sources for the story are late. What is more likely is that having let Columbus slip, and resenting the credit that Spain takes for his success, the Portuguese invented a rival. After all, if they had got there already, why were the Portuguese so sceptical of Columbus when he asked them for money?

Columbus had only a passing interest in discovering new lands. His letters and diaries reveal that he looked on such merely as ports-of-call. His eyes were on the Indies. Asia was his sole aim; and by his own lights his life was a failure.

He was born in Genoa in 1451, the son of a woolcomber, and was brought up to follow in that trade. At the age of fourteen he went to sea. In about 1470 he was shipwrecked in a fight off Cape St Vincent with Tunisian galleys, but reached the shores of Portugal on a plank. By 1474 he had conceived his life's work; a design in which he was enthusiastically supported by Toscanelli.

What inspired his genius is difficult to determine. Initially he seems to have eschewed obvious commercial motives. He was a devout Catholic and he saw his work as missionary. The eastward expansion of the Faith had been checked by the capture of Constantinople and the Turkish advance into the Balkans. Until the infidel could be driven from the east, the peoples of India, China, and Japan would be forever lost to the Church. To reach them by the west would provide an opportunity to reinforce the shrinking ranks of Christendom with potentially millions of converts. Decadent European Catholicism would in turn be invigorated by an access of crusading zeal.

Once formed, Columbus's idea grew into an obsession. Like an artist he wandered restlessly in pursuit of material for its perfection. He went to Galway to study the Atlantic flotsam. According to his son Ferdinand, who wrote his father's *Life*, he was inspired by reports of the 'islands of St Brendan, of which wonderful things are told'. Those 'reports' seem to have been through Portuguese rather than Irish agencies, though. In 1477 he 'sailed 100 leagues beyond Thule'; probably to or beyond Iceland. It has been romantically proposed that there he heard a recital of one of the sagas of Vineland; but it is doubtful whether he had a translator. His discovery of America was made independently of the Norseman Leiv Eriksson's.

Eventually in 1484 Columbus was granted an audience at the Portuguese court. King John II of Portugal, nicknamed the Perfect, shared the seafaring passions of Henry the Navigator. The audience was not a success. John found Columbus intolerably boastful, and was sceptical about his claims for the nearness of Japan. However, he did not refuse Columbus's request for three caravels outright. Instead he prevaricated. He encouraged two of his subjects to make a foray at their own expense. When the ships foundered after running into the westerlies, the king maintained a flicker of interest. What snuffed it was the triumphant return of Bartolomeo Diaz in 1488 from his rounding of the Cape of Good Hope. For close on a century the Portuguese had put their trust in the eastern route to India. On the verge of success they were not to be deflected by an experiment in the opposite direction.

Meanwhile Columbus wrote to Henry VII of England. Henry, even less than John, was not the man to back an untried venture with hard cash. (Later, following Columbus's success Henry promoted a voyage by Columbus's fellow Genoese, John Cabot.)

Next Columbus turned to Spain. The Duke of Medina Coeli referred him to Isabella the Catholic, Queen of Castile. Negotiations with her were more extended. Failure had made Columbus arrogant. The less he was listened to, the more dogmatic his assertions became. His demands were outrageous. Not only did he want money to cover the cost of the trip, he must have ten per cent of all the bounty he picked up along the way. He must be entitled Admiral of the Ocean Sea. He must be appointed to the governorship of the Indies and every other island he discovered; honours which must pass through his eldest son to his heirs 'for evermore'.

True to her most Catholic reputation, Isabella handed Columbus over to the University of Salamanca, to an investigating committee consisting entirely of priests. They rejected the expedition on the grounds that Columbus had under-estimated the distance between Spain and Japan.

So Columbus was repulsed. Then his plans were reconsidered. Then Isabella changed her mind again. And then again. After seven years of alternating encouragement and repudiation Columbus finally got his three caravels. In his final plea to Isabella Columbus quoted from a book recently printed, *The Travels of Marco Polo*. The Orient was a land dripping with spices and paved with gold. It was ruled over by a great Christian prince. If only he could be reached, this prince would ally his forces with those of Spain and surround and defeat the Turk.

Columbus reinforced the testimony of Marco Polo by recounting his own conversations with God. The Almighty could confirm Marco Polo's story. Columbus's eloquence was irresistible. Assured by her treasurer that the cost of three caravels would be rather less than the cost of one banquet, Isabella agreed to underwrite the expense. Columbus's contract, with all his requirements indulged, was signed at Grenada, and, with a royal blessing and a letter to be delivered to the Grand Khan of China, he was exhorted to prepare his expedition 'for gospel and for gold'.

After seven years of negotiations and repeated requests for financial support, Columbus finally received help from Spain; and on the morning of 3 August 1492 his convoy of three ships, the *Santa Maria*, the *Pinta* and the *Niña*, set sail from Pasdos.

The ships achieved the Canary Islands without much difficulty, but when they failed to sight any of the other islands with which cartographers had imaginatively dotted the Atlantic, morale amongst the men sank. After an encounter with the trade winds they were close to mutiny. On 10 October the captains of the two other ships signalled for a rendezvous and begged to be allowed to turn back. Columbus reassured them by showing them his log, which he had faked to reduce the distance they had sailed from Spain. Columbus had underestimated the width of the Atlantic Ocean by half. He promised the captains that if they were still at sea forty-eight hours later, he would allow them to turn back without him. On the night of 11 October he tells us, he 'prayed mightily to the Lord'. On the following day they sighted land.

The land which Columbus saw was Watling's Island in the Bahamas: he believed it to be Asia or one of its offshore islands. He went on to explore Haiti and then Cuba, which he decided was Marco Polo's Zipangu (Japan). He was surprised by the absence of cities, but there were cotton, spices, and strange birds, and the natives were coloured; and they assured him, in sign-language, one supposes, as the Indians assured all succeeding explorers, that inland there were mountains of gold.

Columbus never believed he had reached America. He did, however, reject his original identification of Cuba with Japan: he came to believe it to be a promontory of China instead. On his second voyage to the Indies in 1493 he refused to circumnavigate Cuba on the grounds that it was not an island. His third voyage in 1498 resulted in the discovery of South America. This, Columbus argued, was the boundary of the earthly paradise, as described in the Book of Genesis. On his fourth, last, great voyage (1502–4) along the south side of the Mexique Bay, he touched the isthmus of Panama and said it must be Malaya.

One detail he did recant: South America, he accepted, was not a continent recorded by Marco Polo. In his mental map of the world, the West Indies were the East Indies, and South America a kind of Australia. Columbus believed no more in the existence of America than he did in the isle of St Brendan.

If Columbus had not had his single-minded obsession with Asia, America might have been named after him. Instead the honour went to a dishonest Florentine. Amerigo Vespucci (1451–1512) promoted several voyages to the New World in the wake of Columbus. In an account of his travels, published in 1507, he is represented as having reached America ten years before; a claim based on his own letters in which he says he made four voyages. At least one of those was pure fabrication, and the rest are dubious. The man whose name is echoed everytime America and Americans are mentioned was a charlatan. But he gets the credit for recognizing one truth which Columbus resisted to the end of his life.

A Note on Hakluyt

Many of the pieces in Part Two have been taken from that original anthology of travellers' impressions of America, Hakluyt's *Voyages*.

Richard Hakluyt was born in about 1553. Entering Christ Church, Oxford, in 1570, he started on a course of reading which comprised all the printed or written voyages or discoveries that he could find. Some of these he collected in his *Divers Voyages Touching the Discoverie of America* (London, 1582) including his own translations. While chaplain to the embassy in Paris he started on his most famous work, *The Principall Navigations, Voiages and Discoveries of the English Nation*, the first volume of which appeared in 1589.

Christopher Columbus (1492)

In his log-book, in which he refers to himself as 'the admiral', Columbus records the first historic sighting of the New World and lands on an island of the Bahamas.

Wednesday, 10th of October

The course was west-southwest, and they went at the rate of ten miles an hour, occasionally 12 miles, and sometimes seven.

During the day and night they made 59 leagues, counted as no more than 44. Here the people could endure no longer. They complained of the length of the voyage. But the admiral cheered them up in the best way he could, giving them good hopes of the advantages they might gain from it. He added that, however much they might complain, he had to go to the Indies, and that he would go on until he found them with the help of our Lord.

Thursday, 11th of October

The course was west-southwest, and there was more sea than there had been during the whole of the voyage. They saw sandpipers and a green reed near the ship. Those of the caravel *Pinta* saw a cane and a pole, and they took up another small pole, which appeared to have been worked with iron; also another bit of cane, a land plant, and a small board. The crew of the caravel *Niña* also saw signs of land, and a small branch covered with berries. Everyone breathed afresh and rejoiced at these signs. The run until sunset was 27 leagues.

After sunset the admiral returned to his original west course, and they went along at the rate of 12 miles an hour. Up to two hours after midnight they had gone 90 miles, equal to 22½ leagues. As the caravel *Pinta* was a better sailer and went ahead of the admiral, she found the land, and made the signals ordered by the admiral. The land was first seen by a sailor named Rodrigo de Triana. But the admiral, at ten o'clock, being on the castle of the poop, saw a light, though it was so uncertain that he could not affirm it was land. He called Pedro Gutiérrez, a gentleman of the King's bedchamber, and said that there seemed to be a light, and that he should look at it. He did so and saw it. . . . After the admiral had spoken he saw the light once or twice, and it was like a wax candle rising and falling. It seemed to few to be an indication of land, but the admiral made certain that land was close.

When they said the 'Salve', which all the sailors were accustomed to sing in their way, the admiral asked and admonished the men to keep a good lookout on the forecastle and to watch well for land; and to him who should first cry out that he saw land, he would give a silk doublet, besides the other rewards promised by the Sovereigns – which were 10,000 maravedis [about $67.50; the maravedi was worth less than 7/10 of a cent] to him who should first see it [Columbus received the award]. At two hours after midnight the land was sighted at a distance of two leagues. They shortened sail and lay by under the mainsail without the bonnets.

Friday, 12th of October

The vessels were hove to, waiting for daylight. And on Friday they arrived at a small island of the Lucayos [Bahamas] called, in the language of the Indians, Guanahani [Watling Island]. Presently they saw naked people. The admiral went on shore in the armed boat, and Martín Alonso Pinzón and Vicente Yáñez, his brother, who was captain of the *Niña*. The admiral took the royal standard, and the captains went with two banners of the green cross, which the admiral took in all the ships as a sign, with an F and Y [for 'Fernando' and 'Ysabel'] and a crown over each letter, one on one side of the cross and the other on the other.

Having landed, they saw trees very green and much water and fruits of diverse kinds. The admiral called to the two captains and to the others who leaped on shore and to Rodrigo de Escobedo, secretary of the whole fleet, and to Rodrigo Sánchez of Segovia [the royal inspector], and said that they should bear faithful testimony that he, in presence of all, had taken, as he now took, possession of the said island for the King and for the Queen his Lords, making the declarations that are required, as is now largely set forth in the testimonies which were then made in writing.

Presently many inhabitants of the island assembled. What follows is in the actual words of the admiral in his book of the first navigation and discovery of the Indies: 'I,' he says, 'that we might form great friendship, for I knew that they were a people who could be more easily freed and converted to our holy faith by love than by force, gave to some of them red caps, and glass beads to put round their necks, and many other things of little value, which gave them great pleasure and made them so much our friends that it was a marvel to see. They afterwards came to the ship's boats where we were, swimming and bringing us parrots, cotton threads in skeins, darts, and many other things. And we exchanged them for other things that we gave them, such as glass beads and small bells. In fine, they took all and gave what they had with good will.

'It appeared to me to be a race of people very poor in everything. They go as naked as when their mothers bore them, and so do the women, although I did not see more than one young girl. All I saw were youths, none more than thirty years of age. They are very well made, with very handsome bodies and very good countenances. Their hair is short and coarse, almost like the hairs of a horse's tail. They wear the hairs brought down to the eyebrows, except a few locks behind which they wear long and never cut. They paint themselves black, and they are the colour of the Canarians, neither black nor white. Some paint themselves white, others red, and others of what colour they find. Some paint their faces, others the whole body, some only round the eyes, others only on the nose. They neither carry nor know anything of arms, for I showed them swords, and they took them by the blade and cut themselves through ignorance. . . . They should be good servants and intelligent, for I observed that they quickly took in what was said to them, and I believe that they would easily be made Christians, as it appeared to me that they had no religion.

'I, our Lord being pleased, will take hence, at the time of my departure, six natives for Your Highnesses, that they may learn to speak. I saw no beast of any kind, except parrots, on this island.' The above is in the words of the admiral.

Lorenzo Pasqualio (1497)

John Cabot (1425–1501) was the discoverer of mainland America. He was born in Genoa, naturalized in Venice in 1476, and settled in Bristol about 1490. Under letters-patent from Henry VII of England he set sail with two ships, and accompanied by his three sons sighted Cape Breton Island and Nova Scotia on June 24th 1497.

The Venetian, our countryman, who went with a ship from Bristol to find new islands, has returned, and says that 700 leagues hence he discovered mainland, the territory of the Grand Cham [Great Khan]. He coasted for 300 leagues and landed. He did not see any person, but he has brought hither to the king certain snares which had been set to catch game, and a needle for making nets. He also found some cut trees, wherefore he supposed there were inhabitants. Being in doubt he returned to his ship.

He was three months on the voyage, and this is certain; and on his return he saw two islands but would not land, so as not to lose time, as he was short of provisions. The king is much pleased with this. He says that the tides are slack and do not flow as they do here.

The king has promised that in the spring our countryman shall have ten ships; armed to his order, and at his request has conceded him all the prisoners, except traitors, to go with him as he has requested. The king has also given him money wherewith to amuse himself till then, and he is now at Bristol with his wife, who is also Venetian, and with his sons. His name is Zuam Talbot, and he is styled the great admiral. Vast honour is paid to him. He dresses in silk, and these English run after him like mad people, so that he can enlist as many of them as he pleases, and a number of our own rogues besides.

The discoverer of these things planted on his new-found land a large cross, with one flag of England and another of Saint Mark, by reason of his being a Venetian, so that our banner has floated very far afield.

London, 23 August, 1497.

John Verrazanus (1524)

*'The relation of John Verrazanus (c. 1480–c. 1527) a Florentine, of the land
by him discovered in the name of His Majesty Francis I of France written in
Dieppe the eighth of July, 1524.' (Hakluyt's* Voyages*)*

The 17 of January, the year 1524, by the grace of God we departed from
the dishabited Rock [one of the Deserta islands] by the isle of Madeira,
appertaining to the king of Portugal, with fifty men, with victuals, weapons,
and other ship munitions very well provided and furnished for eight months.
And, sailing westward with a fair easterly wind, in 25 days we ran 500
leagues. And the 20 of February we were overtaken with as sharp and
terrible a tempest as ever any sailors suffered; whereof, with the divine help
and merciful assistance of almighty God and the goodness of our ship,
accompanied with the good hap of her fortunate name, we were delivered,
and with a prosperous wind followed our course west and by north. And
in other 25 days we made above 400 leagues more, where we discovered a
new land [probably the vicinity of Charleston, South Carolina] never before
seen of any man, either ancient or modern. And at the first sight it seemed
somewhat low but, being within a quarter of a league of it, we perceived
by the great fires that we saw by the seacoast that it was inhabited, and saw
that the land stretched to the southward.

In seeking some convenient harbour whereby to come aland and have
knowledge of the place, we sailed 50 leagues in vain; and, seeing the land
to run still to the southward, we resolved to return back again toward the
north, where we found ourselves troubled with the like difficulty. At length,
being in despair to find any port, we cast anchor upon the coast and sent
our boat to shore, where we saw great store of people which came to the
seaside; and seeing us to approach, they fled away, and sometimes would
stand still and look back, beholding us with great admiration. But afterward,
being animated and assured with signs that we made them, some of them
came hard to the seaside, seeming to rejoice very much at the sight of us
and, marvelling greatly at our apparel, shape, and whiteness, showed us by
sundry signs where we might most commodiously come aland with our boat,
offering us also of their victuals to eat.

Now I will briefly declare to Your Majesty their life and manners, as far
as we could have notice thereof: These people go altogether naked, except
only that they cover their privy parts with certain skins of beasts like unto
martens, which they fasten unto a narrow girdle made of grass, very artificially wrought, hanged about with tails of divers other beasts, which round
about their bodies hang dangling down to their knees. Some of them wear
garlands of birds' feathers. The people are of colour russet, and not much
unlike the Saracens, their hair black, thick, and not very long, which they
tie together in a knot behind and wear it like a tail. They are well featured

in their limbs, of mean stature, and commonly somewhat bigger than we; broad breasted, strong arms, their legs and other parts of their bodies well fashioned, and they are disfigured in nothing saving that they have somewhat broad visages, and yet not all of them; for we saw many of them well favoured, having black and great eyes with a cheerful and steady look, not strong of body yet sharp-witted, nimble, and great runners, as far as we could learn by experience. And in those two last qualities they are like to the people of the East parts of the world, and especially to them of the uttermost parts of China. We could not learn of this people their manner of living nor their particular customs by reason of the short abode we made on the shore – our company being but small and our ship riding far off in the sea . . .

We departed from this place, still running along the coast which we found to trend toward the east, and we saw everywhere very great fires by reason of the multitude of the inhabitants. While we rode on that coast, partly because it had no harbour and for that we wanted water, we sent our boat ashore with 25 men; where, by reason of great and continual waves that beat against the shore – being an open coast – without succour none of our men could possibly go ashore without losing our boat. We saw there many people, which came unto the shore making divers signs of friendship and showing that they were content we should come aland, and by trial we found them to be very courteous and gentle, as Your Majesty shall understand by the success.

To the intent we might send them of our things which the Indians commonly desire and esteem, as sheets of paper, glasses, bells, and suchlike trifles, we sent a young man, one of our mariners, ashore; who, swimming toward them and being within three or four yards off the shore, not trusting them, cast the things upon the shore. Seeking afterward to return, he was with such violence of the waves beaten upon the shore that he was so bruised that he lay there almost dead; which the Indians perceiving, ran to catch him and, drawing him out, they carried him a little way off from the sea. The young man, perceiving they carried him being at the first dismayed, began then greatly to fear and cried out piteously. Likewise did the Indians which did accompany him, going about to cheer him and give him courage; and then, setting him on the ground at the foot of a little hill, against the sun, began to behold him with great admiration, marveling at the whiteness of his flesh. And, putting off his clothes, they made him warm at a great fire, not without our great fear which remained in the boat that they would have roasted him at that fire and have eaten him. The young man, having recovered his strength and having stayed awhile with them, showed them by signs that he was desirous to return to the ship. And they, with great love clapping him fast about with many embracings, accompanying him unto the sea and, to put him in more assurance, leaving him alone, they went unto a high ground and stood there beholding him until he was entered into the boat. This young man observed, as we did also, that these are of colour inclining to black, as the other were, with their flesh very shining; of mean stature, handsome visage, and delicate limbs, and of very little strength, but of prompt wit; farther we observed not . . .

And we came to another land, being 15 leagues distant from the island, where we found a passing good haven; wherein, being entered, we found about 20 small boats of the people, which, with divers cries and wonderings, came about our ship. Coming no nearer than 50 paces toward us, they stayed and beheld the artificialness of our ship, our shape and apparel. Then they all made a loud shout together, declaring that they rejoiced. When we had something animated them (using their gests), they came so near us that we cast them certain bells and glasses and many toys, which, when they had received, they looked on them with laughing and came without fear aboard our ship. There were amongst these people two kings of so goodly stature and shape as is possible to declare. The eldest was about forty years of age; the second was a young man of twenty years old. Their apparel was in this manner: the elder had upon his naked body a hart's skin, wrought artificially with divers branches like damask; his head was bare, with the hair tied up behind with divers knots; about his neck he had a large chain garnished with divers stones of sundry colours. The young man was almost apparelled after the same manner. This is the goodliest people, and of the fairest conditions, that we have found in this our voyage. They exceed us in bigness, they are of the colour of brass, some of them incline more to whiteness. Others are of yellow colour, of comely visage, with long and black hair which they are very careful to trim and deck up. They are black- and quick-eyed. I write not to Your Majesty of the other part of their body, having all such proportion as appertaineth to any handsome man. The women are of the like conformity and beauty, very handsome and well favoured. They are as well mannered and continent as any women of good education. They are all naked save their privy parts, which they cover with a deer's skin, branched or embroidered, as the men use. There are also of them which wear on their arms very rich skins of leopards. They adorn their heads with divers ornaments made of their own hair, which hang down before on both sides of their breasts. Others use other kind of dressing themselves, like unto the women of Egypt and Syria; these are of the elder sort. And when they are married they wear divers toys, according to the usage of the people of the East, as well men as women.

Among whom we saw many plates of wrought copper, which they esteem more than gold, which for the colour they make no account of for that among all other it is counted the basest; they make most account of azure and red. The things that they esteemed most of all those which we gave them were bells, crystal of azure colour, and other toys to hang at their ears or about their neck. They did not desire cloth of silk or of gold, much less of any other sort. Neither cared they for things made of steel and iron, which we often showed them in our armour, which they made no wonder at, and, in beholding them, they only asked the art of making them. The like they did at our glasses, which, when they beheld, they suddenly laughed and gave them us again. They are very liberal, for they give that which they have.

We became great friends with these, and one day we entered into the haven with our ship, whereas before we rode a league off at sea by reason of the contrary weather. They came in great companies of their small boats unto the ship, with their faces all bepainted with divers colours showing us that it was a sign of joy, bringing us of their victuals. They made signs unto us where we might safest ride in the haven for the safeguard of our ship, keeping still our company. And after we were come to an anchor, we bestowed 15 days in providing ourselves many necessary things, whither every day the people repaired to see our ship, bringing their wives with them whereof they are very jealous. And they, themselves entering aboard the ship and staying there a good space, caused their wives to stay in their boats; and for all the entreaty we could make, offering to give them divers things, we could never obtain that they would suffer them to come aboard our ship.

And oftentimes one of the two kings coming, with his queen and many gentlemen for their pleasure, to see us, they all stayed on the shore 200 paces from us, sending a small boat to give us intelligence of their coming, saying they would come to see our ship. This they did in token of safety. And as soon as they had answer from us they came immediately; and, having stayed a while to behold it, they wondered at hearing the cries and noise of the mariners. The queen and her maids stayed in a very light boat at an island a quarter of a league off while the king abode a long space in our ship, uttering divers conceits with gestures, viewing with great admiration all the furniture of the ship, demanding the property of everything particularly. He took likewise great pleasure in beholding our apparel, and in tasting our meats, and so, courteously taking his leave, departed. And sometimes, our men staying for two or three days on a little island near the ship for divers necessaries (as it is the use of seamen), he returned with seven or eight of his gentlemen to see what we did, and asked of us oft times if we meant to make any long abode there, offering us of their provision. Then the king, drawing his bow and running up and down with his gentlemen, made much sport to gratify our men.

We were oftentimes within the land five or six leagues, which we found as pleasant as is possible to declare, very apt for any kind of husbandry of corn, wine, and oil, for that there are plains 25 or 30 leagues broad, open and without any impediment of trees, of such fruitfulness that any seed being sown therein will bring forth most excellent fruit. We entered afterward into the woods, which we found so great and thick that any army, were it never so great, might have hid itself therein, the trees whereof are oaks, cypress trees, and other sorts unknown in Europe. We found *Pomi appii* [a kind of apple], damson trees, and nut trees, and many other sorts of fruits differing from ours. There are beasts in great abundance – as harts, deers, leopards, and other kinds – which they take with their nets and bows, which are their chief weapons. The arrows which they use are made with great cunning, and instead of iron, they head them with smeriglio [emery], with jasper stone, and hard marble and other sharp stones; which they use instead of iron to cut trees and make their boats of one whole piece of wood, making it hollow with great and wonderful art, wherein ten or twelve men may be [seated] commodiously. Their oars are short and broad at the end, and they use them in the sea without any danger and by main force of arms, with as great speediness as they list themselves.

We saw their houses, made in circular or round form ten or twelve feet in compass, made with half circles of timber, separate one from another without any order of building, covered with mats of straw wrought cunningly together which save them from the wind and rain. And if they had the order of building and perfect skill of workmanship as we have, there were no doubt but that they would also make eftsoons great and stately buildings.

For all the seacoasts are full of clear and glistering stones and alabaster, and therefore it is full of good havens and harbours for ships. They move the foresaid houses from one place to another, according to the commodity of the place and season wherein they will make their abode; and only taking off the cover they have other houses builded incontinent [at once]. The father and the whole family dwell together in one house in great number; in some of them we saw 25 or 30 persons. They feed as the other do aforesaid, of pulse, which do grow in that country with better order of husbandry than in others.

They observe in their sowing the course of the moon and the rising of certain stars, and divers other customs spoken of by antiquity. Moreover they live by hunting and fishing. They live long and are seldom sick; and if they chance to fall sick at any time, they heal themselves with fire, without any physician; and they say that they die for very age. They are very pitiful and charitable toward their neighbours. They make great lamentations in their adversity, and in their misery the kindred reckon up all their felicity. At their departure out of life they use mourning mixed with singing, which continueth for a long space. This is as much as we could learn of them.

This land is situated in the parallel of Rome, in 41 degrees and two tierces [thirds]; but somewhat more cold, by accidental cause and not of nature (as I will declare unto Your Highness elsewhere). Describing at this present the situation of the foresaid country, which lieth east and west, I say that the mouth of the haven lieth open to the south half a league broad; and, being entered within it, between the east and the north it stretcheth 12 leagues, where it waxeth broader and broader and maketh a gulf about 20 leagues in compass; wherein are five small islands, very fruitful and pleasant, full of high and broad trees; among the which islands any great navy may ride safe without any fear of tempest or other danger. Afterward, turning toward the south and in the entering into the haven, on both sides there are the most pleasant hills, with many rivers of most clear water falling into the sea. In the midst of this entrance there is a rock of freestone, growing by nature, apt to build any castle or fortress there for the keeping of the haven [probably Narragansett Bay].

The 5 of May, being furnished with all things necessary, we departed from the said coast, keeping along in the sight thereof. And we sailed 150 leagues finding it always after one manner, but the land somewhat bigger with certain mountains, all which bear a show of mineral matter. We sought not to land there in any place because the weather served our turn for sailing. But we suppose that it was like to the former. The coast ran eastward for the space of 50 leagues. And trending afterward [to] the north, we found another land: high, full of thick woods, the trees whereof were firs, cypresses, and suchlike as are wont to grow in cold countries [probably New Hampshire or southern Maine]. The people differ much from the other; and look how much the former seemed to be courteous and gentle, so much were these full of rudeness and ill manners, and so barbarous that by no signs that ever we could make we could have any kind of traffic with them. They clothe themselves in bearskins and leopards' and seals' and other beasts' skins. Their food, as far as we could perceive [by their] repairing often unto their dwellings, we suppose to be by hunting and fishing, and of certain fruits which are a kind of roots which the earth yieldeth of her own accord. They have no grain, neither saw we any kind of sign of tillage; neither is the land, for the barrenness thereof, apt to bear fruit or seed.

If at any time we desired by exchange to have any of their commodities, they used to come to the seashore upon certain craggy rocks, and, we standing in our boats, they let down with a rope what it pleased them to give us, crying continually that we should not approach to the land, demanding immediately the exchange, taking nothing but knives, fishhooks, and tools to cut withal; neither did they make any account of our courtesy. And when we had nothing left to exchange with them, when we departed from them, the people showed all signs of discourtesy and disdain as was possible for any creature to invent. We were, in despite of them, two or three leagues within the land, being in number 25 armed men of us. And when we went on shore they shot at us with their bows, making great outcries, and afterward fled into the woods ...

Sailing northeast for the space of 150 leagues, we approached to the land that in times past was discovered by the Britons, which is in fifty degrees [Newfoundland]. Having now spent all our provision and victuals, and having discovered about 700 leagues and more of new countries, and being furnished with water and wood, we concluded to return into France.

Touching the religion of this people which we have found: for want of their language we could not understand, neither by signs nor gesture, that they had any religion or law at all, or that they did acknowledge any First Cause or Mover; neither that they worship the heaven or stars, the sun or moon or other planets, and, much less, whether they be idolators. Neither could we learn whether that they used any kind of sacrifices or other adorations; neither in their villages have they any temples or houses of prayer.

Jacques Cartier (1536–7)

Between 1534 and 1541 the French navigator Jacques Cartier (1491–1557) made three voyages of discovery to North America, discovering and naming the St Lawrence river. In the land of the Huron at St Charles his men were struck down by the scurvy. Cartier's Brief récit et succincte narration de la navigation faicte es ysles de Canada ... *was first printed in 1545. This translation is by Hakluyt.*

In the month of December we understood that the pestilence was come among the people of Stadacona, in such sort that before we knew it, according to their confession, there were dead above 50; whereupon we charged them neither to come near our fort, nor about our ships, or us. And albeit we had driven them from us, the said unknown sickness [scurvy] began to spread itself amongst us after the strangest sort that ever was either heard of or seen, insomuch as some did lose all their strength and could not stand on their feet; then did their legs swell, their sinews shrink as black as any coal. Others also had all their skins spotted with spots of blood of a purple colour; then did it ascend up to their ankles, knees, thighs, shoulders, arms, and neck; their mouth became stinking, their gums so rotten that all the flesh did fall off, even to the roots of the teeth, which did also almost all fall out.

With such infection did this sickness spread itself in our three ships that about the middle of February, of 110 persons that we were, there were not ten whole, so that one could not help the other – a most horrible and pitiful case, considering the place we were in, forsomuch as the people of the country would daily come before our fort and saw but few of us. There were already eight dead and more than 50 sick and, as we thought, past all hope of recovery. Our captain, seeing this our misery and that the sickness was gone so far, ordained and commanded that everyone should devoutly prepare himself to prayer, and, in remembrance of Christ, caused his image to be set upon a tree about a flight shot from the fort amidst the ice and snow, giving all men to understand that on the Sunday following, service should be said there, and that whosoever could go, sick or whole, should go thither in procession singing the seven Psalms of David, with other litanies, praying most heartily that it would please the said our Christ to have compassion upon us. Service being done and as well celebrated as we could, our captain there made a vow that if it would please God to give him leave to return into France, he would go on pilgrimage to our Lady of Rocquemado. That day Philip Rougemont, born in Amboise, died, being twenty-two years old; and, because the sickness was to us unknown, our Captain caused him to be ripped to see if by any means possible we might know what it was, and so seek means to save and preserve the rest of the company; he was found to have his heart white but rotten and more than a quart of red water about it; his liver was indifferent fair, but his lungs black and mortified; his blood was altogether shrunk about the heart so that, when he was opened, great quantity of rotten blood issued out from about his heart; his milt [spleen] toward the back was somewhat perished [deteriorated], rough as [if] it had been rubbed against a stone. Moreover, because one of his thighs was very black without, it was opened, but within it was whole and sound; that done as well as we could, he was buried.

In such sort did the sickness continue and increase that there were not above three sound men in the ships, and none was able to go under hatches to draw drink for himself nor for his fellows. Sometimes we were constrained to bury some of the dead under the snow because we were not able to dig any graves for them, the ground was so hard frozen and we so weak. Besides this, we did greatly fear that the people of the country would perceive our weakness and misery, which to hide, our captain, whom it pleased God always to keep in health, would go out with two or three of the company, some sick and some whole, whom when he saw out of the fort, he would throw stones at them and chide them, feigning that so soon as he came again he would beat them, and then with signs showed the people of the country that he caused all his men to work and labour in the ships, some in calking them, some in beating of chalk, some in one thing and some in another, and that he would not have them come forth till their work was done. And to make his tale seem true and likely, he would make all his men whole and sound to make a great noise with knocking sticks, stones, hammers, and other things together; at which time we were so oppressed and grieved with that sickness that we had lost all hope ever to see France again, if God, of His infinite goodness and mercy, had not with His pitiful eye looked upon us and revealed a singular and excellent remedy against all diseases unto us, the best that ever was found upon earth, as hereafter shall follow.

From the midst of November until the midst of March we were kept in amidst the ice above two fathoms thick and snow above four feet high and more, higher than the sides of our ships, which lasted till that time in such sort that all our drinks were frozen in the vessels, and the ice through all the ship was above a hand-breadth thick, as well above hatches as beneath; and so much of the river as was fresh, even to Hochelaga, was frozen; in which space there died 25 of our best and chiefest men, and all the rest were so sick that we thought they should never recover again, only three or four excepted. Then it pleased God to cast His pitiful eye upon us, and sent us the knowledge of remedy of our healths and recovery in such manner as in the next chapter shall be showed.

Our captain, considering our estate (and how that sickness was increased and hot amongst us), one day went forth of the fort and, walking upon the ice, he saw a troupe of those countrymen coming from Stadacona, among which was Domagaia, who, not passing ten or 12 days afore, had been very sick with that disease and had his knees swollen as big as a child of two years old, all his sinews shrunk together, his teeth spoiled, his gums rotten and stinking. Our captain, seeing him whole and sound, was thereat marvellous glad, hoping to understand and know of him how he had healed himself, to the end he might ease and help his men. So soon as they were come near him, he asked Domagaia how he had done to heal himself; he answered that he had taken the juice and sap of the leaves of a certain tree and therewith had healed himself, for it is a singular remedy against that disease. Then our captain asked of him if any were to be had thereabout, desiring him to show him for to heal a servant of his who, whilst he was in Canada with Donnacona, was striken with that disease. That he did because he would not show the number of his sick men. Domagaia straight sent two women to fetch some of it, which brought ten or 12 branches of it and therewithal showed the way how to use it, and that is thus: to take the bark and leaves of the said tree and boil them together, then to drink of the said decoction every other day and to put the dregs of it upon his legs that is sick; moreover, they told us that the virtue of that tree was to heal any other disease. The tree is in their language called *ameda* or *hanneda*; this is thought to be the sassafras tree. Our captain presently caused some of that drink to be made for his men to drink of it, but there was none durst taste for it except one or two who ventured the drinking of it only to taste and prove it. The others, seeing that, did the like and presently recovered their health and were delivered of that sickness and what other disease soever, in such sort that there were some had been diseased and troubled with the French pox [syphilis] four or five years and with this drink were clean healed. After this medicine was found and proved to be true, there was such strife about it who should be first to take it that they were ready to kill one another, so that a tree as big as any oak in France was spoiled and lopped bare and occupied all in five or six days; and it wrought so well that if all the physicians of Montpellier and Louvain had been there with all the drugs of Alexandria, they would not have done so much in one year as that tree did in six days; for it did so prevail that as many as used of it by the grace of God recovered their health.

Luis Hernandez de Biedma (1539)

Ferdinand De Soto (1496–1542) had made his fortune serving with Pizarro in the conquest of Peru. In 1539 he was given permission by the Holy Roman Emperor Charles V to conquer Florida. He landed at Tampa Bay in May. For three years until he died of a fever on the banks of the Mississippi, de Soto's expedition was harassed by hostile Indians, who resisted enslavement. De Biedma served on the expedition, and his account is part of a report he presented to the Holy Roman Emperor Charles V, when he held a Council of the Indies in 1544.

We entered the town and set it on fire, whereby a number of Indians were burned, and all that we had was consumed, so that there remained not a thing. We fought that day until nightfall, without a single Indian having surrendered to us – they fighting bravely on like lions. We killed them all, either with fire or the sword, or, such of them as came out, with the lance, so that when it was nearly dark there remained only three alive; and these, taking the women that had been brought to dance, placed the twenty in front, who, crossing their hands, made signs to us that we should come for them. The Christians advancing toward the women, these turned aside, and the three men behind them shot their arrows at us, when we killed two of them. The last Indian, not to surrender, climbed a tree that was in the fence, and taking the cord from his bow, tied it about his neck, and from a limb hanged himself.

This day the Indians slew more than twenty of our men, and those of us who escaped only hurt were two hundred and fifty, bearing upon our bodies seven hundred and sixty injuries from their shafts. At night we dressed our wounds with the fat of the dead Indians, as there was no medicine left, all that belonged to us having been burned. We tarried twenty-seven or twenty-eight days to take care of ourselves, and God be praised that we were all relieved. The women were divided as servants among those who were suffering most. We learned from the Indians that we were as many as forty leagues from the sea. It was much the desire that the Governor should go to the coast, for we had tidings of the brigantines; but he dared not venture thither, as it was already the middle of November, the season very cold; and he found it necessary to go in quest of a country where subsistence might be had for the winter; here there was none, the region being one of little food.

We resumed our direction to the northward, and travelled ten or twelve days, suffering greatly from the cold and rain, in which we marched afoot, until arriving at a fertile province, plentiful in provisions, where we could stop during the rigour of the season. The snows fall more heavily there than they do in Castile. Having reached the Province of Chicaza, the warriors came out to interrupt the passage of a river we had to cross. We were detained by them three days. Finally, we went over in a piragua we built, when the Indians fled to the woods. After seven or eight days, messengers from the Cacique arrived, saying that he and all his people desired to come and serve us. The Governor received the message well, and sent word to him to do so without fail, and that he would present him with many of the things he brought. The Cacique came, having with him a number of persons, who bore him upon their shoulders. He gave us some deerskins and little dogs. The people returned, and every day Indians came and went, bringing us many hares, and whatever else the country supplied.

In the night-time we captured some Indians, who, on a footing of peace, came to observe how we slept and guarded. We, unaware of the perfidy that was intended, told the Cacique that we desired the next day to continue our march, when he left, and that night fell upon us. As the enemy knew whereabout our sentinels were set, they got amongst us into the town, without being observed, by twos and fours, more than three hundred men, with fire which they brought in little pots, not to be seen. When the sentinels discovered that more were coming in troop, they beat to arms; but this was not done until the others had already set fire to the town. The Indians did us very great injury, killing fifty-seven horses, more than three hundred hogs, and thirteen or fourteen men; and it was a great mysterious providence of God, that, though we were not resisiting them, nor giving them any cause to do so, they turned and fled; had they followed us up, not a man of all our number could have escaped. Directly we moved to a cottage about a mile off.

We knew that the Indians had agreed to return upon us that night; but, God be praised, in consequence of a light rain, they did not come; for we were in so bad condition, that, although some horses still remained, we had no saddles, lances, nor targets, all having been consumed. We hastened to make them, the best we could with the means at hand; and at the end of five days, the Indians, coming back upon us with their squadrons in order, attacked us with much concert at three points. As we were prepared, and, moreover, aware of their approach, we met them at the onset, beat them back, and did them some injury; so that, thank God, they returned no more. We remained here perhaps two months, getting ready what were necessary of saddles, lances, and targets, and then left, taking the direction to the northwest, toward a Province called Alibamo.

At this time befell us what is said never to have occurred in the Indias. In the highway over which we had to pass, without there being either women to protect or provisions to secure, and only to try our valour with theirs, the Indians put up a very strong stockade directly across the road, about three hundred of them standing behind it, resolute to die rather than give back. So soon as they observed our approach, some came out to shoot their arrows, threatening that not one of us should remain alive. When we had surveyed that work, thus defended by men, we supposed they guarded something – provision perhaps – of which we stood greatly in need; for we had calculated to cross a desert of twelve days' journey in its extent, where we could have nothing to eat but what we carried. We alighted, some forty or fifty men, and put ourselves on two sides, arranging that at the sound of the trumpet we should all enter the barricade at one time. We did accordingly, carrying it, although at some cost, losing on our side seven or eight men, and having twenty-five or twenty-six more wounded. We killed some Indians, and took others, from whom we learned that they had done this to measure themselves with us, and nothing else. We looked about for food, although at great hazard, that we might begin our journey in the wilderness.

We travelled eight days with great care, in tenderness of the wounded and the sick we carried. One mid-day we came upon a town called Quizquiz, and so suddenly to the inhabitants, that they were without any notice of us, the men being away at work in the maize-fields. We took more than three hundred women, and the few skins and shawls they had in their houses. There we first found a little walnut of the country, which is much better than that here in Spain. The town was near the banks of the River Espiritu Santo. They told us that it was, with many towns about there, tributary to a lord of Pacaha, famed throughout all the land. When the men heard that we had taken their women, they came to us peacefully, requesting the Governor to restore them. He did so, and asked them for canoes in which to pass that great river. These they promised, but never gave; on the contrary, they collected to give us battle, coming in sight of the town where we were; but in the end, not venturing to make an attack, they turned and retired.

We left that place and went to encamp by the riverside, to put ourselves in order for crossing. On the other shore we saw numbers of people collected to oppose our landing, who had many canoes. We set about building four large piraguas, each capable of taking sixty or seventy men and five or six horses. We were engaged in the work twenty-seven or twenty-eight days. During this time, the Indians every day, at three o'clock in the afternoon, would get into two hundred and fifty very large canoes they had, well shielded, and come near the shore on which we were; with loud cries they would exhaust their arrows upon us, and then return to the other bank. After they saw that our boats were at the point of readiness for crossing, they all went off, leaving the passage free. We crossed the river in concert, it being nearly a league in width, and nineteen or twenty fathoms deep. We found some good towns on the other side; and once more following up the stream, on the way to that Province of Pacaha, we came first to the province of another lord, called Icasqui, against whom he waged severe war. The Cacique came out peacefully to meet us, saying that he had heard of us for a long time, and that he knew we were men from heaven, whom their arrows could not harm; wherefore, he desired to have no strife, and wished only to serve us. The Governor received him very kindly, and permitting no one to enter the town, to avoid doing mischief, we encamped in sight, on a plain, where we lay two days.

On the day of our arrival, the Cacique said that inasmuch as he knew the Governor to be a man from the sky, who must necessarily have to go away, he besought him to leave a sign, of which he might ask support in his wars, and his people call upon for rain, of which their fields had great need, as their children were dying of hunger. The Governor commanded that a very tall cross be made of two pines, and told him to return the next day, when he would give him the sign from heaven for which he asked; but that the Chief must believe nothing could be needed if he had a true faith in the cross. He returned the next day, complaining much because we so long delayed giving him the sign he asked, and he had good will to serve and follow us. Thereupon he set up a loud wailing because the compliance was not immediate, which caused us all to weep, witnessing such devotion and earnestness in his entreaties. The Governor told him to bring all his people back in the evening, and that we would go with them to his town and take thither the sign he had asked. He came in the afternoon with them, and we went in procession to the town, while they followed us. Arriving there, as it is the custom of the Caciques to have near their houses a high hill, made by hand, some having the houses placed thereon, we set up the cross on the summit of a mount, and we all went on bended knees, with great humility, to kiss the foot of that cross. The Indians did the same as they saw us do, nor more nor less; then directly they brought a great quantity of cane, making a fence about it; and we returned that night to our camp.

In the morning, we took up our course for Pacaha, which was by the river upward. We travelled two days, and then discovered the town on a plain, well fenced about, and surrounded by a water-ditch made by hand. Hastening on as fast as possible, we came near and halted, not daring to enter there; but going about on one side and the other, and discovering that many people were escaping, we assailed and entered the town, meeting no opposition. We took only a few people, for nearly all had fled, without, however, being able to carry off the little they possessed. While we yet halted in sight of the town, before venturing to enter it, we saw coming behind us a large body of Indians, whom we supposed to be advancing to the assistance of the place; but going to meet them, we found they were those we had left behind, among whom we had raised the cross, and were following to lend us their succour, should we need any. We took the Cacique to the town, where he gave the Governor many thanks for the sign we had left him, telling us the rain had fallen heavily in his country the day before, and his people were so glad of it that they wished to follow and not leave us. The Governor put him into the town, and gave him every thing found there, which was great riches for those people – some beads made of sea-snails, the skins of cats and of deer, and a little maize. He returned home with them, much gratified. We remained in this town twenty-seven or twenty-eight days, to discover if we could take a path to the northward, whereby to come out on the South Sea.

Some incursions were made to capture Indians who might give us the information; particularly was one undertaken to the northwest, where we were told there were large settlements, through which we might go. We went in that direction eight days, through a wilderness which had large pondy swamps, where we did not find even trees, and only some wide plains, on which grew a plant so rank and high, that even on horseback we could not break our way through. Finally, we came to some collections of huts, covered with rush sewed together. When the owner of one moves away, he will roll up the entire covering, and carry it, the wife taking the frame of poles over which it is stretched; these they take down and put up so readily, that though they should move anew every hour, they conveniently enough carry their house on their backs. We learned from this people that there were some hamlets of the sort about the country, the inhabitants of which employed themselves in finding places for their dwellings wherever many deer were accustomed to range, and a swamp where were many fish; and that when they had frightened the game and the fish from one place, so that they took them there not so easily as at first, they would all move off with their dwellings for some other part, where the animals were not yet shy. This Province, called Caluç, had a people who care little to plant, finding support in meat and fish.

We returned to Pacaha, where the Governor had remained, and found that the Cacique had come in peacefully, living with him in the town. In this time arrived the Cacique from the place behind, at which we had put up the cross. The efforts of these two chiefs, who were enemies, each to place himself on the right hand when the Governor commanded that they should sit at his sides, was a sight worth witnessing.

Finding that there was no way by which to march to the other sea, we returned towards the south, and went with the Cacique to where was the cross, and thence took the direction to the southwest, to another Province called Quiquate. This was the largest town we found in Florida, and was on an arm of the Rio Grande. We remained there eight or nine days, to find guides and interpreters, still with the intention of coming out, if possible, on the other sea; for the Indians told us that eleven days' travel thence was a province where they subsisted on certain cattle, and there we could find interpreters for the whole distance to that sea.

We departed with guides for the Province called Coligua, without any road, going at night to the swamps, where we drank from the hand and found abundance of fish. We went over much even country and other of broken hills, coming straight upon the town, as much so as if we had been taken thither by a royal highway, instead of which not a man in all time had passed there before. The land is very plentiful of subsistence, and we found a large quantity of dressed cows' tails, and others already cured. We inquired of the inhabitants for a path in the direction we held, or a town on it, near or far. They could give us no sort of information, only that if we wished to go in the direction where there were people, we should have to return upon a west-southwestern course.

We continued to pursue the course chosen by our guides, and went to some scattered settlements called Tatil Coya. Here we found a copious river, which we afterwards discovered empties into the Rio Grande, and we were told that up the stream was a great Province, called Cayas. We went thither, and found it to be a population that, though large, was entirely scattered. It is a very rough country of hills. Several incursions were made; in one of which the Cacique and a large number of people were taken. On asking him about the particulars of the country, he told us that in following up the river we should come upon a fertile Province, called Tula. The Governor, desiring to visit there, to see if it were a place in which he could winter the people, set off with twenty men on horseback, leaving the remainder in the Province at Cayas.

Before coming to the Province of Tula, we passed over some rough hills, and arrived at the town before the inhabitants had any notice of us. In attempting to seize some Indians, they began to yell and show us battle.

They wounded of ours that day seven or eight men, and nine or ten horses; and such was their courage, that they came upon us in packs, by eights and tens, like worried dogs. We killed some thirty or forty of them. The Governor thought it not well to stay there that night with his small force, and returned on the way we had come, going through a bad passage of the ridge, where it was feared the natives would beset us, to a plain in a vale made by the river. The next day we got back to where the people lay; but there were no Indians of ours, nor could any in the province be found, to speak the language of these we brought.

Orders were given that all should make ready to go to that province. We marched thither at once. The next morning after our arrival, at daybreak, three very large squadrons of Indians came upon us by as many directions: we met them and beat them, doing some injury, so much that they returned upon us no more. In two or three days they sent us messengers of peace, although we did not understand a thing they said, for want of an interpreter. By signs we told them to bring persons in there who could understand the people living back of us; and they brought five or six Indians who understood the interpreters we had. They asked who we were, and of what we were in search. We asked them for some great provinces where there should be much provision (for the cold of winter had begun to threaten us sharply), and they said that on the route we were taking they knew of no great town; but they pointed, that if we wished to return to the east and southeast, or go northwest, we should find large towns.

Discovering that we could not prevail against the difficulty, we returned to the southeast, and went to a Province that is called Quipana, at the base of some very steep ridges; whence we journeyed in a direction to the east, and, having crossed those mountains, went down upon some plains, where we found a population suited to our purpose, for there was a town nigh in which was much food, seated by a copious river emptying into the Rio Grande, from whence we came. The Province was called Viranque. We stopped in it to pass the winter. There was so much snow and cold, we thought to have perished. At this town the Christian died whom we had found in the country belonging to the people of Narvaez, and who was our interpreter. We went out thence in the beginning of March, when it appeared to us that the severity of the winter had passed; and we followed down the course of this river, whereon we found other provinces well peopled, having a quantity of food, to a Province called Anicoyanque, which appeared to us to be one of the best we had found in all the country. Here another Cacique, called Guachoyanque, came to us in peace. His town is upon the River Grande, and he is in continual war with the other chief with whom we were.

The Governor directly set out for the town of Guachoyanque, and took its Cacique with him. The town was good, well and strongly fenced. It contained little provision, the Indians having carried that off. Here the Governor, having before determined, if he should find the sea, to build brigantines by which to make it known in Cuba that we were alive, whence we might be supplied with some horses and things of which we stood in need, sent a Captain in the direction south, to see if some road could be discovered by which we might go to look for the sea; because, from the account given by the Indians, nothing could be learned of it; and he got back, reporting that he found no road, nor any way by which to pass the great bogs that extend out from the Rio Grande. The Governor, at seeing himself thus surrounded, and nothing coming about according to his expectations, sickened and died. He left us recommending Luis de Moscoso to be our Governor.

Since we could find no way to the sea, we agreed to take our course to the west, on which we might come out by land to Mexico, should we be unable to find any thing, or a place whereon to settle. We travelled seventeen days, until we came to the Province of Chavite, where the Indians made much salt; but we could learn nothing of them concerning the west: thence we went to another province, called Aguacay, and were three days on the way, still going directly westward. After leaving this place, the Indians told us we should see no more settlements unless we went down in a southwest-and-by-south direction, where we should find large towns and food; that in the course we asked about, there were some large sandy wastes, without any people or subsistence whatsoever.

We were obliged to go where the Indians directed us, and went to a Province called Nisione, and to another called Nondacao, and another, Came; and at each remove we went through lands that became more sterile and afforded less subsistence. We continually asked for a province which they told us was large, called Xuacatino. The Cacique of Nondacao gave us an Indian purposely to put us somewhere whence we could never come out: the guide took us over a rough country, and off the road, until he told us at last he did not know where he was leading us; that his master had ordered him to take us where we should die of hunger. We took another guide, who led us to a Province called Hais, where, in seasons, some cattle are wont to herd; and as the Indians saw us entering their country, they began to cry out: 'Kill the cows – they are coming'; when they sallied and shot their arrows at us, doing us some injury.

We went from this place and came to the Province of Xacatin, which was among some close forests, and was scant of food. Hence the Indians guided us eastward to other small towns, poorly off for food, having said that they would take us where there were other Christians like us, which afterwards proved false; for they could have had no knowledge of any others than ourselves, although, as we made so many turns, it might be in some of them they had observed our passing. We turned to go southward, with the resolution of either reaching New Spain, or dying. We travelled about six days in a direction south and southwest, when we stopped.

Thence we sent ten men, on swift horses, to travel in eight or nine days as far as possible, and see if any town could be found where we might re-supply ourselves with maize, to enable us to pursue our journey. They went as far as they could go, and came upon some poor people without houses, having wretched huts, into which they withdrew; and they neither planted nor gathered any thing, but lived entirely upon flesh and fish. Three or four of them, whose tongue no one we could find understood, were brought back. Reflecting that we had lost our interpreter, that we found nothing to eat, that the maize we brought upon our backs was failing, and it seemed impossible that so many people should be able to cross a country so poor, we determined to return to the town where the Governor Soto died, as it appeared to us there was convenience for building vessels with which we might leave the country.

We returned by the same road we had taken, until we came to the town; but we did not discover so good outfit as we had thought to find. There were no provisions in the town, the Indians having taken them away, so we had to seek another town, where we might pass the winter and build the vessels. I thank God that we found two towns very much to our purpose, standing upon the Rio Grande, and which were fenced around, having also a large quantity of maize. Here we stopped, and with great labour built seven brigantines, which were finished at about the end of six months. We threw them out into the water, and it was a mystery that, calked as they were with the bark of mulberry-trees, and without any pitch, we should find them staunch and very safe. Going down the river, we took with us also some canoes, into which were put twenty-six horses, for the event of finding any large town on the shore of the sea that could sustain us with food, while we might send thence a couple of brigantines to the Viceroy of New Spain, with a message to provide us with vessels in which we could get away from the country.

The second day, descending the stream, there came out against us about forty or fifty very large and swift canoes, in some of which were as many as eighty warriors, who assailed us with their arrows, following and shooting at us. Some who were in the vessels thought it trifling not to attack them; so, taking four or five of the small canoes we brought along, they went after them. The Indians, seeing this, surrounded them, so that they could not get away, and upset the canoes, whereby twelve very worthy men were drowned, beyond the reach of our succour, because of the great power of the stream, and the oars in the vessels being few.

The Indians were encouraged by this success to follow us to the sea, which we were nineteen days in reaching, doing us much damage and wounding many people; for, as they found we had no arms that could reach them from a distance, not an arquebuse nor a crossbow having remained, but only some swords and targets, they lost their fears, and would draw very nigh to let drive at us with their arrows.

We came out by the mouth of the river, and entering into a very large bay made by it, which was so extensive that we passed along it three days and three nights, with fair weather, in all the time not seeing land, so that it appeared to us we were at sea, although we found the water still so fresh that it could well be drunk, like that of the river. Some small islets were seen westward, to which we went: thenceforward we kept close along the coast, where we took shellfish, and looked for other things to eat, until we entered the River of Pánuco, where we came and were well received by the Christians.

Sir John Hawkins (1567)

Sir John Hawkins (1532–95) belonged to a family of Devonshire shipowners and skippers. He was the first Englishman to trade in Negroes. In 1564 he was granted a coat-of-arms with a demi-Moor, or negro, chained, as his crest. His first two voyages were private expeditions; his third, in 1567, was in fact, though not technically, a national venture. Rivalry between England and Spain was becoming intense. As well as abducting negroes, part of his mission was to force the sale of his goods to the Spanish colonies, including Florida. Hawkins's accounts of his voyages were collected and published by Hakluyt.

The Floridians have pieces of unicorns' horns which they wear about their necks, whereof the Frenchmen obtained many pieces. Of those unicorns they have many, for that they do affirm it to be a beast with one horn, which, coming to the river to drink, putteth the same into the water before he drinketh. Of this unicorns' horn there are [some] of our company that, having gotten the same of the Frenchmen, brought home thereof to show. It is therefore to be presupposed that there are more commodities as well as that, which for want of time and people sufficient to inhabit the same cannot yet come to light; but I trust God will reveal the same before it be long, to the great profit of them that shall take it in hand.

Of beasts in this country besides deer, foxes, hares, polecats, conies, ounces, and leopards, I am not able certainly to say; but it is thought that there are lions and tigers as well as unicorns, lions especially, if it be true that is said of the enmity between them and the unicorns, for there is no beast but hath his enemy, as the cony the polecat, a sheep the wolf, the elephant the rhinoceros, and so of other beasts the like, insomuch that whereas the one is, the other cannot be missing. And seeing I have made mention of the beasts of this country, it shall not be from my purpose to speak also of the venomous beasts, as crocodiles, whereof there is great abundance, adders of great bigness, whereof our men killed some of a yard and a half long. Also I heard a miracle of one of these adders, upon the which a falcon seizing, the said adder did clasp her tail about her; which the French captain seeing, came to the rescue of the falcon and took her, slaying the adder; and this falcon being wild, he did reclaim her and kept her for the space of two months, at which time for very want of meat he was fain to cast her off. On these adders the Frenchmen did feed, to no little admiration of us, and affirmed the same to be a delicate meat. And the captain of the Frenchmen saw also a serpent with three heads and four feet, of the bigness of a great spaniel, which for want of a harquebus he durst not attempt to slay.

Of fish also they have in the river pike, rock salmon, trout, and divers other small fishes, and of great fish some of the length of a man and longer, being of bigness accordingly, having a snout much like a sword of a yard long. There be also of sea fishes which we saw coming along the coast flying, which are of the bigness of a smelt, the biggest sort whereof have four wings but the other have but two; of these we saw coming out of Guinea 100 in a company, which, being chased by the giltheads, otherwise called the bonitos, do to avoid them the better take their flight out of the water; but yet are they not able to fly far because of the drying of their wings, which serve them not to fly but when they are moist, and therefore when they can fly no further they fall into the water and, having wet their wings, take a new flight again. These bonitos be of bigness like a carp and in colour like a mackerel, but it is the swiftest fish in swimming that is, and followeth her prey very fiercely, not only in the water but also out of the water; for as the flying fish taketh her flight, so does this bonito leap after them and taketh them sometimes above the water. There were some of those bonitos which, being galled by a fishgig, did follow our ship coming out of Guinea 500 leagues. There is a seafowl also that chaseth this flying fish as well as the bonito; for as the flying fish taketh her flight, so doth this fowl pursue to take her, which to behold is a greater pleasure than hawking, for both the flights are as pleasant, and also more often than 100 times; for the fowl can fly no way but one or other lighteth in her paws, the number of them are so abundant. There is an innumerable young fry of these flying fishes, which commonly keep about the ship and are not so big as butterflies and yet by flying do avoid the unsatiableness of the bonito. Of the bigger sort of these fishes we took many which both night and day flew into the sails of our ship, and there was not one of them which was not worth a bonito; for, being put upon a hook drabbling in the water, the bonito would leap thereat and so was taken. Also, we took many with a white cloth made fast to a hook, which being tied so short in the water that it might leap out and in, the greedy bonito, thinking it to be a flying fish, leapeth thereat and so is deceived. We took also dolphins, which are of very goodly colour and proportion to behold and no less delicate in taste.

Fowls also there be many, both upon land and upon sea; but, concerning them on the land, I am not able to name them because my abode was there so short. But for the fowl of the fresh rivers, these two I noted to be the chief: whereof the flamingo is one, having all red feathers and long red legs like a heron, a neck, according to the bill, red, whereof the upper neb hangeth an inch over the nether; and an egret, which is all white as the swan, with legs like to an heronshaw and of bigness accordingly, but it hath in her tail feathers of so fine a plume that it passeth the ostrich his feather. Of the seafowl, above all other not common in England I noted the pelican, which is feigned to be the lovingest bird that is; which, rather than her young should want, will spare her heartblood out of her belly; but for all this lovingness she is very deformed to behold, for she is of colour russet, notwithstanding in Guinea I have seen of them as white as a swan, having legs like the same and a body like a heron, with a long neck and a thick, long beak, from the nether jaw whereof down to the breast passeth a skin of such a bigness as is able to receive a fish as big as one's thigh, and this her big throat and long bill doth make her seem so ugly.

Sir Francis Drake (1579)

In his account, compiled by Hakluyt, Sir Francis Drake tries to convince the Californian Indians that the English are not gods. Drake (c. 1540–96) never intended to circumnavigate the world on this voyage. He sailed up the western coast of America, trying to find a passage in the Atlantic. Eventually he touched shore near the Golden Gate.

The third day following, *viz.*, the twenty-first, our ship, having received a leak at sea, was brought to anchor nearer the shore that, her goods being landed, she might be repaired; but for that we were to prevent any danger that might chance against our safety, our general first of all landed his men with all necessary provision to build tents and make a fort for the defence of ourselves and goods and that we might under the shelter of it with more safety (whatever should befall) end our business. Which when the people of the country perceived us doing, as men set on fire to war in defence of their country, in great haste and companies with such weapons as they had they came down unto us; and yet with no hostile meaning or intent to hurt us, standing, when they drew near, as men ravished in their minds with the sight of such things as they never had seen or heard of before that time, their errand being rather with submission and fear to worship us as gods than to have any war with us as with mortal men. Which thing, as it did partly show itself at that instant, so did it more and more manifest itself afterwards during the whole time of our abode amongst them. At this time, being willed by signs to lay from them their bows and arrows, they did as they were directed, and so did all the rest, as they came more and more by companies unto them, growing in a little while to a great number, both of men and women.

To the intent, therefore, that this peace which they themselves so willingly sought might, without any cause of the breach thereof on our part given, be continued, and that we might with more safety and expedition end our business in quiet, our general with all his company used all means possible gently to entreat them, bestowing upon each of them liberally good and necessary things to cover their nakedness, withal signifying unto them we were no gods but men and had need of such things to cover our shame; teaching them to use them to the same ends, for which cause also we did eat and drink in their presence, giving them to understand that without that we could not live and therefore were but men as well as they.

Notwithstanding, nothing could persuade them nor remove that opinion which they had conceived of us that we should be gods.

In recompense of those things which they had received of us, as shirts, linen cloth, etc., they bestowed upon our general and divers of our company divers things, as feathers, cauls of network, the quivers of their arrows made of fawn-skins, and the very skins of beasts that their women wore upon their bodies. Having thus had their fill of this time's visiting and beholding of us, they departed with joy to their houses, which houses are digged round within the earth and have from the uppermost brims of the circle clefts of wood set up and joined close together at the top like our spires on the steeple of a church, which, being covered with earth, suffer no water to enter and are very warm. The door in the most part of them performs the office also of a chimney to let out the smoke; it's made in bigness and fashion like to any ordinary scuttle in a ship and standing slopewise. Their beds are the hard ground, only with rushes strewed upon it, and lying round about the house have their fire in the midst, which, by reason that the house is but low vaulted, round, and close, gives a marvellous reflection to their bodies to heat the same.

Their men for the most part go naked; the women take a kind of bulrushes and, combing it after the manner of hemp, make themselves thereof a loose garment which, being knit about their middles, hangs down about their hips and so affords to them a covering of that which Nature teaches should be hidden; about their shoulders they wear also the skin of a deer with the hair upon it. They are very obedient to their husbands and exceedingly ready in all service, yet of themselves offering to do nothing without the consents or being called of the men. . . .

Against the end of three days more (the news having the while spread itself farther and, as it seemed, a great way up into the country) were assembled the greatest number of people which we could reasonably imagine to dwell within any convenient distance round about. Amongst the rest, the king himself, a man of a goodly stature and comely personage, attended with his guard of about 100 tall and warlike men, this day, *viz.*, June 26, came down to see us. . . .

They made signs to our general to have him sit down, unto whom both the king and divers others made several orations, or rather, indeed, if we had understood them, supplications, that he would take the province and kingdom into his hand and become their king and patron, making signs that they would resign unto him their right and title to the whole land and become his vassals in themselves and their posterities; which that they might make us indeed believe that it was their true meaning and intent, the king himself, with all the rest, with one consent and with great reverence joyfully singing a song, set the crown upon his head, enriched his neck with all their chains, and offering unto him many other things, honoured him by the name of *hióh*. Adding thereunto (as it might seem) a song and dance of triumph, because they were not only visited of the gods (for so they still judged us to be), but the great and chief God was now become their God, their king and patron, and themselves were become the only happy and blessed people in the world.

These things being so freely offered, our general thought not meet to reject or refuse the same, both for that he would not give them any cause of mistrust or disliking of him (that being the only place wherein at this present we were of necessity enforced to seek relief of many things), and chiefly for that he knew not to what good end God had brought this to pass or what honour and profit it might bring to our country in time to come.

Wherefore, in the name and to the use of Her Most Excellent Majesty, he took the sceptre, crown, and dignity of the said country into his hand, wishing nothing more than that it had laid so fitly for Her Majesty to enjoy as it was now her proper own, and that the riches and treasures thereof (wherewith in the upland countries it abounds) might with as great conveniency be transported, to the enriching of her kingdom here at home, as it is in plenty to be attained there; and especially that so tractable and loving a people as they showed themselves to be might have means to have manifested their most willing obedience the more unto her, and by her means, as a mother and nurse of the Church of Christ, might by the preaching of the Gospel be brought to the right knowledge and obedience of the true and everliving God.

The ceremonies of this resigning and receiving of the kingdom being thus performed, the common sort, both of men and women, leaving the king and his guard about him with our general, dispersed themselves among our people, taking a diligent view or survey of every man; and finding such as pleased their fancies (which commonly were the youngest of us), they, presently enclosing them about, offered their sacrifices unto them, crying out with lamentable shrieks and moans, weeping and scratching and tearing their very flesh off their faces with their nails; neither were it the women alone which did this, but even old men, roaring and crying out, were as violent as the women were. . . .

After that our necessary businesses were well dispatched, our general, with his gentlemen and many of his company, made a journey up into the land to see the manner of their dwelling and to be the better acquainted with the nature and commodities of the country. Their houses were all such as we have formerly described and, being many of them in one place, made several villages here and there. The inland we found to be far different from the shore, a goodly country and fruitful soil, stored with many blessings fit for the use of man. Infinite was the company of very large and fat deer which there we saw by thousands, as we supposed, in a herd; besides a multitude of a strange kind of conies by far exceeding them in number. Their heads and bodies, in which they resemble other conies, are but small, his tail, like the tail of a rat, exceeding long, and his feet like the paws of a want or mole. Under his chin, on either side, he hath a bag into which he gathereth his meat when he hath filled his belly abroad, that he may with it either feed his young or feed himself when he lists not to travel from his burrow. The people eat their bodies and make great account of their skins, for their king's holiday's coat was made of them.

This country our general named Albion, and that for two causes: the one in respect of the white banks and cliffs which lie toward the sea; the other that it might have some affinity, even in name also, with our own country, which was sometime so called.

Before we went from thence, our general caused to be set up a monument of our being there, as also of Her Majesty's and successors' right and title to that kingdom; namely, a plate of brass, fast nailed to a great and firm post, whereon is engraven Her Grace's name and the day and year of our arrival there and of the free giving-up of the province and kingdom, both the king and people, into Her Majesty's hands, together with Her Highness' picture and arms in a piece of sixpence current English money, showing itself by a hole made of a purpose through the plate. Underneath was likewise engraven the name of our general, etc.

The Spaniards never had any dealing or so much as set a foot in this country, the utmost of their discoveries reaching only to many degrees southward of this place. . . .

Master Philip Amadas and Master Arthur Barlow (1584)

'The first voyage made to the coasts of America, with two barks, wherein were captains Master Philip Amadas and Master Arthur Barlow, who discovered part of the country now called Virginia, anno 1584. Written by one of the said captains, and sent to Sir Walter Raleigh, knight, at whose charge and direction the said voyage was set forth.' (from Hakluyt's Principall Navigations*)*

The second of July we found shoal water, where we smelt so sweet and so strong a smell, as if we had been in the midst of some delicate garden abounding with all kinds of odoriferous flowers; by which we were assured that the land could not be far distant. And keeping good watch and bearing but slack sail, the fourth of the same month we arrived upon the coast, which we supposed to be a continent and firm land, and we sailed along the same hundred and twenty English miles before we could find any entrance, or river issuing into the sea.

The first that appeared unto us we entered, though not without some difficulty, and cast anchor about three arquebus-shot within the haven's mouth, on the left hand of the same; and after thanks given to God for our safe arrival thither, we manned our boats, and went to view the land next adjoining, and to take possession of the same in the right of the Queen's most excellent Majesty, as rightful queen and princess of the same, and after delivered the same over to your use, according to Her Majesty's grant and letters patents, under Her Highness' great seal. Which being performed according to the ceremonies used in such enterprises, we viewed the land about us, being, where as we first landed, very sandy and low towards the water's side, but so full of grapes as the very beating and surge of the sea overflowed them. Of which we found such plenty, as well there as in all places else, both on the sand and on the green soil on the hills, as in the plains, as well on every little shrub, as also climbing towards the tops of high cedars, that I think in all the world the like abundance is not to be found; and myself having seen those parts of Europe that most abound, find such difference as were incredible to be written.

We passed from the sea side towards the tops of those hills next adjoining, being but of mean height; and from thence we beheld the sea on both sides, to the north and to the south, finding no end any of both ways. This land stretching itself to the west, which after we found to be but an island of twenty miles long, and not above six miles broad. Under the bank or hill whereon we stood, we beheld the valleys replenished with goodly cedar trees, and having discharged our arquebus-shot, such a flock of cranes (the most part white) arose under us, with such a cry redoubled by many echoes, as if an army of men had shouted all together.

This island had many goodly woods full of deer, coneys, hares and fowl, even in the midst of summer, in incredible abundance. The woods are not such as you find in Bohemia, Moscovia, or Hercynia, barren and fruitless, but the highest and reddest cedars of the world, far bettering the cedars of the Azores, of the Indies, or Libanus; pines, cypress, sassafras, the lentisk, or the tree that beareth the mastic; the tree that beareth the rind of black cinnamon, of which Master Winter brought from the Straits of Magellan; and many other of excellent smell and quality.

We remained by the side of this island two whole days before we saw any people of the country. The third day we espied one small boat rowing towards us, having in it three persons. This boat came to the island side, four arquebus-shot from our ships; and there two of the people remaining, the third came along the shore side towards us, and we being then all within board, he walked up and down upon the point of the land next unto us. Then the Master and the Pilot of the admiral, Simon Ferdinando, and the Captain, Philip Amadas, myself, and others, rowed to the land; whose coming this fellow attended, never making any show of fear or doubt. And after he had spoken of many things not understood by us, we brought him, with his own good liking, aboard the ships, and gave him a shirt, a hat, and some other things, and made him taste of our wine and our meat, which he liked very well; and, after having viewed both barks, he departed, and went to his own boat again, which he had left in a little cove or creek adjoining. As soon as he was two bow-shot into the water he fell to fishing, and in less than half-an-hour he had laden his boat as deep as it could swim, with which he came again to the point of the land, and there he divided his fish into two parts, pointing one part to the ship and the other to the pinnace. Which, after he had, as much as he might, requited the former benefits received, departed out of our sight.

The next day there came unto us divers boats, and in one of them the King's brother, accompanied with forty or fifty men, very handsome and goodly people, and in their behaviour as mannerly and civil as any of Europe. His name was Granganimeo, and the King is called Wingana; the country, Wingandacoa, and now, by Her Majesty, Virginia. The manner of his coming was in this sort: he left his boats, altogether as the first man did, a little from the ships by the shore, and came along to the place over against the ships, followed with forty men. When he came to the place, his servants spread a long mat upon the ground, on which he sat down, and at the other end of the mat four others of his company did the like; the rest of his men stood round about him somewhat far off. When we came to the shore to him, with our weapons, he never moved from his place, nor any of the other four, nor never mistrusted any harm to be offered from us; but, sitting still, he beckoned us to come and sit by him, which we performed; and, being set, he made all signs of joy and welcome, striking on his head and his breast and afterwards on ours, to show we were all one, smiling and making show the best he could of all love and familiarity. After he had made a long speech unto us we presented him with divers things, which he received very joyfully and thankfully. None of the company durst speak one word all the time; only the four which were at the other end spoke one in the other's ear very softly.

The King is greatly obeyed, and his brothers and children reverenced. The King himself in person was at our being there sore wounded in a fight which he had with the king of the next country, called Winganadacoa, and was shot in two places through the body, and once clean through the thigh, but yet he recovered; by reason whereof, and for that he lay at the chief town of the country, being six days' journey off, we saw him not at all.

After we had presented this his brother with such things as we thought he liked, we likewise gave somewhat to the other that sat with him on the mat. But presently he arose and took all from them and put it into his own basket, making signs and tokens that all things ought to be delivered unto him, and the rest were but his servants and followers. A day or two after this we fell to trading with them, exchanging some things that we had for chamois, buff, and deer skins. When we showed him all our packet of merchandise, of all things that he saw a bright tin dish most pleased him, which he presently took up and clapped it before his breast, and after made a hole in the brim thereof and hung it about his neck, making signs that it would defend him against his enemies' arrows. For those people maintain a deadly and terrible war with the people and king adjoining. We exchanged our tin dish for twenty skins, worth twenty crowns or twenty nobles; and a copper kettle for fifty skins, worth fifty crowns. They offered us good exchange for our hatchets and axes, and for knives, and would have given anything for swords; but we would not depart with any.

After two or three days the King's brother came aboard the ships and drank wine, and ate of our meat and of our bread, and liked exceedingly thereof. And after a few days overpassed, he brought his wife with him to the ships, his daughter, and two or three children. His wife was very well-favoured, of mean stature, and very bashful. She had on her back a long cloak of leather, with the fur side next to her body, and before her a piece of the same. About her forehead she had a band of white coral, and so had her husband many times. In her ears she had bracelets of pearls hanging down to her middle, whereof we delivered your worship a little bracelet, and those were of the bigness of good peas. The rest of her women of the better sort had pendants of copper hanging in each ear, and some of the children of the King's brother and other noblemen have five or six in either ear. He himself had upon his head a broad plate of gold, or copper; for, being unpolished, we knew not what metal it should be, neither would he by any means suffer us to take it off his head, but feeling it, it would bow very easily. His apparel was as his wife's, only the women wear their hair long on both sides, and the men but on one. They are of colour yellowish, and their hair black for the most part; and yet we saw children that had very fine auburn and chestnut-coloured hair.

After that these women had been there, there came down from all parts great store of people, bringing with them leather, coral, divers kinds of dyes very excellent, and exchanged with us. But when Granganimeo, the King's brother, was present, none durst trade but himself, except such as wear red pieces of copper on their heads like himself; for that is the difference between the noblemen and the governors of countries, and the meaner sort. And we both noted there, and you have understood since by these men which we brought home, that no people in the world carry more respect to their king, nobility, and governors than these do. The King's brother's wife, when she came to us (as she did many times), was followed with forty or fifty women always. And when she came into the ship she left them all on land, saving her two daughters, her nurse, and one or two more. The King's brother always kept this order; as many boats as he would come withal to the ships, so many fires would he make on the shore afar off, to the end we might understand with what strength and company he approached. Their boats are made of one tree, either of pine, or of pitch-trees; a wood not commonly known to our people, nor found growing in England. They have no edge-tools to make them withal; if they have any they are very few, and those, it seems, they had twenty years since, which, as those two men declared, was out of a wreck, which happened upon their coast, of some Christian ship, being beaten that way by some storm and outrageous weather, whereof none of the people were saved, but only the ship, or some part of her, being cast upon the sand, out of whose sides they drew the nails and the spikes, and with those they made their best instruments. The manner of making their boats is thus: they burn down some great tree, or take as are windfallen, and, putting gum and rosin upon one side thereof, they set fire into it, and when it hath burnt it hollow they cut out the coal with their shells, and ever where they would burn it deeper or wider they lay on gums, which burn away the timber, and by this means they fashion very fine boats, and such as will transport men. Their oars are like scoops, and many times they set with long poles, as the depth serveth.

The King's brother had great liking of our armour, a sword and divers other things which we had, and offered to lay a great box of pearl in gage for them; but we refused it for this time, because we would not make them know that we esteemed thereof, until we had understood in what places of the country the pearl grew, which now your worship doth very well understand. He was very just of his promise, for many times we delivered him merchandise upon his word, but ever he came within the day and performed his promise. He sent us every day a brace or two of fat bucks, coneys, hares, fish the best in the world. He sent us divers kinds of fruits, melons, walnuts, cucumbers, gourds, pease, and divers roots, and fruits very excellent good, and of their country corn, which is very white, fair, and well tasted, and groweth three times in five months: in May they sow, in July they reap; in June they sow, in August they reap; in July they sow, in September they reap. Only they cast the corn into the ground, breaking a little of the soft turf with a wooden mattock or pickaxe. Ourselves proved the soil, and put some of our peas in the ground, and in ten days they were of fourteen inches high. They have also beans very fair, of divers colours, and wonderful plenty, some growing naturally and some in their gardens; and so have they both wheat and oats. The soil is the most plentiful, sweet, fruitful, and wholesome of all the world. There are above fourteen several sweet-smelling timber-trees, and the most part of their underwoods are bays and suchlike. They have those oaks that we have, but far greater and better.

After they had been divers times aboard our ships, myself with seven more went twenty mile into the river that runneth toward the city of Skicoake, which river they call Occam; and the evening following we came to an island which they call Roanoke, distant from the harbour by which we entered seven leagues; and at the north end thereof was a village of nine houses built of cedar and fortified round about with sharp trees to keep out their enemies, and the entrance into it made like a turnpike very artificially. When we came towards it, standing near unto the water's side, the wife of Granganimeo, the King's brother, came running out to meet us very cheerfully and friendly. Her husband was not then in the village. Some of her people she commanded to draw our boat on shore, for the beating of the billow. Others she appointed to carry us on their backs to the dry ground, and others to bring our oars into the house for fear of stealing. When we were come into the outer room (having five rooms in her house) she caused us to sit down by a great fire, and after took off our clothes and washed them and dried them again. Some of the women plucked off our stockings and washed them, some washed our feet in warm water, and she herself took great pains to see all things ordered in the best manner she could, making great haste to dress some meat for us to eat.

After we had thus dried ourselves, she brought us into the inner room, where she set on the board standing along the house some wheat like frumenty, sodden venison and roasted, fish sodden, boiled, and roasted, melons raw and sodden, roots of divers kinds, and divers fruits. Their drink is commonly water, but while the grape lasteth they drink wine; and for want of casks to keep it, all the year after they drink water, but it is sodden with ginger in it, and black cinnamon, and sometimes sassafras, and divers other wholesome and medicinable herbs and trees. We were entertained with all love and kindness, and with as much bounty (after their manners) as they could possibly devise.

Thomas Harriot (1585)

Thomas Harriot (1560–1621) was tutor to Sir Walter Raleigh at St Mary Hall Oxford. Raleigh appointed him geographer on the second expedition to Virginia in 1585. His account of the country was later published in Haklyut's Principall Navigations. *Here he describes the goodness of Virginia.*

There is an herb which is sowed apart by itself and is called by the inhabitants *uppówoc*. In the West Indies it hath divers names, according to the several places and countries where it groweth and is used. The Spaniards generally call it tobacco. The leaves thereof, being dried and brought into powder, they use to take the fume or smoke thereof by sucking it through pipes made of clay into their stomach and head, from whence it purgeth superfluous phlegm and other gross humours, openeth all the pores and passages of the body: by which means the use thereof not only preserveth the body from obstructions but also, if any be, so that they have not been of too long continuance, in short time breaketh them, whereby their bodies are notably preserved in health and know not many grievous diseases wherewithal we in England are oftentimes afflicted.

This *uppówoc* is of so precious estimation amongst them that they think their gods are marvellously delighted therewith, whereupon sometime they make hallowed fires and cast some of the powder therein for a sacrifice; being in a storm upon the waters, so pacify their gods, they cast some up into the air and into the water; so, a weir for fish being newly set up, they cast some therein and into the air; also, after an escape of danger, they cast some into the air likewise: but all done with strange gestures, stamping, sometime dancing, clapping of hands, holding up of hands, and staring up into the heavens, uttering therewithal and chattering strange words and noises.

We ourselves during the time we were there used to suck it after their manner, as also since our return, and have found many rare and wonderful experiments of the virtues thereof, of which the relation would require a volume by itself; the use of it by so many of late, men and women of great calling as else, and some learned physicians also, is sufficient witness.

And these are the commodities for sustenance of life that I know and can remember they use to husband; all else follow are found growing naturally or wild. . . .

John Brereton (1602)

New England had neither been named nor permanently settled by the time this voyage took place when its promise was fulsomely described by Brereton.

These people, as they are exceeding courteous, gentle of disposition, and well-conditioned, excelling all others that we have seen, so for shape of body and lovely favour I think they excel all the people of America: of stature much higher than we; of complexion or colour much like a dark olive; their eyebrows and hair black, which they wear long, tied up behind in knots, whereon they prick feathers of fowls in fashion of a crownet. Some of them are black, thin-bearded. They make beards of the hair of beasts, and one of them offered a beard of their making to one of our sailors for his that grew on his face, which, because it was of a red colour, they judged to be none of his own. They are quick-eyed and steadfast in their looks; fearless of others' harms, as intending none of themselves; some of the meaner sort given to filching, which the very name of savages (not weighing their ignorance in good or evil) may easily excuse. Their garments are of deerskins, and some of them wear furs round and close about their necks. They pronounce our language with great facility, for one of them one day sitting by me, upon occasion I spake smiling to him these words: 'How now, sirrah, are you so saucy with my tobacco?' Which words (without any further repetition) he suddenly spoke so plain and distinctly as if he had been a long scholar in the language. Many other such trials we had which are here needless to repeat.

Their women (such as we saw, which were but three in all) were but low of stature, their eyebrows, hair, apparel, and manner of wearing like to the men, fat and very well favoured and much delighted in our company. The men are very dutiful towards them. And truly, the wholesomeness and temperature of this climate doth not only argue this people to be answerable to this description but also of a perfect constitution of body, active, strong, healthful, and very witty, as the sundry toys of theirs cunningly wrought may easily witness.

For the agreeing of this climate with us (I speak of myself, and so I may justly do for the rest of our company), that we found our health and strength all the while we remained there so to renew and increase as, notwithstanding our diet and lodging was none of the best, yet not one of our company (God be thanked) felt the least grudging or inclination to any disease or sickness but were much fatter and in better health than when we went out of England . . .

Your Lordship's to command,
John Brereton

Thomas Studley (1608–9)

Captain John Smith (1580–1631) joined an expedition to colonize Virginia in 1606. He organized the first settlement at Jamestown, and it fell to his lot to trade with the Indians for provisions. On 10 December 1608 he set out to discover the source of the River Chickahominy. In this passage, Studley, who was one of the men under Smith's command, describes how Smith's life was saved by the Princess Pocahontas.

. . . And now, the winter approaching, the rivers became so covered with swans, geese, ducks, and cranes that we daily feasted with good bread, Virginia peas, pompions, and putchamins, fish, fowl, and divers sorts of wild beasts, as far as we could eat them: so that none of our tuftaffeta humorists desired to go for England. But our comedies never endured long without a tragedy. Some idle exceptions being muttered against Captain Smith for not discovering the head of Chickahominy River, and taxed by the Council to be too slow in so worthy an attempt, the next voyage he proceeded so far that, with much labour by cutting of trees in sunder, he made his passage. But when his barge could pass no farther he left her in a broad bay out of danger of shot, commanding none should go ashore till his return. Himself with two English and two savages went up higher in a canoe, but he was not long absent.

But his men went ashore, whose want of government gave both occasion and opportunity to the savages to surprise one George Cassen, whom they slew, and much failed not to have cut off the boat and all the rest. Smith, little dreaming of that accident, being got to the marshes at the river's head twenty miles in the desert, had his two men slain (as is supposed) sleeping by the canoe whilst himself by fowling sought them victual; who, finding he was beset with two hundred savages, two of them he slew, still defending himself with the aid of a savage his guide, whom he bound to his arm with his garters and used him as a buckler, yet he was shot in his thigh a little and had many arrows that stuck in his clothes but no great hurt, till at last they took him prisoner.

When this news came to Jamestown, much was their sorrow for his loss, few expecting what ensued. Six or seven weeks those barbarians kept him prisoner; many strange triumphs and conjurations they made of him, yet he so demeaned himself amongst them as he not only diverted them from surprising the fort but procured his own liberty and got himself and his company such estimation amongst them that those savages admired him more than their own quiyouckosucks. The manner how they used and delivered him is as followeth.

The savages, having drawn from George Cassen whither Captain Smith was gone, prosecuting that opportunity, they followed him with three hundred bowmen conducted by the king of Pamunkey, who in divisions searching the turnings of the river found Robinson and Emry by the fire-side; those they shot full of arrows and slew. Then, finding the captain, as is said, that used the savage that was his guide as his shield (three of them being slain and divers other so galled), all the rest would not come near him. Thinking thus to have returned to his boat, regarding them as he marched more than his way, [he] slipped up to the middle in an oozy creek and his savage with him; yet durst they not come to him till, being near dead with cold, he threw away his arms.

Then according to their composition they drew him forth and led him to the fire where his men were slain. Diligently they chafed his benumbed limbs. He demanding for their captain, they showed him Opechancanough, king of Pamunkey, to whom he gave a round ivory double compass dial. Much they marvelled at the playing of the fly and needle, which they could see so plainly and yet not touch it, because of the glass that covered them. But when he demonstrated by that globe-like jewel the roundness of the earth and skies, the sphere of the sun, moon, and stars, and how the sun did chase the night round about the world continually, the greatness of the land and sea, the diversity of nations, variety of complexions, and how we were to them antipodes, and many other such-like matters, they all stood as amazed with admiration. Notwithstanding, within an hour after they tied him to a tree and as many as could stand about him prepared to shoot him; but the king holding up the compass in hand, they all laid down their bows and arrows and in a triumphant manner led him to Orapaks, where he was after their manner kindly feasted and well used.

Their order in conducting him was thus: drawing themselves all in file, the king in the midst had all their pieces and swords borne before him. Captain Smith was led after him by three great savages, holding him fast by each arm, and on each side six went in file with their arrows nocked. But, arriving at the town (which was but only thirty or forty hunting-houses made of mats, which they remove as they please, as we our tents), all the women and children staring to behold him, the soldiers first all in file performed the form of a besom so well as could be, and on each flank officers as sergeants to see them keep their orders. A good time they continued this exercise and then cast themselves in a ring, dancing in such

several postures and singing and yelling out such hellish notes and scree-
ches; being strangely painted, every one his quiver of arrows and at his back
a club; on his arm a fox or an otter's skin, or some such matter for his
vambrace; their heads and shoulders painted red, with oil and puccoon
mingled together, which scarlet-like colour made an exceeding handsome
show; his bow in his hand, and the skin of a bird, with her wings abroad,
dried, tied on his head, a piece of copper, a white shell, a long feather, with
a small rattle growing at the tails of their snakes tied to it, or some such-
like toy. All this while Smith and the king stood in the midst guarded, as
before is said, and after three dances they all departed.

Smith they conducted to a long house, where thirty or forty tall fellows
did guard him, and ere long more bread and venison was brought him than
would have served twenty men; I think his stomach at that time was not
very good. What he left they put in baskets and tied over his head. About
midnight they set the meat again before him. All this time not one of them
would eat a bit with him, till the next morning they brought him as much
more, and then did they eat all the old and reserved the new as they had
done the other, which made him think they would fat him to eat him. Yet
in this desperate estate, to defend him from the cold, one Maocassater
brought him his gown in requital of some beads and toys Smith had given
him at his first arrival in Virginia.

Not long after, early in a morning, a great fire was made in a long house
and a mat spread on the one side, as on the other. On the one they caused
him to sit, and all the guard went out of the house, and presently came
skipping in a great grim fellow, all painted over with coal mingled with oil;
and many snakes and weasels' skins stuffed with moss and all their tails
tied together, so as they met on the crown of his head in a tassel; and round
about the tassel was as a coronet of feathers, the skins hanging round about
his head, back, and shoulders, and in a manner covered his face. With a
hellish voice and a rattle in his hand, with most strange gestures and
passions, he began his invocation and environed the fire with a circle of
meal; which done, three more such-like devils came rushing in with the
like antic tricks, painted half black, half red, but all their eyes were painted
white and some red strokes like mustachios along their cheeks.

Round about him those fiends danced a pretty while, and then came in
three more as ugly as the rest, with red eyes and white strokes over their
black faces; at last they all sat down right against him, three of them on the
one hand of the chief priest and three on the other. Then all with their
rattles began a song, which ended, the chief priest laid down five wheat
corns, then, straining his arms and hands with such violence that he sweat
and his veins swelled, he began a short oration. At the conclusion they all
gave a short groan and then laid down three grains more. After that began
their song again and then another oration, ever laying down so many corns
as before, till they had twice encircled the fire. That done, they took a bunch
of little sticks prepared for that purpose, continuing still their devotion, and
at the end of every song and oration they laid down a stick betwixt the
divisions of corn. Till night, neither he nor they did either eat or drink,
and then they feasted merrily, with the best provisions they could make.
Three days they used this ceremony, the meaning whereof they told him
was to know if he intended them well or no. The circle of meal signified

their country, the circles of corn the bounds of the sea, and the sticks his country. They imagined the world to be flat and round, like a trencher, and they in the midst. After this they brought him a bag of gunpowder, which they carefully preserved till the next spring to plant as they did their corn, because they would be acquainted with the nature of that seed.

Opitchapam, the king's brother, invited him to his house, where, with as many platters of bread, fowl, and wild beasts as did environ him, he bid him welcome; but not any of them would eat a bit with him but put up all the remainder in baskets. At his return to Opechancanough's, all the king's women and their children flocked about him for their parts, as a due by custom to be merry with such fragments.

At last they brought him to Meronocomo, where was Powhatan their emperor. Here more than two hundred of those grim courtiers stood wondering at him, as he had been a monster, till Powhatan and his train had put themselves in their greatest braveries. Before a fire, upon a seat like a bedstead, he sat covered with a great robe, made of raccoon skins and all the tails hanging by. On either hand did sit a young wench of sixteen or eighteen years, and along on each side the house two rows of men, and behind them as many women, with all their heads and shoulders painted red; many of their heads bedecked with the white down of birds, but every one with something, and a great chain of white beads about their necks.

At his entrance before the king, all the people gave a great shout. The queen of Appomattox was appointed to bring him water to wash his hands, and another brought him a bunch of feathers, instead of a towel, to dry them. Having feasted him after their best barbarous manner they could, a long consultation was held, but the conclusion was, two great stones were brought before Powhatan.

Then as many as could laid hands on him, dragged him to them and thereon laid his head, and being ready with their clubs to beat out his brains, Pocahontas, the king's dearest daughter, when no entreaty could prevail, got his head in her arms and laid her own upon his to save him from death. Whereat the emperor was contented he should live to make him hatchets and her bells, beads, and copper; for they thought him as well of all occupations as themselves. For the king himself will make his own robes, shoes, bows, arrows, pots; plant, hunt, or do anything so well as the rest.

Two days after, Powhatan, having disguised himself in the most fearful manner he could, caused Captain Smith to be brought forth to a great house in the woods and there upon a mat by the fire to be left alone. Not long after, from behind a mat that divided the house, was made the most dolefullest noise he ever heard; then Powhatan, more like a devil than a man, with some two hundred more as black as himself, came unto him and told him how they were friends and presently he should go to Jamestown to send him two great guns and a grind-stone, for which he would give him the country of Capahowosick and for ever esteem him as his son, Nantaquoud.

So, to Jamestown with twelve guides Powhatan sent him. That night they quartered in the woods, he still expecting (as he had done all this long time of his imprisonment) every hour to be put to one death or other, for all their feasting. But Almighty God (by His divine providence) had mollified the hearts of those stern barbarians with compassion.

The next morning betimes they came to the fort, where Smith, having used the savages with what kindness he could, he showed Rawhunt, Powhatan's trusty servant, two demi-culverins and a mill-stone to carry Powhatan. They found them somewhat too heavy; but when they did see him discharge them, being loaded with stones, among the boughs of a great tree loaded with icicles, the ice and branches came so tumbling down that the poor savages ran away half dead with fear. But at last we regained some conference with them and gave them such toys and sent to Powhatan, his women and children, such presents as gave them in general full content.

Now in Jamestown they were all in combustion, the strongest preparing once more to run away with the pinnace, which with the hazard of his life with saker, falcon, and musket shot Smith forced now the third time to stay or sink. Some no better than they should be had plotted with the President the next day to have put him to death by the Levitical law for the lives of Robinson and Emry, pretending the fault was his that had led them to their ends. But he quickly took such order with such lawyers that he laid them by the heels till he sent some of them prisoners for England.

Now, ever once in four or five days, Pocahontas with her attendants brought him so much provision that saved many of their lives that else for all this had starved with hunger.

His relation of the plenty he had seen, especially at Werowocomoco, and of the state and bounty of Powhatan (which till that time was unknown), so revived their dead spirits (especially the love of Pocahontas) as all men's fear was abandoned. Thus you may see what difficulties still crossed any good endeavour, and the good success of the business being thus oft brought to the very period of destruction, yet you see by what strange means God hath still delivered it.

As for the insufficiency of them admitted in commission, that error could not be prevented by the electors, there being no other choice and all strangers to each other's education, qualities, or disposition. And if any deem it a shame to our nation to have any mention made of those enormities, let them peruse the histories of the Spaniards' discoveries and plantations, where they may see how many mutinies, disorders, and dissensions have accompanied them and crossed their attempts; which, being known to be particular men's offences, doth take away the general scorn and contempt which malice, presumption, covetousness, or ignorance might produce, to the scandal and reproach of those whose actions and valiant resolutions deserve a more worthy respect.

Written by Thomas Studley, the first cape-merchant in Virginia, Robert Fenton, Edward Harrington, and J. S.

Captain Peter Wynne (1608)

*A letter from Captain Peter Wynne to his patron, Sir John Egerton describes
how Indians sound like Welshmen.*

Most Noble Knight,

I was not so desirous to come into this country as I am now willing here
to end my days, for I find it a far more pleasant and plentiful country than
any report made mention of. Upon the river which we are seated I have
gone six- or sevenscore miles, and so far is navigable; afterward I travelled
between fifty or sixty miles by land into a country called Monacan, who
owe no subjection to Powhatan. This land is very high ground and fertile,
being very full of very delicate springs of sweet water, the air more healthful
than the place where we are seated, by reason it is not subject to such fogs
and mists as we continually have. The people of Monacan speak a far
differing language from the subjects of Powhatan, their pronunciation being
very like Welsh, so that the gentlemen in our company desired me to be
their interpreter. The commodities as yet known in this country, whereof
there will be great store, is pitch, tar, soap-ashes, and some dyes, whereof
we have sent examples. As for things more precious, I omit till time (which
I hope will be shortly) shall make manifest proof of it. As concerning your
request of bloodhounds, I cannot learn that there is any such in this country;
only the dogs which are here are a certain kind of curs like our warreners'
hay-dogs in England, and they keep them to hunt their land-fowls, as
turkeys and such-like, for they keep nothing tame about them. Hereafter I
doubt not but to give you at large a farther relation than as yet I am able
to do, and do therefore desire you to take these few lines in good part and
hold me excused for the rest until fitter opportunity. Thus commending my
service to your good love with good love, with many thanks for all favours
and kindnesses received from you, I do ever remain

Yours most devoted in
all service,
Peter Wynne

Jamestown in Virginia
this 21st of November [1608]

William Bradford (1620)

New England had been named by Captain John Smith, who explored its shores in 1614. The first permanent settlement was made at Plymouth, Massachusetts, in 1620 by the 'Pilgrim Fathers' aboard the Mayflower, whose arrival is described here by William Bradford.

About ten o'clock we came into a deep valley, full of brush, wood-gaile, and long grass, through which we found little paths or tracts, and there we saw a deer, and found springs of fresh water, of which we were heartily glad, and sat us down and drunk our first New England water, with as much delight as ever we drunk drink in all our lives.

When we had refreshed ourselves, we directed our course full south, that we might come to the shore, which within a short while after we did, and there made a fire, that they in the ship might see where we were (as we had direction) and so marched on towards this supposed river: and as we went in another valley, we found a fine clear pond of fresh water, being about a musket shot broad, and twice as long: there grew also many small vines, and fowl and deer haunted there; there grew much sassafras: from thence we went on and found much plain ground about fifty acres, fit for the plow, and some signs where the Indians had formerly planted their corn: after this, some thought it best for nearness of the river to go down and travel on the sea sands, by which means some of our men were tired, and lagged behind, so we stayed and gathered them up, and struck into the land again; where we found a little path to certain heaps of sand, one whereof was covered with old mats, and had a wooden thing like a mortar whelmed on the top of it, and an earthen pot laid in a little hole at the end thereof; we musing what it might be, digged and found a bow, as we thought, arrows, but they were rotten; we supposed there were many other things, but because we deemed them graves, we put in the bow again and made it up as it was, and left the rest untouched, because we thought it would be odious unto them to ransack their sepulchres. We went on further and found new stubble of which they had gotten corn this year, and many walnut trees full of nuts, and great store of strawberries, and some vines; passing thus a field or two, which were not great, we came to another, which had also been new gotten, and there we found where an house had been, and four or five old planks laid together; also we found a great kettle, which had been some ship's kettle and brought out of Europe; there was also an heap of sand, made like the former, but as it was newly done, we might see how they had paddled it with their hands, which we digged up, and in it we found a little old basket full of fair Indian corn, and digged further, and found a fine great new basket full of very fair corn of this year, with some six and thirty goodly ears of corn, some yellow, and some red, and others mixed with blue, which was a very goodly sight: the basket was

round, and narrow at the top, it held about three or four bushels, which
was as much as two of us could lift up from the ground, and was very
handsomely and cunningly made: but whilst we were busy about these
things, we set our men sentinel in a round ring, all but two or three which
digged up the corn. We were in suspense, what to do with it, and the kettle,
and at length after much consultation, we concluded to take the kettle, and
as much of the corn as we could carry away with us: and when our shallop
came if we could find any of the people, and came to parley with them, we
would give them the kettle again, and satisfy them for their corn . . .

When we had marched five or six miles into the woods, and could find
no signs of any people, we returned again another way, and as we came
into the plain ground, we found a place like a grave, but it was much bigger
and longer than any we had yet seen. It was also covered with boards, so
as we mused what it should be, and resolved to dig it up; where we found,
first a mat, and under that a fair bow, and there another mat, and under
that a board about three quarters long, finely carved and painted, with three
tynes, or broaches on the top, like a crown; also between the mats we found
bowls, trays, dishes, and such like trinkets; at length we came to a fair new
mat, and under that two bundles, the one bigger, the other less, we opened
the greater and found in it a great quantity of fine and perfect red powder,
and in it the bones and skull of a man. The skull had fine yellow hair still
on it, and some of the flesh unconsumed; there was bound up with a knife,
a packneedle, and two or three old iron things. It was bound up in a sailor's
canvas cassock, and a pair of cloth breeches; the red powder was a kind of
embalment, and yielded a strong, but not offensive smell; it was as fine as
any flower. We opened the less bundle like wise, and found of the same
powder in it, and the bones and head of a little child, about the legs, and
other parts of it was bound strings, and bracelets of fine white beads; there
was also by it a little bow, about three quarters long, and some other odd
knacks: we brought sundry of the prettiest things away with us, and covered
the corpse up again . . .

We went ranging up and down till the sun began to draw low, and then
we hasted out of the woods, that we might come to our shallop. By that
time we had done, and our shallop come to us it was within night, and we
fed upon such victuals as we had, and betook us to our rest after we had
set out our watch. About midnight we heard a great and hideous cry, and
our sentinel called, 'Arm, Arm.' So we bestirred ourselves and shot off a
couple of muskets and noise ceased: we concluded, that it was a company
of wolves and fox, for one told us he had heard such a noise in New-found-
land. About five a clock in the morning we began to be stirring . . . upon
a sudden we heard a great and strange cry which we knew to be the same
voices, though they varied their notes; one of the company being abroad
came running in, and cried, 'They are men, Indians, Indians'; and withal,
their arrows came flying amongst us, our men ran out with all speed to
recover their arms . . . The cry of our enemies was dreadful, especially,
when our men ran out to recover their arms, their note was after this
manner, 'Woath woach ha ha hach woach': our men were no sooner come
to their arms, but the enemy was ready to assault them.

There was a lusty man, and no whit less valiant, who was thought to be
their captain, stood behind a tree within half a musket shot of us, and there

let his arrows fly at us; he stood three shots off a musket, at length one took as he said full aim at him, after which he gave an extraordinary cry and away they went all, we followed them about a quarter of a mile, but we left six to keep our shallop, for we were careful of our business . . . We tooke up eighteen of their arrows, which we had sent to England by Master Jones, some whereof were headed with brass, others with hartshorn, and others with eagles' claws; many more no doubt were shot, for these we found were almost covered with leaves: yet by the special providence of God, none of them either hit or hurt us . . . On Monday we found a very good harbour for our shipping, we marched also into the land, and found divers corn fields and little running brooks, a place very good for situation, so we returned to our ship again with good news to the rest of our people, which did much comfort their hearts.

Edward Winslow (1621)

Edward Winslow (1595–1655) was one of the Pilgrim Fathers who sailed on the Mayflower. *Here he gives good news from New England.*

New England, 11 December 1621
We have found the Indians very faithful in their covenant of peace, very loving and ready to pleasure us. We often go to them, and they come to us; some of us have been fifty miles by land in the country with them, the occasions and relations whereof you shall understand by our general and more full declaration of such things as are worth the noting. Yea, it hath pleased God so to possess the Indians with a fear of us, and love unto us, that not only the greatest king amongst them, called Massasoit, but also all the princes and peoples round about us, have either made suit unto us or been glad of any occasion to make peace with us, so that seven of them at once have sent their messengers to us to that end. Yea, an isle at sea, which we never saw, hath also, together with the former, yielded willingly to be under the protection and subject to our Sovereign Lord King James, so that there is now great peace among the Indians themselves, which was not formerly, neither would have been but for us. And we for our parts walk as peaceably and safely in the wood as in the highways in England. We entertain them familiarly in our houses, and they as friendly bestowing their venison on us. They are a people without any religion or knowledge of any God, yet very trusty, quick of apprehension, ripe-witted, just. The men and women go naked, only a skin about their middles.

For the temper of the air, here it agreeth well with that in England, and if there be any difference at all, this is somewhat hotter in summer. Some think it to be colder in winter, but I cannot out of experience so say; the air is very clear and not foggy, as hath been reported. I never in my life remember a more seasonable year than we have here enjoyed, and if we have once but kine, horses, and sheep, I make no question but men might

live as contented here as in any part of the world. For fish and fowl, we
have great abundance, fresh cod in the summer is but coarse meat with us;
our bay is full of lobsters all the summer and affordeth variety of other fish,
in September we can take a hogshead of eels in a night, with small labour,
and can dig them out of their beds all the winter. We have mussels and
others at our doors. Oysters we have none near, but we can have them
brought by the Indians when we will. All the springtime the earth sendeth
forth naturally very good sallet herbs. Here are grapes, white and red, and
very sweet and strong also; strawberries, gooseberries, raspas, etc; plums of
three sorts, with black and red being almost as good as damson; abundance
of roses, white, red, and damask, single, but very sweet indeed. The country
wanteth only industrious men to employ, for it would grieve your hearts if,
as I, you had seen so many miles together by goodly rivers uninhabited,
and withal to consider those parts of the world wherein you live to be even
greatly burdened with abundance of people . . .

Be careful to have a very good bread-room to put your biscuits in. Let
your cask for beer and water be iron-bound for the first tire if not more;
let not your meat be dry-salted – none can better do it than the sailors. Let
your meal be so hard trod in your cask that you shall need an adze or
hatchet to work it out with. Trust not too much on us for corn at this time,
for by reason of this last company that came, depending wholly upon us,
we shall have little enough till harvest; be careful to come by some of your
meal to spend by the way – it will much refresh you. Build your cabins as
open as you can, and bring good store of clothes and bedding with you.
Bring every man a musket or fowling-piece, let your piece be long in the
barrel, and fear not the weight of it, for most of our shooting is from stands.
Bring juice of lemons, and take it fasting; it is of good use. For hot waters,
aniseed water is the best, but use it sparingly. If you bring any thing for
comfort in the country, butter or sallet oil, or both, is very good. Our Indian
corn, even the coarsest, maketh as pleasant meat as rice, therefore spare
that unless to spend by the way. Bring paper and linseed oil for your
windows, with cotton yarn for your lamps. Let your shot be most for big
fowls, and bring store of powder and shot.

Captain John Smith (c. 1624)

*The following letter from Captain John Smith, addressed to the Society of
Cordwainers, discusses profits in Virginia for shoemakers.*

To the Worshipful the Master Wardens and Society of the Cordwainers of
the city of London

Worthy gentlemen:
Not only in regard of your courtesy and love, but also of the continual
use I have had of your labours and the hope you may make some use of

mine, I salute you with this chronological discourse, whereof you may understand with what infinite difficulties and dangers these plantations first began, with their yearly proceedings and the plain description and condition of those countries. How many of your company have been adventurers whose names are omitted or not nominated in the alphabet, I know not; therefore I entreat you better to inform me, that I may hereafter imprint you among the rest. But of this I am sure, for want of shoes among the oyster banks we tore our hats and clothes, and, those being worn, we tied barks of trees about our feet to keep them from being cut by the shells among which we must go or starve. Yet how many thousand of shoes have been transported to these plantations, how many soldiers, mariners, and sailors have been and are likely to be increased thereby, what vent your commodities have had and still have, and how many ships and men of all faculties have been and are yearly employed, I leave to your own judgements; and yet by reason of ill managing the returns have neither answered the general expectation nor my desire. The causes thereof you may read at large in this book for your better satisfaction; and I pray you take it not in ill part that I present the same to you in this manuscript epistle so late, for both it and myself have been so overtired by attendances that this work of mine does seem to be superannuated before its birth; notwithstanding let me entreat you to give it lodging in your hall freely to be perused for ever, in memory of your nobleness towards me and my love to God, my country, your society, and those plantations, ever resting

Yours to use,
John Smith.

Francis Higginson (1630)

Francis Higginson landed at Naumkeag, later Salem, in the Massachusetts Bay colony in April 1629 with his wife and seven children. Higginson, a minister of the gospel, was an enthusiastic advocate of emigration to the new country. This tract praising the health-preserving climate of New England was published a few months before Higginson died of tuberculosis in August 1630.

Of the air of New England with the Temper and Creatures in It

The temper of the air of New England is one special thing that commends this place. Experience doth manifest that there is hardly a more healthful place to be found in the world that agrees better with our English bodies. Many that have been weak and sickly in old England by coming hither have been thoroughly healed and grown healthful and strong. For here is an extraordinary clear and dry air that is of a most healing nature to all such as are of a cold, melancholy, phlegmatic, rheumatic temper of body. None can more truly speak hereof by their own experience than myself. My friends that knew me can well tell how very sickly I have been and continually in physic, being much troubled with a tormenting pain, through an extraordinary weakness of my stomach and abundance of melancholic humours; but since I came hither on this voyage I thank God I have had perfect health and freed from pain and vomitings, having a stomach to digest the hardest and coarsest fare who before could not eat finest meat; and whereas my stomach could only digest and did require such drink as was both strong and stale, now I can and do oftentimes drink New England water very well; and I that have not gone without a cap for many years together, neither durst leave off the same, have now cast away my cap and do wear none at all in the day-time; and whereas before-time I clothed myself with double clothes and thick waistcoats to keep me warm, even in the summer-time, I do now go as thin clad as any, only wearing a light stuff cassock upon my shirt and stuff breeches of one thickness without linings. Besides, I have one of my children that was formerly most lamentably handled with sore breaking-out of both his hands and feet of the king's evil, but since he came hither he is very well over he was, and there is hope of perfect recovery shortly, even by the very wholesomeness of the air, altering, digesting, and drying up the cold and crude humours of the body. And therefore I think it is a wise course for all cold complexions to come to take physic in New England; for a sup of New England's air is better than a whole draught of old England's ale.

In the summer-time, in the midst of July and August, it is a good deal hotter than in old England; and in winter, January and February are much colder, as they say; but the spring and autumn are of a middle temper.

Fowls of the air are plentiful here and of all sorts as we have in England, as far as I can learn, and a great many of strange fowls which we know not. Whilst I was writing these things, one of our men brought home an eagle which he had killed in the wood; they say they are good meat. Also here are many kinds of excellent hawks, both sea-hawks and land-hawks; and myself, walking in the woods with another in company, sprung a partridge so big that through the heaviness of his body could fly but a little way; they that have killed them say they are as big as our hens. Here are likewise abundance of turkeys often killed in the woods, far greater than our English turkeys and exceeding fat, sweet, and fleshy, for here they have abundance of feeding all the year long, as strawberries – in summer all places are full of them and all manner of berries and fruits. In the winter-time I have seen flocks of pigeons and have eaten of them. They do fly from tree to tree as other birds do, which our pigeons will not do in England; they are of all colours as ours are, but their wings and tails are far longer, and therefore it is likely they fly swifter to escape the terrible hawks in this country. In winter-time this country does abound with wild geese, wild ducks, and other sea-fowl, that a great part of winter the planters have eaten nothing but roast meat of divers fowls which they have killed.

Thus you have heard of the earth, water, and air of New England, now it may be you expect something to be said of the fire proportionable to the rest of the elements.

Indeed, I think New England may boast of this element more than of all the rest: for though it be here something cold in the winter, yet here we have plenty of fire to warm us, and that a great deal cheaper than they sell billets and faggots in London; nay, all Europe is not able to afford to make so great fires as New England. A poor servant here that is to possess but fifty acres of land may afford to give more wood for timber and fire as good as the world yields than many noblemen in England can afford to do. Here is good living for those that love good fires.

Roger Williams (1643)

Ordained an Anglican clergyman, Roger Williams (c. 1604–83) objected to the innovations of Laud and emigrated to New England in 1630. However, he could not stomach the Boston theocracy either, and was banished from Salem in 1635. He escaped to Narrangansett Bay, where he bought lands from the Indians and founded the city of Providence on the principles of a pure democracy. In 1643 he returned to England briefly to procure a charter for his Rhode Island colony. In England he published a guide to native language and customs.

A Key into the Language of America: Or An help to the Language of the Natives in that part of America, called New-England (1643) To my dear and wellbeloved friends and countrymen, in old and New England:

I present you with a *Key*; I have not heard of the like, yet framed, since it pleased God to bring that mighty continent of America to light. Others of my countrymen have often and excellently and lately written of the country (and none that I know beyond the goodness and worth of it).

This *Key* respects the native language of it, and happily may unlock some rarities concerning the natives themselves not yet discovered.

I drew the materials in a rude lump at sea, as a private help to my own memory, that I might not by my present absence lightly lose what I had so dearly bought in some few years' hardship and charges among the barbarians; yet being reminded by some what pity it were to bury those materials in my grave at land or sea, and withal remembering how oft I have been importuned by worthy friends of all sorts to afford them some helps this way, I resolved (by the assistance of the most high) to cast those materials into this *Key*, pleasant and profitable for all, but especially for my friends residing in those parts.

A little *Key* may open a box, where lies a bunch of keys.

With this I have entered into the secrets of those countries, wherever English dwell, about two hundred miles between the French and Dutch plantations. For want of this, I know what gross mistakes myself and others have run into. . . .

It is expected that, having had so much converse with these natives, I should write some little of them. . . .

From Adam and Noah that they spring, it is granted on all hands.

But as for their later descent, and whence they came into these parts, it seems as hard to find as to find the wellhead of some fresh stream which, running many miles out of the country to the salt ocean, hath met with

many mixing streams by the way. They say themselves that they have sprung
and grown up in that very place, like the very trees of the wilderness.

They say that their great God Cawtantowwit created those parts. They
have no clothes, books, nor letters, and conceive their fathers never had;
and therefore they are easily persuaded that the God that made Englishmen
is a greater God because He hath so richly endowed the English above
themselves. But when they hear that about sixteen hundred years ago,
England and the inhabitants thereof were like themselves, and since have
received from God clothes, books, &c., they are greatly affected with a
secret hope concerning themselves. . . .

They have many strange relations of one Wetucks, a man that wrought
great miracles amongst them, and walking upon the waters, &c., with some
kind of broken resemblance to the Son of God. . . .

For myself, I have uprightly laboured to suit my endeavours to my
pretences, and of later times (out of desire to attain their language) I have
run through varieties of intercourses with them, day and night, summer and
winter, by land and sea.

Many solemn discourses have I had with all sorts of nations of them,
from one end of the country to another (so far as opportunity and the little
language I have could reach).

I know there is no small preparation in the hearts of multitudes of them.
I know their many solemn confessions to myself, and one to another, of
their lost wandering conditions.

I know strong convictions upon the consciences of many of them, and
their desires uttered that way.

I know not with how little knowledge and grace of Christ the Lord may
save, and therefore neither will despair nor report much . . .

Now, because this is the great inquiry of all men, what Indians have been
converted? what have the English done in those parts? what hopes of the
Indians' receiving the knowledge of Christ? and because to this question,
some put an edge from the boast of the Jesuits in Canada and Maryland,
and especially from the wonderful conversions made by the Spaniards and
Portugals in the West Indies, besides what I have here written, . . . I shall
further present you with a brief additional discourse concerning this great
point, being comfortably persuaded that that Father of spirits, who was
graciously pleased to persuade Japhet (the Gentiles) to dwell in the tents
of Shem (the Jews), will in His holy season (I hope approaching) persuade
these Gentiles of America to partake of the mercies of Europe. And then
shall be fulfilled what is written by the Prophet Malachi: 'From the rising
of the sun (in Europe) to the going down of the same (in America), my
name shall be great among the Gentiles.' So I desire to hope and pray,

Your unworthy countryman,
Roger Williams

Taûbotne aunanamêan   *I thank you for your love.*
Observation

I have acknowledged amongst them an heart sensible of kindnesses, and
have reaped kindness again from many, seven years after, when I myself
had forgotten. Hence the Lord Jesus exhorts his followers to do good for
evil: for otherwise sinners will do good for good, kindness for kindness.

Cowàmmaunsh	*I love you.*
Cowammaûnuck	*He loves you.*
Cowámmaus	*You are loving.*
Cowâutam?	*Understand you?*
Nowaûtam	*I understand.*
Cowâwtam tawhitche nippeeyaúmen?	*Do you know why I come?*
Cowannántam?	*Have you forgotten?*
Awanagusàntowosh	*Speak English*
Eeanàntowash	*Speak Indian.*
Cutehanshishaùmo?	*How many were you in company?*
Kúnnishishem?	*Are you alone?*
Nníshishem	*I am alone.*
Naneeshâumo	*There be two of us.*
Nanshwishâwmen	*We are four.*
Npiuckshâwmen	*We are ten.*
Neesneechecktashaûmen	*We are twenty.*
Nquitpausuckowashâwmen	*We are an hundred.*
Comishoonhómmis?	*Did you come by boat?*
Kuttiakewushaùmis?	*Came you by land?*
Mesh nomíshoonhómmin	*I came by boat.*
Meshntiauké wushem	*I came by land.*
Nippenowàntawem	*I am of another language.*
Penowantowawhettûock	*They are of a diverse language.*
Mat nowawtau hettémina	*We understand not each other.*
Nummaûchenèm	*I am sick.*
Cummaúchenem?	*Are you sick?*
Tashúckqunne cummauche-naûmis?	*How long have you been sick?*
Nummauchêmin, *or* Ntannetéimmin	*I will be going.*
Saûop Cummauchêmin	*You shall go tomorrow.*
Maúchish, *or* Anakish	*Be going.*
Kuttannâwshesh	*Depart.*
Mauchéi, *or* Ànittui	*He is gone.*
Kautanaûshant	*He being gone.*
Mauchéhettit, *or* Kautanawshàwhettit	*When they are gone.*
Kukkowêtous	*I will lodge with you.*
Yò Cówish	*Do, lodge here.*
Howúnsheck	*Farewell.*
Chénock wonck cuppee-yeâumen?	*When will you be here again?*
Nétop tattà	*My friend, I cannot tell.*

From these courteous salutations, observe in general: there is a savour of civility and courtesy even amongst these wild Americans, both amongst themselves and towards strangers.

Parched meal, which is a ready wholesome food, which they eat with a little water, hot or cold. I have travelled with near 200 of them at once, near 100 miles through the woods, every man carrying a little basket of this at his back, and sometimes in a hollow leather girdle about his middle sufficient for man three or four days.

With this ready provision, and their bow and arrows, are they ready for war and travel at an hour's warning. With a spoonful of this meal and a spoonful of water from the brook, have I made many a good dinner and supper.

Of eating and entertainment. If any stranger come in, they presently give him to eat of what they have; many a time, and at all times of the night (as I have fallen in travel upon their houses), when nothing hath been ready, they have themselves and their wives risen to prepare me some refreshing.

It is a strange truth that a man shall generally find more free entertainment and refreshing amongst these barbarians than amongst thousands that call themselves Christians.

At whose house did you sleep? I once travelled to an island of the wildest in our parts, where in the night an Indian (as he said) had a vision or dream of the sun (whom they worship for a God) darting a beam into his breast, which he conceived to be the messenger of his death. This poor native called his friends and neighbours, and prepared some little refreshing for them, but himself was kept waking and fasting in great humiliations and invocations for ten days and nights. I was alone (having travelled from my bark, the wind being contrary), and little could I speak to them to their understandings, especially because of the change of their dialect or manner of speech from our neighbours; yet so much (through the help of God) I did speak, of the true and living only wise God, of the creation, of man, and his fall from God, &c., that at the parting many burst forth, 'Oh, when will you come again, to bring us more news of this God?'

From their sleeping. Sweet rest is not confined to soft beds, for not only God gives His beloved sleep on hard lodgings, but also nature and custom gives sound sleep to these Americans on the earth, on a board or mat. Yet how is Europe bound to God for better lodging?

The parts of the body. Nature knows no difference between Europe and Americans in blood, birth, bodies, God having of one blood made all mankind (Acts 17) and all by nature being children of wrath (Ephesians 2) . . .

I am weary with speaking. Their manner is upon any tidings to sit round, double or treble or more, as their numbers be. I have seen near a thousand in a round, where English could not well near half so many have sitten. Every man hath his pipe of their tobacco, and deep silence they make, and attention give to him that speaketh; and many of them will deliver themselves, either in a relation of news or in a consultation, with very emphatical speech and great action, commonly an hour, and sometimes two hours together.

I hear you. They are impatient (as all men and God Himself is) when their speech is not attended and listened to.

I shall never believe it. As one answered me when I had discoursed about many points of God, of the creation, of the soul, of the danger of it and saving of it, he assented; but when I spake of the rising again of the body, he cried out, 'I shall never believe this.'

Of discourse and news. The whole race of mankind is generally infected with an itching desire of hearing news . . .

A stone path. It is admirable to see what paths their naked hardened feet have made in the wilderness in most stony and rocky places.

Be my guide. The wilderness being so vast, it is a mercy that for a hire a man shall never want guides, who will carry provisions and such as hire them over the rivers and brooks, and find out often times hunting-houses or other lodgings at night.

Of travel. As the same sun shines on the wilderness that doth on a garden, so the same faithful and all-sufficient God can comfort-feed and safely guide even through a desolate, howling wilderness ...

Of beasts. The wilderness is a clear resemblance of the world, where greedy and furious men persecute and devour the harmless and innocent as the wild beasts pursue and devour the hinds and roes.

Of the sea. How unsearchable are the depths of the wisdom and power of God in separating from Europe, Asia, and Africa such a mighty vast continent as America is? And that for so many ages? As also, by such a western ocean of about three thousand of English miles' breadth in passage over? ...

The Fire-God. When I have argued with them about their Fire-God: can it, say they, be but this fire must be a God or divine power, that out of a stone will arise in a spark, and when a poor naked Indian is ready to starve with cold in the house, and especially in the woods, often saves his life; doth dress all our food for us; and if it be angry will burn the house about us; yea, if a spark fall into the dry woods, burns up the country (though this burning of the woods to them they count a benefit for destroying of vermin, and keeping down the weeds and thickets)? ...

Besides, there is a general custom amongst them, at the apprehension of any excellency in men, women, birds, beasts, fish, to cry out '*Manittoo*,' that is, it is a God. As thus if they see one man excell others in wisdom, valour, strength, activity, they cry out, '*Manittoo*,' a God. And therefore when they talk amongst themselves of the English ships, and great buildings, of the plowing of their fields, and especially of books and letters, they will end thus: '*Manittowock*,' they are Gods; '*Cummanitoo*,' you are a God, &c. A strong conviction natural in the soul of man, that God is filling all things, and places, and that all excellencies dwell in God and proceed from Him, and that they only are blessed who have that Jehovah their portion.

He is gone to the feast. They have a modest religious persuasion not to disturb any man, either themselves, English, Dutch, or any, in their conscience and worship; and therefore say, 'Peace, hold your peace.'

God's book or writing. After I had (as far as my language would reach) discoursed (upon a time) before the chief sachem or prince of the country, with his archpriests and many others in a full assembly; and being night, wearied with travel and discourse, I lay down to rest; and before I slept, I heard this passage:

A Qunnihticut Indian (who had heard our discourse) told the sachem Miantonomu that souls went not up to heaven or down to hell: 'for,' saith he, 'our fathers have told that our souls go to the southwest.'

The sachem answered, 'But how do you know yourself that your souls go to the southwest; did you ever see a soul go thither?'

The native replied, 'When did he [meaning myself] see a soul go to heaven or hell?'

The sachem again replied, 'He hath books and writings, and one which God Himself made, concerning men's souls, and therefore may well know more than we that have none, but take all upon trust from our forefathers.'

The said sachem and the chief of his people discoursed by themselves of keeping the Englishman's day of worship, which I could easily have brought the country to but that I was persuaded, and am, that God's way is first to turn a soul from its idols, both of heart, worship, and conversation, before it is capable of worship to the true and living God. . . . As also that the two first principles and foundations of true religion or worship of the true God in Christ are repentance from dead works, and faith towards God, before the doctrine of baptism or washing and laying on of hands, which contain the ordinances and practices of worship: the want of which, I conceive, is the bane of millions of souls in England and all other nations professing to be Christian nations, who are brought by public authority to baptism and fellowship with God in ordinances of worship before the saving work of repentance and a true turning to God.

The whole world shall ere long be burned. Upon the relating that God hath once destroyed the world by water, and that He will visit it the second time with consuming fire, I have been asked this profitable question of some of them: 'What then will become of us? Where then shall we be?'

Of their government and justice. I could never discern that excess of scandalous sins amongst them which Europe aboundeth with. Drunkenness and gluttony, generally they know not what sins they be; and although they have not so much to restrain them (both in respect of knowledge of God and laws of men) as the English have, yet a man shall never hear of such crimes amongst them, of robberies, murders, adulteries, &c., as amongst the English. I conceive that the glorious sun of so much truth as shines in England hardens our English hearts; for what the sun softeneth not, it hardens.

Of their trading. O, the infinite wisdom of the most holy, wise God, who hath so advanced Europe above America that there is not a sorry hoe, hatchet, knife, nor a rag of cloth in all America but what comes over the dreadful Atlantic Ocean from Europe! And yet, that Europe be not proud nor America discouraged: what treasures are hid in some parts of America and in our New English parts? How have foul hands (in smoky houses) the first handling of those furs which are after worn upon the hands of queens and heads of princes?

I will owe it you. They are very desirous to come into debt, but then he that trusts them must sustain a twofold loss:

First, of his commodity;

Secondly, of his custom, as I have found by dear experience. Some are ingenuous, plain-hearted, and honest; but the most never pay unless a man follow them to their several abodes, towns, and houses, as I myself have been forced to do, which hardship and travels it hath yet pleased God to sweeten with some experiences and some little gain of language.

I have found a deer, which sometimes they do, taking a wolf in the very act of his greedy prey, when sometimes (the wolf being greedy of his prey) they kill him. Sometimes the wolf, having glutted himself with the one half, leaves the other for his next bait; but the glad Indian, finding of it, prevents him.

And that we may see how true it is that all wild creatures, and many tame, prey upon the poor deer (which are there in a right emblem of God's persecuted, that is, hunted people:

> To harmless roes and does,
> Both wild and tame are foes).

I remember how a poor deer was long hunted and chased by a wolf; at last (as their manner is) after the chase of ten, it may be more, miles' running, the stout wolf tired out the nimble deer, and seizing upon it, killed: in the act of devouring his prey, two English swine, big with pig, passed by, assaulted the wolf, drove him from his prey, and devoured so much of that poor deer as they both surfeited and died that night.

The wolf is an emblem of a fierce, blood-sucking persecutor.

The swine of a covetous, rooting worldling. Both make a prey of the Lord Jesus and His poor servants.

Of their hunting. There is a blessing upon endeavor, even to the wildest Indians; the sluggard roasts not that which he took in hunting, but the substance of the diligent (either in earthly or heavenly affairs) is precious.

Of their gaming. This life is a short minute, eternity follows. On the improvement or dis-improvement of this short minute depends a joyful or dreadful eternity. Yet (which I tremble to think of) how cheap is this invaluable jewel, and how many vain inventions and foolish pastimes have the sons of men in all parts of the world found out, to pass time and post over this short minute of life, until like some pleasant river they have past into *mare mortuum*, the dead sea of eternal lamentation.

Of their war. How dreadful and yet how righteous is it with the most righteous judge of the whole world, that all the generations of men being turned enemies against, and fighting against Him who gives them breath and being and all things (whom yet they cannot reach), should stab, kill, burn, murder, and devour each other?

Of death and burial. O, how terrible is the look, the speedy and serious thought of death to all the sons of men? Thrice happy those who are dead and risen with the Son of God, for they are passed from death to life and shall not see death (a heavenly sweet paradox or riddle), as the Son of God hath promised them . . .

Now, to the most high and most holy, immortal, invisible and only wise God, who alone is Alpha and Omega, the beginning and the ending, the first and last, who was and is and is to come; from whom, and by whom, and to whom are all things; by whose gracious assistance and wonderful supportment in so many varieties of hardship and outward miseries I have had such converse with barbarous nations, and have been mercifully assisted to frame this poor *Key*, which may (through His blessing, in His own holy season) open a door, yea, doors of unknown mercies to us and them, be honour, glory, power, riches, wisdom, goodness, and dominion ascribed by all His in Jesus Christ to eternity. *Amen.*

Jacques Marquette (1674)

In 1673 the French Jesuit missionary Jacques Marquette (1637–1675) was chosen to undertake the exploration of the Mississippi. He caught dysentry, and a further exploration, of the River Illinois, proved fatal. He describes the character of the Illinois tribe.

When one speaks the word 'Illinois' it is as if one said in their language, 'the men,' – As if the other Savages were looked upon by them merely as animals. It must also be admitted that they have an air of humanity which we have not observed in the other nations that we have seen upon our route. The shortness Of my stay among Them did not allow me to secure all the Information that I would have desired; among all Their customs, the following is what I have observed.

They are divided into many villages, some of which are quite distant from that of which we speak, which is called peouarea. This causes some difference in their language, which, on the whole, resembles allegonquin, so that we easily understood each other. They are of a gentle and tractable disposition; we Experienced this in the reception which they gave us. They have several wives, of whom they are Extremely jealous; they watch them very closely, and cut off their noses or ears when they misbehave. I saw several women who bore the marks of their misconduct. Their Bodies are shapely; they are active and very skillful with their bows and arrows. They also use guns, which they buy from our savage allies who Trade with our French. They use them especially to inspire, through their noise and smoke, terror in their Enemies; the latter do not use guns, and have never seen any, since they live too Far toward the West. They are warlike, and make themselves dreaded by the Distant tribes to the south and west, whither they go to procure Slaves; these they barter, selling them at a high price to other Nations, in exchange for other Wares. Those very Distant Savages against whom they war, have no Knowledge of Europeans; neither do they know anything of iron, or of Copper, and they have only stone Knives. When the Illinois depart to go to war, the whole village must be notified by a loud Shout, which is uttered at the doors of their Cabins, the night and The Morning before their departure. The Captains are distinguished from the warriors by wearing red Scarfs. These are made, with considerable Skill, from the Hair of bears and wild cattle. They paint their faces with red ochre, great quantities of which are found at a distance of some days' journey from the village. They live by hunting, game being plentiful in that country, and on Indian corn, of which they always have a good crop; consequently, they have never suffered from famine. They also sow beans and melons, which are Excellent, especially those that have red seeds. Their Squashes are not of the best; they dry them in the sun, to eat them during The winter and spring. Their Cabins are very large, and are Roofed and floored with mats made of Rushes. They make all Their utensils of wood, and Their Ladles out of the heads of cattle, whose Skulls they know so well how to prepare that they use these ladles with ease for eating their sagamité.

They are liberal in cases of illness, and Think that the effect of the medicines administered to them is in proportion to the presents given to the physician. Their garments consist only of skins; the women are always clad very modestly and very becomingly, while the men do not take the trouble to cover themselves. I know not through what superstition some Illinois, as well as some Nadouessi, while still young, assume the garb of women, and retain it throughout their lives. There is some mystery in this, For they never marry and glory in demeaning themselves to do everything that the women do. They go to war, however, but can use only clubs, and not bows and arrows, which are the weapons proper to men. They are present at all the juggleries, and at the solemn dances in honour of the Calumet; at these they sing, but must not dance. They are summoned to the Councils, and nothing can be decided without their advice. Finally, through their profession of leading an Extraordinary life, they pass for Manitous, – that is to say, for Spirits – or persons of Consequence.

There remains no more, except to speak of the Calumet. There is nothing more mysterious or more respected among them. Less honour is paid to the Crowns and sceptres of Kings than the Savages bestow upon this. It seems to be the God of peace and of war, the Arbiter of life and of death. It has but to be carried upon one's person, and displayed, to enable one to walk safely through the midst of Enemies – who, in the hottest of the Fight, lay down Their arms when it is shown. For That reason, the Illinois gave me one, to serve as a safeguard among all the Nations through whom I had to pass during my voyage. There is a Calumet for peace, and one for war, which are distinguished solely by the Colour of the feathers with which they are adorned; Red is a sign of war. They also use it to put an end to Their disputes, to strengthen Their alliances, and to speak to Strangers. It is fashioned from red stone, polished like marble, and bored in such a manner that one end serves as a receptacle for the tobacco, while the other fits into the stem; this is a stick two feet long, as thick as an ordinary cane, and bored through the middle. It is ornamented with the heads and necks of various birds, whose plumage is very beautiful. To these they also add large feathers, – red, green, and other colours, – wherewith the whole is adorned. They have a great regard for it, because they look upon it as the Calumet of the Sun; and, in fact, they offer it to the latter to smoke when they wish to obtain a calm, or rain, or fine weather. They scruple to bathe themselves at the beginning of Summer, or to eat fresh fruit, until after they have performed the dance, which they do as follows:

The Calumet dance, which is very famous among these peoples, is performed solely for important reasons; sometimes to strengthen peace, or to unite themselves for some great war; at other times, for public rejoicing. Sometimes they thus do honour to a Nation who are invited to be present; sometimes it is danced at the reception of some important personage, as if they wished to give him the diversion of a Ball or a Comedy. In Winter, the ceremony takes place in a Cabin; in summer, in the open fields. When the spot is selected, it is completely surrounded by trees, so that all may sit in the shade afforded by their leaves, in order to be protected from the heat of the Sun. A large mat of rushes, painted in various colours, is spread in the middle of the place, and serves as a carpet upon which to place with honour the God of the person who gives the Dance; for each has his own God, which they call their Manitou. This is a serpent, a bird, or other similar thing, of which they have dreamed while sleeping, and in which they place all their confidence for the success of their war, their fishing, and their hunting. Near this Manitou, and at its right, is placed the Calumet in honour of which the feast is given; and all around it a sort of trophy is made, and the weapons used by the warriors of those Nations are spread, namely: clubs, war-hatchets, bows, quivers, and arrows.

Everything being thus arranged, and the hour of the Dance drawing near, those who have been appointed to sing take the most honourable place under the branches; these are the men and women who are gifted with the best voices, and who sing together in perfect harmony. Afterward, all come to take their seats in a circle under the branches; but each one, on arriving, must salute the Manitou. This he does by inhaling the smoke, and blowing it from his mouth upon the Manitou, as if he were offering to it incense. Everyone at the outset, takes the Calumet in a respectful manner, and, supporting it with both hands, causes it to dance in cadence keeping good time with the air of the songs. He makes it execute many differing figures; sometimes he shows it to the whole assembly, turning himself from one side to the other. After that, he who is to begin the Dance appears in the middle of the assembly, and at once continues this. Sometimes he offers it to the sun, as if he wished the latter to smoke it; sometimes he inclines it toward the earth; again, he makes it spread its wings, as if about to fly; at other times, he puts it near the mouths of those present, that they may smoke. The whole is done in cadence; and this is, as it were, the first Scene of the Ballet.

The second consists of a Combat carried on to the sound of a kind of drum, which succeeds the songs, or even unites with them, harmonizing very well together. The Dancer makes a sign to some warrior to come to take the arms which lie upon the mat, and invites him to fight to the sound of the drums. The latter approaches, takes up the bow and arrows, and the war-hatchet, and begins the duel with the other, whose sole defence is the Calumet. This spectacle is very pleasing, especially as all is done in cadence; for one attacks, the other defends himself; one strikes blows; the other parries them; one takes to flight, the other pursues; and then he who was fleeing faces about, and causes his adversary to flee. This is done so well – with slow and measured steps, and to the rhythmic sound of the voices and drums – that it might pass for a very fine opening of a Ballet in France. The third Scene consists of a lofty Discourse, delivered by him who holds the Calumet; for, when the Combat is ended without bloodshed, he recounts the battles at which he has been present, the victories that he has won, the names of the Nations, the places, and the Captives whom he has made. And, to reward him, he who presides at the Dance makes him a present of a fine robe of Beaver-skins, or some other article. Then, having received it, he hands the Calumet to another, the latter to a third, and so on with all the others, until everyone has done his duty; then the President presents the Calumet itself to the Nation that has been invited to the Ceremony, as a token of the everlasting peace that is to exist between the two peoples.

John Miller (1695)

John Miller (1666–1724) served as chaplain to His Majesty's Forces in New York, recently seized from the Dutch, from 1692 to 1695. On the return voyage to England in 1695 his ship was captured by French privateers and Miller was imprisoned at St. Malo, where he wrote his account of the people and the province of New York.

The number of the Inhabitants in the Province are about 3000 families whereof almost one half are naturally Dutch a great part English and the rest French ... As to their Religion they are very much divided. few of them intelligent & sincere but the most part ignorant & conceited, fickle & regardless. As to their wealth & disposition thereto the Dutch are rich & sparing, the English neither very rich nor too great husbands, the French are poor and therefore forced to be penurious: As to their way of trade & dealing they are all generally cunning and crafty but many of them not so just to their words as they should be.

... The wickedness & irreligion of the inhabitants which abounds in all parts of the Province & appears in so many shapes constituting so many sorts of sin that I can scarce tell which to begin withal. But as a great reason of & inlet to the rest I shall first mention the great negligence of divine things that is generally found in most people of what Sect or party soever they pretend to be. Their eternall interests are their least concern & as if Salvation were not a matter of moment when they have opportunities of Serving God they care not for making use thereof if they go to church 'tis but too often out of curiosity & to find out faults in him that preacheth rather than to hear their own or what is yet worse to slight & deride where they should be Serious if they have none of those opportunities they are well contented & regard it little if there be any whom seem otherwise & discontented many of them when they have them make appear by their Actions 'twas but in show; for though at first they will pretend to have a great regard for God's ordinances & a high esteem for the Ministry whether real or pretended a little time will plainly evidence that they were most pleased at the novelty than truly affected with the Benefit when they slight that which they before seemingly so much admired & Speake evil of him who before was the subject of their praise & commendation & that without any other reason than their own fickle temper & envious humour. In a soil so ranke as this no marvail if the Evill one find a ready entertainment. For the seed he is minded to cast in & from a people so inconsistent & regardless of Heaven & holy things no wonder if God withdraw his grace & give them up a prey to those temptations which they so industriously seek to embrace hence is it therefore that their natural corruption without check or hindrance is by frequent acts improved into habits most evill in the practice & Difficult in the correction.

One of which & the first, I am minded to speak of is drunkenness which tho of itself a great sin is yet aggravated in that it is an occasion of many others . . .

. . . many in the City of New York whose daily practice is to frequent the taverns & to Carouse & game their night employment. This course is the ruin & destruction of many merchants especially those of the Younger sort who carrying over with them a stock whether as Factors or on their own Account Spend even to prodigality till they find themselves bankrupt e'er they are aware.

In a town where this course of life is led by many 'tis no wonder if there be other vices in vogue because they are the natural product of it such are cursin & Swearing to both of which People are here much accustomed some doing it in that frequent horrible & dreadful manner as if they prided themselves both as to the number and invention of them this joined with their profane Atheisticall & scoffing method of discourse makes their Company extremely uneasy to sober & religious men who sometimes by reason of their affairs cannot help being of their society & becoming ear-witnesses of their blasphemy & folly. 'tis strange that men should engage themselves so foolishly & run into the Commission of so great a sin unto which they have no sufficient, often no a pretended, provocation & from which they reap no advantage nor any real pleasure: & yet we see them even delight in it & no discourse is thought witty or eloquent except larded with oaths & execrations . . .

Père Mathurin le Petit (1730)

This letter from the French Jesuit missionary, Père Mathurin le Petit to Père D'Avaugour, Procurator of the Missions in North America, gives a report of the Louisiana missions. The event of most importance in it is the massacre by the Natchez Indians (October 28, 1729) of some two hundred French people settled among them.

At New Orleans
The 12th of July, 1730

MY REVEREND FATHER:
The peace of Our Lord.
You cannot be ignorant of the sad event which has desolated that part of the French Colony established at *Natchez*, . . .

After having thus given you a slight idea of the character and customs of the *Natchez* Savages, I proceed, my Reverend Father, as I have promised you, to enter on a detail of their perfidy and treason. It was on the second of December of the year 1729, that we learned that they had surprised the French, and had massacred almost all of them. This sad news was first brought to us by one of the planters, who had escaped their fury. It was confirmed to us on the following day by other French fugitives and finally some French women whom they had made slaves, and were forced afterward to restore, brought us all particulars.

At the first rumour of an event so sad, the alarm and consternation was general in New Orleans. Although the massacre had taken place more than a hundred leagues from here, you would have supposed that it had happened under our own eyes. Each one was mourning the loss of a relative, a friend, or some property; all were alarmed for their own lives, for there was reason to fear that the conspiracy of the Savages had been general.

This unlooked for massacre began on Monday, the 28th of October, about 9 o'clock in the morning. Some cause of dissatisfaction which the *Natchez* thought they had with Monsieur the Commandant, and the arrival of a number of richly laden boats for the garrison and the colonists, determined them to hasten their enterprise, and to strike their blow sooner than they had agreed with the other confederate Tribes. And it was thus that they carried their plan into execution. First they divided themselves, and sent into the Fort, into the Village, and into the two grants, as many Savages as there were French in each of these places; then they feigned that they were going out for a grand hunt, and undertook to trade with the French for guns, powder and ball, offering to pay them as much, even more than was customary; and in truth, as there was no reason to suspect their fidelity, they made at that time an exchange of their poultry and corn, for some arms and ammunition which they used advantageously against us. It is true that some expressed their distrust, but this was thought to have so little foundation, that they were treated as cowards who were frightened of their own shadows. They had been on their guard against the *Tchactas*, but as for the *Natchez*, they had never distrusted them, and they were so persuaded of their good faith that it increased their hardihood. Having thus posted themselves in different houses, provided with the arms obtained from us, they attacked at the same time each his man, and in less than two hours they massacred more than two hundred of the French. The best known are Monsieur de Chepar, Commandant of the post, Monsieur de Codère, Commandant among the *Yazous*, Monsieur des Ursins, Messieurs de Kolly, father and son, Messieurs de Longrays, des Noyers, Bailly, etc.

Father du Poisson had just performed the funeral rites of his associate, Brother Crucy, who had died very suddenly of Sunstroke. He arrived among the *Natchez* on the 26th of November, that is, two days before the massacre. The next day which was the first Sunday of Advent, he said Mass in the parish and preached in the absence of the Curé. He was to have returned in the afternoon to his mission among the *Akensas*, but he was detained by some sick persons, to whom it was necessary to administer the Sacraments. On Monday he was about to say Mass, and to carry the holy Viaticum to one of those sick persons whom he had confessed the evening before, when the massacre began; a gigantic Chief six feet in height, seized him, and having thrown him to the ground, cut off his head with blows of a hatchet. The Father in falling only uttered these words, 'Ah, my God, ah, my God!' Monsieur de Codère drew his sword to defend him, when he was himself killed by a musket-ball from another Savage, whom he did not perceive.

These barbarians spared but two of the French, a Tailor and a Carpenter, who were able to serve their wants. They did not treat badly either the Negro Slaves, or the Savages who were willing to give themselves up; but they ripped up the belly of every pregnant woman, and killed almost all those who were nursing and their children, because they were disturbed by their cries and tears. They did not kill the other women, but made them slaves, and treated them with every indignity during the two or three months that they were their masters. The least miserable were those who knew how to sew, because they kept them busy making shirts, dresses, etc. The others were employed in cutting and carrying wood for cooking, and in pounding the corn of which they make their sagamité. But two things, above all, aggravated the grief and hardness of their slavery; it was, in the first place, to have for masters those same persons whom they had seen dipping their cruel hands in the blood of their husbands, and, in the second place, to hear them continually saying that the French had been treated in the same manner at all the other posts, and that the country was now entirely freed from them.

During the massacre, the great Chief of the *Natchez* was seated quietly under the tobacco shed of the Company. His Warriors brought to his feet the head of the Commandant, about which they ranged those of the principal French of the post, leaving their bodies a prey to the dogs, the buzzards, and other carnivorous birds.

When they were assured that not another Frenchman remained at the post, they applied themselves to plunder the houses, the magazine of the Company of the Indies, and all the boats which were still loaded by the bank of the river. They employed the Negroes to transport the merchandise which they divided among themselves, with the exception of the munitions of war, which they placed for security in a separate cabin. While the brandy lasted, of which they found a good supply, they passed their days and nights in drinking, singing, dancing, and insulting in the most barbarous manner, the dead bodies and the memories of the French.

Some of the French escaped the fury of the Savages by taking refuge in the woods, where they suffered extremely from hunger and the effects of the weather. One of them, on arriving here, relieved us of a little disquietude we felt with regard to the post we occupy among the *Yazous*, which is not more than forty or fifty leagues above the *Natchez* by water, and only 15 or 20 by land. Not being able longer to endure the extreme cold from which he suffered, he left the woods under the cover of night, to go warm himself in the house of a Frenchman. When he was near it he heard the voices of Savages and deliberated whether he should enter. He determined, however, to do so, preferring rather to perish by the hand of these barbarians, than to die of famine and cold. He was agreeably surprised when he found these Savages eager to render him a service, to heap kindnesses upon him, to commiserate him, to console him, to furnish him with provisions, clothes, and a boat to make his escape to New Orleans. These were the *Yazous*, who were returning from chanting the calumet at *Oumas*. The chief charged him to say to Monsieur Perrier, that he had nothing to fear on the part of the *Yazous*, that 'they would not lose their sense,' that is, that they would always remain attached to the French, and that he would be constantly on the watch with his tribe to warn the French pirogues that were descending the river to be on their guard against the *Natchez*.

We believed for a long time that the promises of this Chief were very sincere, and feared no more Indian perfidy for our post among the *Yazous*. But learn, my Reverend Father, the disposition of these savages, and how little one is able to trust their word, even when accompanied by the greatest demonstrations of friendship. Scarcely had they returned to their own village, when, loaded with the presents they received from the *Natchez*, they followed their example and imitated their treachery. Uniting with the *Corroys*, they agreed together to exterminate the French. They began with Father Souel, the Missionary of both tribes, who was then living in the midst of them, in their own village. The fidelity of the *Ofogoulas*, who were then absent at the chase, has never been shaken, and they now compose one Village with the *Tonikas*.

On the 11th of December, Father Souel was returning in the evening from visiting the Chief, and while in a ravine, received many musket-balls, and fell dead on the spot. The Savages immediately rushed to his cabin to plunder it. His Negro, who composed all his family and all his defence, armed himself with a wood-cutter's knife, to prevent the pillage, and even wounded one of the Savages. This zealous action cost him his life, but, happily, he had received Baptism less than a month before, and was living in a most Christian manner.

These Savages, who even to that time seemed sensible of the affection which their Missionary bore them, reproached themselves for his death as soon as they were capable of reflection; but returning again to their natural ferocity, they adopted the resolution of putting a finishing stroke to their crime by the destruction of the whole French post. 'Since the black Chief is dead,' said they, 'it is the same as if all the French were dead - let us not spare any.'

The next day, they executed their barbarous plan. They repaired early in the morning to the fort, which was not more than a league distant, and whose occupants supposed on their arrival, that the savages wished to chant the calumet to the Chevalier des Roches, who commanded the post in the absence of Monsieur de Codère. He had but seventeen men with him, who had no suspicion of any evil design on the part of the Savages, and were therefore all massacred, not one escaping their fury. They, however, granted their lives to four women and five children, whom they found there, and whom they made slaves.

One of the *Yazous*, having stripped the Missionary, clothed himself in his garments and shortly afterward announced to the *Natchez*, that his Nation had redeemed their pledge, and that the French settled among them were all massacred. In this city there was no longer any doubt on that point, as soon they learned what came near of being the fate of Father Doutreleau. This Missionary had availed himself of the time when the Savages were engaged in their winter occupations, to come to see us, for the purpose of regulating some matters relating to his Mission. He set out on the first day of this year, 1730, and not expecting to arrive at the residence of Father Souel, of whose fate he was ignorant, in time to say Mass, he determined to say it at the mouth of the little river of the *Yazous*, where his party had cabined.

As he was preparing for this sacred office, he saw a boat full of savages landing. They demanded from what Nation they were. '*Yazous*, comrades of the French,' they replied, making a thousand friendly demonstrations to the voyageurs who accompanied the Missionary, and presenting them with provisions. While the Father was preparing for his altar, a flock of bustards passed, and the voyageurs fired at them the only two guns they had, without thinking of reloading, as the Mass had already commenced. The Savages noted this and placed themselves behind the voyageurs, as if it was their intention to hear Mass, although they were not Christians.

At the time when the Father was saying the *Kyrie Eleison* the Savages made their discharge. The Missionary perceiving himself wounded in his right arm, and seeing one of the voyageurs killed at his feet, and the four others fled, threw himself on to his knees to receive the last fatal blow, which he regarded as inevitable. In this posture he received two or three discharges. But although the Savages fired while almost touching him, yet they did not inflict on him any new wounds. Finding himself then, as it were, miraculously escaped from so many mortal blows, he took flight, having on still his priestly garments, and without any other defence than an entire confidence in God, whose particular protection was given him, as the event proved. He threw himself into the water, and after advancing some steps, gained the pirogue in which two of the voyageurs were making their escape. They had supposed him to be killed by some of the many balls which they had fired on him. In climbing up into the pirogue, and turning his head to see whether any one of his pursuers was following him too closely, he received in the mouth a discharge of small shot, the greater part of which were flattened against his teeth, although some of them entered his gums, and remained there for a long time. I have myself seen two of them there. Father Doutreleau, all wounded as he was, undertook the duty of steering the pirogue, while his two companions placed themselves at the paddles. Unfortunately, one of them, at setting out, had his thigh broken by a musket ball, from the effects of which he has since remained a cripple.

The *Tchikachas*, a brave Nation but treacherous, and little known to the French, have endeavoured to seduce the Illinois Tribes from their allegiance: they have even sounded some particular persons to see whether they could not draw them over to the party of those Savages who were enemies of our Nation. The Illinois have replied to them that they were almost all 'of the prayer' (that is, according to their manner of expression, that they were Christians); and that in other ways they are inviolably attached to the French, by the alliances which many of that nation had contracted with them, in espousing their daughters. At the first news of the war with the *Natchez* and the *Yazous*, they came hither to weep for the black Robes and the French, and to offer the services of their Nation to Monsieur Perrier, to avenge their death. I happened to be at the governor's house when they arrived, and was charmed with the harangues they made. *Chikagou*, whom you saw in Paris, was at the head of the *Mitchigamias*, and *Mamantouensa* at the head of the *Kaskaskias*.

Chikagou spoke first. He spread out in the hall a carpet of deerskin, bordered with porcupine quills, on which he placed two calumets, with different savage ornaments, accompanying them with a present according to the usual custom. 'There,' he said in showing the two calumets, 'are two messages which we bring you, the one of Religion and the other of peace or war, as you shall determine. We have listened with respect to the Governors, because they bring us the word of the King our Father, and much more to the black Robes, because they bring us the word of God himself, who is the King of Kings. We have come from a great distance to weep with you for the death of the French, and to offer our Warriors to strike those hostile Nations whom you may wish to designate. You have but to speak. When I went over to France, the King promised me his protection for the Prayer, and recommended me never to abandon it. I will always remember it. Grant then your protection to us and to our black Robes.' He then gave utterance to the edifying sentiments with which he was impressed with regard to the Faith, as the Interpreter Baillarjon enabled us to half understand them in his miserable French.

Chikagou guards most carefully, in a bag made expressly for the purpose, the magnificent snuff-box which the late Madame, the Duchess d'Orléans, gave him at Versailles. Notwithstanding all the offers made to him, he has never been willing to part with it, – a degree of consideration very remarkable in a Savage, whose characteristic generally is, to be in a short time disgusted with anything he has, and passionately desire what he sees, but does not own.

Everything *Chikagou* has related to his countrymen with regard to France, has appeared to them incredible. 'They have bribed you,' said some to him, 'to make us believe all these beautiful fictions.' 'We are willing to believe,' said his relatives, and those by whom his sincerity was least doubted, 'that you have really seen all that you tell us, but there must have been some charm which fascinated your eyes, for it is not possible that France can be such as you have painted it.'

When he told them that in France they were accustomed to have five cabins, one on top of the other, and that they were as high as the tallest trees, that there were as many people in the streets of Paris, as there were blades of grass on the Prairies, or mosquitoes in the woods, and that they rode about there and even made long journeys in moving cabins of leather, they did not credit it any more than when he added that he had seen long cabins full of sick people, where skilful Surgeons performed the most wonderful cures. 'Here,' he would say to them in sport, 'you may lose an arm or a leg, an eye, a tooth, a breast, if you are in France, and they will supply you with others, so that it will not be noticed.' What most embarrassed *Mamantouensa*, when he saw the ships, was to know how it was possible to launch them into the water after they had been built on land, where arms enough could be found for this purpose, and above all to raise the anchors with their enormous weights. They explained both these points to him and he admired the genius of the French who were capable of such beautiful inventions.

You can well believe, my reverend Father, that this war has retarded the French colony; nevertheless we flatter ourselves that this misfortune will be productive of benefit, by determining the Court to send the forces necessary to tranquillize the Colony and render it flourishing. Although they have nothing to fear at *New Orleans*, either from the smaller neighbouring tribes, whom our Negroes alone could finish in a single morning, or even from the *Tchactas*, who would not dare to expose themselves on the Lake in any great numbers, yet a panic terror has spread itself over almost every spirit, particularly with the women. They will, however, be reassured by the arrival of the first troops from France, whom we are now constantly expecting. As far as our Missionaries are concerned, they are very tranquil. The perils to which they see themselves exposed seem to increase their joy and animate their zeal.

Gustavus Vassa (1766)

Gustavus Vassa was born c. 1745 in south-eastern Onitsha, in what is now Nigeria. His native language was Ibo. At the age of ten he was captured by traders and sold into slavery. He travelled widely with a Captain Pascal, serving with him in Wolfe's campaign in Quebec and Boscawen's in the Mediterranean during the Seven Years' War. He received some schooling in England, which prepared him for his work as shipping clerk and amateur navigator on the ships of his second master, Robert King, a Quaker from Philadelphia. Though Quakers did not believe in slavery King was reluctant to release him. He sold him for £40 to Captain Farmer, who gave him his freedom in 1766. The Interesting Narrative of the Life of Olaudah Equiano, or Gustavus Vassa the African, written by himself *was published in 1789.*

Mr King dealt in all manner of merchandize and kept from one to six clerks. He loaded many vessels in a year, particularly to Philadelphia, where he was born and was connected with a great mercantile house in that city. He had besides many vessels and droggers of different sizes which used to go about the island and others, to collect rum, sugar, and other goods. I understood pulling and managing these boats very well, and this hard work, which was the first that he set me to, in the sugar season used to be my constant employment. I have rowed the boat and slaved at the oars from one hour to sixteen in the twenty-four, during which I had fifteen pence sterling per day to live on, though sometimes only ten pence. However, this was considerably more than was allowed to other slaves that used to work with me, and belonged to other gentlemen on the island: those poor souls had never more than nine pence per day, and seldom more than six pence, from their masters or owners, though they earned them three or four pisterines: for it is a common practice in the West Indies for men to purchase slaves though they have not plantations themselves, in order to let them out to planters and merchants at so much a piece by the day, and they give what allowance they choose out of this produce of their daily work to their slaves for subsistence; this allowance is often very scanty. My master often gave the owners of these slaves two and a half of these pieces per day, and found the poor fellows in victuals himself, because he thought their owners did not feed them well enough according to the work they did. The slaves used to like this very well, and as they knew my master to be a man of feeling, they were always glad to work for him in preference to any other gentleman, some of whom, after they had been paid for these poor people's labour, would not give them their allowance out of it. Many times have I even seen these unfortunate wretches beaten for asking for their pay, and often severely flogged by their owners if they did not bring them their daily or weekly money exactly to the time, though the poor creatures were obliged to wait on the gentlemen they had worked for sometimes for more than half the day before they could get their pay, and this generally on Sundays, when they wanted the time for themselves. In particular, I knew a countryman of mine who once did not bring the weekly money directly that it was earned, and though he brought it the same day to his master, yet he was staked to the ground for this pretended negligence, and was just going to receive a hundred lashes but for a gentleman who begged him off fifty. This poor man was very industrious, and by his frugality had saved so much money by working on shipboard that he had got a white man to buy him a boat, unknown to his master. Some time after he had this little estate the governor wanted a boat to bring his sugar from different parts of the island, and knowing this to be a negro-man's boat he seized upon it for himself, and would not pay the owner a farthing. The man on this went to his master, and complained to him of this act of the governor, but the only satisfaction he received was to be damned very heartily by his master, who asked him how dared any of his negroes to have a boat. If the justly-merited ruin of the governor's fortune could be any gratification to the poor man he had thus robbed, he was not without consolation. Extortion and rapine are poor providers, and some time after this the governor died in the King's Bench in England, as I was told, in great poverty. The last war favoured this poor negro-man, and he found some means to escape from his Christian master. He came to England, where I saw him afterwards several times. Such treatment as this often drives these miserable wretches to despair, and they run away from their masters at the hazard of their lives. Many of them in this place, unable to get their pay when they have earned it, and fearing to be flogged as usual if they return home without it, run away where they can for shelter, and a reward is often offered to bring them in dead or alive. My master used sometimes, in these cases, to agree with their owners and to settle with them himself, and thereby he saved many of them a flogging.

Once, for a few days, I was let out to fit a vessel, and I had no victuals allowed me by either party; at last I told my master of this treatment and he took me away from it. In many of the estates, on the different islands where I used to be sent for rum or sugar, they would not deliver it to me or any other negro; he was therefore obliged to send a white man along with me to those places, and then he used to pay him from six to ten pisterines a day. From being thus employed during the time I served Mr King, in going about the different estates on the island I had all the opportunity I could wish for to see the dreadful usage of the poor men, usage that reconciled me to my situation and made me bless God for the hands into which I had fallen.

I had the good fortune to please my master in every department in which he employed me, and there was scarcely any part of his business or household affairs in which I was not occasionally engaged. I often supplied the place of a clerk in receiving the delivering cargoes to the ships, in tending stores, and delivering goods: and besides this I used to shave and dress my master when convenient, and take care of his horse, and when it was necessary, which was very often, I worked likewise on board of different

vessels of his. By these means I became very useful to my master, and saved
him, as he used to acknowledge, above a hundred pounds a year. Nor did
he scruple to say I was of more advantage to him than any of his clerks,
though their usual wages in the West Indies are from sixty to a hundred
pounds current a year.

I have sometimes heard it asserted that a negro cannot earn his master
the first cost, but nothing can be further from the truth. I suppose nine-
tenths of the mechanics throughout the West Indies are negro slaves, and
I well know the coopers among them earn two dollars a day, the carpenters
the same and oftentimes more, as also the masons, smiths, and fishermen,
etc. and I have known many slaves whose masters would not take a thousand
pounds current for them. But surely this assertion refutes itself, for if it be
true, why do the planters and merchants pay such a price for slaves? And,
above all, why do those who make this assertion exclaim the most loudly
against the abolition of the slave trade? So much are men blinded, and to
such inconsistent arguments are they driven by mistaken interest! I grant,
indeed, that slaves are sometimes, by half-feeding, half-clothing, over-
working and stripes, reduced so low that they are turned out as unfit for
service and left to perish in the woods or expire on a dunghill.

It was very common in several of the islands, particularly in St Kitt's, for
the slaves to be branded with the initial letters of their master's name, and
a load of heavy iron hooks hung about their necks. Indeed on the most
trifling occasions they were loaded with chains, and often instruments of
torture were added. The iron muzzle, thumbscrews, etc. are so well known
as not to need a description, and were sometimes applied for the slightest
faults. I have seen a negro beaten till some of his bones were broken for
even letting a pot boil over. Is it surprising that usage like this should drive
the poor creatures to despair and make them seek refuge in death from
those evils which render their lives intolerable – while,

> 'With shudd'ring horror pale, and eyes aghast,
> They view their lamentable lot, and find
> No rest!'

This they frequently do. A negro-man on board a vessel of my master,
while I belonged to her, having been put in irons for some trifling misdemeanour and kept in that state for some days, being weary of life, took an
opportunity of jumping overboard into the sea; however, he was picked up
without being drowned. Another whose life was also a burden to him
resolved to starve himself to death, and refused to eat any victuals; this
procured him a severe flogging, and he also, on the first occasion which
offered, jumped overboard at Charleston, but was saved.

Nor is there any greater regard shown to the little property, than there
is to the persons and lives of the negroes. I have already related an instance
or two of particular oppression out of many which I have witnessed, but
the following is frequent in all the islands. The wretched field-slaves, after
toiling all the day for an unfeeling owner who gives them but little victuals,
steal sometimes a few moments from rest or refreshment to gather some
small portion of grass, according as their time will admit. This they
commonly tie up in a parcel, (either a bit, worth six pence, or half a bit's-
worth) and bring it to town or to the market to sell. Nothing is more

common than for the white people on this occasion to take the grass from them without paying for it; and not only so, but too often also to my knowledge our clerks and many others at the same time have committed acts of violence on the poor, wretched, and helpless females, whom I have seen for hours stand crying to no purpose and get no redress or pay of any kind. Is not this one common and crying sin enough to bring down God's judgement on the islands? He tells us the oppressor and the oppressed are both in his hands; and if these are not the poor, the broken-hearted, the blind, the captive, the bruised, which our Saviour speaks of, who are they? One of these depredators once in St Eustatia came on board our vessel and brought some fowls and pigs of me, and a whole day after his departure with the things he returned again and wanted his money back: I refused to give it and not seeing my captain on board, he began the common pranks with me, and swore he would even break open my chest and take my money. I therefore expected, as my captain was absent, that he would be as good as his word, and he was just proceeding to strike me, when fortunately a British seaman on board, whose heart had not been debauched by a West India climate, interposed and prevented him. But had the cruel man struck me I certainly should have defended myself at the hazard of my life, for what is life to a man thus oppressed? He went away, however, swearing, and threatened that whenever he caught me on shore he would shoot me, and pay for me afterwards.

The small account in which the life of a negro is held in the West Indies is so universally known that it might seem impertinent to quote the following extract, if some people had not been hardy enough of late to assert that negroes are on the same footing in that respect as Europeans. By the 329th Act, page 125, of the Assembly of Barbadoes, it is enacted 'That if any negro, or other slave, under punishment by his master, or his order, for running away, or any other crime or misdemeanour towards his said master, unfortunately shall suffer in life or member, no person whatsoever shall be liable to a fine, but if any man shall out of *wantonness, or only of bloody-mindedness, or cruel intention, wilfully kill a negro, or other slave, of his own, he shall pay into the public treasury fifteen pounds sterling.*' And it is the same in most, if not all, of the West India islands. Is not this one of the many acts of the islands which call loudly for redress? And do not the assembly which enacted it deserve the appellation of savages and brutes rather than of Christians and men? It is an act at once unmerciful, unjust, and unwise, which for cruelty would disgrace an assembly of those who are called barbarians, and for its injustice and *insanity* would shock the morality and common sense of a Samoyed or a Hottentot.

Shocking as this and many more acts of the bloody West India code at first view appear, how is the iniquity of it heightened when we consider to whom it may be extended! Mr James Tobin, a zealous labourer in the vineyard of slavery, gives an account of a French planter of his acquaintance in the island of Martinique who showed him many mulattoes working in the fields like beasts of burden, and he told Mr Tobin these were all the produce of his own loins! And I myself have known similar instances. Pray, reader, are these sons and daughters of the French planter less his children by being begotten on a black woman? And what must be the virtue of those legislators and the feelings of those fathers, who estimate the lives of their sons, however begotten, at no more than fifteen pounds, though they should be murdered, as the acts says, *out of wantonness and bloody-mindedness*! But is not the slave trade entirely a war with the heart of man? And surely that which is begun by breaking down the barriers of virtue involves in its continuance destruction to every principle, and buries all sentiments in ruin!

I have often seen slaves, particularly those who were meagre, in different islands, put into scales and weighed, and then sold from three pence to six pence or nine pence a pound. My master, however, whose humanity was shocked at this mode, used to sell such by the lump. And at or after a sale it was not uncommon to see negroes taken from their wives, wives taken from their husbands, and children from their parents, and sent off to other islands, and wherever else their merciless lords chose; and probably never more during life to see each other! Oftentimes my heart had bled at these partings, when the friends of the departed have been at the waterside, and with sighs and tears have kept their eyes fixed on the vessel till it went out of sight.

A poor Creole negro I knew well, who, after having been often thus transported from island to island, at last resided in Montserrat. This man used to tell me many melancholy tales of himself. Generally, after he had done working for his master, he used to employ his few leisure moments to go a-fishing. When he had any fish his master would frequently take them from him without paying him, and at other times some other white people would serve him in the same manner. One day he said to me, very movingly, 'Sometimes when a white man take away my fish I go to my master, and he get me my right; and when my master by strength take away my fishes, what me must do? I can't go to anybody to be righted; then,' said the poor man, looking up above, 'I must look up to God Mighty in the top for right.' This artless tale moved me much and I could not help feeling the just causes Moses had in redressing his brother against the Egyptian. I exhorted the man to look up still to the God on the top since there was no redress below. Though I little thought then that I myself should more than once experience such imposition and read the same exhortation hereafter in my own transactions in the islands, and that even this poor man and I should some time after suffer together in the same manner, as shall be related hereafter.

Nor was such usage as this confined to particular places or individuals, for in all the different islands in which I have been (and I have visited no less than fifteen) the treatment of the slaves was nearly the same; so nearly indeed, that the history of an island or even a plantation, with a few such exceptions as I have mentioned, might serve for a history of the whole. Such a tendency has the slave-trade to debauch men's minds and harden them to every feeling of humanity! For I will not suppose that the dealers in slaves are born worse than other men – No, it is the fatality of this mistaken avarice that it corrupts the milk of human kindness and turns it into gall. And had the pursuits of those men been different, they might have been as generous, as tender-hearted and just, as they are unfeeling, rapacious and cruel. Surely this traffic cannot be good, which spreads like a pestilence and taints what it touches! which violates that first natural right of mankind, equality and independency, and gives one man a dominion over his fellows which God could never intend! For it raises the owner to a state as far above man as it depresses the slave below it, and with all the presumption of human pride, sets a distinction between them, immeasurable in extent and endless in duration! Yet how mistaken is the avarice even of the planters! Are slaves more useful by being thus humbled to the condition of brutes than they would be if suffered to enjoy the privileges of men? The freedom which diffuses health and prosperity throughout Britain answers you – No. When you make men slaves you deprive them of half their virtue, you set them in your own conduct an example of fraud, rapine, and cruelty, and compel them to live with you in a state of war, and yet you complain that they are not honest or faithful! You stupefy them with stripes and think it necessary to keep them in a state of ignorance, and yet you assert that they are incapable of learning, that their minds are such a barren soil or moor that culture would be lost on them, and that they come from a climate where nature, though prodigal of her bounties in a degree unknown to yourselves, has left man alone scant and unfinished and incapable of enjoying the treasures she had poured out for him! – An assertion at once impious and absurd. Why do you use those instruments of torture? Are they fit to be applied by one rational being to another? And are ye not struck with shame and mortification to see the partakers of your nature reduced so low? But above all, are there no dangers attending this mode of treatment? Are you not hourly in dread of an insurrection? Nor would it be surprising: for when

> '– No peace is given
> To us enslav'd, but custody severe;
> And stripes and arbitrary punishment
> Inflicted – and what peace can we return?
> But to our power, hostility and hate;
> Untam'd reluctance, and revenge, though slow.
> Yet ever plotting how the conqueror least
> May reap his conquest, and may least rejoice
> In doing what we most in suffering feel.'

But by changing your conduct and treating your slaves as men every cause of fear would be banished. They would be faithful, honest, intelligent and vigorous; and peace, prosperity, and happiness, would attend you.

Free Man

Every day now brought me nearer to my freedom, and I was impatient till we proceeded again to sea, that I might have an opportunity of getting a sum large enough to purchase it. I was not long ungratified, for in the beginning of 1766 my master brought another sloop, named the *Nancy*, the largest I had ever seen. She was partly laden, and was to proceed to Philadelphia. Our captain had his choice of three, and I was well pleased he chose this, which was the largest, for from his having a large vessel I had more room and could carry a larger quantity of goods with me. Accordingly, when we had delivered our old vessel, the *Prudence*, and completed the lading of the *Nancy*, having made near 300 per cent by four barrels of

---

[1] Paradise Lost, Book I, ll. 332–340 (speech of Beelzebub).

pork I brought from Charleston, I laid in as large a cargo as I could, trusting to God's providence to prosper my undertaking. With these views I sailed for Philadelphia.

We arrived safe and in good time at Philadelphia, and I sold my goods there chiefly to the Quakers. They always appeared to be a very honest discreet sort of people, and never attempted to impose on me; I therefore liked them, and ever after chose to deal with them in preference to any others. One Sunday morning while I was here, as I was going to church, I chanced to pass a meeting-house. The doors being open, and the house full of people, it excited my curiosity to go in. When I entered the house, to my great surprise, I saw a very tall woman standing in the midst of them, speaking in an audible voice something which I could not understand. Having never seen anything of this kind before, I stood and stared about me for some time, wondering at this odd scene. As soon as it was over I took an opportunity to make inquiry about the place and people, when I was informed they were called Quakers. I particularly asked what that woman I saw in the midst of them had said, but none of them were pleased to satisfy me; so I quitted them, and soon after, as I was returning, I came to a church crowded with people: the churchyard was full likewise, and a number of people were even mounted on ladders, looking in at the windows. I thought this a strange sight, as I had never seen churches, either in England or the East Indies, crowded in this manner before. I therefore made bold to ask some people the meaning of all this, and they told me the Rev. Mr George Whitfield was preaching. I had often heard of this gentleman, and had wished to see and hear him; but I had never before had an opportunity. I now therefore resolved to gratify myself with the sight and pressed in amidst the multitude. When I got into the church I saw this pious man exhorting the people with the greatest fervour and earnestness, and sweating as much as I ever did while in slavery on Montserrat beach. I was very much struck and impressed with this; I thought it strange I had never seen divines exert themselves in this manner before, and I was no longer at a loss to account for the thin congregations they preached to.

When we had discharged our cargo here and were loaded again, we left this fruitful land once more and set sail for Montserrat. My traffic had hitherto succeeded so well with me that I thought, by selling my goods when we arrived at Montserrat, I should have enough to purchase my freedom. But as soon as our vessel arrived there, my master came on board and gave orders for us to go to St Eustatia and discharge our cargo there, and from thence proceed for Georgia. I was much disappointed at this, but thinking, as usual, it was of no use to encounter with the decrees of fate, I submitted without repining and we went to St Eustatia. After we had discharged our cargo there we took in a live cargo, as we call a cargo of slaves. Here I sold my goods tolerably well, but not being able to lay out all my money in this small island to as much advantage as in many other places, I laid out only part, and the remainder I brought away with me neat. We sailed from hence for Georgia, and I was glad when we got there though I had not much reason to like the place from my last adventure in Savannah; but I longed to get back to Montserrat and procure my freedom, which I expected to be able to purchase when I returned. As soon as we arrived here I waited on my careful doctor, Mr Brady, to whom I made the most grateful acknowledgments in my power for his former kindness and attention during my illness.

While we were here an odd circumstance happened to the captain and me, which disappointed us both a good deal. A silversmith, whom we had brought to this place some voyages before, agreed with the captain to return with us to the West Indies and promised at the same time to give the captain a great deal of money, having pretended to take a liking to him, and being, as we thought, very rich. But while we stayed to load our vessel this man was taken ill in a house where he worked, and in a week's time became very bad. The worse he grew the more he used to speak of giving the captain what he had promised him, so that he expected something considerable from the death of this man, who had no wife or child, and he attended him day and night. I used also to go with the captain at his own desire, to attend him, especially when we saw there was no appearance of his recovery: and in order to recompense me for my trouble, the Captain promised me ten pounds when he should get the man's property. I thought this would be of great service to me, although I had nearly money enough to purchase my freedom if I should get safe this voyage to Montserrat. In this expectation I laid out above eight pounds of my money for a suit of superfine clothes to dance with at my freedom, which I hoped was then at hand. We still continued to attend this man and were with him even on the last day he lived till very late at night, when we went on board. After we were got to bed, about one or two o'clock in the morning, the captain was sent for and informed the man was dead. On this he came to my bed, and waking me, informed me of it, and desired me to get up and procure a light, and immediately go to him. I told him I was very sleepy and wished he would take somebody else with him; or else, as the man was dead and could want no further attendance, to let all things remain as they were till the next morning. 'No, no,' said he, 'we will have the money tonight, I cannot wait till tomorrow, so let us go.'

Accordingly I got up and struck a light, and away we both went and saw the man as dead as we could wish. The captain said he would give him a grand burial in gratitude for the promised treasure, and desired that all the things belonging to the deceased might be brought forth. Amongst others, there was a nest of trunks of which he had kept the keys whilst the man was ill, and when they were produced we opened them with no small eagerness and expectation; and as there were a great number within one another, with much impatience we took them one out of the other. At last, when we came to the smallest and had opened it, we saw it was full of papers, which we supposed to be notes, at the sight of which our hearts leapt for joy, and that instant the captain, clapping his hands, cried out, 'Thank God, here it is.' But when we took up the trunk and began to examine the supposed treasure and long-looked-for bounty, (alas! alas! how uncertain and deceitful are all human affairs!) what had we found! While we thought we were embracing a substance we grasped an empty nothing. The whole amount that was in the nest of trunks was only one dollar and a half, and all that the man possessed would not pay for his coffin. Our sudden and exquisite joy was now succeeded by as sudden and exquisite pain, and my captain and I exhibited for some time most ridiculous figures – pictures of chagrin and disappointment! We went away greatly mortified and left the deceased to do as well as he could for himself as we had taken so good care of him when alive for nothing.

We set sail once more for Montserrat and arrived there safe, but much out of humour with our friend the silversmith. When we had unladen the vessel and I had sold my venture, finding myself master of about forty-seven pounds I consulted my true friend, the captain, how I should proceed in offering my master the money for my freedom. He told me to come on a certain morning, when he and my master would be at breakfast together. Accordingly, on that morning I went and met the captain there as he had appointed. When I went in I made my obeisance to my master, and with money in my hand and many fears in my heart I prayed him to be as good as his offer to me, when he was pleased to promise me my freedom as soon as I could purchase it. This speech seemed to confound him; he began to recoil: and my heart that instant sunk within me.

'What,' said he, 'give you your freedom? Why, where did you get the money? Have you got forty pounds sterling?' 'Yes, sir,' I answered. 'How did you get it?' replied he. I told him very honestly. The captain then said he knew I got the money very honestly and with much industry, and that I was particularly careful. On which my master replied I got money much faster than he did, and said he would not have made me the promise he did if he had thought I should have got money so soon. 'Come, come,' said my worthy captain, clapping my master on the back, 'Come Robert, (which was his name) I think you must let him have his freedom; you have laid your money out very well; you have received good interest for it all this time, and here is now the principal at last. I know Gustavus has earned you more than an hundred a year, and he will still save you money, as he will not leave you. Come, Robert, take the money.'

My master then said he would not be worse than his promise, and taking the money, told me to go the Secretary at the Register Office and get my manumission drawn up. These words of my master were like a voice from Heaven to me. In an instant all my trepidation was turned into unutterable bliss, and I most reverently bowed myself with gratitude, unable to express my feelings but by the overflowing of my eyes, while my true and worthy friend, the captain, congratulated us both with a peculiar degree of heartfelt pleasure. As soon as the first transports of my joy were over, and that I had expressed my thanks to these my worthy friends in the best manner I was able, I rose with a heart full of affection and reverence and left the room, in order to obey my master's joyful mandate of going to the Register Office. As I was leaving the house I called to mind the words of the Psalmist, in the 126th Psalm, and like him, 'I glorified God in my heart, in whom I trusted.' These words had been impressed on my mind from the very day I was forced from Deptford to the present hour, and I now saw them, as I thought, fulfilled and verified.

My imagination was all rapture as I flew to the Register Office, and in this respect, like the apostle Peter, (whose deliverance from prison was so sudden and extraordinary, that he thought he was in a vision) I could scarcely believe I was awake. Heavens! who could do justice to my feelings at this moment! Not conquering heroes themselves in the midst of a triumph – Not the tender mother who has just regained her long-lost infant, and presses it to her heart – Not the weary, hungry mariner at the sight of the desired friendly port – Not the lover, when he once more embraces his beloved mistress after she had been ravished from his arms! – All within my breast was tumult, wildness, and delirium! My feet scarcely touched the ground, for they were winged with joy, and like Elijah, as he rose to Heaven, they 'were with lightning sped as I went on'. Everyone I met I told of my happiness and blazed about the virtue of my amiable master and captain.

When I got to the office and acquainted the Registrar with my errand he congratulated me on the occasion and told me he would draw up my manumission for half price, which was a guinea. I thanked him for his kindness, and having received it and paid him I hastened to my master to get him to sign it, that I might be fully released. Accordingly he signed the manumission that day, so that before night, I who had been a slave in the morning, trembling at the will of another, was become my own master and completely free. I thought this was the happiest day I had ever experienced; and my joy was still heightened by the blessings and prayers of the sable race, particularly the aged, to whom my heart had ever been attached with reverence.

In short, the fair as well as black people immediately styled me by a new appellation, to me the most desirable in the world, which was Freeman, and at the dances I gave my Georgia superfine blue clothes made no indifferent appearance, as I thought. Some of the sable females who formerly stood aloof now began to relax and appear less coy, but my heart was still fixed on London, where I hoped to be ere long. So that my worthy captain and his owner, my late master, finding that the bent of my mind was towards London, said to me, 'We hope you won't leave us, but that you will still be with the vessels.' Here gratitude bowed me down, and none but the generous mind can judge of my feelings, struggling between inclination and duty. However, notwithstanding my wish to be in London, I obediently answered my benefactors that I could go in the vessel and not leave them, and from that day I was entered on board as an able-bodied sailor at thirty-six shillings per month, besides what perquisites I could make. My intention was to make a voyage or two entirely to please these my honoured patrons, but I determined that the year following, if it pleased God I would see Old England once more and surprise my old master, Capt. Pascal, who was hourly in my mind; for I still loved him, notwithstanding his usage of me, and I pleased myself with thinking of what he would say when he saw what the Lord had done for me in so short a time, instead of being, as he might perhaps suppose, under the cruel yoke of some planter. With these kind of reveries I used often to entertain myself and shorten the time till my return, and now, being as in my original free African state, I embarked on board the *Nancy* after having got all things ready for our voyage. In this state of serenity we sailed for St Eustatia, and having smooth seas and calm weather we soon arrived there: after taking our cargo on board we proceeded to Savannah in Georgia, in August, 1766.

While we were there, as usual, I used to go for the cargo up the rivers in boats, and on this business I have been frequently beset by alligators, which were very numerous on that coast, and I have shot many of them when they have been near getting into our boats; which we have with great difficulty sometimes prevented, and have been very much frightened at them. I have seen a young one sold in Georgia alive for six pence. During our stay at this place, one evening a slave belonging to Mr Read, a merchant of Savannah, came near our vessel, and began to use me very ill. I entreated him, with all the patience I was master of, to desist, as I knew there was little or no law for a free negro here; but the fellow, instead of taking my advice, persevered in his insults, and even struck me. At this I lost all temper, and I fell on him and beat him soundly.

The next morning his master came to our vessel as we lay alongside the wharf, and desired me to come ashore that he might have me flogged all round the town, for beating his negro slave. I told him he had insulted me, and had given the provocation, by first striking me. I had told my captain also the whole affair that morning, and wished him to have gone along with me to Mr Read to prevent bad consequences; but he said that it did not signify, and if Mr Read said anything he would make matters up, and had desired me to go to work which I accordingly did. The captain being on board when Mr Read came, he told him I was a free man; and when Mr Read applied to him to deliver me up, he said he knew nothing of the matter. I was astonished and frightened at this, and thought I had better keep where I was than go ashore and be flogged round the town, without judge or jury. I therefore refused to stir; and Mr Read went away, swearing he would bring all the constables in the town, for he would have me out of the vessel.

When he was gone, I thought his threat might prove too true to my sorrow; and I was confirmed in this belief, as well by the many instances I had seen of the treatment of free negroes, as from a fact that had happened within my own knowledge here a short time before. There was a free black man, a carpenter, that I knew, who, for asking a gentleman that he worked for for the money he had earned, was put into goal; and afterwards the oppressed man was sent from Georgia, with false accusations, of an intention to set the gentleman's house on fire, and run away with his slaves. I was therefore much embarrassed, and very apprehensive of a flogging at least. I dreaded, of all things, the thoughts of being striped, as I never in my life had the marks of any violence of that kind. At that instant a rage seized my soul, and for a little I determined to resist the first man that should offer to lay violent hands on me, or basely use me without a trial; for I would sooner die like a free man, than suffer myself to be scourged by the hands of ruffians, and my blood drawn like a slave.

The captain and others, more cautious, advised me to make haste and conceal myself; for they said Mr Read was a very spiteful man, and he would soon come on board with constables and take me. At first I refused this counsel, being determined to stand my ground; but at length, by the prevailing entreaties of the captain and Mr Dixon, with whom he lodged, I went to Mr Dixon's house, which was a little out of town, at a place called Yea-ma-chra. I was but just gone when Mr Read, with the constables, came for me, and searched the vessel; but, not finding me there, he swore he would have me dead or alive. I was secreted about five days; however, the good character which my captain always gave me as well as some other gentlemen who also knew me, procured me some friends. At last some of them told my captain that he did not use me well, in suffering me thus to be imposed upon, and said they would see me redressed, and get me on board some other vessel. My captain, on this, immediately went to Mr Read, and told him, that ever since I eloped from the vessel his work had been neglected, and he could not go on with her loading, himself and mate not being well; and, as I had managed things on board for them, my absence must retard his voyage, and consequently hurt the owner; he therefore begged of him to forgive me, as he said he never had any complaint of me before, for the many years that I had been with him.

After repeated entreaties, Mr Read said I might go to hell, and that he would not meddle with me; on which my captain came immediately to me at his lodging, and, telling me how pleasantly matters had gone on, he desired me to go on board. Some of my other friends then asked him if he had got the constable's warrant from them; the captain said, No. On this I was desired by them to stay in the house; and they said they would get me on board of some other vessel before the evening. When the captain heard this he became almost distracted. He went immediately for the warrant, and, after using every exertion in his power, he at last got it from my hunters; but I had all the expenses to pay. After I had thanked all my friends for their attention, I went on board again to my work, of which I had always plenty. We were in haste to complete our lading, and were to carry twenty head of cattle with us to the West Indies, where they are a very profitable article.

Part Three
The New Nation 1775–1865

By 1763 Great Britain had emerged as the dominant European power. Her army had defeated her historical enemy, France, in the Seven Years' War; forcing the French to sign the humiliating Treaty of Paris; she had a growing Empire of possessions in all parts of the known world; at home the Hanoverian dynasty had ruled long enough to secure undivided loyalty; the new king, George III, was no foreign impostor, but an Englishman born, who gloried in the name of Briton; and the last vestiges of internal dissent had been wiped away at Culloden. Yet within twenty years Britain's foreign standing had fallen; her internal politics were cut in two; and that once-popular monarch was on the verge of abdication. All this was brought about by the defeat of the British by the Thirteen Colonies of America. Before the British Empire had even achieved its zenith, its most prized possession had broken away. Between 1774 and the final defeat at Yorktown in 1781 fourteen great battles were fought, of which the British lost nine. The same army which had triumphed over the French in Canada was to lay down its arms before the rebel colonists and their French and Spanish allies.

This is not the place to examine the causes of the rebellion or the reasons for its success. Obvious causes there were: the Boston Massacre and the Boston Tea Party; the general repining against economic and commercial interference from London; and one might also mention the fears that were expressed by the overwhelmingly Protestant colonists of the religious toleration that was granted to the former-French Catholics of Quebec. That the rebellion was successful was against all the odds. In 1763 most colonists seemed content with the present set-up; their loyalty to the Crown was guaranteed. Washington had been amongst the most conspicuous of those who had fought against the French in Canada. There was as yet no common identity between the thirteen colonies. The terms 'America' and 'Americans' were only just coming into popular use. (In 1783 so disjointed and disconnected was the new nation that it was possible for two female Messiahs to flourish in New York State without their having apparently heard of each other.) British resources and strength were the Americans' superior. Added to that, Washington was not an outstanding general. He lost more battles than he won; and only at Yorktown was he in a position to dictate the terms of surrender.

The new nation was not the result of centuries of organic growth, it had to be invented and its institutions and Constitution had to be created from scratch. And, as is characteristic of America, the ideas that inspired the new order were not intrinsically American but European. The framers of the new Constitution were not 'foreigners', in the sense that they had been born outside America: most of them came from families which had been settled there for at least three generations. But their guiding lights were from across the Atlantic, and while the physical battle was being fought on

American soil, the issue of independence excited fundamental intellectual debate in the Old World, particularly in England.

To modern readers the Declaration of Independence which brought into being the new nation is not a revolutionary document. Two centuries of use have made it into a conservative one. Framed in language that speaks of universal truth, and, in the West, the object of almost unanimous assent, it is easily forgotten how relative to its age the *Declaration* is.

> We hold these truths to be self-evident, that all men are created equal, that they are endowed by their Creator with certain unalienable rights; that among these are life, liberty and the pursuit of happiness; that to secure these rights, governments are instituted among men, deriving their just powers from the consent of the governed . . .

In Britain the main support for the colonists came from the opposition Whigs. The speeches of Burke and Chatham dealt frankly with the issue as a question of good policy. 'You cannot conquer America,' said Chatham, and in the end he was right. 'I do not know,' said Burke, on his speech on Conciliation with America, 'the method of drawing up an indictment against an whole people.' And he continued: 'Freedom and not servitude is the cure of anarchy . . . Deny them this participation of freedom, and you break that sole bond, which originally made, and must still preserve, the unity of the empire.' In other words, if Britain wants to retain its American colonies, it must give into their just demands.

Rather more emotive support for the colonists came from Thomas Paine, whose *Common Sense* was published in 1776. For him fundamental political principles were much more the issue than whether the war was justifiable by ordinary pragmatic concerns, such as expense. The Patriots of America, he said, should be not only the champions of their own liberty but of the rights of all mankind. Government at best was a 'necessary evil', and governments by monarchs were the worst kind. George III was a deplorable king: 'nothing better than the principal ruffian of some restless gang'. Kings had no divine right to their authority: they simply won power by defeating their rivals. The English people owed no allegiance to them; and neither did the American people owe anything to the English. For the sake of liberty everywhere the time had come for the Americans to break free and govern themselves. 'O! Ye that love mankind! Ye that dare oppose not only tyranny but the tyrant, stand forth! Every spot of the old world is overrun with oppression. Freedom hath been hunted round the globe . . . O! receive the fugitive, and prepare in time an asylum for mankind.'

Such stuff did not win the entire approval of the colonists themselves. John Adams in particular disliked *Common Sense*. But Paine gave voice to many of the feelings which Americans had, and which so far they had not expressed. 'Patriots' throughout the thirteen colonies rose up to demand that America 'stand forth'; and in July, seven months after *Common Sense* was published, the Declaration of Independence was adopted.

Paine's pamphlet had been written partly in answer to the most full-bodied Tory statement of the matter, *Taxation No Tyranny*, written by Dr Johnson, and published the year before.

Unfortunately Johnson's credentials were suspect. He was a pensioner of the government, and *Taxation No Tyranny* was a paid performance. And when Johnson starts attacking the 'Whigs of America' his eyes were possibly rather more focused on the internal scene than on events on the other side of the Atlantic.

Though *Taxation No Tyranny* was written for money, it is not the lamentable performance of which Boswell was ashamed. As Johnson was constitutionally incapable of putting pen to paper except for payment or to meet a deadline, it is not fair to condemn the work as a hack performance, except in so far as to say that everything he wrote falls into this category. For *Taxation No Tyranny* puts in written form the deep-felt political prejudices which Johnson was usually too lazy to expound except from the tavern-seat.

While the war was on, it was natural that Johnson should express his hatred of the rebels: 'I am willing to love all mankind, *except* an American,' he told Boswell on 15 April 1778. But his dislike went further back. As early as 1769 he had told Dr John Campbell: 'Sir, they are a race of convicts, and ought to be thankful for anything we allow them short of hanging.'

To Johnson the American settlers were Englishmen abroad who refused to pay taxes to their government at home.

They allow to the supreme power nothing more than the liberty of notifying to them its demands or its necessities. Of this notification they profess to think for themselves, how far it shall influence their counsels, and of the necessities alleged, how far they shall endeavour to relieve them. They assume the exclusive power of settling not only the mode but the quantity of payment. They are ready to co-operate with all the other dominions of the king; but they will co-operate by no means which they do not like, and at no greater charge than they are willing to bear.

Though refusing to pay taxes, the colonists nevertheless continued to accept the protection of the British Navy.

But it was the conduct of the colonists which Johnson particularly detested. Since the time of Disraeli until Macmillan imperialism and Toryism have been inextricably combined. But in the eighteenth century it was not so. Historically Tories have been 'Little Englanders'; stay-at-homes; suspicious of colonies as of everything else beyond their own parish. The notion that one should sail beyond one's own shores, often in the name of religion, to subjugate a foreign people, and to exploit them and their lands for profit was anathema to Johnson. Not that he was in favour of the primitive life. 'Don't cant in favour of savages,' he once told Boswell, who had swallowed Rousseau (another guiding light of the founding fathers) whole on their noble qualities. Johnson was in favour of civilization; and by this he meant the civilization of eighteenth-century Europe. But this did not mean that those deprived of a classical education were lower forms of creation. Much of Johnson's hatred of Americans comes from his hatred of slavery.

Johnson had a Negro servant, Frank Barber, who was an ex-slave. Whenever Frank left Johnson's service to try his hand at some other job, and failed at it, as he did repeatedly, Johnson took him back. When Frank married, Johnson took on his wife and family as well. Because he was convinced that Frank could not support himself, he made him the principal

legatee in his will. It would only have confirmed Johnson's grim view of
human nature could he have foreseen that Frank was to squander this
money.

Johnson, therefore, had a personal stake in the slave question. His opposition to American independence was based on his view that America was
a large country whose vast resources which might have benefited so many
were being exploited by a handful of planters growing rich by lashing the
backs of slaves. Johnson wanted to punish the planters by lashing them.
One sentence in *Taxation No Tyranny* still cracks with the same force as
when it was first delivered: 'Why is it,' he demanded, 'that we hear the
loudest yelps for liberty from the drivers of the Negroes?'

To Johnson and the classic Tories the current theories of liberty were
all cant: liberty was ensured, not by vague notions of rights, but by strictly
defined and limited duties. Government did not have its authority from
democratic assent but by divine dispensation, to which all men were subject.
Men were arranged in degrees by birth, kinship, and their use of their
natural talents; and this subordination was necessary for the convenience
of society. It was not tyrannical imposition, as Rousseau and Paine had
claimed, but it created a stable system in which the arts of peace could
flourish.

The American experiment was to be quite different. Following Locke,
the founding fathers had a vision of an original paradise of virtuous anarchy,
like Gonzalo's in *The Tempest*, when men lived together according to reason
and obeyed no other superior except the law of nature. Unfortunately, men
were inconsiderate creatures: they disobeyed the natural law and were deaf
to the voice of reason. In order to protect their rights therefore men had
to enter into what Locke called a 'Social Contract'. They would select
instruments of government from amongst themselves to ensure the happiness of all; and that men should be deterred from unreasonable behaviour
by the sanction of the law.

To Johnson such theories showed an almost *unbearable* lack of self-
knowledge. He knew that reason was only one of a complex of energies
that motivated human action, even virtuous action: prejudice, custom, and
self-interest were always more likely to figure first in men's calculations.
The human mind constantly held contradictory impulses simultaneously.
Not only were men not naturally virtuous; they were inherently corrupt.
Happiness, though it was what all men longed for, was a vain pursuit: it
was never to be achieved on earth, which was a place of tearful exile: men's
sufferings were mitigated only by religious consolation, companionship, and
civilized pleasures. The Tories derided the possibility that politics could
alter this state of affairs. 'Most schemes of political improvement are very
laughable things,' said Johnson. He said he would not give sixpence to live
under one political system rather than another. A private citizen's political
duty consisted in obedience to the law and in fighting for his sovereign
when his realm was under threat. The duty of governors was to maintain
order to enable private citizens to pursue their interests in peace. Their
involvement in government was a reckless innovation, likely to upset the
precarious balance which kept the 'great republic of human nature' in some
kind of equilibrium. It was also a great waste of time and energy. One can
imagine the scorn and merriment that Johnson would have made of the fact

that in the United States even the post of the local rat-catcher is decided by popular election. Better to stay at home and read a book.

The theories on which the Declaration of Independence were drawn now command almost unanimous assent, at least in the West. Johnson's views, except on slavery, will strike most modern readers as laughably archaic. He himself foresaw this possibility. In a passage at the end of *Taxation No Tyranny*, deleted from the printed text, he wrote:

Their [the Americans] numbers are, at present, not quite sufficient for the greatness which, in some form of government or other, is to rival the ancient monarchies; but by Dr Franklin's rule of progression, they will, in a century and a quarter, be more than equal to the inhabitants of Europe. When the Whigs of America are thus multiplied, let the Princes of the earth tremble in their palaces. If they should continue to double and to double, their own hemisphere would not contain them. But let not our boldest oppugners of authority look forward with delight to this futurity of Whiggism.

The French Revolution was to bear out this prediction with astonishing quickness. And Thomas Paine was to be strangely in agreement: 'That the principles of America opened the Bastille is not to be doubted.' Burke disagreed. And he broke up his party rather than accept that the principles which had led him to believe that compromising with the Americans would justify the beheading of Marie-Antoinette.

Thomas Gage (1775)

Thomas Gage (1721–87) was appointed commander-in-chief of the British forces in America in 1763, and in 1774 governor of Massachusetts. When the rebellion broke out, he decided to send a column to destroy the cannon and military stores which he had heard were being assembled by the colonists at Concord. To command this expedition he chose Colonel Smith of the 10th Regiment. Here he orders the destruction of the rebels' stores at Concord.

Boston, April 18, 1775

Lieut. Colonel Smith, 10th Regiment Foot.

Sir,

Having received intelligence that a quantity of Ammunition, Provision, Artillery, Tents and small arms, have been collected at Concord, for the Avowed Purpose of raising and supporting a Rebellion against His Majesty, you will march the Corps of Grenadiers and Light Infantry, under your Command, with the utmost expedition and Secrecy to Concord, where you will seize and destroy all Artillery, Ammunition, Provisions, Tents, Small Arms, and all Military Stores whatever. But you will take care the soldiers do not plunder the inhabitants, or hurt private property.

You have a Draught [map] of Concord, on which is marked the Houses, Barns etc. which contain the above military stores. You will order a Trunnion to be knocked off each gun, but if it is found impracticable on any, they must be spiked, and the Carriages destroyed. The Powder and flour must be shook out of the Barrels into the River, the Tents burned, Pork or Beef destroyed in the best way you can devise. And the men may put balls of lead in their pockaps, throwing them by degrees into Ponds, Ditches etc. but no quantity together so that they may be recovered afterwards.

If you meet any brass Artillery, you will order their muzzles to be beat in so as to render them useless.

You will observe by the Draught that it will be necessary to secure the two Bridges as soon as possible, you will therefore order a party of the best Marchers to go on with expedition for the purpose.

A small party on Horseback is ordered out to stop all advice of your March getting to Concord before you, and a small number of Artillery [artillerymen] go out in Chaises to wait for you on the road, with Sledge Hammers, Spikes etc.

You will open your business and return with the Troops as soon as possible, which I must leave to your own Judgment and Discretion. I am, Sir,

Your most obedient humble servant,
Thos. Gage

Captain Harris (1775)

Captain Harris of the 5th Foot Writes to His Cousin Bess.

GRENADIER CAMP,
June 12, 1775

Affairs at present wear a serious aspect. I wish the Americans may be brought to a sense of their duty. One good drubbing, which I long to give them, by way of retaliation, might have a good effect towards it. At present they are so elated by the petty advantage they gained the 19th of April, that they despise the power of Britain, who seems determined to exert herself in the conflict. Troops every day coming in, and such as will soon enable us, I hope, to take the field on the other side the Demel, *alias* the Neck. At present we are completely blockaded, and subsisting almost on salt provision, except such as the Americans (so strong is the old leaven of smuggling in them, about which these troubles arose) bring into us. My garden (*à propos* to gardens, you and I will certainly have one) – what can afford the philosophic mind such food for contemplation? – with salt provisions, what can afford such food for the body? such salads? such excellent greens the young turnip-tops make? Then the spinach and radishes, with the cucumbers, beans, and peas, so promising. All within six weeks from the first turning of the soil, is really surprising. Jonathan is an excellent gardener, though this is his first essay. I was quite Uncle Toby; to plan and to direct was my department, his to execute and improve. My house will be struck over my head if I do not quit it, as a change of ground is to take place immediately. I only wish the movement was towards the Americans, that we might sooner bring this unpleasant business to an issue, and get home to our friends. Near three years since I left you, and but little probability that three years more will bring me back. But a soldier should not complain, and I think, Bess, that yours will be one of the last to do so. The ground is marked out. Holmes says we shall be last, so adieu. May we to the last preserve that friendship that has hitherto been so pleasant to both.

Remember me to all friends,

Yours, etc.,
G. HARRIS

Marie Joseph Paul Yves Roch Gilbert Motier, Marquis de Lafayette (1777)

Lafayette was only twenty when he sailed to America in order to fight beside the colonists. Washington rewarded him by giving him a division.

Letter to his wife

Charleston, 19 June 1777.

My last letter to you, my dear love, has informed you, that I arrived safely in this country, after having suffered a little from sea-sickness during the first weeks of the voyage; that I was then, the morning after I landed, at the house of a very kind officer, that I had been nearly two months on the passage, and that I wished to set off immediately. It spoke of every thing most interesting to my heart; of my sorrow at parting from you, and of our dear children; and it said, besides, that I was in excellent health. I give you this abstract of it, because the English may possibly amuse themselves by seizing it on its way. I have such confidence in my lucky star, however, that I hope it will reach you. This same star has befriended me, to the astonishment of every body here. Trust to it yourself, and be assured that it ought to calm all your fears. I landed after having sailed several days along a coast, which swarmed with hostile vessels. When I arrived, every body said that my vessel must inevitably be taken, since two British frigates blockaded the harbour. I even went so far as to send orders to the captain, both by land and sea, to put the men on shore and set fire to the ship, if not yet too late. By a most wonderful good fortune, a gale obliged the frigates to stand out to sea for a short time. My vessel came in at noon-day, without meeting friend or foe.

At Charleston I have met General (Robert) Howe, an American officer now in the service. The Governor of the State is expected this evening from the country. All with whom I wished to become acquainted here, have shown me the greatest politeness and attention. I feel entirely satisfied with my reception, although I have not thought it best to go into any detail respecting my arrangements and plans. I wish first to see Congress. I hope to set out for Philadelphia in two days. Our route is more than two hundred and fifty leagues by land. We shall divide ourselves into small parties. I have already purchased horses and light carriages for the journey. Some French and American vessels are here, and are to sail together tomorrow morning, taking advantage of a moment when the frigates are out of sight. They are armed, and have promised me to defend themselves stoutly against the small privateers, which they will certainly meet. I shall distribute my letters among the different ships.

I will now tell you about the country and its inhabitants. They are as agreeable as my enthusiasm had painted them. Simplicity of manners, kindness, love of country and of liberty, and a delightful equality everywhere prevail. The wealthiest man and the poorest are on a level; and, although there are some large fortunes, I challenge anyone to discover the slightest difference between the manners of these two classes respectively towards each other. I first saw the country life at the house of Major Huger. I am now in the city, where everything is very much after the English fashion, except that there is more simplicity, equality, cordiality, and courtesy here than in England. The city of Charleston is one of the handsomest and best built, and its inhabitants among the most agreeable, that I have ever seen. The American women are very pretty, simple in their manners and exhibit a neatness, which is everywhere cultivated even more studiously than in England. What most charms me is, that all the citizens are brethren. In America, there are no poor, nor even what we call peasantry. Each individual has his own honest property, and the same rights as the most wealthy landed proprietor. The inns are very different from those of Europe; the host and hostess sit at table with you, and do the honours of a comfortable meal; and, on going away, you pay your bill without higgling. When one does not wish to go to an inn, there are country-houses where the title of a good American is a sufficient passport to all those civilities paid in Europe to one's friend.

As to my own reception, it has been most agreeable in every quarter; and to have come with me secured the most flattering welcome. I have just passed five hours at a grand dinner, given in honour of me by an individual of this city. Generals Howe and Moultrie, and several officers of my suite, were present. We drank healths and tried to talk English. I begin to speak it a little. Tomorrow I shall go with these gentlemen to call on the Governor of the State, and make arrangements for my departure. The next day the commanding officers here will show me the city and its environs, and then I shall set out for the army.

Considering the pleasant life I lead in this country, my sympathy with the people, which makes me feel as much at ease in their society as if I had known them for twenty years, the similarity between their mode of thinking and my own, and my love of liberty and of glory, one might suppose that I am very happy. But you are not with me, my friends are not with me; and there is no happiness for me far from you and them. I ask you, if you still love me; but I put the same question much oftener to myself, and my heart always responds. Yes. I am impatient beyond measure to hear from you. I hope to find letters at Philadelphia. My only fear is that the privateer, which is to bring them, may be captured on her passage. Although I suppose I have drawn upon me the special displeasure of the English, by taking the liberty to depart in spite of them, and by landing in their very face, yet I confess they will not be in arrears with me, should they capture this vessel, my cherished hope, on which I so fondly depend for letters from you. Write frequent and long letters. You do not know the full extent of the joy with which I shall receive them. Embrace Henrietta tenderly. May I say embrace tenderly our children? The father of these poor children is a rover, but a good and honest man at heart; a good father, who loves his family dearly, and a good husband, who loves his wife with all his heart.

Remember me to your friends and my own, to the dear society, once the society of the court, but which by the lapse of time has become the society of the Wooden Sword. We republicans think it all the better. I must leave off for want of paper and time; and if I do not repeat to you ten thousand times that I love you, it is not from any want of feeling, but from modesty; since I have the presumption to hope, that I have already convinced you of it. The night is far advanced, and the heat dreadful. I am devoured by insects; so, you see, the best countries have their disadvantages. Adieu.

Another Letter

I have not for a long time had the honour to address you, either in public or private letters. This has been owing to a tour I made through several parts of Europe, and to a derangement in the packets which, to my great concern, I found to have taken place during my absence.

In the course of a journey to Prussia, Silesia, the Austrian dominions, and back again to Berlin, I could not but have many opportunities to improve myself by the inspection of famous fields of battle, the conversation of the greatest Generals, and the sight of excellent troops – those of Prussia particularly exceeding my expectations. I had occasions not less numerous to lament the folly of nations who can bear a despotic Government, and to pay a new tribute of respect and attachment to the constitutional principles we had the happiness to establish. Wherever I went, America was of course a topic in the conversation. Her efforts during the contest are universally admired; and in the transactions which have so gloriously taken place, there is a large field of enthusiasm for the soldier, of wonder and applause for the politician; and to the philosopher and the philanthropist they are a matter of unspeakable delight, and I could say of admiration. Those sentiments I had the pleasure to find generally diffused. But to my great sorrow, (and I will the more candidly tell it in this letter, as it can hurt none more than it hurts myself), I did not find that every remark equally turned to the advantage of my pride, and of that satisfaction I feel in the admiration of the world for the United States.

In countries so far distant, under constitutions so foreign to republican notions, the affairs of America cannot be thoroughly understood, and such inconveniences as we lament ourselves are greatly exaggerated by her enemies. It would require almost a volume to relate how many mistaken ideas I had the opportunity to set to rights. And it has been painful for me to hear, it is now disagreeable to mention, the bad effect which the want of federal unions, and of effective arrangements for the finances and commerce of a general establishment of militia, have had on the minds of European nations. It is foolishly thought by some that democratical constitutions will not, cannot last, that the States will quarrel with each other, that a King, or at least a nobility, are indispensable for the prosperity of a nation. But I would not attend to those absurdities, as they are answered by the smallest particle of unprejudiced common sense, and will, I trust, be forever destroyed by the example of America. But it was impossible for me to feel so much unconcerned when those points were insisted upon for which I could not but acknowledge within myself there was some ground, although it was so unfairly broached upon by the enemies of the United States. It is an object with the European Governments to check and discourage the spirit of emigration, which, I hope, will increase among the Germans with a more perfect knowledge of the situation of America. And while I was enjoying the admiration and respect of those parts of the world for the character of the United States; while I was obliged to hear some remarks which, although they were exaggerated, did not seem to me quite destitute of a foundation, I heartily addressed my prayers to Heaven that, by her known wisdom, patriotism, and liberality of principles, as well as firmness of conduct, America may preserve the consequence she has so well acquired, and continue to command the admiration of the world . . .

Lafayette

Patrick Ferguson (1780)

Patrick Ferguson was born in Aberdeenshire in 1744. In 1776 he patented his breech-loading rifle, which fired seven shots a minute, and had a range of up to 500 yards. With it he helped to arm a corps of loyalists, who helped at the battle of Brandywine (1777) to inflict a crushing defeat on the Americans. In 1780, isolated in South Carolina, with only 100 men of the American Volunteers and about 1000 militia, a force of 3000 backwoodsmen assembled to crush him. Learning of their attentions, Ferguson tried to rouse Loyalist support by this proclamation. It was issued six days before his death fighting to defend King's Mountain.

DENARD'S FORD. BROAD RIVER,
TRYON COUNTY,
October 1, 1780

GENTLEMAN,

Unless you wish to be eat up by an inundation of barbarians who have begun by murdering an unarmed son before the aged father, and afterwards lopped off his arms, and who, by their shocking cruelties and irregularities, give the best proof of their cowardice and want of discipline: – I say, if you wish to be pinioned, robbed, and murdered, and see your wives and daughters, in four days, abused by the dregs of mankind – in short, if you wish or deserve to live and bear the name of men, grasp your arms in a moment and run to camp.

The Backwater men have crossed the mountains: McDowell, Hampton, Shelby, and Cleveland are at their head: so that you know what you have to depend upon. If you choose to be degraded for ever and ever by a set of mongrels, say so at once, and let your women turn their backs upon you, and look out for real men to protect them.

PAT. FERGUSON
(Major 71st Regiment).

J. Hector St John De Crevecoeur (1782)

Crevecoeur (1735–1813) emigrated to America during the Seven Years' War. He was naturalized in 1765. He bought a farm near the present Chester, New York State, and settled down there with his wife, Mehetable Tippet of Yonkers, until their life was upset by the War of Independence. Crevecoeur was imprisoned; his farmhouse burnt; eventually he was allowed to return to France, where he wrote these Letters from an American Farmer.

As you are the first enlightened European I have ever had the pleasure of being acquainted with, you will not be surprised that I should, according to your earnest desire and my promise, appear anxious of preserving your friendship and correspondence. By your accounts, I observe a material difference subsists between your husbandry, modes, and customs, and ours; everything is local; could we enjoy the advantages of the English farmer, we should be much happier, indeed, but this wish, like many others, implies a contradiction; and could the English farmer have some of those privileges we possess, they would be the first of their class in the world. Good and evil I see is to be found in all societies, and it is in vain to seek for any spot where those ingredients are not mixed. I therefore rest satisfied, and thank God that my lot is to be an American farmer, instead of a Russian boor, or an Hungarian peasant. I thank you kindly for the idea, however dreadful, which you have given me of their lot and condition; your observations have confirmed me in the justness of my ideas, and I am happier now than I thought myself before. It is strange that misery, when viewed in others, should become to us a sort of real good, though I am far from rejoicing to hear that there are in the world men so thoroughly wretched; they are no doubt as harmless, industrious and willing to work as we are. Hard is their fate to be thus condemned to a slavery worse than that of our negroes. Yet when young I entertained some thoughts of selling my farm. I thought it afforded but a dull repetition of the same labours and pleasures. I thought the former tedious and heavy, the latter few and insipid; but when I came to consider myself as divested of my farm, I then found the world so wide, and every place so full, that I began to fear lest there would be no room for me. My farm, my house, my barn, presented to my imagination objects from which I adduced quite new ideas; they were more forcible than before. Why should not I find myself happy, said I, where my father was before? He left me no good books it is true, he gave me no other education than the art of reading and writing; but he left me a good farm, and his experience; he left me free from debts, and no kind of difficulties to struggle with.

I married, and this perfectly reconciled me to my situation; my wife rendered my house all at once cheerful and pleasing; it no longer appeared gloomy and solitary as before; when I went to work in my fields I worked with more alacrity and sprightliness; I felt that I did not work for myself alone, and this encouraged me much. My wife would often come with her knitting in her hand, and sit under the shady trees, praising the straightness of my furrows, and the docility of my horses; this swelled my heart and made everything light and pleasant, and I regretted that I had not married before.

I felt myself happy in my new situation, and where is that station which can confer a more substantial system of felicity than that of an American farmer, possessing freedom of action, freedom of thoughts, ruled by a mode of government which requires but little from us? I owe nothing, but a pepper corn to my country, a small tribute to my king, with loyalty and due respect; I know no other landlord than the lord of all land, to whom I owe the most sincere gratitude. My father left me three hundred and seventy-one acres of land, forty-seven of which are good timothy meadow, an excellent orchard, a good house, and a substantial barn. It is my duty to think how happy I am that he lived to build and to pay for all these improvements; what are the labours which I have to undergo, what are my fatigues when compared to his, who had everything to do, from the first tree he felled to the finishing of his house? Every year I kill from 1500 to 2000 weight of pork, 1200 of beef, half a dozen of good wethers in harvest: of fowls my wife has always a great stock: what can I wish more? My negroes are tolerably faithful and healthy; by a long series of industry and honest dealings, my father left behind him the name of a good man; I have but to read his paths to be happy and a good man like him. I know enough of the law to regulate my little concerns with propriety, nor do I dread its power; these are the grand outlines of my situation, but as I can feel much more than I am able to express, I hardly know how to proceed.

When my first son was born, the whole train of my ideas were suddenly altered; never was there a charm that acted so quickly and powerfully; I ceased to ramble in imagination through the wide world; my excursions since have not exceeded the bounds of my farm, and all my principal pleasures are now centred within its scanty limits; but at the same time there is not an operation belonging to it in which I do not find some food for useful reflections. This is the reason, I suppose, that when you were here, you used, in your refined style, to denominate me the farmer of feelings; how rude must those feelings be in him who daily holds the axe or the plough, how much more refined on the contrary those of the European, whose mind is improved by education, example, books, and by every acquired advantage! Those feelings, however, I will delineate as well as I can, agreeably to your earnest request.

When I contemplate my wife, by my fire-side, while she either spins, knits, darns, or suckles our child, I cannot describe the various emotions of love, of gratitude, of conscious pride, which thrill in my heart and often overflow in involuntary tears. I feel the necessity, the sweet pleasure of acting my part, the part of an husband and father, with an attention and propriety which may entitle me to my good fortune. It is true these pleasing images vanish with the smoke of my pipe, but though they disappear from my mind, the impression they have made on my heart is indelible. When I play with the infant, my warm imagination runs forward, and eagerly antici-pates his future temper and constitution. I would willingly open the book of fate, and know in which page his destiny is delineated; alas! where is the father who in those moments of paternal ecstasy can delineate one half of the thoughts which dilate his heart? I am sure I cannot; then again I fear for the health of those who are become so dear to me, and in their sicknesses I severely pay for the joys I experienced while they were well. Whenever I go abroad it is always involuntary. I never return home without feeling some pleasing emotion, which I often suppress as useless and foolish. The instant I enter on my own land, the bright idea of property, of exclusive right, of independence exalt my mind. Precious soil, I say to myself, by what singular custom of law is it that thou wast made to constitute the riches of the freeholder? What should we American farmers be without the distinct possession of that soil? It feeds, it clothes us, from it we draw even a great exuberancy, our best meat, our richest drink, the very honey of our bees comes from this privileged spot. No wonder we should thus cherish its possession, no wonder that so many Europeans who have never been able to say that such portion of land was theirs, cross the Atlantic to realise that happiness. This formerly rude soil has been converted by my father into a pleasant farm, and in return it has established all our rights; on it is founded our rank, our freedom, our power as citizens, our importance as inhabitants of such a district. These images I must confess I always behold with pleasure, and extend them as far as my imagination can reach: for this is what may be called the true and the only philosophy of an American farmer.

Pray do not laugh in thus seeing an artless countryman tracing himself through the simple modifications of his life; remember that you have required it, therefore with candour, though with diffidence, I endeavour to follow the thread of my feelings, but I cannot tell you all. Often when I plough my low ground, I place my little boy on a chair which screws to the beam of the plough – its motion and that of the horses please him, he is perfectly happy and begins to chat. As I lean over the handle, various are the thoughts which crowd into my mind. I am now doing for him, I say, what my father formerly did for me, may God enable him to live that he may perform the same operations for the same purposes when I am worn out and old! I relieve his mother of some trouble while I have him with me, the odoriferous furrow exhilarates his spirits, and seems to do the child a great deal of good, for he looks more blooming since I have adopted that practice; can more pleasure, more dignity be added to that primary occupation? The father thus ploughing with his child, and to feed his family, is inferior only to the emperor of China ploughing as an example to his kingdom. In the evening when I return home through my low grounds, I am astonished at the myriads of insects which I perceive dancing in the beams of the setting sun. I was before scarcely acquainted with their existence, they are so small that it is difficult to distinguish them; they are carefully improving this short evening space, not daring to expose themselves to the blaze of our meridian sun. I never see an egg brought on my table but I feel penetrated with the wonderful change it would have undergone but for my gluttony; it might have been a gentle, useful hen leading her chickens with a care and vigilance which speaks shame to many women. A cock perhaps, arrayed with the most majestic plumes, tender to its mate, bold, courageous, endowed with an astonishing instinct, with thoughts, with memory, and every distinguishing characteristic of the reason of man. I never see my trees drop their leaves and their fruit in the autumn, and bud again in the spring, without wonder; the sagacity of those animals which have long been the tenants of my farm astonish me: some of them seem to surpass even men in memory and sagacity. I could tell you singular instances of that kind. What then is this instinct which we so debase, and of which we are taught to entertain so diminutive an idea? My bees, above any other tenants of my farm, attract my attention and respect; I am astonished to see that nothing exists but what has its enemy. One species pursues and lives upon the other: unfortunately our kingbirds are the destroyers of those industrious insects; but on the other hand, these birds preserve our fields from the depredation of crows which they pursue on the wing with great vigilance and astonishing dexterity.

Thus divided by two interested motives, I have long resisted the desire I had to kill them, until last year, when I thought they increased too much, and my indulgence had been carried too far; it was at the time of swarming when they all came and fixed themselves on the neighbouring trees, from whence they catched those that returned loaded from the fields. This made me resolve to kill as many as I could, and I was just ready to fire, when a bunch of bees as big as my fist, issued from one of the hives, rushed on one of the birds, and probably stung him, for he instantly screamed, and flew, not as before, in an irregular manner, but in a direct line. He was followed by the same bold phalanx, at a considerable distance, which unfortunately becoming too sure of victory, quitted their military array and disbanded themselves. By this inconsiderate step they lost all that aggregate of force which had made the bird fly off. Perceiving their disorder he immediately returned and snapped as many as he wanted; nay, he had even the impudence to alight on the very twig from which the bees had drove him. I killed him and immediately opened his craw, from which I took 171 bees; I laid them all on a blanket in the sun, and to my great surprise 54 returned to life, licked themselves clean, and joyfully went back to the hive; where they probably informed their companions of such an adventure and escape, as I believe had never happened before to American bees!

I draw a great fund of pleasure from the quails which inhabit my farm; they abundantly repay me, by their various notes and peculiar tameness, for the inviolable hospitality I constantly show them in the winter. Instead of perfidiously taking advantage of their great and affecting distress, when nature offers nothing but a barren universal bed of snow, when irresistible necessity forces them to my barn doors, I permit them to feed unmolested; and it is not the least agreeable spectacle which that dreary season presents, when I see those beautiful birds, tamed by hunger, intermingling with all my cattle and sheep, seeking in security for the poor scanty grain which but for them would be useless and lost. Often in the angles of the fences where the motion of the wind prevents the snow from settling, I carry them both chaff and grain; the one to feed them, the other to prevent their tender feet from freezing fast to the earth as I have frequently observed them to do.

I do not know an instance in which the singular barbarity of man is so strongly delineated, as in the catching and murthering those harmless birds, at that cruel season of the year. Mr -, one of the most famous and extraordinary farmers that has ever done honour to the province of Connecticut, by his timely and humane assistance in a hard winter, saved this species from being entirely destroyed. They perished all over the country, none of their delightful whistlings were heard the next spring, but upon this gentleman's farm; and to his humanity we owe the continuation of their music. When the severities of that season have dispirited all my cattle, no farmer ever attends them with more pleasure than I do; it is one of those duties which is sweetened with the most rational satisfaction. I amuse myself in beholding their different tempers, actions, and the various effects of their instinct now powerfully impelled by the force of hunger. I trace their various inclinations, and the different effects of their passions, which are exactly the same as among men; the law is to us precisely what I am in my barn yard, a bridle and check to prevent the strong and greedy from oppressing the timid and weak. Conscious of superiority, they always strive to encroach on their neighbours; unsatisfied with their portion, they eagerly swallow it in order to have an opportunity of taking what is given to others, except they are prevented. Some I chide, others, unmindful of my admonitions, receive some blows. Could victuals thus be given to men without the assistance of any language, I am sure they would not behave better to one another, nor more philosophically than my cattle do.

The same spirit prevails in the stable; but there I have to do with more generous animals, there my well-known voice has immediate influence, and soon restores peace and tranquillity. Thus by superior knowledge I govern all my cattle as wise men are obliged to govern fools and the ignorant. A variety of other thoughts crowd on my mind at that peculiar instant, but they all vanish by the time I return home. If in a cold night I swiftly travel in my sledge, carried along at the rate of twelve miles an hour, many are the reflections excited by surrounding circumstances. I ask myself what sort of an agent is that which we call frost? Our minister compared it to needles, the points of which enter our pores. What is become of the heat of summer; in what part of the world is it that the N.W. keeps these grand magazines of nitre? When I see in the morning a river over which I can travel, that in the evening before was liquid, I am astonished indeed! What is become of those millions of insects which played in our summer fields, and in our evening meadows; they were so puny and so delicate, the period of their existence was so short, that one cannot help wondering how they could learn, in that short space, the sublime art to hide themselves and their offspring in so perfect a manner as to baffle the rigour of the season, and preserve that precious embryo of life, that small portion of ethereal heat, which if once destroyed would destroy the species! Whence that irresistible propensity to sleep so common in all those who are severely attacked by the frost. Dreary as this season appears, yet it has like all other its miracles, it presents to man a variety of problems which he can never resolve; among the rest, we have here a set of small birds which never appear until the snow falls; contrary to all others, they dwell and appear to delight in that element.

François-René de Chateaubriand (1791)

François-René de Chateaubriand (1768–1848) left France because of the Revolution, and sailed for America in the spring of 1791. This is his landing in the New World, at Chesapeake Bay.

We walked towards the nearest house. Woods of balsam trees and Virginian cedars, mocking-birds, and cardinal tanagers proclaimed by their appearance and shade, their song and colour, that we were in a new clime. The house, which we reached after half an hour, was a cross between an English farmhouse and a West Indian hut. Herds of European cows were grazing in pastures surrounded by fences, on which striped squirrels were playing. Blacks were sawing up logs of wood, whites tending tobacco plants. A Negress of thirteen or fourteen, practically naked and singularly beautiful, opened the gate to us like a young Night. We bought some cakes of Indian corn, chickens, eggs, and milk, and returned to the ship with our demijohns and baskets. I gave my silk handkerchief to the little African girl: it was a slave who welcomed me to the soil of liberty.

Marquise de la Tour du Pin de Gouvermet (1793–6)

Of Irish ancestry, Madame de la Tour du Pin was a lady-in-waiting to Marie-Antoinette. Escaping from France after the Revolution, she and her husband and her family ran a farm at Troy, New York State. This is an extract from her memoirs written in the 1840s.

Mr Geyer was one of the richest men in Boston. Although he had returned after the peace treaty to enjoy his fortune in the country of his birth, he had been among those who supported England and he had taken no part in the revolt against the mother-country. Following the example of many other Boston merchants, he had even taken his family to England. My husband was received by him with a warm friendliness which quite charmed him.

The house in which our Captain had found us lodging was inhabited by three generations of women: Mrs Pierce, her mother and her daughter. It stood on the Market Square, the busiest and most lively part of the town.

We boarded with these good ladies, who fed us very well, in the English style. Sally, the young daughter, was passionately fond of children and she took my small daughter and wanted to look after her. The grandmother took charge of Humbert, already very tall for his age and most unusually intelligent. We could not have had a more fortunate start. By the evening of the first day, we felt as settled there as if no grief or anxiety had ever troubled our lives.

Forty-five years ago, the town was still just like an English colony, yet it was there that the first movements of rebellion against the mother-country had begun to stir. We were shown with pride the column that had been erected on top of the hill where the people had gathered to pass the first resolutions against the unjust taxes with which England was crippling the colony; the part of the harbour where the two shiploads of tea were tipped into the sea rather than pay the exorbitant duty charged on that commodity; the fine lawn where the first armed troops had gathered and the site of the first battle: Bunker's Hill. But the richer and more distinguished inhabitants, although they submitted to the new government, regretted – though they did not disapprove – the separation from the mother-country. They were still linked to England by ties of affection and family. They preserved the customs of that country quite unchanged, and many of them who had taken refuge there, did not return until the peace had been signed. They were known as the Loyalists. Among them was Mr Jeffreys, brother of the famous editor of the *Edinburgh Review*, and a family named Russell who took care to make known their close relationship to the Duke of Bedford. All these people welcomed us with the greatest kindness and took an active interest in our welfare.

We stayed a month in Boston, going nearly every day to visit the kindly people who had showered attentions and kindnesses on us. I also received visits from many Créoles from Martinique who had known my father. One of them, who had married in Boston, made us promise to spend a few days with him in the country, and we did so with great pleasure. He lived in Wrentham, a village half way between Boston and Providence. It was a delightful spot, cool, unspoilt and very fertile. There were lakes strewn with small forested islands which looked like gardens floating on the water; there were great trees, old as time itself, dipping their ancient trunks and their younger shoots into water clear as crystal. It was a place of enchantment.

At Lebanon there was a sulphur bath establishment which was even then quite well known. The inn was very good, and above all, impeccably clean. But the luxury of white sheets was still unknown in that part of the United States. To ask for sheets that had not been used by others would have been considered a quite unreasonable caprice, and when the bed was fairly wide, you would even be asked, as if it were the most normal thing in the world, to allow someone to share it with you. This is what happened to M. de Chambeau that very evening at Lebanon. In the middle of the night, we suddenly heard a stream of French oaths, which could come only from him. In the morning we learned that towards midnight he had been awakened by a gentleman who was sliding, without so much as a 'by your leave' into the empty half of his double bed. Furious at this invasion, he promptly leaped out at the other side and spent the night in a chair listening to his companion's snores, for he had been in no way disturbed by M. de Chambeau's anger. This misadventure led to much teasing from everyone. When we arrived that evening at Albany, a small room was reserved for him alone, and that consoled him.

Two years earlier, the town of Albany had been almost entirely burned down as the result of a negro plot. In the State of New York, slavery had been abolished for children born in the year 1794 and later. They were to be given their freedom when they reached their twentieth year, a very wise measure both for the negroes and the owners of slaves. It obliged the latter to support their slaves during childhood and it compelled the slaves, in their turn, to work sufficiently long for the masters to repay the cost of their upbringing. One negro, a very bad lot, who had hoped that the Government's measure would give him unconditional liberty, resolved to avenge his disappointment. He collected a few other malcontents and they arranged to set fire to the city on a certain day, where most of the buildings were still of wood. This horrible plot succeeded beyond their wildest imaginings. The fire caught hold in twenty places at once and despite the efforts of the inhabitants, led by old General Schuyler and his entire family, houses, shops and merchandise were reduced to ashes. A small twelve-year-old negress was caught in the act of setting fire to her master's hay store. She revealed the names of the plotters and the following day the Court assembled in the smoking débris of the building where it had been accustomed to hold its sessions and condemned the negro leader and six of his accomplices to be hanged. The sentence was carried out there and then.

In September, my husband opened negotiations with a farmer whose land lay two miles inland on the other side of the river, on the road from Troy of Schenectady. It was on a hill overlooking a wide stretch of country, and we thought it a very pleasant situation. The house was new and pretty, and in good condition. Only a part of the land was in cultivation. There were 150 acres under crops, a similar area of woodland and pasture, a small kitchen garden of a quarter of an acre filled with vegetables, and a fine orchard sewn with red clover and planted with ten-year-old cider apple trees, all in fruit. We were told that the price was twelve thousand francs, which General Schuyler thought not excessive. The property was four miles from Albany, on the line of the road which it was planned to build between Albany and Schenectady, a town which was then expanding rapidly. In other words, it was 'in a thriving situation', an all-important phrase in that country.

The owner did not want to move until after the first snows. Since our agreement with the van Burens had been for only two months and since it was clear that they had had enough of us, this meant we had to find other lodgings from the 1st of September to the 1st of November. At Troy, for a modest rent, we found a little wooden house standing in a large yard enclosed by clapboard walls. We moved in and as it would eventually be necessary to buy certain furnishings for the farm, decided to buy them now. These furnishings, added to what we had brought from Europe, made it possible for us to move in without delay. I had engaged a very reliable white girl. She was to be married in two months time and agreed to enter my service while waiting for her future husband to finish building the log house where they were to live after their marriage.

I must explain what is meant by a log house, though it is more easily drawn than described. A site fourteen to fifteen feet square is levelled off, and before any other work is begun, a brick chimney is built. This is the most important part of the house. When it has been completed, the walls are put up, built with large planks of wood still covered in bark and cut to fit very closely together. On top of these walls is set the roof, with a hole for the chimney. A door is then cut into the south wall. You can see many such buildings in Switzerland, in the pastures of the Upper Alps, where they are used only for sheltering the cattle and the herdsmen. In America they represent the first step in settlement – and often the last, for there are always the unlucky ones, and when a town has prospered, these log houses become the refuge of the poor.

One day, towards the end of September, I was out in the yard chopper in hand, busy cutting the bone of a leg of mutton which I was about to roast on the spit for our dinner. As Betsey did not cook, I had been left in charge of everything concerned with food and, with the help of the *Cuisine Bourgeoise*, acquitted myself as best I could. Suddenly from behind me a deep voice remarked in French: 'Never was a leg of mutton spitted with greater majesty.' Turning quickly round, I saw M. de Talleyrand and M. de Beaumetz. They had arrived in Albany the previous day and had learned our whereabouts from General Schuyler. They had come to invite us, on his behalf, to dine and spend the next day with them at his house. These gentlemen were staying only two days in Albany as the English friend who was with them was extremely anxious to return to New York. However, as M. de Talleyrand was so much amused at the sight of my leg of mutton, I insisted that he should return the following day and share it with us. This he promised to do. Leaving the children in the care of M. de Chambeau and Betsey, we went off to Albany.

We had a great deal to talk about on the way, and passed from one subject to another as people do when they meet after a long time. They had returned only the previous evening from their journey to Niagara and had therefore heard none of the latest news, which was worse than ever. Blood flowed everywhere in Paris. Mme Elisabeth had perished. Each of us had relatives and friends among the victims of the terror. Nor could we see an end to it.

When we arrived at the good General's house, he was on the porch making signs to us from afar and shouting: 'Come along, come along. There's fine news from France!' We hurried into the drawing-room and each seized a gazette.

In them we found accounts of the revolt of 9 Thermidor, of the death of Robespierre and his supporters, the end of the murders and the just execution of the members of the Revolutionary Tribunal. We all rejoiced together, though the deep mourning worn by my husband and myself bore sad witness to the fact that, for us, this divine justice had arrived too late. We, personally, had less cause for rejoicing than M. de Talleyrand and M. de Beaumetz.

Between the 25th of October and the 1st of November, the sky would become covered by a mass of cloud so thick that the daylight faded. These clouds were driven violently before a horribly cold north-west wind and everyone began preparing to put under shelter everything that could not be left out and buried under the snow. Boats, canoes, and ferries were hauled out of the water and those which were not decked in were turned keel upwards. It was a time of intense activity for everyone. Then the snow would begin to fall, so thickly that it was impossible to see a man at ten paces. Usually, the river would have frozen hard several days before. The first precaution was to mark out a wide path along one of the river banks with pine branches. Places where the bank was not steep and where it was safe to walk on the ice were similarly marked. It would have been dangerous to walk anywhere but between these markers for in many places the ice at the edge was not very solid.

We had bought moccasins, which are like shoes. They are made by the savages in buffalo-hide. Sometimes, as for instance, when they are embroidered with dyed bark of porcupine quills, they are quite costly.

It was when buying these shoes that I saw the savages for the first time, the last survivors of the Mohawk nation whose territory had been bought or seized by the Americans after the war. At about the same time, the Onondagas, who lived near Lake Champlain, had also sold their forests and dispersed, but now and again some of them were still to be seen. I was rather startled, I must admit, the first time I met a man and a woman, both stark naked, walking calmly along the road. But no one seemed to find it strange and I soon grew used to it. When I was living at the farm, I saw these people nearly every day during the summer time.

During this time, we also bought a negro and this purchase, which seemed so very simple, gave me such a strange sensation that I shall always remember the smallest circumstance connected with it.

As I have said, the Government had decided that negroes born in 1794 would be set free on reaching the age of twenty. But there were some who had already been freed, either by their masters as a reward, or for some other reason. A custom had also been established which no master would have dared to disregard for fear of public displeasure; a negro who was dissatisfied with his situation could go to a Justice of the Peace and send his master an official request to be sold. By common usage, the owner was then compelled to allow him to seek another master willing to pay a certain sum for him. The master could enforce a delay of three months or six, but rarely did so, not usually wishing to keep a worker or servant known to be anxious to leave him. That is what happened to us. Betsey, who was very well thought of, had sung our praises and was very sad at leaving us. A few pieces of ribbon and some old gowns that I had given her had secured me, at very little expense, a surprising reputation for generosity, a reputation which had reached even the farmers in the old Dutch colony. There was a young negro there named Minck, who wished to leave the master on whose property he had been born. He was trying to escape from the severity of his father, a negro like himself, and of his mother. He brought us written permission to find another situation and when we made enquiries, we learned that he had indeed been treated with extreme harshness and as the boy's father himself asked us to buy his son, we agreed to do so.

We climbed in our red and yellow sledge, drawn by our two excellent black horses and drove about four miles to a part of the country where there were eight or ten neighbouring farms, all owned by people named Lansing. This arose probably from the fact that the first man to buy land in those parts would have had to pay only four or five sous an acre for it, since it was covered with forest. He would have begun the work of clearing, and his children would have continued it. The latter would, in due course, build on the land they had cleared, and each house would be exactly like the original one. And that is why it was not uncommon to spend an entire day going from farm to farm, finding in each someone of the same name, but never the person one was seeking.

However, since we knew the baptismal name of our negro – always supposing that he had been baptised – we reached the pretty house of Mr Henry Lansing, a brick house, a sign of prosperity that we ourselves had not yet aspired to. There we asked Mrs Lansing for Minck. True to her Dutch traditions, she was anxious to discover, in her rather halting English, if we had brought the money. My husband counted out on the table the thousand francs I had been holding under my cloak, and at that moment, Mr Lansing came in. He was a very tall man, dressed in a good coat of home-spun grey cloth. He called Minck in, and taking his hand, put it into my husband's saying: 'This is your master.' When that had been done, we told Minck that we were ready to leave. But Mrs Lansing having set out Madeira wine and cake for us, we had to stay a little longer, under pain of being thought unneighbourly. In the course of conversation, Mr Lansing learned that my husband had represented the King of France in Holland, his mother country, as he called it. His opinion of us rose prodigiously. We took our leave, and found Minck already installed in the sledge. He had gone up to his room to put on his best clothes. These belonged to him, for he took away nothing that had been bought with his master's money, not even his moccasins. All his other personal belongings, so few that they could have been carried in the crown of a hat, he put into the sledge locker and then turning to us and touching his hat like any well-trained coachman, he pointed to the horses and asked: 'Are they *my* horses?' Told that they were, he took up the reins and set off at a gallop for his new home, much less preoccupied than I, for it was the first time I had ever bought a man and I still felt quite overcome by the way in which it had been done.

One day we received a visit from a Frenchman who had been an officer in my husband's regiment, M. de Novion. Having come straight from Europe, he was very glad to learn that his former colonel had become a farmer. He had brought some funds with him and would have liked to use them to buy a small farm near us. But as he had no knowledge of agriculture, spoke not a single word of English, and had neither wife nor children, he lacked all the essential qualifications for running a reasonable establishment of that kind. M. de la Tour du Pin explained this to him. But he still wanted to see something of the country, so we went riding together. After a few miles, I realised that I had forgotten my whip. As M. de Novion had no knife with which to cut me a stick he could not help. The undergrowth in the wood was fairly thick and at that moment, seeing one of my Indian friends sitting behind a bush, I called to him: 'Squaw John.'

It is impossible to describe the surprise, almost the horror, of M. de Novion at the apparition which emerged from the bush and came towards us with his hand held out to me: a very tall man wearing only a strip of blue cloth passed between his legs and fixed to a cord about his waist. His astonishment increased when he saw how well we knew one another and the calm way in which we engaged in a conversation of which he could not understand a single word. As we walked our horses on, and before I had time to explain how I knew such an odd person in such extraordinary

garments, Squaw John leaped lightly from the top of a hillock which dominated the road and politely offered me a stick which he had stripped of its
bark with his tomahawk.

I am sure that in that moment M. de Novion resolved, deep in his heart,
never to live in a country where one was exposed to such encounters. 'And
if you had been alone, Madame?' he asked. 'I should have been just as little
alarmed,' I told him, 'and you know, if I had had to defend myself from
you and had told him to throw his tomahawk at you, he would have done
so without hesitation.' Such a manner of life did not seem to please him.
On our return, he told my husband that I had odd friends and that he, for
his part, had decided to go and live in New York, where civilisation seemed
slightly more advanced.

Our ride was rather too long and tired me, with the result that I had a
recurrence of the double tertian fever from which I had been suffering
intermittently for two months.

We reached New York on the morning of the third day and found that
M. de Talleyrand was staying with Mr Law. They gave us a most friendly
welcome, but were shocked by my thinness and changed appearance. I had
planned to travel by the stage coach to Philadelphia with my husband,
spending two nights on the way, but this they absolutely refused to allow.
My husband therefore went alone and I was given into the care of Mrs
Foster, Mr Law's housekeeper. This excellent lady tried every restorative
she knew in her effort to help me out. Four or five times a day she would
arrive with a small cup of broth and, curtseying in the English fashion, say
'Pray, ma'am, you had better take this.' I submitted very willingly to her
care, so tired was I of listening to M. de Talleyrand's lamentations about
my wasting away.

The three weeks that we spent in New York are among my happiest
memories. My husband was away only four days, but had an opportunity
to admire the fine city of Philadelphia and, what I envied still more, to see
my hero, the great Washington. Even today, I still regret not having looked
on the face of that great man of whom I had heard so much from his close
friend, Mr Hamilton.

After three weeks the rumour went around one evening that yellow fever
had broken out in a street very close to Broadway, where we were staying.
That very night, either because we had the first symptoms of the illness or
because we had eaten too many bananas, pineapples and other fruit brought
from the Caribbean in the same ship that had carried the fever, my husband
and I were terribly ill. Fearing to be kept in New York by quarantine
measures, I decided to leave immediately. We packed our trunk and went
at daybreak to reserve places on a sloop which was ready to sail. We then
went to say goodbye to Mr Law. He decided to leave too, on the pretext
of visiting certain properties he had bought in the new town of Washington,
where building had just begun. He had invested the greater part of his
fortune in these purchases. Our departure was so hurried that I did not
even see M. de Talleyrand: by the time he had begun to think of getting
up, we were already far from New York.

I returned to my country tasks with fresh ardour, for the change of air
had cured my fever and I had recovered all my strength. I resumed my
dairy work and the pretty patterns stamped on my butter told my customers

that I was back. Our orchard promised a magnificent crop of apples and our loft held enough grain for the entire year. Our negroes, spurred on by our example, worked with a will. They were better clothed and better fed than any of those belonging to our neighbours.

I was very happy in this life when, suddenly, God dealt me the most unexpected and what seemed to me then the most cruel blow that any mortal could endure. Alas, I have since suffered others far more severe. My small Séraphine was taken from us by a short illness very common in that part of the continent: a sudden paralysis of the stomach and intestines without any accompanying fever or convulsions. She died within a few hours, and was conscious until the very end. The Albany doctor whom M. de Chambeau had ridden to fetch as soon as the illness began, told us immediately he saw her that there was no hope. He said that the illness was very widespread in the country just then and there was no known remedy for it. The Schuylers' small son, who had played with my daughter throughout the afternoon of the previous day, also died a few hours later from the same illness and joined Séraphine in heaven. His mother adored him, and called him my dear child's little husband. This cruel loss threw us all into the deepest sadness and despondency. We brought Humbert home to live with us and I tried to find distraction from my grief in teaching him myself. He was then five and a half years old. His intelligence was very well developed and he spoke English perfectly and read it fluently.

There was no Catholic priest in Albany or anywhere else in the neighbourhood, and as my husband did not want a Protestant minister summoned, he himself performed the last rites for our child and buried her in a small enclosure intended as a cemetery for the people of the farm. It was in the middle of a wood. Nearly every day I went to prostrate myself on that earth which was the last home of a child I had so dearly cherished, and it was there, my beloved son, that God bided His time to work a change of heart in me.

Until then, although far from irreligious, I had not been much concerned with religion. During my childhood, no one had ever talked to me about it. During my early youth, I had been constantly surrounded by the worst possible examples. In the highest circles of Paris society I had seen the same scandalous behaviour repeated so often that it had become familiar and no longer distressed me. It was as if all concern with morality had been stifled in my heart. But the hour had come when I was to be forced to recognise the hand that had stricken me.

I could not describe exactly the change which took place in me. It was as if a voice cried out to me to change my whole nature. Kneeling on my child's grave, I implored her to obtain forgiveness for me from God, Who had taken her back to be with Him, and to give me a little comfort in my distress. My prayer was heard. God granted me the grace of knowing Him and serving Him; he gave me the courage to bow very humbly beneath the blow I had received and to prepare myself to endure without complaint those future griefs, which in his justice, he was to send to try me. Since that day, the divine will has found me submissive and resigned.

Although all the joy had gone from our home, we still had to go about our daily tasks and we encouraged one another, my husband and I, to seek distraction in the need in which we found ourselves to find employment for every single minute. It was almost apple-picking time. The crop promised to be plentiful, for the trees were heavily laden. There were almost as many apples as leaves. The previous autumn we had followed an old Bordeaux custom and hoed a patch four to five feet square around each tree. It was the first time this had been done to them. Indeed, Americans were ignorant of the benefit which this practice has on growth and when we told them that we had owned vines where this operation was repeated three times a year, they thought we were exaggerating. But when spring came and they saw our trees covered in blossom, they began to think it must be due to some kind of magic.

Another idea was also widely remarked upon. Instead of buying new barrels of very porous wood for our cider, we hunted in Albany for a number of Bordeaux casks and for some marked 'Cognac', of a type well known to us. Then we arranged our cellar with as much care as if it had been going to house the wines of Médoc.

We were lent a mill for pressing the apples and to it we harnessed an ancient, twenty-three-year-old horse which General Schuyler had given me. The mill was extremely primitive: there were two interlocking, grooved pieces of wood, like ratchets, and these were turned by the horse, which was harnessed to a wooden bar. The apples fell from a hopper into the interlocking pieces of wood and when there was enough juice to fill a large basket, it was taken to the cellar and poured into the casks.

The whole operation was exceedingly simple and as the weather was very fine, this harvesting became a delightful recreation for us. My son, who spent the whole of every day astride the horse, was convinced that his presence was vital to the task!

When the work was finished, we found that, after putting aside enough for our own use, we had eight or ten casks to sell. Our reputation for honest dealing was a guarantee that not a drop of water had been added to the cider, so that it fetched more than twice the customary price. It was all sold immediately. As for that which we kept for ourselves, we treated it just as we would have done our white wine at Le Bouilh.

The apple picking was followed by the harvesting of the maize. We had an abundance of it, for it is indigenous to the United States and grows there better than any other plant. As the corn must not be left in the husk for more than two days, the neighbours collect to help, and they work without stopping until it is all done. This is called a 'frolic'. First, the floor of the barn is swept with as much care as for a ball. Then, when darkness comes, candles are lit and the people assemble, about thirty of them, both black and white, and they set to work. All night long someone sings or tells stories and in the middle of the night everyone is given a bowl of boiling milk, previously turned with cider, to which have been added cloves, cinnamon, nutmeg and other spices, and five or six pounds of brown sugar, if one is being very grand, or similar quantity of molasses if one feels less grand. We prepared a kitchen boiler full of this mixture and our workers paid us the compliment of drinking it all, eating toast which accompanied it. These good people left us at five o'clock in the morning, going out into the sharp cold saying 'Famous good people, those from the old country!' Our negroes were often asked to similar frolics, but my negress never went.

When all the harvests had been gathered in and stored, we began the ploughing and all the other tasks which had to be finished before winter. The wood which we intended to sell was stacked under a shelter. The sledges were repaired and repainted. I bought a length of coarse blue and white checked flannel to make two shirts each for my negroes. A journeyman tailor installed himself at the farm to make good waistcoats and well-lined cloaks. Being white, this man took his meals with us. He would certainly have refused, had we suggested it, to eat with the 'slaves', though they were incomparably better dressed and far better mannered than he. But I was very careful to avoid even the slightest reference to this custom. My neighbours acted thus and I followed their example, never making in any of our dealings the slightest allusion to my former station. I was the owner of a 250-acre farm and I lived as did all owners of such farms, neither better nor worse. This simplicity and renunciation of the past earned me far more respect and consideration than I would have had if I had tried to 'play the lady'.

The work which tired me most was the laundering. Judith and I did it all between us. Every fortnight, Judith washed the negroes' clothes, her own and the kitchen linen. I washed my own clothes, my husband's and those of M. de Chambeau, and I did all the ironing. This latter task I greatly enjoyed; I excelled at it and could compete with the best. In my early girlhood, before my marriage, I often went to the linen-room at Montfermeil and there, as if by a presentiment, I learned to iron. Being naturally dexterous, I was soon as skilful at it as the girls who taught me.

I never wasted a minute. Every day, winter and summer, I was up at dawn and my toilet took very little time. Before the negroes went to their work, they helped the negress to milk the cows, of which we had at one time as many as eight. While they were doing that, I busied myself in the dairy, skimming the milk. On the days when there was butter to be made, which was twice a week, Minck stayed behind to turn the handle of the churn, a task too heavy for a woman. All the remainder of the butter-making, and much other tiring work which still remained to be done, fell to me. I had a remarkable collection of bowls, ladles and wooden spatulae, all made by my good friends the savages. My dairy was reputed the cleanest and even the most elegant in the country.

Towards the end of the winter of 1795–1796, I caught measles. It was a fairly severe attack, aggravated by the fact that I was in the first months of pregnancy. We were afraid Humbert would catch it, but he did not, although he slept in my room. I recovered quickly and was no sooner better than we received letters from Bonie in France telling us that he and M. de Brouquens had, by their combined efforts, succeeded in having the sequestration removed from Le Bouilh.

The property of those who had been condemned was being restored. My mother-in-law, with the assistance of her daughter's husband, the Marquis de Lameth, had acted on behalf of her children and again taken possession of the properties of Tesson and Ambleville, as well as of the house at Saintes which had been held by the Department of Charente-Inférieure. But when they asked for the removal of the seals on Le Bouilh, they were told that this could not be done in the owner's absence. They replied that he had gone to America *with a valid passport*, and that neither M. de La Tour de Pin nor I, who owned a house in Paris, had been on the list of émigrés. After much discussion, the authorities agreed to allow us one year's grace in which to present ourselves. If we did not do so within that period, Le Bouilh would be offered for sale as national property, unless M. de Lameth was able to prove his own children's rights as the grandchildren of the former owner. We were urged, therefore, to return as soon as possible. However, as the stability of the French government of the day inspired little confidence, we were also advised to take passage to a Spanish port instead of a French one, for the Republic had just signed a treaty of peace with Spain which seemed likely to last for a while.

The arrival of these letters at our peaceful farm had somewhat the effect of a firebrand, for in the hearts of all about me they suddenly set aflame thoughts of a return to our homeland, glimpses of a better life, hopes of achieving our ambitions, in short, they armed all those sentiments which animate the life of man. My own feelings were quite different. France had left me only memories of horror. It was there that I had lost my youth, crushed out of being by numberless, unforgettable terrors. Only two sentiments had remained alive in me, and to this day they are the only ones that remain with me: love of my husband and love of my children. However, religion, which from that time forward was my only guide in all my problems, prevented me from setting the slightest obstacle in the way of a departure which terrified me and filled me with dismay. I had a presentiment that I was embarking on a fresh series of troubles and anxieties. M. de La Tour du Pin never realised the intensity of my regret when I knew that the day on which we would leave the farm had been fixed. I set only one condition to our departure: that our negroes should be given their freedom. My husband agreed, and reserved the joy of telling them to me alone.

When these poor people saw the letters arriving from Europe, they feared there would be changes in our way of life. They were anxious and frightened, so that it was in trembling that they came, all four of them, to the drawing-room in answer to my summons.

Judith was holding her small daughter, three-year-old Maria, in her arms: she was soon to give birth to her second child. They found me alone in the drawing room and I said to them with much emotion: 'My friends, we are returning to Europe. What are we to do with you?' The poor things were stricken. Judith sank on to a chair, sobbing, and the three men hid their faces in their hands. All four remained motionless. I went on: 'We have been so pleased with you that it is right that you should be rewarded. My husband has charged me to tell you that he gives you your freedom.' Hearing this, our good servants were so amazed that they remained silent for some seconds. Then, falling at my feet, they cried: 'Is it possible? Do you mean that we are free?' I answered: 'Yes, upon my honour. From this moment you are as free as I am myself.'

The poignancy of such a scene cannot be described. Never in my life have I known a happier moment. These people whom I had just freed, surrounded me and wept. They kissed my hands, my feet, my gown; and then, suddenly, their joy vanished and they said: 'We would prefer to remain slaves all our lives and for you to stay here.'

The following day, my husband took them before the Justice in Albany, for the ceremony of manumission, which had to take place in public. All the negroes in town gathered to watch. The Justice of the Peace, who was also the manager of Mr Renslaer's properties, was very displeased. He tried to object that since Prime was fifty years of age, he could not, under the law, be given his freedom unless he had an assured pension of one hundred dollars. But Prime had foreseen this difficulty, and produced his certificate of baptism, which showed that he was only forty-nine. They were told to kneel in front of my husband who laid his hand on the head of each in turn in token of liberation, exactly as used to be done in ancient Rome.

We leased our house and land to the man from whom we had bought it, and sold most of the furnishings and stock. The horses fetched quite good prices. I distributed many small pieces of porcelain that I had brought with me from Europe as souvenirs. To my poor Judith, I left some of my old silk gowns, which will doubtless have been handed down to her descendants.

William Cobbett (1792–1800)

Cobbett's visit to the United States (1792–1800) was not a sudden resolution; when serving as a sergeant-major in New Brunswick he had decided to settle there.

A desire of seeing a country, so long the theatre of a war of which I had heard and read so much; the flattering picture given of it by Raynal; and, above all, an inclination for seeing the world, led me to this determination. It would look like coaxing for me to say that I had imbibed principles of republicanism, and that I was ambitious to become a citizen of a free state, but this was really the case. I thought that men enjoyed here a greater degree of liberty than in England; and this, if not the principal reason, was at least one, for my coming to this country.

Cobbett landed in Philadelphia in October 1792, provided with a letter of recommendation from the American Ambassador in Paris to Thomas Jefferson, then Secretary of State. This he forwarded with the following note:

Ambitious to become the citizen of a free state, I have left my native country, England, for America. I bring with me youth, a small family, a few useful literary talents, and that is all.

Thomas Jefferson to William Cobbett
PHILADELPHIA, *November 5, 1792.*

SIR, – In acknowledging the receipt of your favour of the 2nd instant, I wish it were in my power to announce to you any way in which I could be useful to you. Mr. Short's assurance of your merit would be a sufficient inducement to me. Public Offices in our Government are so few, and of so little value, as to offer no resource to talents. When you shall have been here some small time, you will be able to judge in what way you can set out with the best prospect of success, and if I can serve you in it, I shall be very ready to do it. – I am, Sir, your very humble servant, TH. JEFFERSON.

Cobbett at first set up as a teacher of English to the French refugees.

William Cobbett to Miss Rachel Smither, 156 Houndsditch

PHILADELPHIA, July 6, 1794.

This country is good for getting money, that is to say, if a person is industrious and enterprising. In every other respect the country is miserable. Exactly the contrary of what I expected it. The land is bad, rocky; houses wretched; roads impassable after the least rain. Fruit in quantity, but good for nothing. One apple or peach in England or France is worth a bushel of them here. The seasons are detestable. All is burning or freezing. There is no spring or autumn. The weather is so very inconstant that you are never sure for an hour, a single hour at a time. Last night we made a fire to sit by, and to-day it is scorching hot. The whole month of March was so hot that we could hardly bear our clothes, and three parts of the month of June there was a frost every night, and so cold in the day-time that we were obliged to wear great-coats. The people are worthy of the country - cheating, sly, roguish gang. Strangers make fortunes here in spite of all this, particularly the English. The natives are by nature idle, and seek to live by cheating, while foreigners, being industrious, seek no other means than those dictated by integrity, and are sure to meet with encouragement even from the idle and roguish themselves; for, however roguish a man may be, he always loves to deal with an honest man. You have perhaps heard of the plague being at Philadelphia last year. It was no plague; it was a fever of the country, and is by no means extraordinary among the Americans. In the fall of the year almost every person, in every place, has a spell of the fever that is called the fall-fever. It is often fatal, and the only way to avoid it is to quit the country. But this fever is not all. Every month has its particular malady. In July, for example, everybody almost, or at least one half of the people, are taken with vomitings for several days at a time; they often carry off the patient, and almost always children. In short, the country altogether is detestable.

The greatest part of my acquaintance in this country are French merchants from St. Domingo and Martinico. To one of those Islands I shall probably go in about eight or nine months; and in that case, if I live so long, I shall be in England in about three years. For I do not intend to stay much above a couple of years in the Islands. Take care of my trunk and box, if you please, till you see me or hear from me. My Nancy's kind love to you all, and accept of mine at the same time. Doctor Priestley is just arrived here from England. He has attacked our English laws and Constitution in print, and declared his sentiments in favour of those butchers in France. He has, however, been attacked in his turn by an Englishman here. I will send you one of these pieces by another ship. Accept my love, and God bless you.

WM. COBBETT.

> *On June 12th 1794 there arrived in New York, Dr Joseph Priestley, one of the most ardent English supporters of the French Revolution. England was not a safe residence for one holding such opinions. Cobbett wrote later:*

Newspapers were a luxury for which I had little relish, and which, if I had been ever so fond of, I had not time to enjoy. The manifestos, therefore, of the Doctor, upon his landing in that country, and the malicious attacks upon the monarchy and the monarch of England which certain societies in America thereupon issued through the press, would, had it not been for a circumstance purely accidental, have escaped, probably for ever, not only my animadversions, but my knowledge of their existence. One of my scholars, who was a person that we in England should call a Coffee-house politician, chose for once to read his newspaper by way of lesson; and it happened to be the very paper which contained the addresses presented to Dr. Priestley at New York, together with his replies. My scholar, who was a sort of republican, or, at best, but half a monarchist, appeared delighted with the invectives against England, to which he was very much disposed to add. Those Englishmen who have been abroad, particularly if they have had time to make a comparison between the country they are in and that which they have left, well know how difficult it is, upon occasions such as I have been describing, to refrain from expressing their indignation and resentment; and there is not, I trust, much reason to suppose that I should, in this respect, experience less difficulty than another. The dispute was as warm as might reasonably be expected between a Frenchman, and an Englishman not unremarkable for *sang froid*; and the result was a declared resolution on my part to write and publish a pamphlet in defence of my country, which pamphlet he pledged himself to answer: his pledge was forfeited: it is known that mine was not. Thus, Sir, it was that I became a writer on politics.

I could have no hope of gain from the proposed publication [*Observations on Priestley's Emigration*] itself, but, on the contrary, was pretty certain to incur a loss; no hope of remuneration, for not only had I never seen any agent of the British Government in America, but I was not acquainted with any one British subject in the country. I was actuated, perhaps, by no very exalted notions of either loyalty or patriotism; the act was not so much an act of refined reasoning or of reflection, it arose merely from feeling, but it was that sort of feeling, that jealousy for the honour of my native country, which I am sure you will allow to have been highly meritorious, especially when you reflect on the circumstances of the times and the places in which I ventured before the public.

> *During this time Cobbett was under suspicion by the American authorities for being an English spy. The Post Office took to opening his parcels and letters. Cobbett published the following proclamation in his paper, Porcupine's Gazette.*

Thursday, October 26 [1797]

REPUBLICAN POST OFFICE, – This is to notify the postmasters and others, between this place and New York inclusive, that, if the next package brought me by the English packet come to my hands *broken open* and *I am not able to discover the persons who may break it open* it is my resolution to *prosecute the postmaster-general*. I have no objection to people talking about *liberty* and the *rights of man* as long as they please, but I do not like that they should proceed so far *in the practice of them* as to ransack what comes under seal to my address.

WM. COBBETT.

This is Cobbett's farewell address, printed in the American newspapers:

When people care not two straws for each other, ceremony at parting is mere grimace; and as I have long felt the most perfect indifference with regard to a vast majority of those whom I now address, I shall spare myself the trouble of a ceremonious farewell. Let me, however, not part from you in indiscriminating contempt. If no man ever had so many and such malignant foes, no one ever had more friends, and those more kind, more sincere, and more faithful. If I have been unjustly villified by some, others have extolled me far beyond my merits; if the savages of the city have scared my children in the cradle, those children have, for their father's sake, been soothed and caressed by the affectionate, the gentle, the generous inhabitants of the country, under whose hospitable roofs I have spent some of the happiest hours of my life.

Thus and *thus*, Americans, will I ever speak of you. In a very little time I shall be beyond the reach of your friendship and your malice; beyond the hearing of your commendations of your curses, but being out of your power will alter neither my sentiments nor my words. As I have never spoken anything but truth *to* you, so I will never speak anything but truth *of* you; the heart of a Briton revolts at an emulation in baseness, and although you have as a nation treated me most ungratefully and unjustly, I scorn to repay you with ingratitude and injustice.

To my friends, who are also the real friends of America, I wish that peace and happiness which virtue ought to ensure, but which I greatly fear they will not find; and as to my enemies, I can wish them no severer scourge than that which they are preparing for themselves and their country. With this I depart for my native land, where neither the moth of democracy, nor the rust of federalism, doth corrupt, and where thieves do not with impunity break through and steal five thousand dollars at a time.

Frances Trollope (1827)

Frances Trollope (1780–1863) was the mother of Anthony. In 1827, somewhat impoverished, she and her husband emigrated to Cincinnati to open a fancy-goods shop. It was not a success. But the book that came out of it, Domestic Manners of the Americans, *published in England in 1832, set her up for life; the first book in a prodigious literary career. It is still her best-known work: because of it, according to Una Pope-Hennessey, the name of Frances Trollope is still held in execration in the United States.*

I hardly know any annoyance so deeply repugnant to English feelings, as the incessant, remorseless spitting of Americans. I feel that I owe my readers an apology for the repeated use of this, and several other odious words; but I cannot avoid them, without suffering the fidelity of description to escape me. It is possible that in this phrase, 'Americans', I may be too general.

The United States form a continent of almost distinct nations, and I must now, and always, be understood to speak only of that portion of them which I have seen. In conversing with Americans I have constantly found that if I alluded to anything which they thought I considered as uncouth, they would assure me it was local, and not national; the accidental peculiarity of a very small part, and by no means a specimen of the whole. 'That is because you know so little of America,' is a phrase I have listened to a thousand times, and in nearly as many different places. *It may be so* – and having made this concession, I protest against the charge of injustice in relating what I have seen.

The gentlemen in the cabin (we had no ladies) would certainly, neither from their language, manners, nor appearance, have received that designation in Europe; but we soon found their claim to it rested on more substantial ground, for we heard them nearly all addressed by the titles of general, colonel, and major. On mentioning these military dignitaries to an English friend some time afterwards, he told me that he too had made the voyage on a steamboat on the Mississippi with the same description of company, but remarking that there was not a single captain among them; he made the observation to a fellow-passenger, and asked how he accounted for it. 'Oh, sir, the captains are all on deck,' was the reply.

Our honours, however, were not all military, for we had a judge among us. I know it is equally easy and invidious to ridicule the peculiarities of appearance and manner in people of a different nation from ourselves; we may, too, at the same moment, be undergoing the same ordeal in their estimation; and, moreover, I am by no means disposed to consider whatever is new to me as therefore objectionable; but, nevertheless, it was impossible not to feel repugnance to many of the novelties that now surrounded me.

The total want of all the usual courtesies of the table, the voracious rapidity with which the viands were seized and devoured, the strange uncouth phrases and pronunciation; the loathsome spitting, from the contamination of which it was absolutely impossible to protect our dresses; the frightful manner of feeding with their knives, till the whole blade seemed to enter into the mouth; and the still more frightful manner of cleaning the teeth afterwards with a pocket knife, soon forced us to feel that we were not surrounded by the generals, colonels, and majors of the old world; and that the dinner hour was to be anything rather than an hour of enjoyment.

The little conversation that went forward while we remained in the room, was entirely political, and the respective claims of Adams and Jackson to the presidency were argued with more oaths and more vehemence than it had ever been my lot to hear. Once a colonel appeared on the verge of assaulting a major, when a huge seven-foot Kentuckian gentleman horse-dealer, asked of the heavens to confound them both, and bade them sit still and be d – d. We too thought we should share this sentence; at least, sitting still in the cabin seemed very nearly to include the rest of it, and we never tarried there a moment longer than was absolutely necessary to eat.

We were soon settled in our new dwelling in Cincinnati, which looked neat and comfortable enough, but we speedily found that it was devoid of nearly all the accommodation that Europeans conceive necessary to decency and comfort. No pump, no cistern, no drain of any kind, no dustman's cart, or any other visible means of getting rid of rubbish, which vanishes with such celerity in London, that one has no time to think of its existence; but which accumulated so rapidly at Cincinnati, that I sent for my landlord to know in what manner refuse of all kinds was to be disposed of.

'Your Help will just have to fix them all into the middle of the street, but you must mind, old woman, that it is the middle. I expect you don't know as we have got a law what forbids throwing such things at the sides of the streets; they must just all be cast right into the middle, and the pigs soon takes them off.'

In truth the pigs are constantly seen doing Herculean service in this way through every quarter of the city; and though it is not very agreeable to live surrounded by herds of these unsavoury animals, it is well they are so numerous, and so active in their capacity of scavengers, for without them the streets would soon be choked up with all sorts of substances, in every stage of decomposition.

I observed everywhere throughout the slave States that all articles which can be taken and consumed are constantly locked up, and in large families, where the extent of the establishment multiplies the number of keys, these are deposited in a basket, and consigned to the care of a little negress, who is constantly seen following her mistress's steps with this basket on her arm, and this, not only that the keys may be always at hand, but because, should they be out of sight one moment, that moment would infallibly be employed for the purposes of plunder. It seemed to me in this instance, as in many others, that the close personal attendance of these sable shadows, must be very annoying; but whenever I mentioned it, I was assured that no such feeling existed, and that use rendered them almost unconscious of their presence.

I had, indeed, frequent opportunities of observing this habitual indifference to the presence of their slaves. They talk of them, of their condition, of their conduct, exactly as if they were incapable of hearing. I once saw a young lady, who, when seated at table between a male and a female, was induced by her modesty to intrude on the chair of her female neighbour to avoid the indelicacy of touching the elbow of *a man*. I once saw this very young lady lacing her stays with the most perfect composure before a negro footman. A Virginian gentleman told me that ever since he had married, he had been accustomed to have a negro girl sleep in the same chamber with himself and his wife. I asked for what purpose this nocturnal attendance was necessary? 'Good heaven!' was the reply, 'if I wanted a glass of water during the night, what would become of me?'

In relating all I know of America, I surely must not omit so important a feature as the cooking. There are sundry anomalies in the mode of serving even a first-rate table; but as these are altogether matters of custom, they by no means indicate either indifference or neglect in this important business; and whether castors are placed on the table or on the side-board; whether soup, fish, patties, and salad be eaten in orthodox order or not, signifies but little. I am hardly capable, I fear, of giving a very erudite critique on the subject; general observations therefore must suffice. The ordinary mode of living is abundant, but not delicate. They consume an extraordinary quantity of bacon. Ham and beef-steaks appear morning, noon and night. In eating, they mix things together with the strangest incongruity imaginable. I have seen eggs and oysters eaten together; the sempiternal ham with apple-sauce; beef-steak with stewed peaches; and salt fish with onions. The bread is everywhere excellent, but they rarely enjoy it themselves, as they insist upon eating horrible half-baked hot rolls both morning and evening. The butter is tolerable; but they have seldom such cream as every little dairy produces in England; in fact, the cows are very roughly kept, compared with ours. Common vegetables are abundant and very fine. I never saw sea-kale or cauliflowers, and either from the want of summer rain, or the want of care, the harvest of green vegetables is much sooner over than with us. They eat the Indian corn in a great variety of forms; sometimes it is dressed green, and eaten like peas; sometimes it is broken to pieces when dry, boiled plain, and brought to table like rice; this dish is called hominy. The flour of it is made into at least a dozen different sorts of cakes; but in my opinion all bad. This flour, mixed in the proportion of one-third with fine wheat, makes by far the best bread I have ever tasted.

I never saw turbot, salmon, or fresh cod; but the rock and shad are excellent. There is a great want of skill in the composition of sauces; not only with fish, but with everything. They use very few made dishes, and I never saw any that would be approved by our savants. They have an excellent wild duck, called the Canvass Back, which, if delicately served, would surpass the black cock; but the game is very inferior to ours; they have no hares, and I never saw a pheasant. They seldom indulge in second courses, with all their ingenious temptations to the eating a second dinner; but almost every table has its dessert, (invariably pronounced desart) which is placed on the table before the cloth is removed, and consists of pastry, preserved fruits, and creams. They are 'extravagantly fond', to use their own phrase, of puddings, pies, and all kinds of 'sweets', particularly the ladies; but are by no means such connoisseurs in soups and ragoûts as the gastronomes of Europe. Almost every one drinks water at table, and by a strange contradiction, in the country where hard drinking is more prevalent than in any other, there is less wine taken at dinner; ladies rarely exceed one glass, and the great majority of females never take any. In fact, the hard drinking, so universally acknowledged, does not take place at jovial dinners, but, to speak in plain English, in solitary dram-drinking. Coffee is not served immediately after dinner, but makes part of the serious matter of tea-drinking, which comes some hours later. Mixed dinner parties of ladies and gentlemen are very rare, and unless foreigners are present, but little conversation passes at table. It certainly does not, in my opinion, add to the well ordering a dinner table, to set gentlemen at one end of it, and the ladies at the other; but it is very rarely that you find it otherwise.

Their large evening parties are supremely dull; the men sometimes play cards by themselves, but if a lady plays, it must not be for money; no écarté, no chess; very little music, and that little lamentably bad. Among the blacks, I heard some good voices, singing in tune; but I scarcely ever heard a white American, male or female, go through an air without being out of tune before the end of it; nor did I ever meet any trace of science in the singing I heard in society. To eat inconceivable quantities of cake, ice, and pickled oysters – and to show half their revenue in silks and satins, seem to be the chief object they have in these parties.

The most agreeable meetings, I was assured by all young people, were those to which no married women are admitted; of the truth of this statement I have not the least doubt. These exclusive meetings occur frequently, and often last to a late hour; on these occasions, I believe, they generally dance. At regular balls, married ladies are admitted, but seldom take much part in the amusement. The refreshments are always profuse and costly, but taken in a most uncomfortable manner. I have known many private balls, where everything was on the most liberal scale of expense, where the gentlemen sat down to supper in one room, while the ladies took theirs, standing, in another.

What we call pic-nics are very rare, and when attempted, do not often succeed well. The two sexes can hardly mix for the greater part of a day without great restraint and ennui; it is quite contrary to their general habits; the favourite indulgences of the gentlemen (smoking cigars and drinking spirits), can neither be indulged in with decency, nor resigned with complacency.

The ladies have strange ways of adding to their charms. They powder themselves immoderately, face, neck, and arms, with pulverised starch; the effect is indescribably disagreeable by day-light, and not very favourable at any time. They are also unhappily partial to false hair, which they wear in surprising quantities; this is the more lamented, as they generally have very fine hair of their own. I suspect this fashion to arise from an indolent mode of making their toilet, and from accomplished ladies' maids not being very abundant; it is less trouble to append a bunch of waving curls here, there, and everywhere, than to keep their native tresses in perfect order.

Though the expense of the ladies' dress greatly exceeds, in proportion to their general style of living, that of the ladies of Europe, it is very far (excepting Philadelphia) from being in good taste. They do not consult the seasons in the colours or in the style of their costume; I have often shivered at seeing a young beauty picking her way through the snow with a pale rose-coloured bonnet, set on the very top of her head: I knew one young lady whose pretty little ear was actually frost-bitten from being thus exposed. They never wear muffs or boots, and appear extremely shocked at the sight of comfortable walking shoes and cotton stockings, even when they have to step to their sleighs over ice and snow. They walk in the middle of winter with their poor little toes pinched into a miniature slipper, incapable of excluding as much moisture as might bedew a primrose. I must say in their excuse, however, that they have, almost universally, extremely pretty feet. They do not walk well, nor, in fact, do they even appear to advantage when in movement. I know not why this should be, for they have an abundance of French dancing-masters among them but somehow or other it is the fact. I fancied I could often trace a mixture of affectation and of shyness in their little mincing unsteady step, and the ever-changing position of the hands. They do not dance well; perhaps I should rather say they do not look well when dancing; lovely as their faces are, they cannot, in a position that exhibits the whole person, atone for the want of *tournure*, and for the universal defect in the formation of the bust, which is rarely full, or gracefully formed.

At length, however, we found ourselves alive on board the boat which was to convey us down the Raraton River to New York.

We fully intended to have gone to bed, to heal our bones, on entering the steam-boat, but the sight of a table neatly spread determined us to go to dinner instead. Sin and shame would it have been, indeed, to have closed our eyes upon the scene which soon opened before us. I have never seen the bay of Naples, I can therefore make no comparison, but my imagination is incapable of conceiving anything of the kind more beautiful than the harbour of New York. Various and lovely are the objects which meet the eye on every side, but the naming them would only be to give a list of which, without conveying the faintest idea of the scene. I doubt if even the pencil of Turner could do it justice, bright and glorious as it rose upon us. We seemed to enter the harbour of New York upon waves of liquid gold, and we darted past the green isles which rise from its bosom, like guardian sentinels of the fair city, the setting sun stretched his horizontal beams farther and farther at each moment, as if to point out to us some new glory in the landscape.

New York, indeed, appeared to us, even when we saw it by a sober light, a lovely and a noble city. To us who had been so long travelling through half-cleared forests, and sojourning among an 'I'm-as-good-as you' population, it seemed, perhaps, more beautiful, more splendid, and more refined than it might have done, had we arrived there directly from London; but making every allowance for this, I must still declare that I think New York one of the finest cities I ever saw, and as much superior to every other in the Union (Philadelphia not excepted), as London to Liverpool, or Paris to Rouen. Its advantages of position are, perhaps unequalled anywhere. Situated on an island, which I think it will one day cover, it rises, like Venice, from the sea, and like that fairest of cities in the days of her glory, receives into its lap tribute of all the riches of the earth.

The southern point of Manhattan Island divides the waters of the harbour into the north and east rivers; on this point stands the city of New York, extending from river to river, and running northward to the extent of three or four miles. I think it covers nearly as much ground as Paris, but is much less thickly peopled. The extreme point is fortified towards the sea by a battery, and forms an admirable point of defence; but in these piping days of peace, it is converted into a public promenade, and one more beautiful, I should suppose, no city could boast. From hence commences the splendid Broadway, as the fine avenue is called, which runs through the whole city. This noble street may vie with any I ever saw, for its length and breadth, its handsome shops, neat awnings, excellent *trottoir*, and well-dressed pedestrians. It has not the crowded glitter of Bond Street equipages, nor the gorgeous fronted palaces of Regent Street; but it is magnificent in its extent, and ornamented by several handsome buildings, some of them surrounded by grass and trees. The Park, in which stands the noble cityhall, is a very fine area. I never found that the most graphic description of a city could give me any feeling of being there; and even if others have the power, I am very sure I have not, of setting churches and squares, and long drawn streets, before the mind's eye. I will not, therefore, attempt a detailed description of this great metropolis of the new world, but will only say that during the seven weeks we stayed there, we always found something new to see and to admire; and were it not so very far from all the old-world things which cling about the heart of an European, I should say that I never saw a city more desirable as a residence.

The dwelling houses of the higher classes are extremely handsome, and very richly furnished. Silk or satin furniture is as often, or oftener, seen than chintz; the mirrors are as handsome as in London; the chiffoniers, slabs, and marble tables as elegant; and in addition, they have all the pretty tasteful decoration of French porcelain, and ormolu in much greater abundance, because at a much cheaper rate. Every part of their houses is well carpeted, and the exterior finishing, such as steps, railings, and door-frames, are very superior. Almost every house has handsome green blinds on the outside; balconies are not very general, nor do the houses display, externally, so many flowers as those of Paris and London; but I saw many rooms decorated within, exactly like those of an European *petite maîtresse*. Little tables, looking and smelling like flower beds, portfolios, nick-nacks, bronzes, busts, cameos, and alabaster vases, illustrated copies of lady-like rhymes bound in silk, and, in short, all the pretty coxcomalities of the drawing-room scattered about with the same profuse and studied negligence as with us.

Captain Basil Hall (1827–8)

Captain Basil Hall, R.N. (1788–1844) was an inveterate traveller. He was one of the first Englishmen to visit Korea, on which he wrote a book. His Travels in America, *from which the following is taken, was a popular book in England, when it was published in 1829.*

At this stage of the journey, I find from my notes that the most striking circumstance in the American character, which had come under our notice, was the constant habit of praising themselves, their institutions, and their country, either in downright terms, or by some would-be indirect allusions, which were still more tormenting. I make use of this sharp-edged word, because it really was exceedingly teasing, when we were quite willing and ready to praise all that was good, and also to see everything, whether good or bad, in the fairest light, to be called upon so frequently to admit the justice of such exaggerations. It is considered, I believe, all over the world, as bad manners for a man to praise himself or his family. Now, to praise one's country appears, to say the least of it, in the next degree of bad taste.

It was curious to see with what vigilant adroitness the Americans availed themselves of every little circumstance to give effect to this self laudatory practice. I happened one day to mention to a lady, that I had been amused by observing how much more the drivers of the stages managed their horses by word of mouth, than by touch of the whip. Upon which she replied, 'Oh yes, sir, the circumstance you relate is very interesting, as it shows both intelligence in the men, and sagacity in the animals.' This was pretty well;

but I merely smiled and said nothing, being somewhat tickled by this amiable interchange of human wisdom and brute sagacity. The lady's suspicions however instantly took fire on seeing the expression of my countenance, and she answered my smile by saying, 'Nay, sir, do you not think the people in America, upon the whole, particularly intelligent?'

Thus it ever was, in great things as well as in small, on grave or ludicrous occasions; they were eternally on the defensive, and gave us to understand that they suspected us of a design to find fault, at times when nothing on earth was farther from our thoughts. Whenever any thing favourable happened, by chance or otherwise, to be stated with respect to England, there was straightway a fidget, till the said circumstance was counterbalanced by something equally good, or much better, in America. To such an extent was this jealous fever carried, that I hardly recollect above half-a-dozen occasions during the whole journey, when England was mentioned, that the slightest interest of an agreeable kind was manifested on the part of the audience; or that a brisk cross fire was not instantly opened on all hands, to depreciate what had been said; or which was still more frequent, to build up something finer, or taller, or larger, in America to overmatch it. It always occurred to me, that they paid themselves and their institutions the very poorest description of compliment by this course of proceeding; and it would be quite easy to show why.

Alexis Henri Charles Maurice Clevel, Comte de Tocqueville (1831)

Alexis Henri Charles Maurice Clevel, Comte de Tocqueville (1805–59), was of noble descent, but followed the legal profession. In 1831, as an assistant magistrate, he obtained from the French government a mission to examine prisons and penitentiaries in America, where he went with his friend, Gustave de Beaumont. The result of his trip was his Democracy in America *(1835), which established a European reputation, and was a great influence on liberal thinking in England throughout the nineteenth century.*

To Louise-Madeleine-Marguerite Le Pelletier de Rosanbo, Countess de Tocqueville

December 25, 1831
on the Mississippi

Finally, finally, my dear mama, the signal is given; and here we are descending the Mississippi with all the swiftness that steam and current together can give to a vessel. We were beginning to despair of ever getting out of the wilderness in which we were confined. If you wish to go to the trouble of examining the map, you will see that our position was not cheerful. Before us, the Mississippi half-frozen over and no boat for descending the river, above our heads, a Russian sky pure and ice cold. One could retrace one's steps, you say. That last recourse escaped us. During our stay in Memphis, the Tennessee had frozen over, so that wagons were no longer crossing it. So we found ourselves in the middle of a triangle formed by the Mississippi, the Tennessee, and by impenetrable wilderness to the south, as isolated as on a rock in the ocean, living in a little world made deliberately for us, without newspapers, without news of the rest of mankind, with the prospect of a long winter. We spent a week this way. The anxiety aside, those days, nonetheless, were spent in a quite pleasant way. We were living with good people, who did everything possible to make us feel comfortable. Within twenty paces from our house began the most admirable forest, even beneath the snow, the most sublime and most picturesque place in the world. We had guns, powder, and shot without limit. Some miles from the village lived an Indian nation (the Chickasaws); once on their lands, we always discovered some of them who asked no more than to hunt with us. Hunting and warfare are the sole occupations, and the sole pleasures, of the Indians. One would have to go too far to find real game in quantity. But we killed, on the other hand, a host of pretty birds unknown in France: this hardly raised us in the esteem of our allies, but had the merit of amusing us thoroughly. And so I killed red, blue, yellow birds, not to forget the most brilliant parrots I have ever seen. And so our time passed, lightly with regard to the present; but the future did not leave us calm. Finally, one fine day, a little smoke was seen on the Mississippi, on the limits of the horizon; the cloud drew near little by little, and there emerged from it, neither a giant nor a dwarf as in fairy tales, but a huge steamboat, coming from New Orleans, and which, after parading before us for a quarter of an hour, as if to leave us in uncertainty as to whether it would stop or continue on its route, after spouting like a whale, finally headed toward us, broke through the ice with its huge framework and was tied to the bank. The entire population of our universe made its way to the riverside, which, as you know, then formed one of the furthest frontiers of our empire. The whole city of Memphis was in a flutter; no bells were rung because there are no bells, but people cried out hurrah! and the newcomers alighted on the bank in the manner of Christopher Columbus.

We were not yet saved, however; the boat's destination was to go up the Mississippi to Louisville, and our purpose was to go to New Orleans. We happily had about fifteen companions in adversity who desired no more than we did to make their winter quarters in Memphis. So we made a general *push* on the captain. What was he going to do up the reaches of the Mississippi? He was certainly going to be stopped by the ice. The Tennessee, the Missouri, the Ohio were closed. There was not one of us who did not affirm having ascertained as much by his own eyes. He certainly would be stopped, damaged, smashed perhaps by the ice. As for us, we were speaking only in his interest. That goes without saying: in his own interest properly understood ... Love of our fellow man gave so much warmth to the speeches that at last we began to shake up our man. I am nevertheless of the conviction that he would not have turned in his tracks, without a fortunate event, to which we owe our not becoming citizens of Memphis. As we were thus debating on the bank, an infernal music resounded in the forest; it was a noise composed of drums, the neighing of horses, the barking of dogs. Finally a great troop of Indians, elderly people, women, children, baggage, all conducted by a European and heading toward the capital of our triangle. These Indians were the Chactas (or Choctaws) . . . you undoubtedly wish to know why these Indians had arrived there, and how they could be of use to us; patience, I beg you, now that I have time and paper, I want nothing to hurry me. You will thus know that the Americans of the United States, rational and unprejudiced people, moreover, great philanthropists, supposed, like the Spanish, that God had given them the new world and its inhabitants as complete property.

They have discovered, moreover, that, as it was proved (listen to this well) that a square mile could support ten times more civilized men than savage men, reason indicated that wherever civilized men could settle, it was necessary that the savages cede the place. You see what a fine thing logic is. Consequently, when the Indians begin to find themselves a little too near their brothers the whites, the President of the United States sends them a messenger, who represents to them that in their interest, properly understood, it would be good to draw back ever so little toward the West. The lands they have inhabited for centuries belong to them, undoubtedly: no one refuses them this incontestable right; but these lands, after all, are uncultivated wilderness, woods, swamps, truly poor property. On the other side of the Mississippi, by contrast, are magnificent regions, where the game has never been troubled by the noise of the pioneer's axe, where the Europeans will *never* reach. They are separated from it by more than a hundred leagues. Add to that gifts of inestimable price, ready to reward their compliance; casks of brandy, glass necklaces, pendant earrings and mirrors; all supported by the insinuation that if they refuse, people will perhaps see themselves as constrained to force them to move. What to do? The poor Indians take their old parents in their arms; the women load their children on their shoulders; the nation finally puts itself on the march, carrying with it its greatest riches. It abandons forever the soil on which, perhaps for a thousand years, its fathers have lived, in order to go settle in a wilderness where the whites will not leave them ten years in peace.

Do you observe the results of a high civilization? The Spanish, truly brutal, loose their dogs on the Indians as on ferocious beasts; they kill, burn, massacre, pillage the new world as one would a city taken by assault, without pity as without discrimination. But one cannot destroy everything; fury has a limit. The rest of the Indian population ultimately becomes mixed with its conquerors, takes on their mores, their religion; it reigns today in several provinces over those who formerly conquered it. The Americans of the United States, more humane, more moderate, more respectful of law and legality, never bloodthirsty, are profoundly more destructive, and it is impossible to doubt that within a hundred years there will remain in North America, not a single nation, not even a single man belonging to the most remarkable of the Indian races. . . .

But I no longer know at all where I am in my story. It had to do, I think, with the Choctaws. The Choctaws formed a powerful nation that inhabited the frontier of the state of Alabama and that of Georgia. After long negotiations, they finally managed, this year, to persuade them to leave their country and to emigrate to the right bank of the Mississippi. Six to seven thousand Indians have already crossed the great river; those who arrived in Memphis came there with the aim of following their compatriots. The agent of the American government who accompanied them and was charged with paying for their passage, knowing that a steamboat had just arrived, hurried down to the bank. The price he offered for transporting the Indians sixty leagues down river managed to settle the shaken mind of the captain; the signal to depart was given. The prow was turned toward the south and we cheerfully climbed the ladder down which descended the poor passengers who, instead of going to Louisville, saw themselves forced to await the thaw in Memphis. So goes the world.

But we had not yet left; there was still the matter of embarking our exiled tribe, its horses and its dogs. Here began a scene which was something truly lamentable. The Indians came forward toward the shore with a despondent air; they first made the horses go, several of which, little accustomed to the forms of civilized life, took fright and threw themselves into the Mississippi, from which they could be pulled out only with difficulty. Then came the men, who, following their usual custom, carried nothing except their weapons; then the women, carrying their children attached to their backs or wrapped up in the blankets that covered them; they were, moreover, overburdened with loads that contained all their riches. Finally the old people were led on. There was among them a woman of a hundred and ten years of age. I have never seen a more frightening figure. She was naked, with the exception of a blanket that allowed one to see, in a thousand places, the most emaciated body that one can imagine. She was escorted by two or three generations of grandchildren. To leave her country at that age to go seek her fate in a strange land, what misery! There was, amidst the old people, a young girl who had broken her arm a week before; for want of care, the arm was frostbitten below the fracture. She nonetheless had to follow the common march. When all had gone by, the dogs advanced toward the bank; but they refused to enter the boat and took to making frightful howls. Their masters had to lead them by force.

There was, in the whole of this spectacle, an air of ruin and destruction, something that savoured of a farewell that was final and with no return; no one could witness this without being sick at heart; the Indians were calm, but sombre and taciturn. There was one of them who knew English and of whom I asked why the Choctaws were leaving their country – 'To be free,' he answered – I could never draw anything else out of him. We will deposit them tomorrow in the solitudes of Arkansas. It has to be confessed that this is a singular accident, that made us come to Memphis to witness the expulsion, one might say the dissolution, of one of the most celebrated and most ancient American nations.

But this is enough on the savages. It is time to return to civilized people. Only one word more on the Mississippi, which, in truth, hardly merits being preoccupied with it. It is a great river, yellow, rolling rather gently in the deepest solitudes, in the midst of forests that it inundates in the spring and fertilizes with its mud. Not a hill is seen on the horizon, but woods, then woods, and still more woods: reeds, creepers; a perfect silence; no vestige of man, not even the smoke of an Indian camp.

Thomas Hamilton (1833)

Thomas Hamilton (1789–1842) was born in Glasgow; a city he abjured for Edinburgh when he retired from the army. He had one successful novel, Cyril Thornton, *behind him, and was on the staff of* Blackwood's *Magazine, when he visited the United States. Here are two extracts from his* Men and Manners in America, *a book which in title and tone seems very much an attempt to cash in on the scandalous success of Mrs Trollope.*

The poles are not more diametrically opposed, than a native of the States south of the Potomac, and a New Englander. They differ in everything of thought, feeling, and opinion. The latter is a man of regular and decorous habits, shrewd, intelligent, and persevering; phlegmatic in temperament, devoted to the pursuits of gain, and envious of those who are more successful than himself. The former – I speak of the opulent and educated – is distinguished by a high-mindedness, generosity, and hospitality, by no means predictable of his more eastern neighbours. He values money only for the enjoyments it can procure, is fond of gaiety, given to social pleasures, somewhat touchy and choleric, and as eager to avenge an insult as to show a kindness. To fight a duel in the New England States would, under almost any circumstances, be disgraceful. To refuse a challenge, to tolerate even an insinuation derogatory from personal honour, would be considered equally so in the South.

In point of manner, the Southern gentlemen are decidedly superior to all others of the Union. Being more dependent on social intercourse, they are at greater pains perhaps to render it agreeable. There is more spirit and vivacity about them, and far less of that prudent caution, which, however advantageous on the exchange, is by no means prepossessing at the dinner-table, or in the drawing-room. When at Washington, I was a good deal thrown into the society of members from the South, and left it armed, by their kindness, with a multitude of letters, of which I regret that my hurried progress did not permit me to avail myself. Many of them were men of much accomplishment, and I think it probable that Englishmen unconnected with business would generally prefer the society of gentlemen of this portion of the Union to any other which the country affords.

In regard to the passengers, truth compels me to say, that any thing so disgusting in human shape I had never seen. Their morals and their manners were alike detestable. A cold and callous selfishness, a disregard of all the decencies of society, were so apparent in feature, word, and action, that I found it impossible not to wish that their catalogue of sins had been enlarged by one more – hypocrisy. Of hypocrisy, however, they were not guilty. The conversation in the cabin was interlarded with the vilest blasphemy, not uttered in a state of mental excitement, but with a coolness and deliberation truly fiend-like. There was a Baptist clergyman on board, but his presence did not seem to operate as a restraint. The scene of drinking and gambling had no intermission. It continued day and night. The captain of the vessel, so far from discouraging either vice, was one of the most flagrant offenders in both. He was decidedly the greatest gambler on board; and was often so drunk as to be utterly incapable of taking command of the vessel. There were a few female passengers, but with their presence we were only honoured at meals. At all other times, they prudently confined themselves to their own cabins.

One circumstance may be mentioned, which is tolerably illustrative of the general habits of the people. In every steam-boat there is a *public* comb and hair-brush suspended by a string from the ceiling of the cabin. These utensils are used by the whole body of the passengers, and their condition, the pen of Swift could alone adequately describe. There is no tooth-brush, simply, I believe, because the article is entirely unknown to the American toilet. A common towel, however, passes from hand to hand, and suffices for the perfunctory ablutions of the whole party on board. It was often with great difficulty that I procured the exclusive usufruct of one, and it was evident that the demand was not only unusual but disagreeable.

One day at dinner, my English fellow-traveller, who had resided many years in the United States, enquired whether I observed an ivory hilt protruded from beneath the waistcoat of a gentleman opposite. I answered in the affirmative, and he then informed me that the whole population of the Southern and Western States are uniformly armed with daggers. On my expressing some doubt of this singular fact, he pointed to a number of sticks collected in one corner of the cabin, and offered a wager that every one of these contained either a dagger or a sword. I took the bet, and lost it: and my subsequent observations confirmed the truth of his assertion in every particular. Even in travelling in the State of New York, I afterwards observed that a great number of passengers in stage-coaches and canal boats were armed with this unmanly and assassin-like weapon.

Fanny Kemble (1834)

Fanny Kemble (1809–93) came from a famous acting family. She followed the family profession and went to America with her father's company in 1832. After a much-acclaimed tour she married, in 1834, Pierce Butler, the owner of a Georgia plantation. Slavery revolted her, and from the first there was an inherent friction in the marriage, which eventually bust up in 1846.

I had a most ludicrous visit this morning from the midwife of the estate – rather an important personage both to master and slave, as to her unassisted skill and science the ushering of all the young Negroes into their existence of bondage is entrusted. I heard a great deal of conversation in the dressing room adjoining mine while performing my own toilet, and presently Mr

Butler opened my room door, ushering in a dirty, fat, good-humored looking old Negress, saying: 'The midwife, Rose, wants to make your acquaintance.'

'Oh massa!' shrieked out the old creature, in a paroxysm of admiration, 'where you get this lilly alabaster baby!'

For a moment I looked round to see if she was speaking of my baby; but no, my dear, this superlative apostrophe was elicited by the fairness of *my skin*: so much for degrees of comparison. Now I suppose that if I chose to walk arm in arm with the dingiest mulatto through the streets of Philadelphia, nobody could possibly tell by my complexion that I was not his sister, so that the mere quality of mistress must have had a most miraculous effect upon my skin in the eyes of poor Rose. But this species of outrageous flattery is as usual with these people as with the low Irish, and arises from the ignorant desire, common to both the races, or propitiating at all costs the fellow creature who is to them as a Providence – or rather, I should say, a fate – for 'tis a heathen and no Christian relationship.

Soon after this visit, I was summoned into the wooden porch or piazza of the house, to see a poor woman who desired to speak to me. This was none other than the tall, emaciated-looking Negress who, on the day of our arrival, had embraced me and my nurse with such irresistible zeal. She appeared very ill today, and presently unfolded to me a most distressing history of bodily afflictions. She was the mother of a very large family, and complained to me that, what with child-bearing and hard field labour, her back was almost broken in two. With an almost savage vehemence of gesticulation, she suddenly tore up her scanty clothing, and exhibited a spectacle with which I was inconceivably shocked and sickened. The facts, without any of her corroborating statements, bore tolerable witness to the hardships of her existence. I promised to attend to her ailments and give her proper remedies; but these are natural results, inevitable and irremediable ones, of improper treatment of the female frame; and, though there may be alleviation, there cannot be any cure when once the beautiful and wonderful structure has been thus made the victim of ignorance, folly, and wickedness.

After the departure of this poor woman, I walked down the settlement toward the infirmary or hospital, calling in at one or two of the houses along the row. These cabins consist of one room, about twelve feet by fifteen, with a couple of closets smaller and closer than the staterooms of a ship, divided off from the main room and each other by rough wooden partitions, in which the inhabitants sleep. They have almost all of them a rude bedstead, with a gray moss of the forests for mattress, and filthy, pestilential-looking blankets for covering. Two families (sometimes eight and ten in number) reside in one of these huts, which are mere wooden frames pinned, as it were, to the earth by a brick chimney outside, whose enormous aperture within pours down a flood of air, but little counteracted by the miserable spark of fire, which hardly sends an attenuated thread of lingering smoke up its huge throat. A wide ditch runs immediately at the back of these dwellings, which is filled and emptied daily by the tide. Attached to each hovel is a small scrap of ground for a garden, which, however, is for the most part untended and uncultivated.

Such of these dwellings as I visited today were filthy and wretched in the extreme, and exhibited the most deplorable consequence of ignorance and an abject condition, the inability of the inhabitants to secure and improve even such pitiful comfort as might yet be achieved by them. Instead of the order, neatness, and ingenuity which might convert even these miserable hovels into tolerable residences, there was the careless, reckless, filthy indolence which even the brutes do not exhibit in their lairs and nests, and which seemed incapable of applying to the uses of existence the few miserable means of comfort yet within their reach. Firewood and shavings lay littered about the floors, while the half-naked children were cowering round two or three smouldering cinders. The moss with which the chinks and crannies of their ill-protecting dwellings might have been stuffed was trailing in dirt and dust about the ground, while the back door of the huts, opening upon a most unsightly ditch, was left wide open for the fowls and ducks, which they are allowed to raise, to travel in and out, increasing the filth of the cabin by what they brought and left in every direction.

In the midst of the floor, or squatting round the cold hearth, would be four or five little children from four to ten years old, the latter all with babies in their arms, the care of the infants being taken from the mothers (who are driven afield as soon as they recover from child labour), and devolved upon these poor little nurses, as they are called, whose business it is to watch the infant, and carry it to its mother whenever it may require nourishment. To these hardy human little beings I addressed my remonstrances about the filth, cold, and unnecessary wretchedness of their room, bidding the older boys and girls kindle up the fire, sweep the floor, and expel the poultry. For a long time my very words seemed unintelligible to them, till, when I began to sweep and make up the fire, etc., they first fell to laughing, and then imitating me. The incrustations of dirt on their hands, feet, and faces were my next object of attack, and the stupid Negro practice (by-the-by, but a short time since nearly universal in enlightened Europe) of keeping the babies with their feet bare, and their heads, already well capped by nature with their woolly hair, wrapped in half a dozen hot, filthy coverings.

Thus I travelled down the 'street', in every dwelling endeavouring to awaken a new perception, that of cleanliness, sighing, as I went, over the futility of my own exertions, for how can slaves be improved? Nathless, thought I, let what can be done; for it may be that, the two being incompatible, improvement may yet expel slavery; and so it might, and surely would, if, instead of beginning at the end, I could but begin at the beginning of my task. If the mind and soul were awakened, instead of mere physical good attempted, the physical good would result, and the great curse vanish away; but my hands and feet are tied fast, and this corner of the work is all that I may do. Yet it cannot be but, from my words and actions, some revelations should reach these poor people; and going in and out among them perpetually, I shall teach, and they learn involuntarily a thousand things of deepest import. They must learn, and who can tell the fruit of that knowledge alone, that there are beings in the world, even with skins of a different colour from their own, who have sympathy for their misfortunes, love for their virtues, and respect for their common nature – but oh! my heart is full almost to bursting as I walk among these most poor creatures.

The infirmary is a large two-storey building, terminating the broad orange-planted space between the two rows of houses which form the first settlement; it is built of whitewashed wood, and contains four large-sized rooms. But how shall I describe to you the spectacle which was presented to me on entering the first of these? But half the casements, of which there were six, were glazed, and these were obscured with dirt, almost as much as the other windowless ones were darkened by the dingy shutters, which the shivering inmates had fastened to in order to protect themselves from the cold. In the enormous chimney glimmered the powerless embers of a few sticks of wood, round which, however, as many of the sick women as could approach were cowering, some on wooden settles, most of them on the ground, excluding those who were too ill to rise; and these last poor wretches lay prostrate on the floor, without bed, mattress, or pillow, buried in tattered and filthy blankets, which, huddled round them as they lay strewed about, left hardly space to move upon the floor. And here, in their hour of sickness and suffering, lay those whose health and strength are spent in unrequited labour for us – those who, perhaps even yesterday, were being urged on to their unpaid task – those whose husbands, fathers, brothers, and sons were even at that hour sweating over the earth, whose produce was to buy for us all the luxuries which health can revel in, all the comforts which can alleviate sickness. I stood in the midst of them, perfectly unable to speak, the tears pouring from my eyes at this sad spectacle of their misery, myself and my emotion alike strange and incomprehensible to them. Here lay women expecting every hour the terrors and agonies of childbirth, others who had just brought their doomed offspring into the world, others who were groaning over the anguish and bitter disappointment of miscarriages – here lay some burning with fever, others chilled with cold and aching with rheumatism, upon the hard cold ground, the draughts and dampness of the atmosphere increasing their sufferings, and dirt, noise, and stench, and every aggravation of which sickness is capable, combined in their condition – here they lay like brute beasts, absorbed in physical suffering; unvisited by any of those Divine influences which may ennoble the dispensations of pain and illness, forsaken, as it seemed to me, of all good; and yet, O God, Thou surely hadst not forsaken them! Now pray take notice that this is the hospital of an estate where the owners are supposed to be humane, the overseer efficient and kind, and the Negroes remarkedly well cared for and comfortable.

Richard Cobden (1835)

From Cobden's American Diary. *The English politician Richard Cobden (1804–65) made his fortune as a calico-merchant and factory-owner. However, he had little formal education, and decided to remedy this defect by a course of study and travel. His first trip to the United States was from June to August 1835.*

July 11
   At breakfast see the only truly handsome girl I have met in America – Enquiring of Mr Cozzens the landlord of the Hotel I find this lovely creature

to be the daughter of an *English* gentleman named Oakley – after breakfast converse with Mr Cozzens – he tells me of Captain Hamilton whilst at his house transgressed the rules of the hotel by smoking in the parlour for which he was called upon to reprove the Author of Cyril Thornton & to talk of ejecting him go to see the Cadets on parade – am stuck with the more than ever lean & tall figures of the young men – in England such a number of thin subjects would excite ridicule – Call on Mr Leslie to present a letter from Mr Burtsall house in good taste with a very few well selected proof plates hanging on the walls – Mr Leslie a mild & gentlemanly man with a sweet expression of eye and an intellectual smile – find him a gentleman – we go to the point of view called Fort Putnam – a glorious & inspiring sight – below is Westpoint upon a peninsula formed by a bend of the river whose winding stream above & below is seen pursuing its tortuous course till it abruptly disappears behind one of the numerous heights that here constitute the scenery called the highlands – the gradually sloping banks covered with forest trees – with here & there a little glen or valley breaking away from between these mountains & presenting patches of ripe corn or shining green pasture – the innumerable little sailing boats with their white canvas reflecting the morning sunbeams – the lively looking snowy cottages that are sprinkled over the landscape – all these charms shut in by a near horizon of mountains that formed a rolling graceful outline to the scene make the view from Fort Putnam one of the loveliest perhaps though not the grandest in America

Proceed by the Steam Boat at 11 o'clock for Catskill – the high banks continue to offer an ever varying scene – what exhilaration there is in the sight of mountains & vallies rocks & wild forests! enormous cabin – two tables each 110 feet long at dinner - dexterity of the crew in lowering & hauling in the boat with passengers at the landing places

Land at Catskill village & go by a coach to the mountain house twelve miles which takes four hours & a half – coach the 'Rip Van-Winkle' – driver had not read Irving's tale half way house – a little hotel & a good church where are the inhabitants? for we saw the Mountain house in the cleft of the undulating ridge of the range of hills above – the road all the way runs through an uncultivated forest no break in the foliage even to afford a glimpse of the scene below – met a man with oxen who enquires of our driver for some rattlesnake oil to cure the rheumatism with - on reaching the mountain house a splendid prospect is opened out upon a vast extent of plain country stretching in all directions as far as the eye can reach whilst in the midst is seen the Hudson winding its clear current in a stream of light upon the bosom of the dark landscape – Large Hotel with 100 beds – billiard room – handsomely furnished & yet in a position not tenantable for one half of the year!

Harriet Martineau (1836)

The English writer Harriet Martineau (1802–76) paid a long visit to the United States between 1834 and 1837. Her strong support of the Abolitionist party, then a small and unpopular force in American politics, gave great offence. However, she seems to have been a fearless traveller, except for this one occasion.

To a certain extent, my travels in America answered my purposes of self-discipline in undertaking them. Fearing that I was growing too much accustomed to luxury, and to an exclusive regularity in the modes of living, I desired to 'rough it' for a considerable time. The same purpose would have been answered as well, perhaps, and certainly more according to my inclination, if I could have been quiet, instead of travelling, after my great task was done; – if I could have had repose of body and peace of mind, in freedom from all care. This was impossible; and the next best thing was such a voyage and journey as I took. America was the right country too, (apart from the peculiar agitation it happened to be in when I arrived); the national boast being a perfectly true one, – that a woman may travel alone from Maine to Georgia without dread of any kind of injury. For two ladies who feared nothing, there was certainly nothing to fear. We had to 'rough it' sometimes, as everybody must in so new and thinly peopled a country; but we always felt ourselves safe from ill usage of any kind. One night, at New Orleans, we certainly did feel as much alarmed as could well be; but that was nobody's fault. From my childhood up, I believe I have never felt so desolating a sense of fear as for a few moments on that occasion, – which was simply this.

A cousin of mine whom I saw at Mobile had a house at New Orleans, inhabited by himself or his partner, as they happened to be there or at Mobile. My cousin kindly offered us the use of this house during our stay saying that we might thus obtain some hours of coolness and quiet in the morning which would be unattainable in a boarding-house, or in the capacity of guests. The 'people,' that is, the slaves, received orders to make us comfortable, and the partner saw that all orders were obeyed. We arrived at about ten in the forenoon, – exceedingly tired, – not only by long travel in the southern forests, but especially by the voyage of the preceding night, – in hot, thundery weather, a rough sea, and in a steamboat which so swarmed with cockroaches that we could not bring ourselves to lie down. – It was a day of considerable excitement. We found a great heap of letters from home; we saw many friends in the course of the day; and at night I wrote letters so late that my companion, for once, went to bed before me. We had four rooms forming a square, or nearly: – two sitting-rooms, front and back; and two bedrooms opening out of them, and also reaching, like them, from the landing at the top of the stairs to the street front. On account of the heat, we decided to put all our luggage (which was of considerable bulk) into one room, and sleep in the other. The beds were very large, and as hard as the floor, – as they should be in such a climate. Mosquito nets hung from the top; and the room was plentifully provided with sponging baths and water. – Miss J. was in bed before I finished my writing: and I therefore did not call her when I found that the French window opening on the balcony could not be shut, as the spring was broken. Anyone could reach the balcony from the street easily enough; and here was an entrance which could not be barred! I set the heaviest chair against it, with the heaviest things piled on it that I could lay my hands on. I need not explain that New Orleans is, of all cities in the civilised world, the most renowned for night robbery and murder. The reputation is deserved; or was at that time: and we have been in the way of hearing some very painful and alarming stories from some of our friends who spoke from their own experience. Miss. J. was awake when I was about to step into bed, and thoughtlessly put out the candle. I observed on my folly in doing this, and on our having forgotten to inquire where the slave-quarter was. Here we were, alone in the middle of New Orleans, with no light, no bell, no servants within reach if we had had one, and no idea where the slaves were to be found! We could only hope that nothing would happen: but I took my trumpet with me within the mosquito curtain, and laid it within reach of Miss J.'s hand, in case of her having to tell me any news. I was asleep in a trice. Not so Miss J.

She gently awoke me after what seemed to her a very long time; and, put the cup of my tube close to her mouth, whispered slowly, so that I could hear her, 'There is somebody or something walking about the room.' I whispered that we could do nothing: and that, in our helpless state, the safest way was to go to sleep. 'But I can't,' replied she. I cannot describe how sorry I was for her, sitting up listening to fearful sounds that I could not hear. I earnestly desired to help her: but there was nothing that I could do. To sit up, unable to hear anything, and thus losing nerve every minute, was the worst thing of all for us both. I told her to rouse me again if she had the slightest wish: but that I really advised her going to sleep, as I meant to do. She again said she could not. I did; and it must be remembered how remarkably tired I was. After another space, Miss J. woke me again, and in the same cautious manner said, 'It is a man without shoes; and he is just at your side of the bed. We each said the same thing as before; and again I went to sleep. Once more she woke me; and this time she spoke with a little less caution. She said he had been walking about all that time, – for hours. He had pushed against the furniture, and especially the washstand, and seemed to be washing his hands: and now he had gone out at the door nearest the stairs. What did I think of her fastening the door? I feared she would let the mosquitoes in if she got up; and there were two other doors to the room; so I did not think we should gain much. She was better satisfied to try; and she drove a heavy trunk against the door, returned without letting in any mosquitoes, and at last obtained some sleep. In the morning we started up to see what we had lost. My watch was safe on the table. My rings were not there; but we soon spied them rolled off to the corners of the room. The water from the baths was spilled; and our clothes were on the floor; but we missed nothing.

We agreed to say and do nothing ungracious to the servants, and to make no complaint; but to keep on the watch for an explanation of the mystery; and, if evening came without any light being thrown on the matter, to consult our friends the Porters about spending another night in that room. – At breakfast, the slave women, who had been to market, and got us some young green peas and other good things, hung over our chairs, and were ready to gossip, as usual. I could make nothing of their jabber; and Miss J. not much: but she persevered on this occasion; and, before breakfast was over, she gave me a nod which showed me that our case was explained. She had been playing with a little black dog the while: and she told me at length that this little black dog belonged to the personage at the back of my chair; and that the big dog, chained up in the yard, belonged to my cousin; and that the big dog was the one which was unchained the last thing at night, and allowed the range of the premises, to deal with the rats, which abounded in that house as in every other in New Orleans. The city being built in a swamp, innumerable rats are a necessary consequence. The intruder was regarded very differently the next night; and we had no more alarms. I own that the moments when my companion told me that a man without shoes was walking about the room, and, when, again, she heard him close by my bedside, were those of very painful fear. I have felt nothing like it, on any other occasion, since I grew up.

George Combe (1838–40)

George Combe (1788–1858) was a practising phrenologist until 1837. After his retirement he made a 'Phrenological Visit' to the United States. He published Notes on the United States *in 1841, including this perception of the Image of Liberty.*

In your vast unoccupied territory, a fruitful soil presents its attractions to those individuals in whom Acquisitiveness and Ambition predominate. . . . In your political institutions, Self-esteem and Love of Approbation find unlimited scope. . . . Some persons appear to conceive liberty to consist in the privilege of unlimited exercise of the animal propensities. The head of Liberty stamped on the earlier medals, commemorative of the French Revolution, is the very personification of this idea. She is a female figure with a villainously small, low, and retreating forehead, deficient moral organs, and ample development of the base and posterior regions of the brain, devoted to the propensities. Her hair is flying back in loose disorder, and her countenance expresses vivacity and passion, but neither morality nor wisdom. The same figure appears on the earlier coins of the United States. Liberty as I should draw her, would possess large moral and intellectual organs, with moderate propensities. I should arrange her hair in simple elegance, and imprint serene enjoyment, benignity, and wisdom on her brow. She should represent moral liberty, or the unlimited freedom to accomplish all that is good, and the absence of every desire to do evil. Such alone is the liberty after which you should aspire.

Captain Frederick Marryat (1839)

Captain Frederick Marryat, R.N. (1792–1848) is best known for his series of novels on the sea of naval life during the Napoleonic period. He toured the United States and Canada in 1837–9. On his return he published the diary he had kept. His book did not go down well in America, and an effigy of him was burned in Detroit.

They object to everything nude in statuary. When I was at the house of Governor Everett, at Boston, I observed a fine cast of the Apollo Belvedere, but, in compliance with general opinion, it was hung with drapery, although Governor Everett himself is a gentleman of refined mind and high classical attainments, and quite above such ridiculous sensitiveness. In language it is the same thing: there are certain words which are never used in America, but an absurd substitute is employed. I cannot particularize them after this preface, lest I should be accused of indelicacy myself. I may, however, state one little circumstance, which will fully prove the correctness of what I say.

When at Niagara Falls, I was escorting a young lady with whom I was on friendly terms. She had been standing on a piece of rock, the better to view the scene, when she slipped down, and evidently hurt by the fall; she had in fact grazed her shin. As she limped a little in walking home, I said, 'Did you hurt your leg much?' She turned from me, evidently much shocked, or much offended; and not being aware that I had committed any very heinous offence, I begged to know what was the reason of her displeasure. After some hesitation, she said that as she knew me well, she would tell me that the word *leg* was never mentioned before ladies. I apologized for my want of refinement, which was attributable to my having been accustomed only to *English* society, and added, that as such articles must occasionally be referred to, even in the most polite circles of America, perhaps she would inform me by what name I might mention without shocking the company. Her reply was, that the word *limb* was used; 'Nay,' continued she, 'I am not so particular as some people are, for I know those who always say limb of a table, or limb of a piano-forte.'

There the conversation dropped; but a few months afterwards I was obliged to acknowledge that the young lady was correct when she asserted that some people were more particular than even she was.

I was requested by a lady to escort her to a seminary for young ladies, and on being ushered into the reception-room, conceive my astonishment at beholding a square piano-forte with four *limbs*. However, that the ladies who visited their daughters, might feel in its full force the extreme delicacy of the mistress of the establishment, and her care to preserve in their utmost

purity the ideas of the young ladies under her charge, she had dressed all
these four limbs in modest little trousers, with frills at the bottom of them!

James Silk Buckingham (1839)

*The English journalist, James Silk Buckingham (1786–1855) was the author
of several travel books, including* The Slaves States of America in 1839, *from
which this extract is taken. He describes the American physiognomy.*

The men are generally tall and slender in figure, more frequently above
five feet ten inches than below it, and rarely exceeding three feet in circum-
ference about the waist; the arms are long, the legs small, the chest narrow,
the form not so frequently erect, as slightly stooping, rising from carelessness
of gait and hurry in walking; the head is small, but the features are long,
the complexion pale, the eyes small and dark, the hair straight, the cheeks
generally smooth or without whiskers or beard, and the whole expression
and deportment is grave and serious. The women of America are not so
tall in stature as the women of Europe generally, being often below five feet
four inches than above it; of slender figure, without the fullness of rotundity
and flowing lines of the Medicean statue, imperfect development of bust,
small hands and feet, small and pretty features, pale complexions, dark eyes,
a mincing gait, delicate health, and a grave rather than a gay or animated
expression. If the men seem to be marked by a general uniformity of
standard in personal appearance, the women are still more alike.

Thomas Colley Grattan (1840s)

*Irish-born Thomas Colley Grattan (1792–1864) was appointed British Consul
at Massachusetts in 1839. At the period the controversy between the United
States and the British provinces in Canada over the north-eastern boundary was
the absorbing topic. Grattan later assisted in the negotiations which settled the
dispute. This extract from* Civilized America, *which he published in 1859,
concerns an issue, however, which many find irksome to this day.*

The method of heating many of the best houses is a terrible grievance to
persons not accustomed to it, and a fatal misfortune to those who are.
Casual visitors are nearly suffocated, and constant occupiers killed. An
enormous furnace in the cellar sends up, day and night, streams of hot air,
through apertures and pipes, to every room in the house. No spot is free
from it, from the dining-parlour to the dressing-closet. It meets you the

moment the street-door is opened to let you in, and it rushes after you when you emerge again, half-stewed and parboiled, into the wholesome air. The self-victimized citizens, who have a preposterous affection for this atmosphere, undoubtedly shorten their lives by it. Several elderly gentlemen of my acquaintance, suddenly cut off, would assuredly have had a verdict of 'died of a furnace' pronounced on their cases, had a coroner been called, and had a jury decided on fair evidence. But no citizen is inclined to condemn the instrument which everyone in 'high life' patronizes, and which is congenial to the frigid temperament of all classes. Half the sickness in the Atlantic cities, north of Washington, is to be attributed to the extreme heat of the houses, without which the cold external air would do good instead of harm. Large fires of anthracite coal and close stoves are common, in houses of moderate pretensions, where the cruel luxury of a furnace is not found. And independent of the mischief done to the health of both sexes and all ages, there is something inexpressibly cheerless, whether it be in Germany, Holland, or the United States, in the look of a house heated by a furnace, particularly if the rooms have grates unfilled and useless.

Charles Dickens (1842)

Annoyed by the pirating of his books by American publishers, which involved him in considerable financial losses, Dickens's first lecture-tour of the United States concerned the necessity of an international copyright law. The Americans he met were not inclined to apologize for the current anomaly. In his American Notes *he fiercely criticized many aspects of their customs and manners, though the following extract is favourable in tone.*

When I landed in America, I could not help being strongly impressed by the contrast their Custom-house presented, and the attention, politeness and good humour with which its officers discharged their duty.

Boston
The city is a beautiful one, and cannot fail, I should imagine, to impress all strangers very favourably. The private dwelling-houses are, for the most part, large and elegant; the shops extremely good; and the public buildings handsome. The State House is built upon the summit of a hill, which rises gradually at first, and afterwards by a steep ascent, almost from the water's edge. In front is a green enclosure, called the Common. The site is beautiful: and from the top there is a charming panoramic view of the whole town and neighbourhood. In addition to a variety of commodious offices, it contains two handsome chambers; in one the House of Representatives of the State hold their meetings: in the other, the Senate. Such proceedings as I saw here, were conducted with perfect gravity and decorum; and were certainly calculated to inspire attention and respect.

There is no doubt that much of the intellectual refinement and superiority of Boston is referable to the quiet influence of the University of Cambridge, which is within three or four miles of the city. The resident professors at that university are gentlemen of learning and varied attainments; and are, without one exception that I can call to mind, men who would shed a grace upon, and do honour to, any society in the civilised world.

... Whatever the defects of American universities may be, they disseminate no prejudices; rear no bigots; dig up the buried ashes of no old superstitions; never interpose between the people and their improvement; exclude no man because of his religious opinions; above all, in their whole course of study and instruction, recognise a world, and a broad one too, lying beyond the college walls.

It was a source of inexpressible pleasure to me to observe the almost imperceptible, but not less certain effect, wrought by this institution among the small community of Boston, and to note at every turn the humanising tastes and desires it has engendered; the affectionate friendships to which it has given rise; the amount of vanity and prejudice it has dispelled. The golden calf they worship at Boston is a pigmy compared with the giant effigies set up in other parts of that vast counting-house which lies beyond the Atlantic; and the almighty dollar sinks into something comparatively insignificant, amidst a whole Pantheon of better gods.

Above all, I sincerely believe that the public institutions and charities of this capital of Massachusetts are as nearly perfect, as the most considerate wisdom, benevolence, and humanity, can make them. I never in my life was more affected by the contemplation of happines, under circumstances of privation and bereavement, than in my visits to these establishments ...

At South Boston, as it is called, in a situation excellently adapted for the purpose, several charitable institutions are clustered together. One of these is the State Hospital for the insane; admirably conducted on those enlightened principles of conciliation and kindness, which twenty years ago would have been worse than heretical, and which have been acted upon with so much success in our own Pauper Asylum at Hanwell. 'Evince a desire to show some confidence, and repose some trust, even in mad people,' said the resident physician, as we walked along the galleries, his patients flocking round us unrestrained. Of those who deny or doubt the wisdom of this maxim after witnessing its effects, if there be such people still alive, I can only say that I hope I may never be summoned as a Juryman on a Commission of Lunacy whereof they are the subjects; for I should certainly find them out of their senses, on such evidence alone.

Each ward in this institution is shaped like a long gallery or hall, with the dormitories of the patients opening from it on either hand. Here they work, read, play at skittles, and other games; and when the weather does not admit of their taking exercise out of doors, pass the day together. In one of these rooms, seated, calmly, and quite as a matter of course, among a throng of mad-women, black and white, were the physician's wife and another lady, with a couple of children. These ladies were graceful and handsome; and it was not difficult to perceive at a glance that even their presence there, had a highly beneficial influence on the patients who were grouped about them ...

Every patient in this asylum sits down to dinner every day with a knife and fork; and in the midst of them sits the resident physician ... At every meal, moral influence alone restrains the more violent among them from cutting the throats of the rest; but the effect of that influence is reduced to an absolute certainty, and is found, even as a means of restraint, to say nothing of it as a means of cure, a hundred times more efficacious than all the strait-waistcoats, fetters, and handcuffs, that ignorance, prejudice, and cruelty have manufactured since the creation of the world ...

Once a week they have a ball, in which the Doctor and his family, with all the nurses and attendants, take an active part. Dances and marches are performed alternately, to the enlivening strains of a piano; and now and then some gentleman or lady (whose proficiency has been previously ascertained) obliges the company with a song. ...

America, as a new and not over-populated country, has in all her prisons, the one great advantage, of being enabled to find useful and profitable work for the inmates; whereas, with us, the prejudice against prison labour is naturally very strong, and almost insurmountable, when honest men who have not offended against the laws are frequently doomed to seek employment in vain. Even in the United States, the principle of bringing convict labour and free labour into a competition which must obviously be to the disadvantage of the latter, has already found many opponents, whose number is not likely to diminish with access of years.

In an American state prison or house of correction, I found it difficult at first to persuade myself that I was really in a jail: a place of ignominious punishment and endurance. And to this hour I very much question whether the humane boast that it is not like one has its root in the true wisdom or philosophy of the matter.

The House of Correction which has led to these remarks, is not walled, like other prisons, but is palisaded round about with tall rough stakes, something after the manner of an enclosure for keeping elephants in, as we see it represented in Eastern prints and pictures. The prisoners wear a parti-coloured dress; and those who are sentenced to hard labour, work at nail-making, or stone-cutting. When I was there, the latter class of labourers were employed upon the stone for a new custom-house in course of erection at Boston. They appeared to shape it skilfully and with expedition, though there were very few among them (if any) who had not acquired the art within the prison gates. ...

Such are the Institutions at South Boston! In all of them, the unfortunate or degenerate citizens of the State are carefully instructed in their duties both to God and man; are surrounded by all reasonable means of comfort and happiness that their condition will admit of; are appealed to, as members of the great human family, however afflicted, indigent, or fallen; are ruled by the strong Heart, and not by the strong (though immeasurably weaker) Hand. ... I mean to take them for a model, and to content myself with saying of others we may come to, whose designs and purpose are the same, that in this or that respect they practically fail, or differ ...

The tone of society in Boston is one of perfect politeness, courtesy, and good breeding. The ladies are unquestionably very beautiful – in face: but there I am compelled to stop. Their education is much as with us; neither better nor worse. I had heard some very marvellous stories in this respect; but not believing them, was not disappointed. Blue ladies there are, in

Boston; but like philosophers of that colour and sex in most other latitudes, they rather desire to be thought superior than to be so. Evangelical ladies there are, likewise, whose attachment to the forms to religion, and horror of theatrical entertainments, are most exemplary. Ladies who have a passion for attending lectures are to be found among all classes and all conditions. In the kind of provincial life which prevails in cities such as this, the Pulpit has great influence. The peculiar province of the Pulpit in New England (always excepting the Unitarian Ministry) would appear to be the denouncement of all innocent and rational amusements. The church, the chapel, and the lecture-room, are the only means of the excitement excepted; and to the church, the chapel, and the lecture-room, the ladies resort in crowds.

Wherever religion is resorted to, as a strong drink, and as an escape from the dull monotonous round of home, those of its ministers who pepper the highest will be the surest to please. They who strew the Eternal Path with the greatest amount of brimstone, and who most ruthlessly tread down the flowers and leaves that grow by the wayside, will be voted the most righteous; and they who enlarge with the greatest pertinacity on the difficulty of getting into heaven, will be considered by all true believers certain of going there: though it would be hard to say by what process of reasoning this conclusion is arrived at. It is so at home, and it is so abroad. With regard to the other means of excitement, the Lecture, it has at least the merit of being always new. One lecture treads so quickly on the heels of another, that none are remembered; and the course of this month may be safely repeated next, with its charm of novelty unbroken, and its interest unabated. . . . Such of its [Boston's] social customs as I have not mentioned. . . . may be told in a very few words.

The usual dinner-hour is two o'clock. A dinner party takes place at five; and at an evening party, they seldom sup later than eleven; so that it goes hard but one gets home, even from a rout, by midnight. I never could find out any difference between a party at Boston and a party in London, saving that at the former place all assemblies are held at more rational hours; that the conversation may possibly be a little louder and more cheerful; and a guest is usually expected to ascend to the very top of the house and take his cloak off; that he is certain to see, at every dinner, an unusual amount of poultry on the table; and at every supper, at least two mighty bowls of hot stewed oysters, in any one of which a half-grown Duke of Clarence might be smothered easily.

There are two theatres in Boston, of good size and construction, but sadly in want of patronage. The few ladies who resort to them, sit, as of right, in the front rows of the boxes.

The bar is a large room with a stone floor, and there people stand and smoke, and lounge about, all the evening: dropping in and out as the humour takes them. There too the stranger is initiated into the mysteries of Gin-sling, Cock-tail, Sangaree, Mint Julep, Sherrycobbler, Timber Doodle, and other rare drinks. The house is full of boarders, both married and single, many of whom sleep upon the premises, and contract by the week for their board and lodging: the charge for which diminishes as they go nearer the sky to roost. A public table is laid in a very handsome hall for breakfast, and for dinner, and for supper. The party sitting down together to these meals will vary in number from one or two hundred:

sometimes more. The advent of each of these epochs in the day is proclaimed by an awful gong, which shakes the very window-frames as it
reverberates through the house, and horribly disturbs nervous foreigners.
There is an ordinary for ladies, and an ordinary for gentlemen.

In our private room the cloth could not, for any earthly consideration,
have been laid for dinner without a huge glass dish of cranberries in the
middle of the table; and breakfast would have been no breakfast unless the
principal dish were a deformed beef-steak with a great flat bone in the
centre, swimming in hot butter, and sprinkled with the very blackest of all
possible pepper. Our bedroom was spacious and airy, but (like every
bedroom on this side of the Atlantic) very bare of furniture, having no
curtains to the French bedstead or to the window. It had one unusual
luxury, however, in the shape of a wardrobe of painted wood, something
smaller than an English watch-box; or if this comparison should be insuf-
ficient to convey a just idea of its dimensions, they may be estimated from
the fact of my having lived for fourteen days and nights in the firm belief
that it was a shower-bath.

Frank Marryat (1850)

*Frank Marryat was the youngest of four sons of Captain Frederick Marryat, and
the only one to survive him, though not by long. According to the Dictionary of
National Biography, Frank 'died of decline in his twenty-ninth year' in 1855.
He sounds a most intriguing young man. This description of the San Francisco
fire of 1850 is taken from a book called* Recollections of a Burnt Journal, *which was published in the year of his death.*

We have arrived at the moment of the great June Fire of 1850, and San
Francisco is again in ashes! ... although four hundred houses have been
destroyed, they were but of wood or thin sheet iron, and the 'devouring
element' has made a clean sweep of everything, except a few brick chimneys
and iron pots. Everybody seems to be in good humour ... so soon as the
embers cool, the work of rebuilding will commence.

I found it amusing the next day to walk over the ground and observe the
effects of the intense heat on the articles which were strewed around. Gun-
barrels were twisted and knotted like snakes; there were tons of nails welded
together by the heat, standing in the shape of the kegs which had contained
them; small lakes of molten glass of all the colours of the rainbow; tools of
all descriptions from which the wood-work had disappeared, and pitch-pots
filled with melted lead and glass. Here was an iron house that had collapsed
with the heat, and even an iron fire-proof safe that had burst under the
same influence; spoons, knives, forks and crockery were melted up together
in heaps; crucibles even had cracked; preserved meats had been unable to
stand this second cooking, and had exploded in every direction. The loss
was very great by this fire, as the houses destroyed had been for the most

part filled with merchandise; but there was little time wasted in lamentation, the energy of the people showed itself at once in action, and in forty-eight hours after the fire the whole district resounded to the din of busy workmen.

William Makepeace Thackeray (1852)

Thackeray was forty-one when he embarked on a lecture-tour of the United States on the subject of the English Humourists of the Eighteenth Century.

New York, The Clarendon Hotel

23 December 1852

My Dear Lady:

I send you a little line and shake your hand across the water. God bless you and yours. . . .

The passage is nothing, now it is over; I am rather ashamed of gloom and disquietude about such a trifling journey. I have made scores of new acquaintances and lighted on my legs as usual. I didn't expect to like people as I do, but am agreeably disappointed and find many most pleasant companions, natural and good; natural and well read and well bred too; and I suppose am none the worse pleased because everybody has read all my books and praises my lectures; (I preach in a Unitarian Church, and the parson comes to hear me. His name is Mr Bellows, it isn't a pretty name), and there are 2000 people nearly who come, and the lectures are so well liked that it is probable I shall do them over again. So really there is a chance of making a pretty little sum of money for old age, imbecility, and those young ladies afterwards.

Had Lady Ashburton told you of the moving tables? Try, six or seven of you, a wooden table without brass castors; sit around it, lay your hands flat on it, not touching each other, and in half an hour or so perhaps it will begin to turn round and round. It is the most wonderful thing, but I have tried twice in vain since I saw it and did it at Mr Bancroft's. I have not been into fashionable society yet, what they call the upper ten thousand here, but have met very likeable of the lower sort. On Sunday I went into the country, and there was a great rosy jolly family of sixteen or eighteen people, round a great tea-table; and the lady of the house told me to make myself at home – remarking my bashfulness, you know – and said, with a jolly face, and twinkling of her little eyes, 'Lord bless you, we know you all to pieces!' and there was sitting by me. Oh! such a pretty girl, the very picture of Rubens's second wife, and face and figure. Most of the ladies, all except this family, are as lean as greyhounds; they dress prodigiously fine, taking for their models the French actresses, I think, of the Boulevard theatres.

Broadway is miles upon miles long, a rush of life such as I never have seen; not so full as the Strand, but so rapid. The houses are always being torn down and built up again, the railroad cars drive slap into the midst of the city. There are barricades and scaffoldings banging everywhere. I have not been into a house except the fat country one, but something new is being done to it, and the hammerings are clattering in the passage, or a wall, or steps are down, or the family is going to move. Nobody is quiet here, no more am I. The rush and restlessness pleases me, and I like, for a little, the dash of the stream. I am not received as a god, which I like too. There is one paper which goes on every morning saying I am a snob, and I don't say no. Six people were reading it at breakfast this morning, and the man opposite me popped it under the table cloth. But the other papers roar with approbation . . .

Here comes in a man with a paper I hadn't seen; I must cut out a bit just as the actors do, but then I think you will like it, and that is why I do it. There was a very rich biography about me in one of the papers the other day, with an account of a servant, maintained in the splendour of his menial decorations – Poor old John whose picture is in Pendennis. And I have filled my paper, and I shake my dear lady's hand across the roaring sea, and I know that you will be glad to know that I prosper and that I am well, and that I am yours

W.M.T.

This welcome day brought me a nice long letter from K.E.P., and she must know that I write from the most comfortable quarters I have ever had in the United States. In a tranquil old city, wide-streeted, tree-planted, with a few cows and carriages toiling through the sandy road, a few happy negroes sauntering here and there, a red river with a tranquil little fleet of merchant-men taking in cargo, and tranquil ware-houses barricaded with packs of cotton, – no row, no tearing northern bustle, no ceaseless hotel racket, no crowds drinking at the bar, – a snug little languid audience of three or four hundred people, far too lazy to laugh or applaud; a famous good dinner, breakfast etc., and leisure all the morning to think and do and sleep and read as I like. The only place I say in the States where I can get these comforts – all free gratis – is in the house of my friend Andrew Low of the great house of A. Low and Co., Cotton Dealers, Brokers, Merchants – what's the word? Last time I was here he was a widower with two daughters in England, about whom - and other two daughters – there was endless talk between us. Now there is a pretty wife added to the establishment, and a little daughter number three crowing in the adjoining nursery. They are tremendous men these cotton merchants.

When I had finished at Charleston I went off to a queer little rustic city called Augusta – a great broad street 2 miles long - old quaint looking shops – houses with galleries – ware-houses - trees – cows and negroes strolling about the side walks – plank roads – happy dirty tranquillity generally prevalent. It lies 130 miles from Charleston. You take 8½ hours to get there by the railway, about same time and distance to come here, over endless plains of swampy pine-lands – a village or two here and there in a clearing. I brought away a snug little purse from snug little Augusta, though I had a rival – A Wild man, lecturing in the very same hall: I tell you it is not a dignified metier, that which I pursue.

What is this about the Saturday Review? After giving Vernon Harcourt

2/6 to send me the first 5 numbers, and only getting No. 1, it is too bad
they should assault me – and for what? My lecture is rather extra loyal
whenever the Queen is mentioned, – and the most applauded passage in
them I shall have the honour of delivering to-night in the Lecture on
George II, where the speaker says, 'In laughing at these old-world follies
and ceremonies shall we not acknowledge the change of to-day? As the
mistress of St James passes me now I salute the sovereign, wise, moderate,
exemplary of life, the good mother, the good wife, the acomplished Lady,
the enlightened friend of Art, the tender sympathizer in her people's glories
and sorrows.'

I can't say more, can I? and as for George III, I leave off just with the
people on the crying point. And I never for one minute should think that
my brave old Venables would hit me; or if he did that he hadn't a good
cause for it. . . .

From *A Mississippi Bubble*

. . . . How they sang; how they laughed and grinned; how they scraped,
bowed, and complimented you and each other, those negroes of the critics
of the Southern parts of the then United States! My business kept me in
the towns; I was but in one negro-plantation village, and there were only
women and little children, the men being out a-field. But there was plenty
of cheerfulness in the huts, under the great trees – I speak of what I saw
– and amidst the dusky bondsmen of the cities. I witnessed a curious gaiety;
heard amongst the black folk endless singing, shouting, and laughter; and
saw on holidays black gentlemen and ladies arrayed in such splendour and
comfort as freeborn workmen in our towns seldom exhibit. What a grin and
bow that dark gentleman performed, who was the porter at the colonel's,
when he said, 'You write your name, mas'r, else I will forget.' I am not
going into the slavery question, I am not an advocate for the 'institution,'
as I know, madam, by that angry toss of your head, you are about to declare
me to be. For domestic purposes, my dear lady, it seemed to me about the
dearest institution that can be devised. In a house in a Southern city you
will find fifteen negroes doing the work which John, the cook, the house-
maid, and the help, do perfectly in your own comfortable London house.
And these fifteen negroes are the pick of a family of some eighty or ninety.
Twenty are too sick, or too old for work, let us say; twenty too clumsy:
twenty are too young, and have to be nursed and watched by ten more.
And master has to maintain the immense crew to do the work of half a
dozen willing hands. No, no; let Mitchell, the exile from poor dear enslaved
Ireland, wish for a gang of 'fat niggers'; I would as soon you should make
me a present of a score of Bengal elephants, when I need but a single stout
horse to pull my brougham.

How hospitable they were, those Southern men! In the North itself the
welcome was not kinder, as I, who have eaten Northern and Southern salt,
can testify. As for New Orleans, in spring-time – just when the orchards
were flushing over with peach-blossoms, and the sweet herbs came to
flavour the juleps – it seemed to me the city of the world where you can
eat and drink the most and suffer the least. At Bordeaux itself, claret is not
better to drink than at New Orleans. It was all good – believe an expert

Robert – from the half dollar Médoc of the public hotel table, to the private gentleman's choicest wine. Claret is, somehow, good in that gifted place at dinner, at supper, and at breakfast in the morning. It is good: it is super-abundant – and there is nothing to pay. Find me speaking ill of such a country! When I do. . . . smother me in a desert, or let Mississippi or Garonne drown me! At that comfortable tavern on Pontchartrain we had a bouillabaisse than which a better was never eaten at Marseilles: and not the least headache in the morning, I give you my word; on the contrary, you only wake with a sweet refreshing thirst for claret and water. They say there is fever there in the autumn; but not in the spring-time, when the peach-blossoms blush over the orchards, and the sweet herbs come to flavour the juleps . . .

Mounting the stream it chanced that we had very few passengers. How far is the famous city of Memphis from New Orleans? I do not mean the Egyptian Memphis, but the American Memphis, from which to the Amer-ican Cairo we slowly toiled up the river – to the American Cairo at the confluence of the Ohio and Mississippi rivers. And at Cairo we parted company from the boat, and from some famous and gifted fellow-passengers who joined us at Memphis, and whose pictures we had seen in many cities of the South. I do not give the names of these remarkable people, unless, by some wondrous chance, in inventing a name I should light upon that real one which some of them bore; but if you please I will say that our fellow-passengers whom we took in at Memphis were no less personages than the Vermont Giant and the famous Bearded Lady of Kentucky and her son. Their pictures I had seen in many cities through which I travelled with my own little performance. I think the Vermont Giant was a trifle taller in his pictures than he was in life (being represented in the former as, at least, some two stories high): but the lady's prodigious beard received no more than justice at the hands of the painter; that portion of it which I saw being really most black, rich, and curly – I say the portion of beard, for this modest or prudent woman kept I don't know how much of the beard covered up with a red handkerchief, from which I suppose it only emerged when she went to bed, or when she exhibited it professionally.

The Giant, I must think, was an overrated giant. I have known gentlemen, not in the professional, better made, and I should say taller, than the Vermont gentleman. A strange feeling I used to have at meals; when, on looking round our little society, I saw the Giant, the Bearded Lady of Kentucky, the little Bearded Boy of three years old, the Captain, (this I think; but at this distance of time I would not like to make the statement on affidavit) and the three other passengers, all with their knives in their mouths making play at the dinner – a strange feeling I say it was, and as though I was in a castle of ogres. But, after all, why so squeamish? A few scores of years back, the finest gentlemen and ladies of Europe did the like . . . Have you ever looked at Gilray's print of the Prince of Wales, a languid voluptuary, retiring after his meal, and noted the toothpick which he uses? . . . You are right, madam; I own that the subject is revolting and terrible. I will not pursue it. Only – allow that a gentleman, in a shaky steamboat, on a dangerous river, in a far-off country, which caught fire three times during the voyage – (of course I mean the steamboat, not the country,) – seeing a giant, a voracious supercargo, a bearded lady, and a little boy, not three years of age, with a chin already quite black and curly, all plying their victuals down their throats with their knives – allow, madam, that in such a company a man had a right to feel a little nervous. I don't know whether you have ever remarked the Indian jugglers swallowing their knives, or seen, as I have, a whole table of people performing the same trick, but if you look at their eyes when they do it, I assure you there is a roll in them which is dreadful.

Apart from this usage, which they practise in common with many thousand most estimate citizens, the Vermont gentleman, and the Kentucky whiskered lady – or did I say the reverse? – whichever you like, my dear sir – were quite quiet, modest, unassuming people. She sat working with her needle, if I remember right. He, I suppose, slept in the great cabin, which was seventy feet long at the least, nor, I am bound to say, did I hear in the night any snores or roars, such as you would fancy ought to accompany the sleep of ogres. Nay, this giant had quite a small appetite, (unless, to be sure, he went forward and ate a sheep or two in private with his horrid knife – oh, the dreadful thought! – but in public, I say, he had quite a delicate appetite,) and was also a tee-totaller. I don't remember to have heard the lady's voice, though I might, not unnaturally, have been curious to hear it. Was her voice a deep, rich, magnificent bass, or was it soft, flutey, and mild? I shall never know now. Even if she comes to this country, I shall never go and see her. I have seen her, and for nothing.

You would have fancied that, as after all we were only some half-dozen on board, she might have dispensed with her red handkerchief, and talked, and eaten her dinner in comfort; but in covering her chin there was a kind of modesty. That beard was her profession: that beard brought the public to see her: out of her business she wished to put that beard aside as it were: as a barrister would wish to put off his wig. I know some who carry theirs into private life, and who mistake you and me for jury-boxes when they address us: but these are not your modest barristers, not your true gentlemen.

Well, I own I respected the lady for the modesty with which, her public business over, she retired into private life. She respected her life, and her beard. That beard having done its day's work, she puts it away in her handkerchief, and becomes, as far as in her lies, a private ordinary person. All public men and women of good sense, I should think, have this modesty. When, for instance, in my small way, poor Mrs Brown comes simpering up to me, with her album in one hand, a pen in the other, and says, 'Ho, ho, dear Mr Roundabout, write us one of your amusing,' &c. &c., my beard drops behind my handkerchief instantly. Why am I to wag my chin and grin for Mrs Brown's good pleasure? My dear madam, I have been making faces all day. It is my profession. I do my comic business with the greatest pains, seriousness, and trouble: and with it make, I hope, a not dishonest livelihood. If you ask Mons. Blondin to tea, you don't have a rope stretched from your garret window to the opposite side of the square, and request Monsieur to take his tea out on the centre of the rope? I lay my hand on this waistcoat, and declare that not once in the course of our voyage together did I allow the Kentucky Giant to suppose I was speculating on his stature, or the Bearded Lady to surmise that I wished to peep under the handkerchief which muffled the lower part of her face.

'And the more fool you,' says some cynic. (Faugh, those cynics, I hate 'em!) Don't you know, sir, that a man of genius is pleased to have his genius recognized; that a beauty likes to be admired; that an actor likes to be applauded; that stout old Wellington himself was pleased, and smiled when the people cheered him as he passed? Suppose you had paid some respectful compliment to that lady? Suppose you had asked that giant, if, for once, he would take anything at the liquor-bar? you might have learned a great deal of curious knowledge regarding giants and bearded ladies, about whom you evidently now know very little. There was that little boy of three years old, with a fine beard already, and his little legs and arms, as seen out of his little frock, covered with a dark down. What a queer little capering satyr! He was quite good-natured, childish, rather solemn. . . .

Thomas Richard Weld (1855)

Thomas Richard Weld was born in Dublin in 1813. He was active at the bar and later worked for the Royal Society. His Vacation Tour of the United States and Canada *was one of a series of 'Vacation Tour' books he wrote of foreign countries. Here he visits the slave market at Richmond, Virginia.*

. . . I must give a sketch of an interesting sight which I witnessed in the afternoon. I was on my way to the Armoury, when I met Captain Dimmock. 'You are fortunate,' he observed, 'for the ceremony of adult negro baptisms has just commenced.' Proceeding towards the James River, we soon fell in with crowds of negroes going to the scene of attraction; and on coming within sight of the water, we beheld the banks covered by thousands of blacks of both sexes. A small wooden house near the river contained numerous candidates for baptismal regeneration, clad in linen trousers, and a shirt. They were led into the stream, and received by the officiating minister and his assistants, who, after a short prayer, plunged them deep beneath the water. Before immersion the assembled multitude sang at the top of their voices spirit-stirring hymns. The sudden transition from the swelling and not inharmonious chorus to profound silence, had a curious effect; for the minister, whom I recognized as the preacher I heard in the morning,–

–'Stretch his arms and call'd
Across the tumult, and the tumult fell.'

Every eye was on him, and the moment a negro emerged from the water, a mighty cry arose from the excited multitude, welcoming a brother's advent into their fold. It was a touching spectacle. For all present were firmly persuaded salvation attended the ceremony, which in spirit at least lifted the souls of these poor bondsmen above the power of oppression.

Not, assuredly, greater is the contrast between a fair landscape illumined by brilliant summer sunshine, and steeped in the purple gloom of an impending thunder-storm, than that present by the baptismal scene on the banks of the James River and the Richmond slave market.

I visited this place with mingled feelings of sadness and curiosity. The market consists of three human shambles, situated in the lower part of the town, far from the dwelling of the whites, easily distinguished by red flags over the entrances, to which are attached particulars of the slaves for sale. The number greatly varies, sometimes amounting to about fifty, and occasionally falling to one or two. On the day of my visit, fourteen males, and seven female '*likely*' slaves, with their children, were advertised to be sold by auction. The first establishment I entered, consisted of a large barn-like room, about forty feet square, furnished with rude wooden benches and chairs; a platform for the display of the human goods; a desk, and a screen across the upper end of the room. The floor, walls, and indeed every object, were befouled by tobacco juice. About a score of ill-looking fellows were present, engaged, with scarcely an exception, in perpetual chewing and whittling. The benches, chairs, and all the wood work, exhibited abundant marks how vigorously the latter practice had been carried on. The pillars were in many cases nearly severed. One man, who had tilted his chair back, was whittling one of the raised legs, with such energy of purpose, as to speedily threaten the amputation of that most important member of a chair's economy.

By degrees more people arrived. When about fifty were present, the slaves were brought in from the neighbouring jail, where they had been confined. There were four men and two girls. The former were immediately led behind the screen, stripped stark naked, and examined with great minuteness. Marks were criticized with the knowing air assumed by horse dealers, and pronounced to be the results of flogging, vermin, or scrofula. Little value was apparently attached to the answers of the slaves, though considerable pains were taken to ascertain their ages, (of which, by the way, they were generally very ignorant,) and the cause of their sale; with one exception, none could assign any reason. The exceptional case was a youth, who stated he was the slave of a tobacco manufacturer, and that although his master treated him well, the overseer was harsh and cruel, and frequently beat him. In proof of this he exhibited a scar on his shoulder. His master, he added, had consented to allow him to be sold. The women were more tenderly dealt with. Personal examination was confined to the hands, arms, legs, bust, and teeth. Searching questions were put respecting their age, and whether they had children. If they replied in the negative, their bosoms were generally handled in a repulsive and disgusting manner.

When sufficient time had been given for the examination of the slaves, the auctioneer left his desk, and desired his assistant, who was a slave, to bring up the first lot. This was a male negro about thirty years of age, who had been working on a tobacco plantation. He was ordered to ascend the platform, and the auctioneer stood on a chair by his side. The assistant now tucked up the slave's trousers, bared his neck and breast, and the sale commenced. 'Here,' said the auctioneer, 'is a likely young nigger, used to all sorts of farm work; what will ye bid, gentlemen? He's worth a thousand dollars. Who'll bid? come, 500 dollars to begin. Thank ye sir: 500 dollars - 500 doll'r - doll'r - doll'r-' (uttered with bewildering rapidity), '500 doll'r - doll'r - doll'r: 600, thank ye sir.' Here the bidding hung fire, and the auctioneer, after expatiating on the good qualities of the lot, ordered him to be walked up and down the room before the people, who now amounted to about 200. During his progress, he was frequently stopped by the parties who examined him. On returning to the platform, the biddings were renewed with greater spirit, until they reached 858 dollars, at which sum the man was sold. The next lot – also a male, who stated he was worn out, and unable to do good work, though apparently under fifty years of age – sold for 630 dollars; the third male, about thirty years old, who had been working in a plantation, for 940 dollars; and the fourth, the young man who was sold at his own request, for 750 dollars. In all these cases the same process was gone through, each slave being trotted up and down the room precisely like a horse.

Now came the women's turn. The first put up was a good-looking girl, gaily-dressed, her hair adorned with ribbons, – who, according to her statement, was nineteen years old, and was skilful in the use of her needle. 'Can you make shirts?' was a question put to her by a dozen men. 'Yes,' she replied, 'and wash them too.' The auctioneer expatiated at great length on the excellent qualities of this 'prime lot', for which he expected 1000 dollars at least. He obtained more – the first bid was 500, and she was knocked down for 1005. The second woman, aged twenty-five, who had been a domestic servant, realized only 700 dollars, on account of some scars on her shoulders, which a man near me was confident were produced by the whip.

As all the slaves present were now sold, I thought business was over in this establishment; but just as the last woman was led away, a mulatto entered the room with another woman followed by two little children about three and four years old, and carrying a third still younger in her arms. These were the children announced for sale. The circumstances of this woman, or lot, as she and the children were called, being brought in alone, led me to suppose there was some distinction between her and the preceding slaves like those just sold; but in appearance the difference was great. She was a remarkably handsome mulatto, and her children were nearly, if not fully, as white as the fairest Americans. If any doubt existed in my mind respecting the revolting nature of this human traffic, the case of this woman would have determined my judgement. Her story was brief: she was not married, and the man whose passions had made her his mistress as well as slave, willed that she should be sold with *his* children. More she would not divulge; nor would she answer questions relative to her occupation. All attempts at extracting further information were met by a scornful refusal to divulge ought of her past life, and when her small soft hands and bosom were examined, on which her infant was reposing, her eyes flashed fire, and I sincerely believe, had a knife been within her grasp she would have plunged it in the hearts of her tormentors. Followed by her two little children, who clung to her dress like scared lambs, shrinking from the gaze of the rough men who pressed round them, she ascended the platform, and the auctioneer recommenced his business.

Whether he dreaded a scene, or that he deemed it unnecessary, I am unable to say; but he limited his prefatorial harangue to the simple announcement that he had a fine young woman to offer, with her children, who would not be sold separate, adding that in a few years the boys would be fit for work. What could he say of her, whose heart's finest affections were perhaps at that moment lacerated to satisfy the greed of a man? He set a high price on the woman and her children, declaring he expected at least 2500 dollars for the lot. The first bid was 800; languid biddings succeeded, until the amount reached 900 dollars. The woman was then ordered down, and followed by her little children, was made to walk up and down the room. On resuming her place on the platform, the biddings became a little brisker; but as no eloquence on the part of the auctioneer could raise them above 1100 dollars, the lot was withdrawn. I was informed the woman alone would have realized more than this amount, but there is a strong aversion against purchasing white children.

Isabella Lucy Bird (1856)

Isabella Lucy Bird was born in Edinburgh in 1832. She was an indefatigable traveller and writer of travel-books. She died in 1904. Here she encounters American hotels.

It will not be out of place here to give a sketch of the peculiarities of the American hotel system, which constitutes such a distinctive feature of life in the States, and is a requirement arising out of the enormous extent of their territory, and the nomad life led by vast numbers of the most restless and energetic people under the sun.

'People will turn hastily over the pages when they come to this' was the remark of a lively critic on reading this announcement; but while I promise my readers that hotels shall only be described *once*, I could not reconcile it to myself not to give them information on 'Things as they are in America', when I had an opportunity of acquiring it.

The American House at Boston, which is a fair specimen of the best class of hotels in the States, though more frequented by mercantile men than by tourists, is built of grey granite, with a frontage to the street of 100 feet. The ground floor to the front is occupied by retail stores, in the centre of which a lofty double doorway denotes the entrance, marked in a more characteristic manner by groups of gentlemen smoking before it. This opens into a lofty and very spacious hall, with a chequered floor of black and white marble; there are lounges against the wall, covered over with buffalo-skins; and, except at meal-times, this capacious apartment is a scene of endless busy life, from two to three hundred gentlemen constantly thronging it, smoking at the door, lounging on the settees, reading the newspapers, standing in animated groups discussing commercial matters, arriving, or departing. Piles of luggage, in which one sees with dismay one's light travelling valise crushed under a gigantic trunk, occupy the centre; porters seated on a form wait for orders; peripatetic individuals walk to and fro; a confused Babel of voices is ever ascending to the galleries above; and at the door, hacks, like the '*eilwagon*' of Germany, are ever depositing fresh arrivals. There is besides this a private entrance for ladies. Opposite the entrance is a counter, where four or five clerks constantly attend, under the superintendence of a cashier, to whom all applications for rooms are personally made. I went up to this functionary, wrote my name in a book, he placed a number against it, and, giving me a key with a corresponding number attached, I followed a porter down a long corridor, and up to a small clean room on the third story, where to all intents and purposes my identity was lost – merged in a mere numeral. At another side of the hall is the bar, a handsomely decorated apartment, where lovers of such beverages can procure 'toddy,' 'nightcaps,' 'mint julep,' 'gin sling,' &c. On the door of my very neat and comfortable bed-room was a printed statement of the rules, times of meals, and charge per diem. I believe there are nearly 300 rooms in this house, some of them being bed-rooms as large and commodious as in a private mansion in England.

On the level of the entrance is a magnificent eating saloon, principally devoted to male guests, and which is 80 feet long. Upstairs is a large room furnished with a rare combination of splendour and taste, called 'The Ladies' Ordinary,' where families, ladies, and their invited guests take their meals. Breakfast is at the early hour of seven, and remains on the table till nine; dinner is at one, and tea at six. At these meals 'every delicacy of the season' is served in profusion; the daily bill of fare would do credit to a banquet at the Mansion House; the *chef de cuisine* is generally French, and an epicure would find ample scope for the gratification of his palate. If people persist in taking their meals in a separate apartment, they are obliged to pay dearly for the indulgence of their exclusiveness. There are more than 100 waiters, and the ladies at table are always served first, and to the best pieces.

Though it is not part of the hotel system, I cannot forbear mentioning the rapidity with which the Americans despatch their meals. My next neighbour has frequently risen from his seat after a substantial and varied dinner while I was sending away my soup-plate. The effect of this at a *table-d'hôte*, where 400 or 600 sit down to dine, is unpleasant, for the swing-door is incessantly in motion. Indeed, the utter absence of repose is almost the first thing which strikes a stranger. The incessant sound of bells and gongs, the rolling of hacks to and from the door, the arrivals and departures every minute, the trampling of innumerable feet, the flirting and talking in every corridor, make these immense hotels more like a human beehive than anything else.

The drawing-rooms are always kept very hot by huge fires of anthracite coal, and the doors are left open to neutralise the effect. The temperance at table filled me with surprise. I very seldom saw any beverage but pure iced-water. There are conveniences of all descriptions for the use of the guests. The wires of the electric telegraph, constantly attended by a clerk, run into the hotel; porters are ever ready to take your messages into the town; pens, paper, and ink await you in recesses in the lobbies; a man is ever at hand to clean and brush soiled boots – in short, there is every contrivance for abridging your labour in mounting up stairs. But the method of avoiding the confusion and din of two or three hundred bells must not be omitted. All the wires from the different rooms centre at one bell, which is located in a case in the lobby, with the mechanism seen on one side through a sheet of plate-glass. The other side of the case is covered with numbers in rows. By each number is a small straight piece of brass, which drops and hangs down where the bell is sounded, displaying the number to the attention of the clerk, who sends a waiter to the apartment, and places the piece of brass in its former position.

Steam laundries are connected with all the large hotels. At American House the laundry is under the management of a clerk, who records all the minor details. The linen is cleansed in a churn-like machine moved by steam, and wrung by a novel application of the principle of centrifugal force, after which the articles are dried by being passed through currents of hot air, so that they are washed and ironed in the space of a few minutes. The charge varies from six to ten shillings a dozen. There are also suites of hot and cold baths, and barbers' shops.

Before I understood the mysteries of these hotels, I used to be surprised to see gentlemen travelling without even carpet-bags, but it soon appeared that razors and hair-brushes were superfluous, and that the possessor of one shirt might always pass as the owner of half a dozen, for, while taking a bath, the magic laundry would reproduce the article in its pristine glories of whiteness and starch. Every attention to the comfort and luxury of the guest is paid at American House, and its spirited proprietor, Mr. Rice, deserves the patronage which the travelling public so liberally bestow upon him. On ringing my bell it was answered by a garçon, and it is rather curious seldom or never to see a chambermaid.

William Howard Russell (1861)

William Howard Russell (1820–1907) made his reputation as The Times *correspondent during the Crimean War, when he exposed the appalling conditions in which the British soldiers served. In March 1861 he sailed for the United States to report for* The Times *the dispute between North and South, which culminated in the Civil War.* The Times *supported the 'Confederate cause', but Russell had not been long in the country before he decided that his sympathies were with the 'Yankees'.*

May 3rd. I bade good-bye to Mr Green, who with several of his friends came down to see me off, at the terminus or depot of the Central Railway, on my way to Montgomery – and looking my last on Savannah, its squares and leafy streets, its churches, and institutes with a feeling of regret that I could not see more of them, and that I was forced to be content with the outer aspect of the public buildings.

From Savannah to Macon, 191 miles, the road passes through level country only partially cleared. That is, there are patches of forest still intruding on the green fields, where the jagged black teeth of the destroyed trees rise from above the maize and cotton. There were but few Negroes visible at work, nor did the land appear rich, but I was told the rail was laid along the most barren part of the country.

Among the passengers to whom I was introduced was the Bishop of Georgia, the Rev Mr Elliott, a man of exceeding fine presence, of great stature, and handsome face, with a manner easy and graceful, but we got on the unfortunate subject of slavery, and I rather revolted at hearing a Christian prelate advocating the institution on scriptural grounds.

This application of Biblical sanction and ordinance as the basis of slavery was not new to me, though it is not much known at the other side of the Atlantic. I had read in a work on slavery, that it was permitted by both the Scriptures and the Constitution of the United States, and that it must, therefore, be doubly right.

Whenever the Southern Confederacy shall achieve its independence – no matter what its resources, its allies, or its aims – it will have to stand face to face with civilized Europe on this question of slavery, and the strength which it derived from the aegis of the Constitution – 'the league with the devil and covenant with Hell' – will be withered and gone.

The train halted at a snug little wood-embowered restaurant, surrounded by trellis and lattice-work, and in the midst of a pretty garden, which presented a marked contrast to the 'surroundings' we had seen. The dinner, served by slaves, was good of its kind, and the charge not high. On tendering the landlord a piece of gold for payment, he looked at it with disgust, and asked, 'Have you no Charleston money? No Confederate notes?' 'Well, no! Why do you object to gold?' 'Well, do you see, I'd rather have our own paper! I don't care to take any of the United States' gold. I don't want their stars and their eagles; I hate the sight of them.' The man was quite sincere – my companion gave him notes of some South Carolina bank.

It was dark when the train reached Macon, one of the principal cities of the state. We drove to the best hotel, but the regular time for dinner-hour was over, and that for supper not yet come. The landlord directed us to a subterranean restaurant, in which were a series of crypts closed by dirty curtains, where we made a very extraordinary repast, served by a half-clad little Negress, who watched us at the meal with great interest through the curtains – the service was of the coarsest description; thick French earthenware, the spoons of pewter, the knives and forks steel or iron, with scarce a pretext of being cleaned. On the doors were the usual warnings against pickpockets, and the customary internal police regulations and ukases. Pickpockets and gamblers abound in American cities and thrive greatly at the large hotels and the lines of railways.

May 4th. In the morning I took a drive about the city, which is loosely built in detached houses over a pretty undulating country covered with wood and fruit-trees. Many good houses of dazzling white, with bright green blinds, verandahs, and doors, stand in their own grounds or gardens. In the course of the drive I saw two or three signboards and placards announcing that 'Smith & Co. advanced money on slaves, and had constant supplies of Virginian Negroes on sale or hire.' These establishments were surrounded by high walls enclosing the slave-pens or large rooms, in which the slaves are kept for inspection. The train for Montgomery started at 9:45 AM, and I had no time to stop and visit them.

It is evident we are approaching the Confederate capital, for the candidates for office begin to show, and I detected a printed testimonial in my room in the hotel.

The people are all hearty Secessionists here – the Bars and Stars are flying at the road-stations and from the pine-tops, and there are lusty cheers for Jeff Davis and the Southern Confederacy. Troops are flocking towards Virginia from the Southern States in reply to the march of volunteers from Northern States to Washington; but it is felt that the steps taken by the Federal Government to secure Baltimore have obviated any chance of successfully opposing the 'Lincolnites' going through that city. There is a strong disposition on the part of the Southerners to believe they have many friends in the North, and they endeavour to attach a factious character to the actions of the Government by calling the volunteers and the war party in the North 'Lincolnites,' 'Lincoln's Mercenaries,' 'Black Republicans,' 'Abolitionists,' and the like. General Scott would, it was fondly believed, retire from the United States Army, and either remain neutral or take command under the Confederate flag, but now that it is certain he will not follow any of these courses, he is assailed in the foulest manner by the press and in private conversation. Heaven help the idol of a democracy!

At one of the junctions General Beauregard, attended by Mr Manning, and others of his staff, got into the car, and tried to elude observation, but the conductors take great pleasure in unearthing distinguished passengers for the public, and the General was called on for a speech by the crowd of idlers. The General hates speech-making, he told me, and he had besides been bored to death at every station by similar demands. But a man must be popular or he is nothing. So, as next best thing, Governor Manning made a speech in the General's name, in which he dwelt on Southern Rights, Sumter, victory, and abolitiondom, and was carried off from the cheers of his auditors by the train in the midst of an unfinished sentence.

Towards evening, having thrown out some slight out-works against accidental sallies of my fellow-passengers' salivas, I went to sleep, and woke up at 11 PM to hear we were in Montgomery. A very rickety omnibus took the party to the hotel, which was crowded to excess. The General and his friends had one room to themselves. Three gentlemen and myself were crammed into a filthy room which already contained two strangers, and as there were only three beds in the apartment it was apparent that we were intended to 'double up considerably'; but after strenuous efforts, a little bribery and cajoling, we succeeded in procuring mattresses to put on the floor, which was regarded by our neighbours as proof of miserable aristocratic fastidiousness. Had it not been for the flies, the fleas would have been intolerable, but one nuisance neutralized the other. Then, as to food – nothing could be had in the hotel – but one of the waiters led us to a restaurant, where we selected from a choice bill of fare, which contained, I think, as many odd dishes as ever I saw, some unknown fishes, oyster-plants, 'possums, raccoons, frogs, and other delicacies, and, eschewing toads and the like, really made a good meal off dirty plates on a vile tablecloth, our appetites being sharpened by the best of condiments.

Colonel Pickett has returned up here, having made his escape from Washington just in time to escape arrest – travelling in disguise on foot through out-of-the-way places until he got among friends.

May 6th. I forgot to say that yesterday before dinner I drove out with some gentlemen and the ladies of the family of Mr George N. Sanders, once United States consul at Liverpool, now a doubtful man here, seeking some office from the Government, and accused by a portion of the press of being a Confederate spy – *Porcus de grege epicuri* – but a learned pig withal, and weather-wise, and mindful of the signs of the times, catching straws and whisking them upwards to detect the currents.

After breakfast I walked down with Senator Wigfall to the capitol of Montgomery – one of the true Athenian Yankee-ized structures of this novo-classic land, erected on a site worthy of a better fate and edifice. By an open cistern, on our way, I came upon a gentleman engaged in disposing of some living ebony carvings to a small circle, who had more curiosity than cash, for they did not at all respond to the energetic appeals of the auctioneer.

The sight was a bad preparation for an introduction to the legislative assembly of a Confederacy which rests on the institution as the cornerstone of the social and political arch which maintains it. But there they were, the legislators or conspirators, in a large room provided with benches and seats, and listening to such a sermon as a Balfour or Burley might have preached to his Covenanters – resolute and massive heads, and large frames – such men as must have a faith to inspire them.

The chaplain, a venerable old man, loudly invoked curses on the heads of the enemy, and blessings on the arms and councils of the New State. When he was done, Mr Howell Cobb, a fat, double-chinned, mellow-eyed man, rapped with his hammer on the desk before the chair on which he sat as speaker of the assembly, and the house proceeded to business. I could fancy that, in all but garments, they were like the men who first conceived the great rebellion which led to the independence of this wonderful country – so earnest, so grave, so sober, and so vindictive.

The word 'liberty' was used repeatedly in the short time allotted to the public transaction of business and the reading of documents; the Congress was anxious to get to its work, and Mr Howell Cobb again thumped his desk and announced that the house was going into 'secret session,' which intimated that all persons who were not members should leave. I was introduced to what is called the floor of the house, and had a delegate's chair, and of course I moved away with the others, and with the disappointed ladies and men from the galleries, but one of the members, Mr Rhett, I believe, said jokingly 'I think you ought to retain your seat. If *The Times* will support the South, we'll accept you as a delegate.' I replied that I was afraid I could not act as a delegate to a Congress of Slave States. And, indeed, I had been much affected at the slave auction held just outside the hotel, on the steps of the public fountain, which I had witnessed on my way to the capitol. The auctioneer, who was an ill-favoured, dissipated-looking rascal, had his 'article' beside him on, not in, a deal packing-case – a stout young Negro badly dressed and ill-shod, who stood with all his goods fastened in a small bundle in his hand, looking out at the small and listless gathering of men, who, whittling and chewing, had moved out from the shady side of the street as they saw the man put up.

A man in a cart, some volunteers in coarse uniform, a few Irish labourers in a long van, and four or five men in the usual black coat, satin waistcoat, and black hat, constituted the audience, whom the auctioneer addressed volubly: 'A prime fieldhand! Just look at him – good-natured, well-tempered; no marks, nary sign of bad about him! En-i-ne hunthered – only nine hun-ther-ed and fifty dol'rs for 'em! Why it's quite rad-aklous! Nine hundred and fifty dol'rs! I can't raly – That's good. Thank you, sir. Twenty five bid – nine hun-therd and seventy-five dol'rs for this most useful hand.' The price rose to one thousand dollars, at which the useful hand was knocked down to one of the black hats near me. The auctioneer and the Negro and his buyer all walked off together to settle the transaction, and the crowd moved away.

'That nigger went cheap,' said one of them to a companion, as he walked towards the shade. 'Yes, *Sirr!* Niggers is cheap now – that's a fact.'

On my return, the Hon W. M. Browne, Assistant Secretary of State, came to visit me – a cadet of an Irish family, who came to America some years ago, and having lost his money in land speculations, turned his pen to good account as a journalist, and gained Mr Buchanan's patronage and support as a newspaper editor in Washington. There he became intimate with the Southern gentlemen, with whom he naturally associated in prefer-ence to the Northern members; and when they went out, he walked over along with them. He told me the Government had already received numerous – I think he said four hundred – letters from shipowners applying for letters of marque and reprisal. Many of these applications were from merchants in Boston, and other maritime cities in the New England States. He further stated that the President was determined to take the whole control of the Army, and the appointments to command in all ranks of officers into his own hands.

The press is fanning the flame on both sides: it would be difficult to say whether it or the telegraphs circulate lies most largely; but that as the papers print the telegrams they must have the palm. The Southerners are told there is a reign of terror in New York – that the 7th New York Regiment has been captured by the Baltimore people – that Abe Lincoln is always drunk – that General Lee has seized Arlington Heights, and is bombarding Washington. The New York people are regaled with similar stories from the South. The coincidence between the date of the skirmish at Lexington and the attack on the 6th Massachusetts Regiment at Baltimore is not so remarkable as the fact that the first man who was killed at the latter place eighty-six years ago, was the direct descendant of the first of the colonists who was killed by the royal soldiery. Baltimore may do the same for the South which Lexington did for all the Colonies. Headshaving, forcible deportations, tarring and feathering are recommended and adopted as specifics to produce conversion from erroneous opinions. The President of the United States has called into service of the Federal Government 42,000 volunteers, and increased the regular Army by 22,000 men, and the Navy by 18,000 men. If the South secedes, they ought certainly to take over with them some Yankee hotel keepers. This 'Exchange' is in a frightful state – nothing but noise, dirt, drinking, wrangling.

May 7th. Today the papers contain a proclamation by the President of the Confederate States of America, declaring a state of war between the Confederacy and the United States, and notifying the issue of letters of marque and reprisal. I went out with Mr Wigfall in the forenoon to pay my respects to Mr Jefferson Davis at the State Department. Mr Seward told me that but for Jefferson Davis the Secession plot could never have been carried out. No other man of the party had the brain, or the courage and dexterity, to bring it to a successful issue. All the persons in the Southern States spoke of him with admiration, though their forms of speech and thought generally forbid them to be respectful to anyone.

There before me was 'Jeff Davis's State Department' – a large brick building, at the corner of a street, with a Confederate flag floating above it. The door stood open, and 'gave' on a large hall white-washed, with doors plainly painted belonging to small rooms, in which was transacted the most important business, judging by the names written on sheets of paper and applied outside, denoting bureaus of the highest functions. A few clerks were passing in and out, and one or two gentlemen were on the stairs, but there was no appearance of any bustle in the building.

We walked straight upstairs to the first floor, which was surrounded by doors opening from a quadrangular platform. On one of these was written simply, 'The President.' Mr Wigfall went in, and after a moment returned and said, 'The President will be glad to see you; walk in, sir.' When I entered, the President was engaged with four gentlemen, who were making some offer of aid to him. He was thanking them 'in the name of the Government'. Shaking hands with each, he saw them to the door, bowed them and Mr Wigfall out, and turning to me said, 'Mr Russell, I am glad to welcome you here, though I fear your appearance is a symptom that our affairs are not quite prosperous,' or words to that effect. He then requested me to sit down close to his own chair at his office-table, and proceeded to speak on general matters, adverting to the Crimean War and the Indian Mutiny, and asking questions about Sebastopol, The Redan, and the Siege of Lucknow.

I had an opportunity of observing the President very closely: he did not impress me as favourably as I had expected, though he is certainly a very different looking man from Mr Lincoln. He is like a gentleman – has a slight, light figure, little exceeding middle height, and holds himself erect and straight. He was dressed in a rustic suit of slate-coloured stuff, with a black silk handkerchief round his neck; his manner is plain, and rather reserved and drastic; his head is well-formed, with a fine full forehead, square and high, covered with innumerable fine lines and wrinkles, features regular, though the cheek-bones are too high, and the jaws too hollow to be handsome; the lips are thin, flexible, and curved, the chin square, well-defined; the nose very regular, with wide nostrils; and the eyes deep set, large and full – one seems nearly blind, and is partly covered with a film, owing to excruciating attacks of neuralgia and tic. Wonderful to relate, he does not chew, and is neat and clean-looking, with hair trimmed and boots brushed. The expression of his face is anxious, he has a very haggard, care-worn, and pain-drawn look, though no trace of anything but the utmost confidence and greatest decision could be detected in his conversation. He asked me some questions respecting the route I had taken in the States.

I mentioned that I had seen great military preparations through the South, and was astonished at the alacrity with which the people sprang to arms. 'Yes, sir,' he remarked, and his tone of voice and manner of speech are rather remarkable for what are considered Yankee peculiarities, 'in Europe' (Mr Seward also indulges in that pronunciation) 'they laugh at us because of our fondness for military titles and displays. All your travellers in this country have commented on the number of generals, and colonels, and majors all over the States. But the fact is, we are a military people, and these signs of the fact were ignored. We are not less military because we have had no great standing armies. But perhaps we are the only people in the world where gentlemen go to a military academy, who do not intend to follow the profession of arms.'

In the course of our conversation, I asked him to have the goodness to direct that a sort of passport or protection should be given to me, as I might possibly fall in with some guerilla leader on my way northwards, in whose eyes I might not be entitled to safe conduct. Mr Davis said, 'I shall give such instructions to the Secretary of War as shall be necessary. But, sir, you are among civilized, intelligent people who understand your position, and appreciate your character. We do not seek the sympathy of England by unworthy means, for we respect ourselves, and we are glad to invite the scrutiny of men into our acts; as for our motives, we meet the eye of Heaven.' I thought I could judge from his words that he had the highest idea of the French as soldiers, but that his feelings and associations were more identified with England, although he was quite aware of the difficulty of conquering the repugnance which exists to slavery.

Mr Davis made no allusion to the authorities at Washington, but he asked me if I thought it was supposed in England there would be war between the two States? I answered that I was under the impression the public thought there would be no actual hostilities. 'And yet you see we are driven to take up arms for the defence of our rights and liberties.'

As I saw an immense mass of papers on his table, I rose and made my bow, and Mr Davis, seeing me to the door, gave me his hand and said, 'As long as you may stay among us you shall receive every facility it is in our power to afford to you, and I shall always be glad to see you.' Colonel Wigfall was outside, and took me to the room of the Secretary of War, Mr Walker, whom we found closeted with General Beauregard and two other officers in a room full of maps and plans. He is the kind of man generally represented in our types of a 'Yankee' – tall, lean, straight-haired, angular, with fiery, impulsive eyes and manner – a ruminator of tobacco and a profuse spitter – a lawyer, I believe, certainly not a soldier; ardent, devoted to the cause, and confident to the last degree of its speedy success.

The news that two more States had joined the Confederacy, making ten in all, was enough to put them in good humour. 'Is it not too bad these Yankees will not let us go our own way, and keep their cursed Union to themselves? If they force us to it, we may be obliged to drive them beyond the Susquehanna.' Beauregard was in excellent spirits, busy measuring off miles of country with his compass, as if he were dividing empires.

From this room I proceeded to the office of Mr Benjamin, the Attorney-General of the Confederate States, the most brilliant perhaps of the whole of the famous Southern orators. He is a short, stout man, with a full face, olive-coloured, and most decidedly Jewish features, with the brightest large black eyes, one of which is somewhat diverse from the other, and a brisk, lively, agreeable manner, combined with much vivacity of speech and quickness of utterance. He is one of the first lawyers or advocates in the United States, and had a large practice at Washington, where his annual receipts from his profession were not less than £8,000 to £10,000 a year. But his love of the card-table rendered him a prey to older and cooler hands, who waited till the sponge was full at the end of the session, and then squeezed it to the last drop.

Mr Benjamin is the most open, frank, and cordial of the Confederates whom I have yet met. In a few seconds he was telling me all about the course of Government with respect to privateers and letters of marque and reprisal, in order probably to ascertain what were our views in England on the subject. I observed it was likely the North would not respect their flag, and would treat their privateers as pirates. 'We have an easy remedy for that. For any man under our flag whom the authorities of the United States dare to execute, we shall hang two of their people.' 'Suppose, Mr Attorney-General, England, or any of the great powers which decreed the abolition of privateering, refuses to recognize your flag?' 'We intend to claim, and do claim, the exercise of all the rights and privileges of an independent sovereign State, and any attempt to refuse us the full measure of those rights would be an act of hostility to our country.' 'But if England, for example, declared your privateers were pirates?' 'As the United States never admitted the principle laid down at the Congress of Paris, neither have the Confederate States. If England thinks fit to declare privateers under our flag pirates, it would be nothing more or less than a declaration of war against us, and we must meet it as best we can.' In fact, Mr Benjamin did not appear afraid of anything; but his confidence respecting Great Britain was based a good deal, no doubt, on his firm faith in her cotton interest and manufactures. 'All this coyness about acknowledging a slave power will come right at last. We hear our commissioners have gone on to Paris, which looks as if they had met with no encouragement at London; but we are quite easy in our minds on this point at present.'

Being invited to attend a levee or reception held by Mrs Davis, the President's wife, I returned to the hotel to prepare for the occasion. On my way I passed a company of volunteers, 120 artillerymen, and three field-pieces, on their way to the station for Virginia, followed by a crowd of 'citizens' and Negroes of both sexes, cheering vociferously. The band was playing that excellent quick-step 'Dixie.' The men were stout, fine fellows, dressed in coarse grey tunics with yellow facings, and French caps. They were armed with smooth-bore muskets, and their knapsacks were unfit for marching, being waterproof bags slung from the shoulders. The guns had no caissons, and the shoeing of the troops was certainly deficient in soleing.

The modest villa in which the President lives is painted white – another 'White House' – and stands in a small garden. The door was open. A coloured servant took in our names, and Mr Browne presented me to Mrs Davis, whom I could just make out in the *demi-jour* of a moderately-sized parlour, surrounded by a few ladies and gentlemen, the former in bonnets, the latter in morning dress *à la midi*. There was no affectation of state or ceremony in the reception. Mrs Davis, whom some of her friends call 'Queen Varina,' is a comely, sprightly woman, verging on matronhood, of good figure and manners, well-dressed, lady-like, and clever, and she seemed a great favourite with those around her, though I did hear one of them say, 'It must be very nice to be the President's wife, and be the first lady in the Confederate States.' Mrs Davis, whom the President C.S. married *en secondes noces*, exercised considerable social influence in Washington, where I met many of her friends. She was just now inclined to be angry, because the papers contained a report that a reward was offered in the North for the head of the arch rebel Jeff Davis. 'They are quite capable, I believe,' she said, 'of such acts.' There were not more than eighteen or twenty persons present, as each party came in and stayed only for a few moments, and, after a time, I made my bow and retired, receiving from Mrs Davis an invitation to come in the evening, when I would find the President at home.

At sundown, amid great cheering, the guns in front of the State Department fired ten rounds, to announce that Tennessee and Arkansas had joined the Confederacy.

In the evening I dined with Mr Benjamin and his brother-in-law, a gentleman of New Orleans, Colonel Wigfall coming in at the end of dinner. The New Orleans people of French descent, or 'Creoles,' as they call themselves, speak French in preference to English, and Mr Benjamin's brother-in-law laboured considerably in trying to make himself understood in our vernacular. The conversation, Franco-English, very pleasant, for Mr Benjamin is agreeable and lively. He is certain that the English law authorities must advise the Government that the blockade of the Southern ports is illegal so long as the President claims them to be ports of the United States. 'At present,' he said, 'their paper blockade does no harm; the season for shipping cotton is over; but in October next, when the Mississippi is floating cotton by the thousands of bales, and all our wharves are full, it is inevitable that the Yankees must come to trouble with this attempt to coerce us.' Mr Benjamin walked back to the hotel with me, and we found our room full of tobacco-smoke, filibusters, and conversation, in which, as sleep was impossible, we were obliged to join. I resisted a vigorous attempt of Mr G. N. Sanders and a friend of his to take me to visit a planter who had a beaver-dam some miles outside Montgomery.

May 8th. I tried to write, as I have taken my place in the steamer to Mobile tomorrow, and I was obliged to do my best in a room full of people, constantly disturbed by visitors. Early this morning, as usual, my faithful Wigfall comes in and sits by my bedside, and passing his hands through his locks, pours out his ideas with wonderful lucidity and of affectation of logic all his own. 'We are a peculiar people, sir! You don't understand us, and you can't understand us, because we are known to you only by Northern writers and Northern papers, who know nothing of us themselves, or misrepresent what they do know. We are an agricultural people; we are a primitive but a civilized people. We have no cities – we don't want them. We have no literature – we don't need any yet. We have no press – we are glad of it. We do not require a press, because we go out and discuss all public questions from the stump with our people. We have no commercial marine – no navy – we don't want them. We are better without them. Your ships carry our produce, and you can protect your own vessels. We want no manufactures: we desire no trading, no mechanical or manufacturing classes. As long as we have our rice, our sugar, our tobacco, and our cotton, we can command wealth to purchase all we want from those nations with which we are in amity, and to lay up money besides. But with the Yankees we will never trade – never. Not one pound of cotton shall ever go from the South to their accursed cities; not one ounce of their steel or their manufactures shall ever cross our border.' And so on. What the Senator who is preparing a bill for drafting the people into the army fears is that the North will begin active operations before the South is ready for resistance. 'Give us till November to drill our men, and we shall be irresistible.' He deprecates any offensive movement, and is opposed to an attack on Washington, which many journals here advocate.

Mr Walker sent me over a letter recommending me to all officers of the Confederate States, and I received an invitation from the President to dine with him tomorrow, which I was much chagrined to be obliged to refuse. In fact, it is most important to complete my Southern tour speedily, as all mail communication will soon be suspended from the South, and the blockade effectually cuts off any communication by sea. Rails torn up, bridges broken, telegraphs down – trains searched – the war is begun.

I expressed a belief in a letter, written a few days after my arrival (March 27th), that the South would never go back into the Union. The North think that they can coerce the South, and I am not prepared to say they are right or wrong; but I am convinced that the South can only be forced back by such a conquest as that which laid Poland prostrate at the feet of Russia. It may be that such a conquest can be made by the North, but success must destroy the Union as it has been constituted in times past. A strong Government must be the logical consequence of victory, and the triumph of the South will be attended by a similar result, for which, indeed, many Southerners are very well disposed.

Neither party – if such a term can be applied to the rest of the United States, and to those States which disclaim the authority of the Federal Government – was prepared for the aggressive or resisting power of the other. Already the Confederate States perceive that they cannot carry all before them with a rush, while the North have learnt that they must put forth all their strength to make good a tithe of their lately uttered threats.

In the matter of slave-labour, South Carolina argues pretty much in the following manner: England and France (she says) require our products. In order to meet their wants, we must cultivate our soil. There is only one way of doing so. The white man cannot live on our land at certain seasons of the year; he cannot work in the manner required by the crops. He must, therefore, employ a race suited to the labour, and that is a race which will only work when it is obliged to do so. That race was imported from Africa, under the sanction of the law, by our ancestors, when we were a British colony, and it has been fostered by us, so that its increase here has been as great as that of the most flourishing people in the world. In other places, where its labour was not productive or imperatively essential, that race has been made free, sometimes with disastrous consequences to itself and to industry. But we will not make it free. We cannot do so. We hold that slavery is essential to our existence as producers of what Europe requires; nay more, we maintain it is in the abstract right in principle; and some of us go so far as to maintain that the only proper form of society, according to the law of God and the exigencies of man, is that which has slavery as its basis. As to the slave, he is happier far in his state of servitude, more civilized and religious, than he is or could be if free or in his native Africa. For this system we will fight to the end.

In the evening I paid farewell visits, and spent an hour with Mr Toombs, who is unquestionably one of the most original, quaint, and earnest of the Southern leaders, and whose eloquence and power as a debater are greatly esteemed by his countrymen. He is something of an Anglo-maniac, and an Anglo-phobist – a combination not unusual in America – that is, he is proud of being connected with and descended from respectable English families, and admires our mixed constitution, whilst he is an enemy to what is called English policy, and is a strong pro-slavery champion. Wigfall and he are very uneasy about the scant supply of gunpowder in the Southern States, and the difficulty of obtaining it.

In the evening had a little reunion in the bedroom as before – Mr Wigfall, Mr Keitt, an eminent Southern politician, Colonel Pickett, Mr Browne, Mr Benjamin, Mr George Sanders, and others.

May 9th. My faithful Wigfall was good enough to come in early, in order to show me some comments on my letters in the *New York Times*. It appears the papers are angry because I said that New York was apathetic when I landed, and they try to prove I was wrong by showing there was a 'glorious outburst of Union feeling,' after the news of the fall of Sumter.

Before my departure I had a little farewell leave – Mr Toombs, Mr Browne, Mr Benjamin, Mr Walker, Major Deas, Colonel Pickett, Major Calhoun, Captain Ripley, and others – who were exceedingly kind with letters of introduction and offers of service. Dined as usual on a composite dinner – Southern meat and poultry bad – at three o'clock, and at four PM drove down to the steep banks of the Alabama River, where the castle-like hulk of the *Southern Republic* was waiting to receive us. I bade good-bye to Montgomery without regret.

Anthony Trollope (1862)

Thirty years after his mother's controversial tour, the novelist Anthony Trollope (1815–82) visited America during the Civil War. Perhaps because he was on official business for the Post Office his account of his journey was considerably less hostile than hers. When in St. Louis, he experienced Martial Law.

The material growth of the States has been so quick, that the political growth has not been able to keep pace with it. In commerce, in education, in all municipal arrangements, in mechanical skill, and also in professional ability, the country has stalked on with amazing rapidity; but in the art of governing, in all political management and detail, it has made no advance. The merchants of our country and of that country have for many years met on terms of perfect equality, but it has never been so with their statesmen

and our statesmen, with their diplomatists and our diplomatists. Lombard
Street and Wall Street can do business with each other on equal footing,
but it is not so between Downing Street and the State-office at Washington.
The science of statesmanship has yet to be learned in the States – and
certainly the highest lesson of that science, which teaches that honesty is
the best policy.

I trust that the war will have left such a lesson behind it. If it do so, let
the cost in money be what it may, that money will not have been wasted.
If the American people can learn the necessity of employing their best men
for their lightest work – if they can recognise honest men when they meet
them and trust them when they are so recognised – then they may become
as great in politics as they have become great in commerce and in social
institutions.

St. Louis, and indeed the whole State of Missouri, was at the time of
my visit under martial law. General Halleck was in command, holding his
head-quarters at St. Louis, and carrying out, at any rate as far as the city
was concerned, what orders he chose to issue. I am disposed to think that,
situated as Missouri then was, martial law was the best law. No other law
could have had force in a town surrounded by soldiers, and in which half
of the inhabitants were loyal to the existing Government, and half of them
were in favour of rebellion. The necessity for such power is terrible, and
the power itself in the hands of one man must be full of danger; but even
that is better than anarchy. I will not accuse General Halleck of abusing
his power, seeing that it is hard to determine what is the abuse of such
power and what its proper use. When we were at St. Louis a tax was being
gathered of £100 a head from certain men presumed to be secessionists,
and as the money was not of course very readily paid, the furniture of these
suspected secessionists was being sold by auction. No doubt such a measure
was by then regarded as a great abuse. One gentleman informed me that,
in addition to this, certain houses of his had been taken by the Government
at a fixed rent, and that the payment of the rent was now refused unless
he would take the oath of allegiance. He no doubt thought that an abuse
of power! But the worst abuse of such power comes not at first, but with
long usage.

Up to the time however at which I was at St. Louis, martial law had
chiefly been used in closing grog-shops and administering the oath of
allegiance to suspected secessionists. Something also had been done in the
way of raising money by selling the property of convicted secessionists, and
while I was there eight men were condemned to be shot for destroying
railway bridges. 'But will they be shot?' I asked of one of the officers. 'Oh
yes. It will be done quietly, and no one will know anything about it. We
shall get used to that kind of thing presently.' And the inhabitants of
Missouri were becoming used to martial law. It is surprising how quickly a
people can reconcile themselves to altered circumstances, when the change
comes upon them without the necessity of any expressed opinion on their
own part. Personal freedom has been considered as necessary to the American of the States as the air he breathes. Had any suggestion been made to
him of a suspension of the privilege of habeas corpus, of a censorship of the
press, or of martial law, the American would have declared his willingness to
die on the floor of the House of Representatives, and have proclaimed with

ten million voices his inability to live under circumstances so subversive of his rights as a man. And he would have thoroughly believed the truth of his own assertions. Had a chance been given of an argument on the matter, of stump speeches, and caucus meetings, these things could never have been done. But as it is, Americans are, I think, rather proud of the suspension of the habeas corpus. They point with gratification to the uniformly loyal tone of the newspapers, remarking that any editor who should dare to give even a secession squeak, would immediately find himself shut up. And now nothing but good is spoken of martial law. I thought it a nuisance when I was prevented by soldiers from trotting my horse down Pennsylvania Avenue in Washington, but I was assured by Americans that such restrictions were very serviceable in a community. At St. Louis martial law was quite popular. Why should not General Halleck be as well able to say what was good for the people as any law or any lawyer? He had no interest in the injury of the State, but every interest in its preservation. 'But what,' I asked, 'would be the effect were he to tell you to put out all your fires at eight o'clock?' 'If he were so to order, we should do it; but we know that he will not.' But who does know to what General Halleck or other generals may come; or how soon a curfew-bell may be ringing in American towns? The winning of liberty is long and tedious, but the losing it is a downhill easy journey.

It was here, in St. Louis, that General Fremont had held his military court. He was a great man here during those hundred days through which his command lasted. He lived in a great house, had a body-guard, was inaccessible as a great man should be, and fared sumptuously every day. He fortified the city – or rather he began to do so. He constructed barracks here, and instituted military prisons. The fortifications have been discontinued as useless, but the barracks and the prisons remain. In the latter there were 1,200 secessionist soldiers who had been taken in the State of Missouri. 'Why are they not exchanged?' I asked. 'Because they are not exactly soldiers,' I was informed. 'The secessionists do not acknowledge them.' 'Then would it not be cheaper to let them go?' 'No,' said my informant; 'because in that case we should have to catch them again.' And so the 1,200 remain in their wretched prison – thinned from week to week and from day to day by prison disease and prison death.

George Augustus Sala (1865)

George Augustus Sala (1828–95) served as special Correspondent of the Daily Telegraph *in the United States during the Civil War.*

What impression does the first glimpse of America make on a stranger? Absolutely that of large box full of German toys. I saw the state of Massachusetts to begin with from Boston harbour. The shows were wonderfully toy-like – everything spick and span, and shining and new-looking. Trim, chalet-looking wooden houses, painted in all kinds of gay colours, dotted about like ornaments on a twelfth-cake. Toy trees, slim in the stem, straight in the branches, light and feathery in foliage; toy road, serpentine, dazzling, sparkling; the kind of roads you see in a Valentine, with a lady and a gentleman meandering towards the Temple of Hymen in the middle distance. Toy carriages: so crank and slender and brightly varnished are they – they all look as though they were made of painted tin; toy fences and palisades, and curious little toy churches, with bright green jalousies to the windows, and wooden steeples. Only give me the run of Mr Cremer's toy warehouse in Regent street, and I would build you up a model of the environs of Boston in half an hour. As a background you must have sky not *quite* Italian blue . . . – a Sèvres porcelain sky, in fact. Let this sky be thoroughly clear from cloud or murk; let the air be as clear as a silver bell, – a wry, high-toned rarefied atmosphere, not bracing, however, but stimulating, lung-lifting, pulse-inclining, stringing your nerves to a degree of tension which is perhaps not very salutary, and of which the reaction may be languor, exhaustion, and ennui. Make the outlines clear of every object sharply defined; make the shadows cast by the sun clear and incisive, and in their texture luminous, instead of (as in our umbrageousness) heavy and woolly. Do this, *pictor ignotus*, and with your toy houses, toy gardens, toy fences, toy trees, and toy carriages, you may get up a suburban Boston to the very life.

Schenectady! There are throughout the North five hundred Schenectadys feeding like one. A broad, dusty main thoroughfare, bordered with trees and irregularly paved. No three houses of the same size together; but the same types of many-windowed factory, tumbledown shanty, shingle villa whitewashed, and packing-case-looking shop of dun brick, repeated over and over again *ad nauseam*. To the whitewashed shingle villas green venetians. No knockers to the doors; but bell-pulls, and name-plates, electro-silvered. At some gates, a ragged, dirty negress, dully babbling with an Irish help – not ragged she, but dirtier. High steps, or 'stoops' to the private houses, and towards evening the entire family sitting, standing, or lounging thereupon: the father, spectacles on nose, reading the local newspaper, in which there is nothing to read save advertisements, eight lines of telegraphic despatches, mostly apocryphal, and sixteen lines of editorial, setting forth how the local contemporary – if it have one – is a liar and scoundrel, and that it's brother-in-law suffered two years in the penitentiary for stealing a horse; the young ladies, in grand evening toilette, staring other young ladies who may happen to pass, out of countenance; mamma, grandmamma, and two or three maiden aunts, or acidulated cousins, knitting socks for the Sanitary Commission; and the younger branches of the family yelling over contested candy, beating upon drums, or – if any of them are girls, and above six years old, fanning themselves and twirling their skirts in imitation of their elders. I dare say were you rude enough to peep through the window at the table laid out for supper, you would find there was Pie. To this, add the jangling of half-a-dozen pianofortes, and the familiar strains of the waltz from *Faust*.

It [Washington] contains, certainly, some notable public buildings, but they are scattered far and wide, with all kinds of incongruous environments, producing upon the stranger a perplexed impression that the British Museum has suddenly migrated to the centre of an exhausted brickfield, where rubbish may be shot; or that St Paul's Cathedral, washed quite white, and stuck upon stone stilts, has been transferred to the middle of the Libyan desert, and called a Capitol. There is a perpetual solution of continuity at Washington. There is no cohesion about Pennsylvania Avenue. Its houses are Hudibras' story of the Bear and the fiddle - begun and broke off in the middle. It is an architectural conundrum which nobody can guess, and in which I candidly believe there is no meaning. The Vitruviuses and Palladios of America have perpetrated a vast practical joke, and called it Washington. It is the most 'bogus' of towns – a shin-plaster in brick and mortar, and with a delusive frontispiece of marble. The inhabitants seem to be very fond of building houses, but when they have run up three or four stories which threaten to attain the altitude of the Tower of Babel, the confusion of tongues sets in; the builders abandon their work; but, nothing disheartened, erect three or four stories of fresh houses elsewhere. It is said of those patrons of the drama who habitually avail themselves of half-price, that they have seen nothing but *dénouements*. Washington, on the contrary, is a collection of first acts without any catastrophes . . . Washington will be, I have no doubt, some day uproariously splendid; but at present it isn't anything. It is in the District of Columbia and the State of the Future.

Part Four
The Great Wave 1865–1988

The original thirteen states of the Union had a combined population of about four million. Of these about half a million were slaves. By 1912, when Wyoming became the forty-eighth 'star' to be added to the American flag, there were ninety two million people in the United States.

This huge expansion of population was never due to the westward movement of the Union except at the beginning, with the absorption of the former French and Spanish colonies in the early nineteenth century. Outside the old colonial settlements population was sparse: the increase in numbers was almost entirely due to mass immigration from Europe.

There always had been a steady trickle of new settlers. Between 1790 and 1820 five to six thousand Europeans settled in America every year. One suspects that the numbers would have been greater had it not been for the wars in Europe during that period; for after 1820 there was a sudden increase to about 90,000 immigrants every year.

But the great wave of immigration began with the econoomic slump and political disorders that affected Europe in the 1840s. The first enormous influx came from Ireland. Ironically two of the factors which brought the Irish over came from America itself. The increasing competitiveness of American agriculture forced small farmers in Ireland to shift from tillage to grazing, on barren ground. And the potato blight crossed the Atlantic from America in 1845, devastating the potato crop two years in succession.

If hunger was the spur in Ireland, the blight elsewhere was politics. Revolutions, successful and failed, undermined Austria, Germany, France, and Italy. America, with strenuous impartiality, welcomed refugee German liberals as it had once welcomed French aristocrats fleeing from the Terror. From 1847 to 1854 immigration averaged about 300,000 per year; approximately three million people in all; twice the total number that had come during the previous seventy years.

Left to its own devices, the momentum could only increase. Temporary checks were provided by the Civil War and the U.S. financial crisis of 1893, but in each case the upward trend was speedily resumed. Between 1891 and 1914 the total number of immigrants was 16,500,000; the biggest number in any one year, 1,285,000 in 1907.

These figures included people who did not remain permanently; sadly we have no idea of the proportion of the total formed by those who returned to Europe. Estimates range as high as 30%. Few of these 're-emigrants' were the travellers whose accounts make up the majority of the pieces in this section. In the late nineteenth century the 'amateur emigrant', as Stevenson called him, mostly came from the leisured classes; men and women who had the time and money to study America properly. Inevitably they formed a different class from the 'huddled masses' whose transit ships choked up New York harbour.

Once anchored, these immigrant convoys were inspected by health

officials, who began the bitter process of weeding out 'undesirable aliens'.
Sufferers from contagious diseases were taken off in a quarantine boat to
await deportation.

In theory the United States had always been welcoming to immigrants.
Its founding fathers were of immigrant stock, and one of the original
grievances of the Declaration of Independence was 'that the king was
endeavoured to prevent the population of these States; for that purpose
obstructing the Laws of Naturalisation of Foreigners; refusing to pass others
to encourage their migrations hither, and raising the conditions of new
Appropriations of Lands.' The bigness of America, with its vast undomesti-
cated spaces, and its moral atmosphere of self-help unfettered by restrictions, encouraged a feeling of unlimited opportunity.

In practice there arose in the nineteenth century a strong tendency in
the opposite direction. As America matured into nationhood, it became
increasingly nationalistic. Organized attacks on immigrants were commonplace in the 1850s; Irish 'Papists' and German 'red republicans' being
particularly disliked. The nativist movement petered out in the Civil War,
when Americans started attacking each other instead, but it asserted itself
again in the 1890s. Until then the chief settlers - the 'old' immigration –
had come from north-west Europe: Irish, then Germans and Scandinavians.
Now the main settlers – the 'new' immigration – were Poles and Jews.

But racial and religious antipathy were not the only reasons for the
demand for restrictions. The new impetus to control was primarily based
on economic grounds. Between 1870 and 1890 the population of the United
States west of the Mississippi nearly trebled. Anyone was entitled to 160
acres of 'free' land simply by going west and homesteading it. But by 1890
agricultural mass migration was approaching its end; the free public lands
had almost all been taken. No more Red Indians or buffalo could be
eliminated. There were limits to the United States after all. The frontier had
disappeared. Now, as America began its period of economic and industrial
dominance, there was a huge movement from the country to the cities.
Unemployment increased. The trades unions, ever in the forefront of
bigoted insularity, resented the competition of cheap, docile labour from
Europe. They probably were the single most important influence in bringing
about the restrictive measures.

Already 'undesirable classes' of immigrants had been excluded by the
Immigration Act of 1882. This forbad entry to criminals, paupers, cripples,
and mental defectives. The Contract Labor Law of 1885 forbad the entry
of any person under a contract made previously to perform work or service
of any kind in the United States. (Foreign lecturers, presumably, could sign
up for tours only once they had got in.)

Those immigrants not suspected of having contagious diseases were
allowed on to Ellis Island, where a doctor summarily diagnosed their
condition. (This did not apply to first-class passengers, who were ensured
a clean bill of health.) Those suspected of disease were marked with a piece
of chalk: 'H' for heart disease; 'F' for facial rash; 'L' for rickets. One
particular mark guaranteed deportation; a circle with a cross in the middle,
for feeble-minded.

Eight out of ten came through this scrutiny. The final process was an

unvarying catechism of questions by an immigration inspector. Up his sleeve
he had that catch question: 'Do you have a job waiting for you?'

Those who passed this examination entered their new country through a
door marked 'Push for New York'. Often they began their new lives with
different names from the ones they had left behind. The inspectors could
often not spell these strange exotic names, and put down an approximation
instead. Often the immigrants could not spell them themselves, for it was
not until 1917 that admission was refused to those who could not read and
write.

These regulations, with their distinction between 'desirable' and 'undesirable' immigrants, failed to bring about the required reduction. Over a
million new settlers came to America in 1920 and 1921. A higher standard
of admissibility would have been impossible to implement without the erection of a substantial bureaucracy: besides, 'quality' controls did not necessarily preclude those ethnic groups which the authorities wished to prevent.
Therefore the quota system was introduced to obtain reductions directly.

The 'Johnson Act' of 1924 introduced the following restriction. Every
year, it said, not more than 2% of the number of foreign-born individuals
of each nationality could enter the country. And the number of those
resident of each nationality was to be based on the 1890 Census. The 2%
made up each country's quota. By placing the operating date at 1890 this
automatically biassed the quota against the 'new' immigrants.

No doubt the quota system played some part in the substantial reduction
of immigration to the United States between the wars. But it was less
important than other factors. According to the quota system about three
million immigrants could have been admitted to America during the twenty
years it operated between 1930 and 1949, but only 800,000 of these places
were taken up. Even discounting the war years, the north-east European
nations were particularly loath to use their high annual quota; on average
only a fifth of these places was used up every year. When the depression
set in, even the quotas for southern and eastern Europe were often unfilled.
Between 1932 and 1935 more people left the United States than came in.

The balance was restored in the late thirties by an influx of refugees
from Nazi Germany, but immigration was not to revive on a large scale
until after the war. And then the authorities relaxed the quotas to admit
another new wave; those characteristic products of the war, Displaced
Persons and G.I. Brides.

John Maguire (1866)

John Maguire, an Irish journalist and politician, visited America in 1866 to survey the conditions of his fellow countrymen in the New World. In his book, The Irish in America, *he recounts this tale of the plight of two new immigrants.*

The law also attempted to regulate the charges in boarding-houses, and protect the luggage of the emigrant from the clutches of the proprietors of these establishments; but it appeared only to render the lot of the emigrant one of still greater hardship; for what could no longer be legally retained was illegally made away with. In their Report for 1848, the Commissioners refer to the new system adopted in these houses:- 'Of late, robberies of luggage from emigrant boarding-houses have become of frequent occurrence, so as to have excited the suspicion that in some instances the keepers of the houses are not altogether free from participation in the robbery. If the tavern keeper has reason to apprehend that the lodger will not be able to pay his bill, and knowing that the law prohibits his retaining the luggage, he may think it proper to secure his claim without law.'

I must confess to being immensely amused at hearing from one who had passed through the ordeal how he had been dealt with in the fine old time of unrestricted plunder, when the emigrant was left to his fate – that fate assuming the substantial form of the runner and the boarding-house keeper. My informant was a great, broad-shouldered, red-haired Irishman, over six feet 'in his stocking vamps,' and who, I may add, on the best authority, bore himself gallantly in the late war, under the banner of the Union. He was but a very young lad when, in 1848, he came to New York, with a companion of his own age, 'to better his fortune,' as many a good Irishman had endeavoured to do before him. He possessed, besides splendid health and a capacity for hard work, a box of tools, a bundle of clothes, and a few pounds in gold – not a bad outfit for a good-tempered young Irishman, with a red head, broad shoulders, grand appetite, and fast rising to the six feet.

The moment he landed his luggage was pounced upon by two runners, one seizing the box of tools, the other confiscating the clothes. The future American citizen assured his obliging friends that he was quite capable of carrying his own luggage; but no, they should relieve him – the stranger, the guest of the Republic - of that trouble. Each was in the interest of a different boarding-house, and each insisted that the young Irishman with the red head should go with him – a proposition that, to any but a New York runner, would seem, if not altogether impossible, at least most difficult of accomplishment. Not being able to oblige both the gentlemen, he could only oblige one; and as the tools were more valuable than the clothes, he followed in the path of the gentleman who had secured that portion of the 'plunder'. He remembers that the two gentlemen wore very pronounced green neckties, and spoke with a richness of accent that denoted special if not conscientious cultivation; and on his arrival at the boarding-house, he was cheered with the announcement that its proprietor was from 'the ould counthry, and loved every sod of it, God bless it!' In a manner truly paternal the host warned the two lads against the danger of the streets; and so darkly did he paint the horrors, and villainies, and murders of all kinds, that were sure to rain down upon their innocent heads, that the poor boys were frightened into a rigid seclusion from the world outside, and occupied their time as best they could, not forgetting 'the eating and the drinking' which the house afforded. The young Irishman with the red head imparted to the host the fact of his having a friend in Canal Street – 'wherever Canal Street was;' and that the friend had been some six years in New York, and knew the place well, and was to procure employment for him as soon as they met; and he concluded by asking how he could get to Canal Street. 'Canal Street! – is it Canal Street? – why then what a mortal pity, and the stage to go just an hour before you entered this very door! My, my! that's unfortunate; isn't it? Well, no matter, there'll be another in two days' time, or three at farthest, and I'll be sure to see you sent there all right – depend your life on me when I say it,' said the jovial kindly host. For full forty-eight hours the two lads, who were as innocent as a brace of young goslings, endured the irksome monotony of the boarding-house, even though that abode of hospitality was cheered by the presence of its jovial host, who loved every sod of the 'ould counthry;' but human nature cannot endure beyond a certain limit – and the two lads resolved, in sheer desperation, to break bounds at any hazard. They roamed through the streets for some time, without any special ill befalling them. Meeting a policeman, the young fellow with the red head suggested to his companion the possibility of the official knowing something about Canal Street; and as his companion had nothing to urge against it, they approached that functionary, and boldly propounded the question to him – where Canal Street was, and how it could be reached? 'Well, then, my man,' replied the policeman, who also happened to be a compatriot, 'if you only follow your nose for the space of twenty minutes in that direction, you'll come to Canal Street, and no mistake about it; you'll see the name on the corner, in big letters, if you can read – as I suppose you can, for you look to be two decent boys.' Canal Street in twenty minutes! Here indeed was a pleasant surprise for the young fellows, who had been told to wait for the stage, which, according to the veracious host, 'was due in about another day.'

Of course they did follow their respective noses until they actually reached Canal Street, found the number of the house in which their friend resided, and discovered the friend himself, to whom they recounted their brief adventures in New York. Thanks to the smartness of their acclimated friend, they recovered their effects, but not before they disbursed to the jovial host, who 'loved every sod of the ould counthry, God bless it!' more than would have enabled them to fare sumptuously at the Astor. And as the great strapping fellow – who had since seen many a brave man die with his face to the foe – told the tale of his first introduction to the Empire City, he actually looked sheepish at its recollection, and then laughed heartily at a simplicity which had long since become, with him, a weakness of the past.

Jacques Offenbach (1876)

In 1876 the United States celebrated the centenary of its independence. Among France's official contributions to the festivities was the gift of the Statue of Liberty. The French composer, Jacques Offenbach (1819–1880) was not of the official party, but he went anyway. A rich South American businessman, one Lino Bacquero, offered him a thousand dollars a performance for thirty concerts. Offenbach needed the money and accepted. His account of his visit is neither a journal nor a memoir; it consists of a series of articles on the peculiarities of the American scene.

The Races

I went to the races at Jerome Park. The field where the steeplechase takes place is a continuation of Central Park which I described earlier. It belongs to a rich banker, Mr. De Belmont. You must not expect me to talk cleverly about this sport, with the *savoir-faire* of my friend Milton of *Le Figaro*; I do not know the special language of the turf; I scarcely know what a starter is. All that I can tell you is that I saw at Jerome Park a rather muddy track and the things you see at every racecourse: lots of horses, lots of jockeys, lots of ladies, lots of gentlemen. If the horses seemed to be a little too fat, the jockeys on the other hand affected me as being a little too thin. But I will state nothing definitely. There is only one thing I can be sure of: here, as everywhere else, there is always a horse and a jockey who come in first, so that some men become very happy at winning and others very unhappy at losing – there is betting here just as everywhere else.

It was my impression that the spectators were not very enthusiastic. The finish of a race, as the seven or eight horses competing drew near to the post, always in France and in England excites cries, acclamations, and hurrahs. One feels that for a few seconds everybody is, as it were, seized by a whirlwind of speed, carried away by the excitement of the spectacle and the emotions of gambling. Even our most correct sportsmen cannot witness this moment without revealing in some way, more often than not by making a noise, what intense interest they take in the result. At Jerome Park, nothing of the kind. A little shiver of interest, immediately suppressed, at the start and at the finish; in between a glacial silence. The noise, the bravos, the hurrahs that give life and gaiety to Longchamp and to Chantilly are completely lacking at Jerome Park.

Because I had only the slightest interest in the spectacle, I had leisure to look around me to observe, and so witnessed a curious and characteristic little scene.

Between two races, a man was walking quietly along the track; suddenly a little thread of smoke was seen to rise from his clothes, an almost imperceptible blue vapour, which immediately spread and became a veritable whirlwind. The man's pocket was burning. Almost immediately there was a spurt of flame. 'You're on fire,' they cried to him from all sides. He certainly must have felt it because the flames were already licking his coat-tails, but with the *sang-froid* of a true Yankee, his first thought was to save his pocketbook. Fortunately, at the very same moment he was drawing it from his inside pocket, several policemen threw themselves upon him and tore off his burning coat. He went off in his shirt sleeves, still quite calm, thanking the public and the policemen with a glance.

I have already described the distinction with which the charming American women dress. I had the occasion on that day to observe it again. They had come to the races in their freshest, their most brilliant *toilettes*, and I cannot tell you how delightful was the sight of the race track embellished with the presence of these elegant ladies. I am sorry that I cannot give the same praise to the American men, who all dress, I will not say simply, but very informally, so much so that at the theatre or at a concert, you can see them wearing clothes – frightful suits – such as we hardly dare to wear in the country or at the seaside. The soft hat is traditional. Even the most distinguished man does not hesitate to go out for the evening or to attend a dinner with a very elegant woman on his arm, wearing a soft hat of the most grotesque kind.

It astonished me to see that many of them wear white ties at all hours of the day and night. At six o'clock in the morning the Yankee winds around his neck a strip of batiste which he does not remove all day long. The ceremonial white tie and informal costume which accompanies it are in strange contrast.

It amazes foreigners also to see that all American men have under the skirts of their frock coat, near the belt, a rather prominent bulge. This is the place where these gentlemen generally carry their revolvers or sometimes quite unimportant business papers.

The American Press

Newspapers have a much greater importance in America than they do in Europe. You must not conclude, however, that the press is more free in the New World than in the Old. With us it is the government that watches over and controls the newspapers; in the United States, the religious sects and political parties tyrannize over the editors, who, it must be said, rather cultivate this servitude and even take advantage of it.

Knowing as well as I do the set-up of the chief French papers, I was eager to visit the offices of some of the New York dailies. American reporters are certainly better off than ours with respect to office space. Imagine immense buildings, grandiose constructions, and in these journalistic palaces a continual going and coming like a laborious beehive.

In New York, as in Paris, the newspapers have chosen for their offices buildings situated in the liveliest part of the city. In order to be well and quickly informed, a paper must be in close proximity to the business centre, in a populous district; so the great American press has chosen Broadway for its home.

The offices are easy to find. If you look for a newspaper during the daytime, raise your head, see which is the tallest building, and walk boldly in. This is the place. To cite only one example, the *New York Tribune* building has nine stories. If it is night time, open your eyes. The edifice which is best illuminated, which sheds its light over the whole district, that is the one you are looking for. Behind those brilliantly lighted windows, the journalists are at work. They say sometimes in France, figuratively, that a newspaper is a lighthouse – in America, lighthouse is the appropriate word.

As for the interior arrangements of the building, it leaves nothing to be desired from the point of view of comfort. The telegraph machines are installed right in the building, enlivening everything with their perpetual tremolo. The typesetting rooms, the room for making the illustrations, the printing shop are wonderfully outfitted.

Here are a few details about some of the principal newspapers of New York. Let's begin with the *New York Herald*, founded about thirty years ago by James Gordon Bennett. Its approximate circulation at present is 70,000 copies. Each edition is composed, according to circumstances, of eight, sixteen, or even twenty-four pages. Its format is about one-fourth larger than that of Parisian papers. Since small type is widely used in America, you can easily perceive how many news items, articles, and advertisements, on the average, you will find in this paper – twenty-eight columns of advertising goes up to sixty. The price of space varies between twenty-five cents and a dollar a line.

The advertising, the news stories, and circulation of the *New York Herald* make it the foremost journal in the United States. It is hard to get an idea of the number of personnel which the administration and exploitation of a sheet of this importance demands: seventy typesetters, twenty pressmen, twenty clerks, a legion of workmen. So much for the manual labour – without counting a whole regiment of delivery men and newspaper sellers. The *New York Herald* naturally has also a numerous editorial staff scattered over all parts of the world. Amongst its oldest collaborators, I might mention Mr. Connery, a musical critic of great talent. But without fear of contradiction, the most interesting personage connected with this newspaper is Mr. Bennett, Jr., its editor and proprietor. I have consecrated a few lines to him in my pen portraits.

After the *New York Herald*, comes the *New York Times*, which publishes 40,000 copies. Its opinion and its literary excellence have given it great authority over the public. It was founded by Messieurs Raymond, Jones, and Wesley. Mr. Raymond, a very distinguished statesman, remained as editor-in-chief until his death. Mr. Jennings of the *London Times* succeeded him. Actually, the principal owner is Mr. Jones, who enjoys very great influence. He has firmly maintained the good traditions of the paper and is very careful that his journal shall shine among all American papers by the purity and elegance of its style. To remain faithful to his tradition, he could have chosen for its editor no more distinguished writer than Mr. Foord nor any more competent musical and dramatic critic than Mr. Schwab.

The *New York Times* uses Walker Presses which need only two men to service them and which print 15,000 to 17,000 copies per hour.

The *New York Tribune* was founded by Horace Greeley, philanthropist and eminent journalist, one of the bitterest enemies of slavery. As candidate for the presidency in 1872, Greeley failed miserably, and died of shame and sorrow as a result.

The *Tribune* is really a forum open to all apostles of new theories. At the present moment a lively campaign in favour of women's rights is being carried on. Though it is still very well edited, this journal has lost something of its influence since it has become the property of Mr. Jay Gould, a former associate of Colonel Fisk. His musical critic is Mr. Hassard, who is mad about Wagner; his dramatic critic is Mr. Winter, an excellent literary man and most agreeable socially.

The *World*, organ of the Democrats; circulation, 12,000 to 15,000; editor-in-chief, Mr. W Hurlbut. Mr. Hurlbut has travelled widely, seen much and retained much. An accomplished man of the world, a writer of merit, nothing he does can be ignored; he has only one fault in the eyes of his fellow journalists – he is somewhat changeable in politics. Is that really a fault in an age like ours? The musical critic of the *World* is Mr. Wheeler, a witty writer.

The *Sun* – editor and principal proprietor, Mr . . . [C. A. Dana], a first-class journalist who speaks every language, excellent at condensing any new scandals that come to hand. His newspaper sells for two cents instead of four. Average edition, 120,000.

Continuing my review of the press, I arrive at the evening newspapers:

The *Evening Post*, edited by Mr. William Cullen Bryant, the great American poet. Republican opinions. Considerable clientele.

The *Advertiser-Evening Telegram* is distinguished from the others in that it appears in a continuous stream. It is always being composed, always in the press, always on sale. Just as soon as a piece of news arrives, an edition is brought out immediately; and since news is arriving all day long . . . The *New York Herald* publishes this sheet.

Among the foreign-language newspapers in New York, the *Courrier des États-Unis* must be mentioned. Forty years of existence. It owes its first prosperity to M. Frédéric Gaillardet, who sold it to M. Charles LaSalle. M. LaSalle is still the owner and has brought into the paper his son-in-law, M. Léon Meunier, the present editor. The *Courrier des États-Unis*, carefully edited, is highly esteemed as a newspaper. Its critic is M. Charles Villa.

The *Messager Franco Américain* is a weekly newspaper about ten years old and ultra-Republican. Its owner is M. De Mavil, and its editor is M. Louis Cortambert.

The *Staats-Zeitung*, written in German, has as its director Mr. Oswald Ollendorf, an Austrian politician and literary man, who has resided for twenty-five years in America. It has complete news coverage, is well written, and possesses great influence on local politics. Its superb office is directly across from the *New York Times*. Approximate circulation, 25,000 to 30,000. The *Staats-Zeitung* was founded about thirty years ago by Madame Uhl, an exceptionally energetic woman. Its beginnings were somewhat difficult. Like the elder Bennett in the early days of his newspaper, it was often the editor herself who made the deliveries.

In addition to these newspapers, one should mention the Associated Press, corresponding to our Agence Havas, and the Association of Reporters, which latter deserves special mention. The reporters, about forty of them for every newspaper, have organized to send in accounts of accidents, of crimes, etc. They all wait in police headquarters, which is connected with the precinct stations by telegraph, until they receive news of some happening and then they go immediately to the place. Two or three of them cover the civil courts; about fifteen more meet morning and evening at the office of the newspaper and are sent to the different quarters of the city by the editor. They all know how to take pictures and are experts in telegraphy. With the help of the telegraph, they can give an immediate account of any event which may have happened a thousand leagues away, so that the speech, the crime, or the accident which they have witnessed the evening before will have five or six columns in small type in next morning's paper.

To Niagara

Pullman Cars

What a beautiful journey from New York to Niagara. Especially as far as Albany the landscape is exquisite, as the track runs along beside the admirable Hudson River. I have been searching my memory for some European river which I might compare with this American one. Certain places recall the most beautiful spots along the Rhine, others surpass in grandeur and charm everything that I have ever seen.

The journey takes place under the best conditions. The Pullman cars are an excellent institution; to be on the train and to be subjected to none of the inconveniences of the train, that is the great problem which has been solved by these wonderful coaches. You are not confined as you are in Europe in narrow compartments, nor exposed to the itching which you get in the legs after a few hours of immobility, nor do you have to fear the paralysis caused in your tired members by staying too long in the same position. In the American train, you can walk up and down through the carriages, one after the other from the baggage car to the rear bumper; when you are tired of walking, you find an elegant drawing-room, and soft chairs where you can take your ease; you have within reach everything that makes life agreeable. I could do no better in summing up my admiration for the American railroads than to say that they are really cradles on wheels.

But I certainly don't like the perpetual bell which accompanies you during the whole journey with its funereal tolling, but perhaps one can get the habit. One must not have a very sensitive ear when travelling in America, since one is continually plagued by annoying noises.

At Utica where we stopped a few minutes for lunch, I saw – and heard, alas! – a big Negro pounding on a tom-tom. Clearly he was making up the tune, for sometimes he beat loud, sometimes with astonishing speed, sometimes with measured slowness. He played, I will not say with fine nuances, but with different meanings. I forgot to eat lunch, because I was examining this interesting musician. During his last piece – for him it must have been a piece of music – I was all eyes and ears. He began with a deafening *fortissimo*, for this Negro was strong and he went at it vigorously. After this brilliant beginning, the music continued with a *decrescendo* which became *piano* and then *pianissimo* and then . . . silence. At that moment the train started, and I barely had time to jump on the step when it was off at full speed.

We arrived at Albany and stopped for dinner. In front of the restaurant at Albany, I found another big Negro almost exactly like the other and also playing a tom-tom. They seemed to be everywhere; this country must passionately love the tom-tom.

'A hungry stomach has no ears,' says one of our proverbs. I am sorry to put myself down as contradicting a saying founded on the wisdom of nations; for in spite of my formidable appetite the Negro's music haunted me during the whole meal. He was playing exactly like his colleague at Utica; his piece was composed of the same succession of *forte, piano*, and *pianissimo*. Astonished at this strange coincidence, I was just about to ask if the Negroes thought that solos on the tom-tom were music and if they were playing their national anthem, when one of my friends forestalled me.

'You're interested in the Negro,' he said to me. 'You can expect to find one just like him at every station on this line.'

'Is it a delicate attention on the part of the railroad company?'

'No, it is the restaurant keepers that maintain them. They play the whole time that the train remains in the station, and their music serves to keep the travellers who have gone into the restaurant informed as to the time. As long as the tom-tom is sounding at full speed, you can be easy; when the noise diminishes, that's the sign that you must hurry. When it almost fades away, the travellers know that they've got to rush to the train, which like Louis XIV never waits, and what is still more disagreeable, never gives any warning of its going. Too bad for those who miss the train!'

I am not certain whether or not I prefer the American system to the one used by a restaurant keeper at Morceux between Bordeaux and Biarritz. Not having any Negro the proprietor himself shouts at intervals in a stentorian voice, 'You still have five minutes! You have four minutes more! You have three minutes more!' Basically, the two systems are alike. The only difference is that one man deafens you by shouts in his restaurant, the other overwhelms you by his music in the open air.

Sarah Bernhardt (1881)

The most celebrated actress of her time, Bernhardt's piece from her autobiography is most memorable for the overwhelming vanity it displays in her treatment of her visit to New York and all points west.

Finally the ship arrived on October 27, at half-past six in the morning. I was asleep, worn out by three days and nights of wild storms. My maid had some difficulty in rousing me. I could not believe that we had arrived, and I wanted to go on sleeping until the last minute. I had to give in to the evidence, however, as the screw had stopped, and I heard a sound of dull thuds echoing in the distance. I put my head out of my porthole, and saw some men endeavouring to make a passage for us through the river. The Hudson was frozen hard, and the heavy vessel could only advance with the aid of pick-axes cutting away the blocks of ice.

This sudden arrival delighted me, and everything seemed to be transformed in a minute. I forgot all my discomforts and the weariness of the twelve days' crossing. The sun was rising, pale but rose-tinted, dispersing the mists and shining over the ice, which, thanks to the efforts of our pioneers, was splintered into a thousand luminous pieces. I had entered the New World in the midst of a display of ice-fireworks. It was fairy-like and somewhat crazy, but it seemed to me that it must be a good omen.

I am so superstitious that if I had arrived when there was no sunshine I should have been wretched and most anxious until after my first performance. It is a perfect torture to be superstitious to this degree, and, unfortunately for me, I am ten times more so now than I was in those days, for besides the superstitions of my own country, I have, thanks to my travels, added to my stock all the superstitions of the other countries. I know them all now, and in any critical moment of my life they all rise up in armed legions, for or against me. I cannot walk a single step or make any movement or gesture, sit down, go out, look at the sky or the ground, without finding some reason for hope or for despair, until at last, exasperated by the trammels put upon my actions by my thought, I defy all my superstitions and just act as I want to act. Delighted, then, with what seemed to me to be a good omen, I began to dress gleefully . . .

On arriving at the Albemarle Hotel I felt tired and nervous, and wanted to be left quite alone. I hurried away at once to my room in the suite that had been engaged for me, and fastened the doors. There was neither lock nor bolt on one of them, but I pushed a piece of furniture against it, and then refused emphatically to open it. There were about fifty people waiting in the drawing-room, but I had that feeling of awful weariness which makes one ready to go to the most violent extremes for the sake of an hour's repose. I wanted to lie down on the rug, cross my arms, throw my head back, and close my eyes. I did not want to talk any more, and I did not want to have to smile or look at any one. I threw myself down on the floor, and was deaf to the knocks on my door and to Jarrett's supplications. I did not want to argue the matter, so I did not utter a word. I heard the murmur of grumbling voices, and Jarrett's words tactfully persuading the visitors to stay. I heard the rustle of paper being pushed under the door, and Madame Guerard whispering to Jarrett, who was furious.

'You don't know her, Monsieur Jarrett,' I heard her say. 'If she thought you were forcing the door open, against which she has pushed the furniture, she would jump out of the window!'

Then I heard Felicie talking to a French lady who was insisting on seeing me.

'It is quite impossible,' she was saying. 'Madame would be quite hysterical. She needs an hour's rest, and everyone must wait!'

For some little time I could hear a confused murmur which seemed to get farther away, and then I fell into a delicious sleep, laughing to myself as I went off, for my good temper returned as I pictured the angry, nonplussed expression on the faces of my visitors.

I woke in an hour's time, for I have the precious gift of being able to sleep ten minutes, a quarter of an hour, or an hour, just as I like, and I then wake up quite peacefully without a shake at the time I choose to rouse up. Nothing does me so much good as this rest to body and mind, decided upon and regulated merely by my will.

Very often when among my intimate friends I have lain down on the bear-skin hearth-rug in front of the fire, telling everyone to go on talking, and to take no notice of me. I have then slept perhaps for an hour, and on waking have found two or three new-comers in the room, who, not wishing to disturb me, have taken part in the general conversation whilst waiting until I should wake up and they could present their respects to me. Even now I lie down on the huge wide sofa in the little Empire salon which leads into my dressing-room, and I sleep whilst waiting for the friends and artistes with whom I have made appointments to be ushered in. When I open my eyes I see the faces of my kind friends, who shake hands cordially, delighted that I should have had some rest. My mind is then tranquil, and I am ready to listen to all the beautiful ideas proposed to me, or to decline the absurdities submitted to me without being ungracious.

I woke up then at the Albemarle Hotel an hour later, and found myself lying on the rug. I opened the door of my room, and discovered my dear Guerard and my faithful Felicie seated on a trunk.

'Are there any people there still?' I asked.

'Oh, Madame, there are about a hundred now,' answered Felicie.

'Help me to take my things off then quickly,' I said, 'and find me a white dress.'

In about five minutes I was ready, and I felt that I looked nice from head to foot. I went into the drawing-room where all these unknown persons were waiting. Jarrett came forward to meet me, but on seeing me well dressed and with a smiling face he postponed the sermon that he wanted to preach to me.

My first impression was a joyful one, and I clapped my hands with delight as I entered the drawing-room, which I had not yet seen. The busts of Racine, Molière, and Victor Hugo were on pedestals surrounded with flowers. All around the large room were sofas laden with cushions, and, to remind me of my home in Paris, there were tall palms stretching out their branches over the sofas. Jarrett introduced Knoedler, who had suggested this piece of gallantry. He was a very charming man. I shook hands with him, and we were friends from that time forth.

The visitors soon went away, but the reporters remained. They were all seated, some of them on the arms of the chairs, others on the cushions. One of them had crouched down tailor-fashion on a bear-skin, and was leaning back against the steam heater. He was pale and thin, and coughed a great deal. I went towards him, and had just opened my lips to speak to him, although I was rather shocked that he did not rise, when he addressed me in a bass voice.

'Which is your favourite rôle, Madame?' he asked.

'That is no concern of yours,' I answered, turning my back on him. In doing so I knocked against another reporter, who was more polite.

'What do you eat when you wake in the morning, Madame?' he inquired.

I was about to reply to him as I had done to the first one, but Jarrett, who had had difficulty in appeasing the anger of the crouching man, answered quickly for me, 'Oatmeal.' I did not know what that dish was, but the ferocious reporter continued his questions.

'And what do you eat during the day?'

'Mussels.'

He wrote down phlegmatically, 'Mussels during the day.'

I moved towards the door, and a female reporter in a tailor-made skirt, with her hair cut short, asked me in a clear, sweet voice 'Are you a Jewess-Catholic-Protestant-Mohammedan-Buddhist-Atheist-Zoroaster-Theist-or-Deist?' I stood still, rooted to the spot in bewilderment. She had said all that in a breath, accenting the syllables haphazard, and making of the whole one word so wildly incoherent that my impression was that I was not in safety near this strange, gentle person. I must have looked uneasy, and as my eyes fell on an elderly lady who was talking gaily to a little group of people, she came to my rescue, saying in very good French, 'This young lady is asking you, Madame, whether you are of the Jewish religion or whether you are a Catholic, a Protestant, a Mohammedan, a Buddhist, an Atheist, a Zoroastrian, a Theist, or a Deist.'

I sank down on a couch.

'Oh, Heavens!' I exclaimed, 'will it be like this in all the cities I visit?'

'On no,' answered Jarrett placidly; 'your interviews will be wired throughout America.'

'What about the mussels?' I thought to myself, and then in an absent-minded way I answered, 'I am a Catholic, Mademoiselle.'

'A Roman Catholic, or do you belong to the Orthodox Church?' she asked.

I jumped up from my seat, for she bored me beyond endurance, and a very young man then approached timidly.

'Will you allow me to finish my sketch, Madame?' he asked.

I remained standing, my profile turned towards him at his request. When he had finished I asked to see what he had done, and, perfectly unabashed, he handed me his horrible drawing of a skeleton with a curly wig. I tore the sketch up and threw it at him, but the following day that horror appeared in the papers, with a disagreeable inscription beneath it. Fortunately I was able to speak seriously about my art with a few honest and intelligent journalists, but twenty-five years ago reporters' paragraphs were more appreciated in America than serious articles, and the public, very much less literary then than at present, always seemed ready to echo the turpitudes invented by reporters hard up for copy. I should think that no creature in the world, since the invention of reporting, has ever had as much to endure as I had during that first tour. The basest calumnies were circulated by my enemies long before I arrived in America, there was all the treachery of the friends of the Comedie, and even of my own admirers, who hoped that I should not succeed on my tour, so that I might return more quickly to the fold, humiliated, calmed down, and subdued. Then there were the exaggerated announcements invented by my impresario Abbey and my representative Jarrett. These announcements were often outrageous and always ridiculous; but I did not know their real source until long afterwards, when it was too late – much too late – to undeceive the public, who were fully persuaded that I was the instigator of all these inventions. I therefore did not attempt to undeceive them. It matters very little to me whether people believe one thing or another.

Life is short, even for those who live a long time, and we must live for the few who know and appreciate us, who judge and absolve us, and for whom we have the same affection and indulgence. The rest I look upon as a mere crowd, lively or sad, loyal or corrupt, from whom there is nothing to be expected but fleeting emotions, either pleasant or unpleasant, which leave no trace behind them. We ought to hate very rarely, as it is too fatiguing; remain indifferent to a great deal, forgive often and never forget. Forgiving does not mean forgetting – at least, it does not with me. I will not mention here any of the outrageous and infamous attacks that were made upon me, as it would be doing too great an honour to the wretched people who were responsible for them, from beginning to end dipping their pen in the gall of their own souls. All I can say is that nothing kills but death, and that anyone who wishes to defend himself or herself from slander can do it. For that one must live. It is not given to everyone to be able to do it, but it depends on the will of God who sees and judges.

We were to remain a fortnight in Chicago. Our success exceeded all expectations. These two weeks seemed to me the most agreeable days I had had since my arrival in America. First of all, there was the vitality of the city in which men pass each other without ever stopping, with knitted brows, with one thought in mind, 'the end to attain'. They move on and on, never turning for a cry or prudent warning. What takes place behind them matters little. They do not wish to know why a cry is raised, and they have no time to be prudent: 'the end to attain' awaits them.

Women here, as everywhere else in America, do not work, but they do not stroll about the streets, as in other cities: they walk quickly: they also are in a hurry to seek amusement. During the day time I went some distance into the surrounding country in order not to meet the sandwich-men advertising the whale.

One day I went to the pigs' slaughter-house. Ah, what a dreadful and magnificent sight! There were three of us, my sister, myself, and an Englishman, a friend of mine.

On arrival we saw hundreds of pigs hurrying, bunched together, grunting and snorting, along a small narrow raised bridge.

Our carriage passed under this bridge, and stopped before a group of men who were waiting for us. The manager of the stock-yards received us and led the way to the special slaughter-houses. On entering into the immense shed, which is dimly lighted by windows with greasy and ruddy panes, an abominable smell gets into your throat, a smell that only leaves one several days afterwards. A sanguinary mist rises everywhere, like a light cloud floating on the side of a mountain and lit up by the setting sun. An infernal hubbub drums itself into your brain: the almost human cries of the pigs being slaughtered, the violent strokes of the hatchets lopping off the limbs, the repeated shouts of the 'ripper', who with a superb and sweeping gesture lifts the heavy hatchet, and with one stroke opens from top to bottom the unfortunate, quivering animal hung on a hook. During the terror of the moment one hears the continuous grating of the revolving razor which in one second removes the bristles from the trunk thrown to it by the machine that has cut off the four legs; the whistle of the escaping steam from the hot water in which the head of the animal is scalded; the rippling of the water that is constantly renewed; the cascade of the waste water; the rumbling of the small trains carrying under wide arches trucks loaded with hams, sausages, &c., and the whistling of the engines warning one of the danger of their approach, which in this spot of terrible massacre seems to be the perpetual knell of wretched agonies.

Nothing was more Hoffmanesque than this slaughter of pigs at the period I am speaking about, for since then a sentiment of humanity has crept, although still somewhat timidly, into this temple of porcine hecatombs.

I returned from this visit quite ill. That evening I played in Phèdre. I went on to the stage quite unnerved, and trying to do everything to get rid of the horrible vision of the stock-yard. I threw myself heart and soul into my role, so much so that at the end of the fourth act I absolutely fainted on the stage.

On the last day of my last performance a magnificent collar of camellias in diamonds was handed me on behalf of the ladies of Chicago. I left that city fond of everything in it; its people; its lake, as big as a small inland sea; its audiences, who were so enthusiastic; everything, everything – except its stock-yards.

I did not even bear any ill-will towards the Bishop, who also, as had happened in other cities, had denounced my art and French literature. By the violence of his sermons he had, as a matter of fact, advertised us so well that Mr Abbey, the manager, wrote the following letter to him:

'Your Grace –, Whenever I visit your city, I am accustomed to spend four hundred dollars in advertising. But as you have done the advertising for me, I send you two hundred dollars for your poor.

Henry Abbey'

We left Chicago to go to St Louis, where we arrived after having covered 283 miles in fourteen hours.

In the drawing-room of my car, Abbey and Jarrett showed me the state-ment of the sixty-two performances that had been given since our arrival. The gross receipts were $227,459, that is to say 1,137,295 francs, an average of 18,343 francs per performance. This gave me great pleasure on Henry Abbey's account, for he had lost all he had in his previous tour with an admirable troup of opera artistes, and greater pleasure still on my own account, as I was to receive a good share of the takings.

We stayed at St Louis all the week, from January 24 to 31. I must admit that this city, which was specially French, was less to my liking than the other American cities, as it was dirty and the hotels were not very comfort-able. Since then St Louis has made great strides, but it was the Germans who planted there the bulb of progress. At the time of which I speak, the year 1881, the city was repulsively dirty. In those days, alas! we were not great at colonising, and all the cities where French influence preponderated were poor and behind the times. I was bored to death at St Louis, and I wanted to leave the place at once, after paying an indemnity to the manager, but Jarrett, the upright man, the stern man of duty, the ferocious man, said to me, holding my contract in his hand:

'No, Madame; you must stay. You can die of ennui here if you like, but stay you must.'

By way of entertaining me he took me to a celebrated grotto where we were to see some millions of fish without eyes. The light had never penetrated into this grotto, and as the first fish who lived there had no use for their eyes, their descendants had no eyes at all. We went to see this grotto. It was a long way off. We went down and groped our way to the grotto very cautiously, on all fours like cats. The road seemed to me interminable, but at last the guide told us that we had arrived at our destination. We were able to stand upright again, as the grotto itself was higher. I could see nothing, but I heard a match being struck, and the guide then lighted a small lantern. Just in front of me, nearly at my feet, was a rather deep natural basin. 'You see,' remarked our guide phlegmatically, 'that is the pond, but just at present there is no water in it; neither are there any fish. You must come again in three months' time.'

Jarrett made such a fearful grimace that I was seized with an uncontrollable fit of laughter, of that kind of laughter which borders on madness. I was suffocated with it, and I choked and laughed till the tears came. I then went down into the basin of the pond in search of a relic of some kind, a little skeleton of a dead fish, or anything, no matter what. There was nothing to be found, though – absolutely nothing. We had to return on all fours, as we came. I made Jarrett go first, and the sight of his big back in his fur coat and of him walking on hands and feet, grumbling and swearing as he went, gave me such delight that I no longer regretted anything, and I gave ten dollars to the guide for his ineffable surprise.

We returned to the hotel, and I was informed that a jeweller had been waiting for me more than two hours. 'A jeweller!' I exclaimed; 'but I have no intention of buying any jewellery. I have too much as it is.' Jarrett, however, winked at Abbey, who was there as we entered. I saw at once that there was some understanding between the jeweller and my two impresarii. I was told that my ornaments needed cleaning, that the jeweller would undertake to make them look like new, repair them if they required it, and in a word exhibit them. I rebelled, but it was of no use. Jarrett assured me that the ladies of St Louis were particularly fond of shows of this kind. He said it would be an excellent advertisement; that my jewellery was very much tarnished, that several stones were missing, and that this man would replace them for nothing, 'What a saving!' he added. 'Just think of it!'

I gave up, for discussions of that kind bore me to death, and two days later the ladies of St Louis went to admire my ornaments in this jeweller's show-cases under a blaze of light. Poor Madame Guerard, who also went to see them, came back horrified.

'They have added to your things,' she said, 'sixteen pairs of ear-rings, two necklaces, and thirty rings; a lorgnette studded with diamonds and rubies, a gold cigarette-holder set with turquoises; a small pipe, the amber mouthpiece of which is encircled with diamond stars; sixteen bracelets, a tooth-pick studded with sapphires, a pair of spectacles with gold mounts ending with small acorns of pearls.'

'They must have been made specially,' said poor Guerard, 'for there can't be anyone who would wear such glasses, and, on them were written the words, "Spectacles which Madame Sarah Bernhardt wears when she is at home." '

I certainly thought that this was exceeding all the limits allowed to advertisement. To make me smoke pipes and wear spectacles was going rather too far, and I got into my carriage and drove at once to the jeweller's. I arrived just in time to find the place closed. It was five o'clock on Saturday afternoon; the lights were out, and everything was dark and silent. I returned to the hotel, and spoke to Jarrett of my annoyance. 'What does it all matter, Madame?' he said tranquilly. 'So many girls wear spectacles; and as to the pipe, the jeweller tells me he has received five orders from it, and that it is going to be quite the fashion. Anyhow, it is of no use worrying about the matter, as the exhibition is now over. Your jewellery will be returned to-night, and we leave here the day after to-morrow.'

That evening the jeweller returned all the objects I had lent him, and they had been polished and repaired so that they looked quite new. He had included with them a gold cigarette-holder set with turquoises, the very one that had been on view. I simply could not make that man understand anything, and my anger cooled down when confronted by his pleasant manner and his joy.

This advertisement, though, came very near costing me my life. Tempted by this huge quantity of jewellery, the greater part of which did not belong to me, a little band of sharpers planned to rob me, believing that they would find all these valuables in the large hand-bag which my steward always carried.

We arrived at Cincinnati safe and sound. We gave three performances there, and set off once more for New Orleans.

Oscar Wilde (1882)

Lecture on Art Decoration (11th May 1882); one of a series of lectures on aesthetic philosophy which Wilde gave in the United States.

When I appeared before you on a previous occasion, I had seen nothing of American art save the Doric columns and Corinthian chimney-pots visible on your Broadway and Fifth Avenue. I find that what your people need is not so much high imaginative art, but that which hallows the vessels of everyday use. I suppose that the poet will sing and the artist will paint regardless whether the world praises or blames. He has his own world and is independent of his fellow-men. But the handicraftsman is dependent on your pleasure and opinion. He needs your encouragement and he must have beautiful surroundings. Your people love art, but you do not sufficiently honour the handicraftsman. Of course, those millionaires who can pillage Europe for their pleasure need have no care to encourage such; but I speak for those whose desire for beautiful things is larger than their means. I find that one great trouble all over is that your workmen are not given to noble designs. You cannot be indifferent to this, because art is not something which you can take or leave. It is a necessity of human life . . .

Now, what America wants today is a school of rational design. Bad art is a great deal worse than no art at all. You must show your workmen, specimens of good work, so that they may come to know what is simple and true and beautiful. To that end I would you have a museum attached to these schools – not one of those dreadful modern institutions where there are a stuffed and very dusty giraffe and a case or two of fossils, but a place where there are gathered examples of art decoration from various periods and countries. Such a place is the South Kensington Museum in London, whereon we build greater hopes for the future than on any other one thing. There I go every Saturday night, when the Museum is opened later than usual, to see the handicraftsman, the wood-worker, the glass-blower and the worker in metals. And it is here that the man of refinement and culture comes face to face with the workman who ministers to this joy. He comes to know more of the nobility of the workman, and the workman, feeling the appreciation, comes to know more of the nobility of his work.

You have too many white walls. More colour is wanted. You should have such men as Whistler among you to teach you the beauty and joy of colour. Take Mr Whistler's *symphony in white*, which you no doubt have imagined to be something quite bizarre. It is nothing of the sort. Think of a cool, grey sky, flecked here and there with white clouds, a grey ocean and three wonderfully beautiful figures robed in white leaning over the water and dropping white flowers from their fingers. Here are no extensive intellectual schemes to trouble you and no metaphysics, of which we have had quite enough in art. But if the simple and unaided colour strikes the right keynote, the whole conception is made clear. I regard Mr Whistler's famous peacock room as the finest thing in colour and art decoration which the world has known since Correggio painted that wonderful room in Italy where the little children are dancing on the walls. Mr Whistler finished another room just before I came away – a breakfast-room in blue and yellow. The ceiling was a light blue, the cabinet furniture was of yellow wood, the curtains at the windows were white and worked in yellow, and when the table was set for breakfast with dainty blue china, nothing can be conceived at once so simple and joyous.

The fault which I have observed in most of your rooms is that there is apparently no definite scheme of colour. Everything is not attuned to a keynote as it should be. The apartments are crowded with pretty things which have no relation to each other. Again, your artists must decorate what is more simply useful. In your art schools I found no attempt to decorate such things as the vessels for water. I know of nothing uglier than the ordinary jug or pitcher. A museum could be filled with the different kinds of water vessels which are used in hot countries. Yet we continue to submit to the depressing jug with the handle all on one side. I do not see the wisdom of decorating dinner-plates with sunsets and soup-plates with moonlight scenes. I do not think it adds anything to the pleasure of canvas-back duck to take it out of such glories. Besides, we do not want a soup-plate whose bottom seeks to vanish in the distance. One neither feels safe nor comfortable under such conditions. In fact, I did not find in the art schools of the country that the difference was explained between decorative and imaginative art.

The conditions of art should be simple. A great deal more depends upon the heart than the head. Appreciation of art is not secured by any elaborate scheme of learning. Art requires a good healthy atmosphere. The motives for art are still around about us as they were around about the ancients. And the subjects are also easily found by the earnest sculptor and the painter. Nothing is more picturesque and graceful than a man at work. Only idle people are ungraceful. The artist who goes to the children's playground, watches them at their sport, sees the boy stoop to tie his shoe, will find the same themes that engaged the attention of the ancient Greeks. And such observation and the illustrations which follow will do much to correct that foolish impression that mental and physical beauty are always divorced.

To you more than perhaps to any other country has nature been generous in furnishing materials for art workers to work in. You have marble quarries where the stone is more beautiful in colour than the Greeks ever had for their beautiful work, and yet day after day I am confronted with the great building of some stupid man who has used the beautiful material as if it were not precious almost beyond speech. Marble should not be used save by noble workmen. There is nothing which gave me a greater sense of barrenness in travelling through the country than the entire absence of wood-carving on your houses. Wood-carving is the simplest of the decorative arts. In Switzerland the little barefooted boy beautifies the porch of his father's house with examples of skill in this direction. Why should not American boys do a great deal more and better than Swiss boys?

There is nothing to my mind more coarse in conception and more vulgar in execution than modern jewelry. This is something that can be easily corrected. Something better should be made out of the beautiful gold which is stored up in your mountain hollows and strewn along your river beds. When I was at Leadville and reflected that all the shining silver I saw coming from the mines would be made into ugly dollars, it made me sad. It should be made into something more permanent. The golden gates at Florence are as beautiful today as when Michael Angelo saw them.

We should see more of the workman than we do. We should not be content to have the salesman stand between us, who knows nothing of what he is selling save that he is charging a great deal too much for it. And watching workmen will teach that most important lesson, the nobility of all rational workmanship.

I said in my last lecture that art would create a new brotherhood among men by furnishing a universal language. I said that under its beneficient influences war might pass away. Thinking this, what place can I ascribe to art in our education? If children grow up among all fair and lovely things, they will grow to love beauty and detest ugliness before they know the reason why. If you go into a house where everything is coarse you find things chipped and broken and unsightly. Nobody exercises any care. If everything is dainty and delicate, gentleness and refinement of manner are unconsciously acquired. When I was in San Francisco I used to visit the Chinese quarters frequently. There I used to watch a great hulking Chinese workman at his task of digging, and used to see him every day drink his tea from a little cup as delicate in texture as the petal of a flower. Whereas in all the grand hotels of the land, where thousands of dollars have been lavished on great gilt mirrors and gaudy columns, I have been given my coffee or my chocolate in cups an inch and a quarter thick. I think I have deserved something nicer.

The art systems of the past have been devised by philosophers who looked upon human beings as obstructions. They have tried to educate boys' minds before they had any. How much better would it be in these early years to teach children to use their hands in the rational service of mankind! I would have a workshop attached to every school, and one hour a day given up to the teaching of simple decorative arts. It would be a golden hour to the children. And you would soon raise up a race of handicraftsmen who would transform the face of your country. I have seen only one such school in the United States, and this was in Philadelphia, and was founded by my friend Mr Leland. I stopped there yesterday and have brought some of their work here this afternoon to show you. [Mr Wilde here turned from the stand to an adjoining table and held up the different articles he spoke of.] Here are two discs of beaten brass; the designs on them are beautiful, the workmanship is simple and the entire result is satisfactory. The work was done by a little boy twelve years old. This is a wooden bowl, decorated by a little girl of thirteen. The design is lovely, and the colouring delicate and pretty. [The bowl was painted black and yellow, and looked like a sunflower with the colours run into each other.] Here you see a piece of beautiful wood-carving, accomplished by a little boy of nine. [This was a small rectangular piece of wood, and the carving was not visible to the audience.] In such work as this children learn sincerity in art. They learn to abhor the liar in art – the man who paints wood to look like iron, or iron to look like stone. It is a practical school of morals. No better way is there to learn to love Nature than to understand Art. It dignifies every flower of the field. And a boy who sees the thing of beauty which a bird on the wing becomes when transferred to wood or canvas will probably not throw the customary stone. What we want is something spiritual added to life. Nothing is so ignoble that art cannot sanctify it.

Robert Louis Stevenson (1883)

While living at Barbizon, a village near Fontainebleau, Robert Louis Stevenson (1850–1894) met the American divorcée Fanny Osbourne. He followed her back to America in 1880 when he married her. She, however, makes no appearance in the following narrative, from The Amateur Emigrant.

New York

As we drew near to New York I was at first amused, and then somewhat staggered, by the cautions and the grisly tales that went the round. You would have thought we were to land upon a cannibal island. You must speak to no one in the streets, as they would not leave you till you were rooked and beaten. You must enter a hotel with military precautions; for the least you had to apprehend was to awake next morning without money or baggage, or necessary raiment, a lone forked radish in a bed; and if the worst befell, you would instantly and mysteriously disappear from the ranks of mankind.

I have usually found such stories correspond to the least modicum of fact. Thus I was warned, I remember, against the roadside inns of the Cevennes, and that by a learned professor; and when I reached Pradelles the warning was explained; it was but the far-away rumour and reduplication of a single terrifying story already half a century old, and half forgotten in the theatre of the events. So I was tempted to make light of these reports against America. But we had on board with us a man whose evidence it would not do to put aside. He had come near these perils in the body; he had visited a robber inn. The public has an old and well-grounded favour for this class of incident, and shall be gratified to the best of my power.

My fellow-passenger, whom we shall call M'Naughten, had come from New York to Boston with a comrade, seeking work. They were a pair of rattling blades; and, leaving their baggage at the station, passed the day in beer-saloons, and with congenial spirits, until midnight struck. Then they applied themselves to find a lodging, and walked the streets till two, knocking at houses of entertainment and being refused admittance, or themselves declining the terms. By two the inspiration of their liquor had begun to wear off; they were weary and humble, and after a great circuit found themselves in the same street where they had begun their search, and in front of a French hotel where they had already sought accommodation. Seeing the house still open, they returned to the charge. A man in a white cap sat in an office by the door. He seemed to welcome them more warmly than when they had first presented themselves, and the charge for the night had somewhat unaccountably fallen from a dollar to a quarter. They thought him ill-looking, but paid their quarter apiece, and were shown upstairs to the top of the house. There, in a small room, the man in the white cap wished them pleasant slumbers ...

The Plains of Nebraska

It had thundered on the Friday night, but the sun rose on Saturday without a cloud. We were at sea – there is no other adequate expression – on the plains of Nebraska. I made my observatory on the top of a fruit-waggon, and sat by the hour upon that perch to spy about me, and to spy in vain for something new. It was a world almost without a feature; an empty sky, an empty earth; front and back, the line of railway stretched from horizon to horizon, like a cue across a billiard-board; on either hand, the green plain ran till it touched the skirts of heaven. Along the track innumerable wild sunflowers, no bigger than a crown-piece, bloomed in a continuous flower-bed; grazing beasts were seen upon the prairie at all degrees of distance and diminution; and now and again we might perceive a few dots beside the railroad, which grew more and more distinct as we drew nearer, till they turned into wooden cabins, and then dwindled and dwindled in our wake until they melted into their surroundings, and we were once more alone upon the billiard-board. The train toiled over this infinity like a snail; and being the one thing moving, it was wonderful what huge proportions it began to assume in our regard. It seemed miles in length, and either end of it within but a step of the horizon. Even my own body or my own head seemed a great thing in that emptiness. I note the feeling the more readily as it is the contrary of what I have read of in the experience of others. Day and night, above the roar of the train, our ears were kept busy with the incessant chirp of grasshoppers – a noise like the winding up of countless clocks and watches, which began after a while to seem proper to that land.

To one hurrying through by steam there was a certain exhilaration in this spacious vacancy, this greatness of the air, this discovery of the whole arch of heaven, this straight, unbroken, prison-line of the horizon. Yet one could not but reflect upon the weariness of those who passed by there in old days, at the foot's pace of oxen, painfully urging their teams, and with no landmark but that unattainable evening sun for which they steered, and which daily fled them by an equal stride. They had nothing, it would seem, to overtake; nothing by which to reckon their advance; no sight for repose or for encouragement; but stage after stage, only the dead green waste under foot, and the mocking, fugitive horizon. But the eye, as I have been told, found differences even here; and at the worst the emigrant came, by perseverance, to the end of his toil. It is the settlers, after all, at whom we have a right to marvel. Our consciousness, by which we live, is itself but the creature of variety. Upon what food does it subsist in such a land? What livelihood can repay a human creature for a life spent in this huge sameness? He is cut off from books, from news, from company, from all that can relieve existence but the prosecution of his affairs. A sky full of stars is the most varied spectacle that he can hope for. He may walk five miles and see nothing; ten, and it is as though he had not moved; twenty, and still he is in the midst of the same great level, and has approached no nearer to the one object within view, the flat horizon which keeps pace with his advance. We are full at home of the question of agreeable wall-papers, and wise people are of opinion that the temper may be quieted by sedative surroundings. But what is to be said of the Nebraskan settler? His is a wall-paper with a vengeance – one quarter of the universe laid bare in all its gauntness. His eyes must embrace at every glance the whole seeming concave of the visible world; it quails before so vast an outlook, it is tortured by distance; yet there is no rest or shelter, till the man runs into his cabin, and can repose his sight upon things near at hand. Hence, I am told, a sickness of the vision peculiar to these empty plains.

Yet perhaps with sunflowers and cicadæ, summer and winter, cattle, wife and family, the settler may create a full and various existence. (We exaggerate the difficulties of a situation when we conceive and criticise it in fancy; for we forget that people live in this world by the day or week. Theory shows us an unbroken tenor to the last sickness; but the actual man lives it in pieces, and begins afresh with every morning. The blind can comfortably exist while seeing nothing; but there is this difference that they are not blind by choice. A man who is married is no longer master of his destiny, and carries a compensation along with him wherever he may go. But what can bring to Nebraska a lone, unfettered bachelor, who has all the world before him and might starve, if he preferred, in London or New York?)

One person at least I saw upon the plains who seemed in every way superior to her lot. This was a woman who boarded us at a way-station, selling milk. She was largely formed; her features were more than comely; she had that great rarity – a fine complexion which became her; and her eyes were kind, dark, and steady. She sold milk with patriarchal grace. There was not a line in her countenance, not a note in her soft and sleepy voice, but spoke of an entire contentment with her life. It would have been fatuous arrogance to pity such a woman. Yet the place where she lived was to me almost ghastly. Less than a dozen wooden houses, all of a shape and all nearly of a size stood planted along the railway lines. Each stood apart in its own lot. Each opened direct off the billiard-board, as if it were a billiard-board indeed, and these only models that had been set down upon it ready-made. Her own, into which I looked, was clean but very empty, and showed nothing home-like but the burning fire. This extreme newness, above all in so naked and flat a country, gives a strong impression of artificiality. With none of the litter and discolouration of human life; with the paths unworn, and the houses still sweating from the axe, such a settlement as this seems purely scenic. The mind is loth to accept it for a piece of reality; and it seems incredible that life can go on with so few properties, or the great child, man, find entertainment in so bare a playroom.

And truly it is as yet an incomplete society in some points; or at least it contained, as I passed through, one person incompletely civilised. At North Platte, where we supped that evening, one man asked another to pass the milk-jug. This other was well dressed, and of what we should call a respectable appearance; a darkish man, high-spoken, eating as though he had some usage of society; but he turned upon the first speaker with extraordinary vehemence of tone -

'There's a waiter here!' he cried.

'I only asked you to pass the milk,' explained the first.

Here is the retort verbatim -

'Pass? Hell! I'm not paid for that business; the waiter's paid for it. You should use civility at table, and, by God, I'll show you how!'

(He would show him how! I wonder what would be his charge for the twelve lessons. And this explosion, you will not forget, was to save himself the trouble of moving a milk jug a distance of perhaps thirty inches.)

The other man very wisely made no answer, and the bully went on with his supper as though nothing had occurred. It pleases me to think that some day soon he will meet with one of his own kind; and that perhaps both may fall.

The Desert of Wyoming

To cross such a plain is to grow home-sick for the mountains. I longed for the Black Hills of Wyoming, which I knew we were soon to enter, like an ice-bound whaler for the spring. Alas! and it was a worse country than the other. All Sunday and Monday we travelled through these sad mountains, or over the main ridge of the Rockies, which is a fair match to them for misery of aspect. Hour after hour it was the same unhomely and unkindly world about our onward path; tumbled boulders, cliffs that drearily imitate the shape of monuments and fortifications – how drearily, how tamely, none can tell who has not seen them; not a tree, not a patch of sward, not one shapely or commanding mountain form; sage-brush, eternal sage-brush; over all, the same weariful and gloomy colouring, greys warming into brown, greys darkening towards black; and for sole sign of life, here and there a few fleeing antelopes; here and there, but at incredible intervals, a creek running in a cañon. The plains have a grandeur of their own; but here there is nothing but a contorted smallness. Except for the air, which was light and stimulating, there was not one good circumstance in that God-forsaken land.

(I had, as I must tell you, been suffering a good deal all the way, from what the gentleman at New York was pleased to call my liver. The hot weather and the fever put into my blood by so much continuous travel, had aggravated these symptoms till they were strangely difficult to bear. When the fit was on me, I grew almost light headed. I had to make a second cigarette before the first was smoked, for tobacco alone gave me self command under these paroxysms of irritation. Fancy will give you no clue to what I endured; the basis was, as you might say, a mere annoyance; but when an annoyance is continued day and night and assumes by starts an absolute control upon your mind, not much remains to distinguish it from pain. I am obliged to touch upon this, but with a delicacy which the reader will appreciate, not only because it is part of emigrant experience, but because it must stand as my excuse for many sins of omission in this chronicle.)

I had been suffering in my health a good deal all the way; and at last, whether I was exhausted by my complaint or poisoned in some wayside eating-house, the evening we left Laramie I fell sick outright. That was a night which I shall not readily forget. The lamps did not go out; each made a faint shining in its own neighbourhood, and the shadows were confounded together in a long, hollow box of the car. The sleepers lay in uneasy attitudes; here two chums alongside, flat upon their backs like dead folk; there a man sprawling on the floor, with his face upon his arm; there another half-seated with his head and shoulders on the bench. The most passive were continually and roughly shaken by the movement of the train; others stirred, turned, or stretched out their arms like children; it was surprising how many groaned and murmured in their sleep; and as I passed to and fro, stepping across the prostrate, and caught now a snore, now a gasp, now a half-formed word, it gave me a measure of the worthlessness of rest in that unresting vehicle. Although it was chill, I was obliged to open my window, for the degradation of the air soon became intolerable to one who was awake and using the full supply of life. Outside, in a glimmering night, I saw the black, amorphous hills shoot by unweariedly into our wake. They that long for morning have never longed for it more earnestly than I.

And yet when day came, it was to shine upon the same broken and unsightly quarter of the world. Mile upon mile, and not a tree, a bird, or a river. Only down the long, sterile cañons, the train shot hooting, and awoke the resting echo. That train was the one piece of life in all the deadly land; it was the one actor, the one spectacle fit to be observed in this paralysis of man and nature. And when I think how the railroad has been pushed through this unwatered wilderness and haunt of savage tribes, and now will bear an emigrant for some twelve pounds from the Atlantic to the Golden Gates; how at each stage of the construction, roaring, impromptu cities, full of gold and lust and death, sprang up and then died away again, and are now but wayside stations in the desert; how in these uncouth places pig-tailed Chinese pirates worked side by side with border ruffians and broken men from Europe, talking together in a mixed dialect, mostly oaths, gambling, drinking, quarrelling, and murdering like wolves; how the plumed hereditary lord of all America heard, in this last fastness, the scream of the 'bad medicine-waggon' charioting his foes; and then when I go on to remember that all this epical turmoil was conducted by gentlemen in frock-coats, and with a view to nothing more extraordinary than a fortune and a subsequent visit to Paris, it seems to me, I own, as if this railway were the one typical achievement of the age in which we live, as if it brought together into one plot all the ends of the world and all the degrees of social rank, and offered to some great writer the busiest, the most extended, and the most varied subject for an enduring literary work. If it be romance, if it be contrast, if it be heroism that we require, what was Troy town to this? But, alas! it is not these things that are necessary – it is only Homer.

Here also we are grateful to the train, as to some god who conducts us swiftly through these shades and by so many hidden perils. Thirst, hunger, the sleight and ferocity of Indians, are all no more feared, so lightly do we skim these horrible lands; as the gull, who wings safely through the hurricane and past the shark.

Fellow-passengers

At Ogden we changed cars from the Union Pacific to the Central Pacific line of railroad. The change was doubly welcome; for, first we had better cars on the new line; and, second, those in which we had been cooped for more than ninety hours had begun to stink abominably. Several yards away, as we returned, let us say from dinner, our nostrils were assailed by air. I have stood on a platform while the whole train was shunting; and as the dwelling-cars drew near, there would come a whiff of pure menagerie, only a little sourer, as from men instead of monkeys. I think we are human only in virtue of open windows. Without fresh air, you only require a bad heart, and a remarkable command of the Queen's English, to become such another as Dean Swift; a kind of leering, human goat, leaping and wagging your scut on mountains of offence. I do my best to keep my head the other way, and look for the human rather than the bestial in this Yahoo-like business of the emigrant train. But one thing I must say: the car of the Chinese was notably the least offensive, (and that of the women and children by a good way the worst. A stroke of nature's satire.)

The cars on the Central Pacific were nearly twice as high, and so proportionally airier; they were freshly varnished, which gave us all a sense of cleanliness as though we had bathed; the seats drew out and joined in the centre, so that there was no more need for bed-boards; and there was an upper tier of berths which could be closed by day and opened by night. (Thus in every way the accommodation was more cheerful and comfortable, and everyone might have a bed to lie on if he pleased. The company deserve our thanks. It was the first sign I could observe of any kindly purpose towards the emigrant. For myself it was, in some ways, a fatal change; for it fell to me to sleep in one of the lofts; and that I found to be impossible. The air was always bad enough at the level of the floor. But my bed was four feet higher, immediately under the roof, and shut into a kind of Saratoga trunk with one side partly open. And there, unless you were the

Prince of Camby, it were madness to attempt to sleep. Though the fumes were narcotic and weighed upon the eyelids, yet they so smartly irritated the lungs that I could only lie and cough. I spent the better part of one night walking to and fro and envying my neighbours.)

I had by this time some opportunity of seeing the people whom I was among. They were in rather marked contrast to the emigrants I had met on board ship while crossing the Atlantic. (There was both less talent and less good manners; I believe I should add less good feeling, though that is implied. Kindness will out; and a man who is gentle will contrive to be a gentleman.) They were mostly lumpish fellows, silent and noisy, a common combination; somewhat sad, I should say, with an extraordinary poor taste in humour, and little interest in their fellow-creatures beyond that of a cheap and merely external curiosity. If they heard a man's name and business, they seemed to think they had the heart of that mystery; but they were as eager to know that much as they were indifferent to the rest. Some of them were on nettles till they learned your name was Dickson and you a journeyman baker; but beyond that, whether you were Catholic or Mormon, dull or clever, fierce or friendly, was all one to them. Others who were not so stupid gossiped a little, and, I am bound to say, unkindly. A favourite witticism was for some lout to raise the alarm of 'All aboard!' while the rest of us were dining, thus contributing his mite to the general discomfort. Such a one was always much applauded for his high spirits. When I was ill coming through Wyoming, I was astonished – fresh from the eager humanity on board ship – to meet with little but laughter. One of the young men even amused himself by incommoding me, as was then very easy; and that not from ill-nature, but mere clod-like incapacity to think, for he expected me to join the laugh. I did so, but it was phantom merriment. Later on, a man from Kansas had three violent epileptic fits, and though, of course, there were not wanting some to help him, it was rather superstitious terror than sympathy that his case evoked among his fellow-passengers. 'Oh, I hope he's not going to die!' cried a woman; 'it would be terrible to have a dead body!' And there was a very general movement to leave the man behind at the next station. This, by good fortune, the conductor negatived.

There was a good deal of story-telling in some quarters; in others, little but silence. In this society, more than any other that ever I was in, it was the narrator alone who seemed to enjoy the narrative. It was rarely that any one listened for the listening. If he lent an ear to another man's story, it was because he was in immediate want of a hearer for one of his own. Food and the progress of the train were the subjects most generally treated; many joined to discuss these who otherwise would hold their tongues. One small knot had no better occupation than to worm out of me my name; and the more they tried, the more obstinately fixed I grew to baffle them. They assailed me with artful questions and insidious offers of correspondence in the future; but I was perpetually on my guard, and parried their assaults with inward laughter. I am sure Dubuque would have given me ten dollars for the secret. He owed me far more, had he understood life, for thus preserving him a lively interest throughout the journey. I met one of my fellow-passengers months after, driving a street tramway car in San Francisco; and, as the joke was not out of season, told him my name without subterfuge. You never saw a man more chapfallen. But had my name been Demogorgon, after so prolonged a mystery he had still been disappointed.

There were no emigrants direct from Europe – save one German family and a knot of Cornish miners who kept grimly by themselves, one reading the New Testament all day long through steel spectacles, the rest discussing privately the secrets of their old-world, mysterious race. Lady Hester Stanhope believed she could make something great of the Cornish; for my part, I can make nothing of them at all. A division of races, older and more original than that of Babel, keeps this close, esoteric family apart from neighbouring Englishmen. Not even a Red Indian seems more foreign in my eyes. This is one of the lessons of travel – that some of the strangest races dwell next door to you at home.

The rest were all American born, but they came from almost every quarter of that continent. All the States of the North had sent out a fugitive to cross the plains with me. From Virginia, from Pennsylvania, from New York, from far western Iowa and Kansas, from Maine that borders on the Canadas, and from the Canadas themselves – some one or two were fleeing in quest of a better land and better wages. The talk in the train, like the talk I heard on the steamer, ran upon hard times, short commons, and hope that moves ever westward. I thought of my shipful from Great Britain with a feeling of despair. They had come 3000 miles, and yet not far enough. Hard times bowed them out of the Clyde, and stood to welcome them at Sandy Hook. Where were they to go? Pennsylvania, Maine, Iowa, Kansas? These were not places for immigration, but for emigration, it appeared; not one of them, but I knew a man who had lifted up his heel and left it for an ungrateful country. And it was still westward that they ran. Hunger, you would have thought, came out of the east like the sun, and the evening was made of edible gold. And, meantime, in the car in front of me, were there not half a hundred emigrants from the opposite quarter? Hungry Europe and hungry China, each pouring from their gates in search of provender, had here come face to face. The two waves had met; east and west had alike failed; the whole round world had been prospected and condemned; there was no El Dorado anywhere; and till one could emigrate to the moon, it seemed as well to stay patiently at home. Nor was there wanting another sign, at once more picturesque and more disheartening; for as we continued to steam westward toward the land of gold, we were continually passing other emigrant trains upon the journey east; and these were as crowded as our own. Had all these return voyagers made a fortune in the mines? Were they all bound for Paris, and to be in Rome by Easter? It would seem not, for, whenever we met them, the passengers ran on the platform and cried to us through the windows, in a kind of wailing chorus, to 'come back.' On the plains of Nebraska, in the mountains of Wyoming, it was still the same cry, and dismal to my heart, 'Come back!' That was what we heard by the way 'about the good country we were going to'. And at that very hour the Sand-lot of San Francisco was crowded with the unemployed, and the echo from the other side of Market Street was repeating the rant of demagogues.

If in truth it were only for the sake of wages that men emigrate, how many thousands would regret the bargain! But wages, indeed, are only one consideration out of many; for we are a race of gipsies, and love change and travel for themselves.

Rudyard Kipling (1890s)

In 1892 the English writer Rudyard Kipling (1865–1936) married Caroline, the sister of the American publisher, Wolcott Balestier. For a while they decided to live in Mrs Kipling's native state, Vermont. But because of Kipling's incompatibility with his in-laws and his neighbours, they went back to England in 1899. It is hard to think of Kipling as a Bohemian, but that seemingly is how he was treated by the local people.

As the New England summer flamed into autumn I piled cut spruce boughs all round the draughty cottage sill, and helped to put up a tiny roofless verandah along one side of it for future needs. When winter shut down and sleigh-bells rang all over the white world that tucked us in, we counted ourselves secure. Sometimes we had a servant. Sometimes she would find the solitude too much for her and flee without warning, one even leaving her trunk. This troubled us not at all. There are always two sides to a plate, and the cleaning of frying- and saucepans is as little a mystery as the making of comfortable beds. When our lead pipe froze, we would slip on our coon-skin coats and thaw it out with a lighted candle. There was no space in the attic bedroom for a cradle, so we decided that a trunk-tray would be just as good. We envied no one – not even when skunks wandered into our cellar and, knowing the nature of the beasts, we immobilised ourselves till it should please them to depart.

But our neighbours saw no humour in our proceedings. Here was a stranger of an unloved race, currently reported to 'make as much as a hundred dollars out of a ten-cent bottle of ink,' and who had 'pieces in the papers' about him, who had married a 'Balestier girl'. Did not her grandmother still live on the Balestier place, where 'old Balestier' instead of farming had built a large house, and there had dined late in special raiment, and drunk red wines after the custom of the French instead of decent whisky? And behold this Britisher, under pretext of having lost money, had settled his wife down 'right among her own folk' in the Bliss Cottage. It was not seemly on the face of it; so they watched as secretively as the New England of English peasant can, and what toleration they extended to the 'Britisher' was solely for the sake of 'the Balestier girl'.

Peter Tchaikovsky (1891)

The opening of the Carnegie Hall in New York was celebrated by a three-day Tchaikovsky festival which the composer himself travelled from Russia to attend.

Peter Tchaikovsky to Vladimir Davidov

April 30, 1891

Just received letters from Modia, Annette, and Jurgenson. It is impossible to express how precious letters are for one in my state. I was infinitely glad. From day to day I keep a detailed diary and on my return will give it to all of you to read – therefore, I will not go into particulars. All in all, New York, American customs, American hospitality, the very sight of the city, and the unusual comforts of the surroundings – all this is quite to my liking, and if I were younger, I would probably derive great pleasure from staying in this interesting, youthful country. But I bear all this as if it were an easy punishment, softened by favourable circumstances. Thought and aspiration are one: homeward, homeward, homeward!!! There is some hope that I will leave on the 12th. Everyone here pampers, honours, and entertains me. It turns out that I am ten times better known in America than in Europe. At first, when they told me that, I thought that it was an exaggerated compliment, but now I see that it is the truth. Works of mine that are still unknown in Moscow, are performed here several times a season, and whole reviews and commentaries are written on them (e.g., *Hamlet*). I am far more a big shot here than in Russia. Is it not curious!!! I was enthusiastically received by musicians at the rehearsal (till now there has been only one). But you will learn all the precise details from my diary. Now I'll say a few words about New York itself. This is a vast city, more strange and original than handsome. There are long one-story houses, 11-storey buildings, and one building (a brand-new hotel) that is 17 stories high. But in Chicago they went even further. There is a 21-story building there!!! As for New York, this phenomenon can be simply explained. The city is situated on a narrow peninsula, surrounded by water on three sides, and can't grow any wider; therefore, it grows up. They say that in 10 years all the buildings will reach at least 10 floors. But for you the most interesting convention in New York is this: every little apartment, every hotel accommodation has a lavatory with a basin, bath, and washstand installed with hot and cold running water. Splashing in the bath in the morning I always think of you. Lighting is by electricity and gas. Candles are not used at all. In case of need, one acts differently than in Europe – namely, one rings and then says what is required through a tube, with one's mouth by the bell. Vice versa, if someone asks for me downstairs, they ring and then report through the tube who came or what they asked about. This is uncomfortable in view of my lack of

English. No one except servants ever walks upstairs. The elevator runs constantly, going up and down at an incredible speed, to let the hotel's inhabitants and visitors in and out. As for the streets, but for the novelty that little houses alternate with huge buildings – except for that peculiarity, the street itself is neither especially noisy nor especially crowded. The explanation is that there are hardly any cabbies or fiacres here. The traffic goes either by horsecars or on an actual railroad, with branches stretching over the whole vast city. Besides, in the morning, the entire population rushes to the East where 'Downtown' is located, i.e., the part of the city with merchants' offices. In the evening all of them return home. They live as in London; every apartment is a separate house with several stories, in a word, extending vertically, not laterally. That's enough for the time being. Soon I will write again to one of you. I embrace you, my dear one, also Modia and Kolia.

How soon, how soon?

Diary

May 5

The servant Max, who brings my morning's tea, spent all his childhood in Nizhnyi-Novgorod and studied in a school there. Since the age of fourteen he has lived in either Germany or New York. Now he is 32 and has forgotten so much Russian that he expresses himself with great difficulty, even though he knows most of the ordinary words. It's pleasant for me to talk a little Russian with him. At 11 o'clock the pianist Rummel appeared (my old Berlin acquaintance) still with the same entreaty that I conduct at his concert on the 17th, for which purpose he'd come once before to me. Then came a reporter – very affable and bland. He asked me whether my wife likes her stay in New York. They have often asked me this question. It turns out, that in some newspapers it was said on the day after my arrival that I came with a young and pretty wife. This happened because two reporters saw me getting into a carriage with Alice Reno, near the steamship dock. Had breakfast downstairs in the hotel. Walked on Broadway. Dropped in at the Viennese café recommended to me, but had the misfortune to encounter the conductor Seidl, and was obliged to talk with him. But I had other things on my mind. I was worried about my upcoming first appearance for an evening concert, before an audience of five thousand . . . I will have to deliberate with Reno. At 7:30 Reno's son-in-law dropped by for me. In an overcrowded trolley we approached the Music Hall. Illuminated and filled with an audience, it had unusually impressive and grand appearance. . . .

 . . . I sat in a box with the Reno family. The concert began with Reno's speech (about which the poor fellow was terribly worried before). After him they sang the national hymn. Then a pastor made what was said to be an unusually dull speech in honour of the founders of the edifice, and especially in honour of Carnegie. Next the Leonore Overture was very well performed. Intermission. I came down. Excitement. My turn. Was loudly received. The March went by very well. Great success. For the rest of the concert I listened from the Hyde's box. 'Te Deum' by Berlioz is dullish; only at the end did I taste the intense pleasure of it. The Renos carried me away to their home. An improvised supper. Slept like a dead man.

May 6

'Tchaikovsky is a tall, gray, well built, interesting man, well on the sixty(?!!). He seems a trifle embarrassed and responds to the applause by a succession of brusque and jerky bows. But as soon as he grasps the baton his self-confidence returns.' That is what I read today in the *Herald*. It angers me that they write not only about the music but about my person, too. I cannot abide when others notice my embarrassment and are surprised at my 'brusque and jerky bows'.

At 7.30 Hyde and his wife drove to get me. Second concert. The oratorio 'Elijah' by Mendelssohn was performed. Beautiful but somehow long-winded thing. During intermission was dragged to boxes of the various big shots of this place. Carnegie (likeable millionaire, founder of the Music Hall) invited me to dine at his home Sunday, but I couldn't accept for I have to go to Mr. Smoll's out in a suburb for the entire day. Having disposed of everyone, I went home on foot. Had supper in the restaurant downstairs. Letters from Modia and brother Kolia. A big fire somewhere.

May 7

My 51st year. Awfully excited this morning. The concert with the suite lies before me at 2 o'clock. A surprising thing is this peculiar fright. How many times have I conducted this very suite! It goes beautifully. What's to be afraid of? And yet I am suffering unbearably!

My sufferings proceeded in crescendo. It seems I have never been so afraid. Is it because they will heed my appearance here and at that point my shyness will show itself? For good or ill after enduring a few difficult hours (particularly the last, when I was forced to hold conversation with Mrs. Mielke etc., while waiting to come out), I came out, was again splendidly received, and, as it's said in today's newspapers, made a sensation. After the suite I sat in Reno's office and gave audiences to reporters (ah, these reporters!) including, by the way, the very famous Jackson. Went up to the box of Mrs. Reno, who sent me a mass of flowers this morning as if in foreknowledge that today is my birthday. Feeling the necessity for being alone, I squeezed my way through the crowd of ladies who surrounded me in the corridor and goggled at me with eyes in which, unwittingly but with pleasure, I read rapt sympathy, then passed up invitations from the Reno family, and ran home. Here, I wrote a message to Botkin that I can't dine with him as I'd promised; then, relieved and happy as much as could be, headed off to roam, dine, drop into cafés, – in short, devoted myself to the enjoyment of silence and solitude. Retired very early.

May 8

Am beginning to have difficulty finding time for writing letters and this diary. Visitors besiege me: reporters, composers, librettists, one of whom, a little old man, – brought me an opera, *Wlast,* and moved me very much with the story of the death of his only son: but chiefly – whole piles of letters from every corner of America with requests for autographs, to which I very conscientiously respond. Was at the rehearsal of the piano concerto. Was angry at Damrosch, who, taking all the best time, gives me the leftover part of the rehearsal. And yet the rehearsal went off all right . . . Hurried home. Visitors are endless, including two Russian ladies . . . Just when I had my first occasion to have a heart-to-heart talk with a Russian woman, – a painful thing happened. Suddenly tears came, my voice began to tremble, and I couldn't restrain my sobs. I ran out into the other room and for a long time didn't come out. Am burning with shame remembering this unexpected thing . . . Slept a little before the concert. My little choruses went well, but were I less embarrassed and worried, they would have gone better. Sat in the boxes of Reno and Hyde during the performance of the beautiful oratorio 'Sulamith' by Damrosch, the father. On the way to supper at Damrosch's, I walked with Reno and Carnegie. This little arch-million-aire is awfully kind to me and was all the time talking about an invitation for the next year. There was a very original supper at Damrosch's. The men went to the table alone and the poor ladies stayed at a distance. The supper was copious, but the cuisine was American, i.e., unusually distasteful. We drank a lot of champagne. I sat in between the host and the concert-master, Dannreuther. Speaking with him about his brother, I must have seemed either crazy or a desperate liar during the whole two hours. He sat with mouth open in surprise and was perplexed. It turned out that I'd confused in my memory Dannreuther, the pianist, with Hartvigson, the pianist. My absent-mindedness becomes unbearable and, it seems, attests to my old age. By the way, all the gathering was surprised when I said that yesterday I'd reached 51. Carnegie was especially surprised; they all thought (except those who knew my biography) that I was much older. Have I grown old lately? Quite possibly. I feel something in me had gone to pieces. I was driven in the Carnegie carriage. Influenced by talk of my aged appearance, I saw dreadful dreams the whole night long. [In the original ten lines are crossed out.] On a gigantic rocky slope I rolled unceasingly down to the sea clutching at a small jut of some cliff. I believe all this mirrors yesterday's talk of my old age.

Mr. Romaiko sends me every day heaps of newspaper clippings about myself. Without exception they are all laudatory in the highest degree. They exalt to the skies my Third Suite, and my conducting perhaps even more. Do I really conduct so well? Or do the Americans overdo it too much?!!!

May 9

The weather has become tropical. Max, that most lovely German from Nizhnyi-Novgorod, arranged my apartment so that it appears ideally comfortable. No doubt it's impossible anywhere in Europe to have such indescribable comfort and peace in a hotel. He has added two tables and vases for the masses of flowers sent to me, and also rearranged the furniture. To my dismay, it comes just before the beginning of my wanderings. In general I detect a curious difference between the attitude of all the hotel employees at the beginning of my stay and now. At first they treated me with that coldness and slightly insulting indifference that verge on hostility.

Now everyone smiles, all are ready to run to the end of the earth at my first word, and even young men, attached to the elevator, speak to me about the weather on each of my journeys up or down. But I am far from convinced that all this is the result of tips, which I hand out quite generously. No, even without that, all servants are very grateful when they receive friendly treatment . . . I was also visited by the violinist Rietzel, who came for my portrait and related how the orchestra musicians had grown fond of me. That moved me very much. After changing I went to Mayer with that other big portrait. From there to Schirmer, and then – impetuously to the Music Hall, where my last appearance before an audience was due. These visits before the concert show how little I was worried this time. Why? I have no idea . . . My concerto, perfectly performed by Adele Aus der Ohe, went off splendidly. There was enthusiasm of a kind that never arises even in Russia. They called for me again and again, shouted 'upwards', waved their handkerchiefs – in a word it was evident that I am greatly loved by the Americans. But especially precious to me was the delight of the orchestra. In consequence of the heat, the copious sweat caused by it, and my waving of the baton, I was unable to stay at the concert, and, to my regret, didn't hear the scene from *Parsifal*. At home took a bath and changed. Breakfasted (or dined) at five o'clock at my place downstairs. At the final evening concert of the festival I sat in turn in the boxes of Carnegie, Hyde, Smolls, and Reno. The oratorio *Israel in Egypt* by Handel was performed completely, and the performance was excellent. In the middle of the concert an ovation for the architect of the building. After the concert went with Damrosch to von Sachs's for supper. This luxurious supper was given at the Manhattan Club. The building is grand and luxurious. We sat in a separate hall. Although the cuisine of this club is famous, I found it distasteful. On a delicate vignette-menu a little piece of some composition of mine was written for all those invited . . . On the whole the supper passed very gaily and that was no lack of consideration for me. We broke up at 2 o'clock.

Diary

                                                                    May 10

It's been a very difficult and heavy day. In the morning I was harried by visitors. Who has not come? Suave, interesting Mr. Korbay; a young, very handsome composer, Klein; von Sachs; the pianist friend with gold in her teeth; Mr. Suro with his beautiful wife, a doctor of laws; and I don't know who else. I was simply driven into unconsciousness. At 1 o'clock came out to visit the nihilist Stark-Stoleshnikov, but he lives at such a distance and the heat was so awful, – that I had to postpone it. Dropped in at Hoffman's and there met Mr. Parris, a ship companion, – the one who provided me with cigarettes. He hates America and thinks only of leaving. From there hurried for lunch at Dr. Neftel's. Was barely in time. Dr. Neftel turned out to be a Russian or at least was brought up in Russia. His wife, as I finally found out, is a Georgian princess, a cousin of Igor Ivanovich. They have lived in America since 1860. They often go to Europe, but have not been in Russia since then. Why do they avoid it – it was embarrassing to inquire. Both are fierce patriots, and love Russia with a genuine love. I took more liking to the husband than to the wife. There was something gentle, kind, nice, and sincere to be felt in each Russian word pronounced (not without difficulty) and in each idle motion made by this weary and somewhat sorrowful old man. Concerning Russia he spoke always of how despotism and bureaucratic administration prevent it from standing at the head of mankind. He repeated that idea with other variations countless times. His wife is a type of breezy Moscow mistress. Wants to look clever and independent but overall, it seems, she has neither intellect nor independence. Both love music very much and know it well. Once Neftel became famous for something in the field of medicine and is very much respected in New York. I think that he is a freethinker, who once drew the wrath of government upon himself and opportunely escaped from Russia; but apparently his present-day liberalism is far from nihilism and anarchism. Both repeated several times that they don't hob-nob with local nihilists.

After breakfast at their place (about 3 o'clock) ran (for lack of cabmen one has to run all the time) to V. N. MacGahan. If one could say that the Neftels live luxuriously, the surroundings of this correspondent for Russian newspapers and magazines are quite like a student's. She lives in a boarding room, that is, in a clean furnished house, where all share a common parlour and a common dining room downstairs, and have living quarters on the upper floors. In her place I found a very strange young Russian man named Griboedov, who spoke in broken Russian but perfect French and English. He has the appearance of a modern dandy and slightly puts on airs. Later the well-known sculptor Kamensky appeared, who has lived in America twenty years already (I don't know why). He is an old man, with a deep scar on his forehead, ailing, and quite lamentable to see. He startled me by asking me to tell all that I know of present-day Russia. I was quite lost before that formidable task, but, fortunately, Varvara Nikolaevna began to talk of my musical affairs and then I glanced at my watch and saw that it was time to run home and change for the dinner at Carnegie's. On Sundays all the cafés are closed. Since they are the only places where one can: 1) buy cigarettes, and 2) fulfill a certain need of nature, and I was in extreme need of both, one can just imagine how great were my sufferings until at last I ran home. Traces of English Puritanism, revealed in such absurd trifles as, for instance, the fact that it's impossible to get a shot of whisky or a glass of beer on Sundays other than by fraud, are quite revolting to me. People say that the legislators who issued the law in New York State are themselves awful drunkards.

Barely managed to change and then went to Carnegie in a carriage (which I had to call specially and pay dearly for). Overall, this ultra-rich man lives no more luxuriously than others. Dining with us were the Renos, the Damroschs, the architect of the Music Hall with his wife, an unknown gentleman, and a fat ladyfriend of Mrs. Damrosch. I again sat next to this very aristocratic lady, so graceful in her air. Carnegie, this remarkable original who rose from telegraph boy to become in the course of years one of America's foremost men of wealth, but remained a modest and simple man, never one to turn his nose up – inspires in me unusual warm feelings, probably because he is also filled with kindly feelings for me. During the whole evening, he showed his love to me in an extraordinarily peculiar way. He clasped my hands, shouting that I am the uncrowned but still genuine king of music; embraced me (without kissing – men never kiss here); he stood on tiptoe and raised his hands up high to express my greatness; and finally threw all the company in delight by imitating my conducting. He did this so seriously, so well, and so accurately, that I myself was enraptured. His wife, an extremely simple and pretty young lady, also showed her sympathy for me in every way. All this was pleasing and somehow embarrassing at the same time. I was very glad to depart for home at 11 o'clock. Reno walked me home. I packed for the tomorrow's trip.

Diary

May 11

Mayer called for me at 8:15. What indeed would I have done without Mayer? How would I have gotten myself a ticket of the exact kind that's required; how would I have approached the railroad; how would I have found out at which hours, how, and what I have to do? I boarded the car-salon. This is like our armchaired car, except that the armchairs are set closer together and against the windows, but in such a way that it's possible to spin around. The windows are big and the view on both sides is entirely open. Next to this car was the car-restaurant, and several cars further was the smoking car with a buffet. The traffic from car to car is absolutely free and much more comfortable than with us, for the passages are covered. The servants, that is, the conductors, the waiters in the car-restaurant, and at the buffet of the smoking compartment, are Negroes; all very obliging and polite. At 12 o'clock I had breakfast (the price of the breakfast is one dollar) by menu, entitling me to eat as much as I want of dishes featured in menu. Dined at 6, again choosing from among several dozen dishes anything I wanted and in whatever amount – all for one dollar. The cars are far more luxurious than ours, despite the absence of classes. The luxury is actually quite superfluous, e.g., the frescoes, the crystal decorations, etc. There are numerous toilets, that is, sections with washing-sets, with installed cold and hot water, towels (there is, in general, amazing plentifulness regarding towels here), cakes of soap, brushes, etc. One can roam about on the train and wash as much as one wants. There is a bath and a barber's shop. All this is convenient and comfortable – and yet our cars are more attractive to me for some reason. But probably this is the aftermath of my homesickness, which oppressed and gnawed at me again yesterday, all day long to the point of madness.

At 8.30 o'clock we arrived in Buffalo. Here two gentlemen were waiting for me, whom Mayer had asked to see me off one train and onto another. It is indeed quite difficult to find the right track in this labyrinthine junction of various railways lines. One of the men was a Polish pianist. The rendez-vous with these gentlemen lasted only 10 minutes. In 50 minutes after leaving Buffalo, I was already in Niagara Falls. Was booked at the Hotel Kaltenbach, where accommodations were prepared again through Mayer. The hotel is modest, in the style of small Swiss ones – but very clean and, most importantly, quite suitable for me, since everyone speaks German here. Drank tea, unfortunately with some gentleman who annoyed me with talk. Felt unusually tired, I think, because the air in the train was terribly stuffy. Americans, especially women, are afraid of draughts, in consequence of which, the windows are closed all the time and outside air is not permitted to circulate. And then you have to sit longer than we do. Hardly any stops at all. It was especially tiresome, since only the first hours of the trip, on the bank of Hudson River, were interesting for the eye; during all the remaining time the region was flat and scarcely attractive. I retired early. The noise of waterfalls in the night's silence is quite audible.

Emma Goldman (1892)

The Russian-born anarchist, Emma Goldman (1869–1940), arrived in the United States in 1886. In this excerpt she recalls an attempt to secure money to pay for her friend, Alexander 'Sasha' Berkman's, plan to assassinate the industrialist, Henry Clay Frick Chairman of the board of Camegic Bros. During the Homestead Strike at Pittsburgh in 1892, Berkman shot and stabbed Frick but Frick survived.

I woke up with a very clear idea of how I could raise the money for Sasha. I would go on the street. I lay wondering how such a notion could have come to me. I recollected Dostoyevsky's *Crime and Punishment*, which had made a profound impression on me, especially the character of Sonya, Marmeladov's daughter. She had become a prostitute in order to support her little brothers and sisters and to relieve her consumptive stepmother of worry. I visioned Sonya as she lay on her cot, face to the wall, her shoulders twitching. I could almost feel the same way. Sensitive Sonya could sell her body; why not I? My cause was greater than hers. It was Sasha – his great deed – the people. But should I be able to do it, to go with strange men – for money? The thought revolted me. I buried my face in the pillow to shut out the light. 'Weakling, coward,' an inner voice said. 'Sasha is giving his life, and you shrink from giving your body, miserable coward!' It took me several hours to gain control of myself. When I got out of bed my mind was made up.

My main concern now was whether I could make myself attractive enough to men who seek out girls on the street. I stepped over to the mirror to inspect my body. I looked tired, but my complexion was good. I should need no make-up. My curly blond hair showed off well with my blue eyes. Too large in the hips for my age, I thought; I was just twenty-three. Well, I came from Jewish stock. Besides, I would wear a corset and I should look taller in high heels (I had never worn either before).

Corsets, slippers with high heels, dainty underwear – where should I get money for it all? I had a white linen dress, trimmed with Caucasian embroidery. I could get some soft flesh-coloured material and sew the underwear myself. I knew the stores on Grand Street carried cheap goods.

I dressed hurriedly and went in search of the servant in the apartment who had shown a liking for me, and she lent me five dollars without any question. I started off to make my purchases. When I returned, I locked myself in my room. I would see no one. I was busy preparing my outfit and thinking of Sasha. What would he say? Would he approve? Yes, I was sure he would. He had always insisted that the end justified the means, that the true revolutionist will not shrink from anything to serve the Cause.

Saturday evening, July 16, 1892, I walked up and down Fourteenth Street, one of the long procession of girls I had so often seen plying their trade. I felt no nervousness at first, but when I looked at the passing men and saw their vulgar glances and their manner of approaching the women, my heart sank. I wanted to take flight, run back to my room, tear off my cheap finery, and scrub myself clean. But a voice kept on ringing in my ears: 'You must hold out; Sasha – his act – everything will be lost if you fail.'

I continued my tramp, but something stronger than my reason would compel me to increase my pace the moment a man came near me. One of them was rather insistent, and I fled. By eleven o'clock I was utterly exhausted. My feet hurt from the high heels, my head throbbed. I was close to tears from fatigue and disgust with my inability to carry out what I had come to do.

I made another effort. I stood on the corner of Fourteenth Street and Fourth Avenue, near the bank building. The first man that invited me – I would go with him, I had decided. A tall, distinguished-looking person, well dressed, came close. 'Let's have a drink, little girl,' he said. His hair was white, he appeared to be about sixty, but his face was ruddy. 'All right,' I replied. He took my arm and led me to a wine house on Union Square which Most had often frequented with me. 'Not here!' I almost screamed; 'please, not here.' I led him to the back entrance of a saloon on Thirteenth Street and Third Avenue. I had once been there in the afternoon for a glass of beer. It had been clean and quiet then.

That night it was crowded, and with difficulty we secured a table. The man ordered drinks. My throat felt parched and I asked for a large glass of beer. Neither of us spoke. I was conscious of the man's scrutiny of my face and body. I felt myself growing resentful. Presently he asked: 'You're a novice in the business, aren't you?' 'Yes, this is my first time – but how did you know?' 'I watched you as you passed me,' he replied. He told me that he had noticed my haunted expression and my increased pace the moment a man came near me. He understood then that I was inexperienced; whatever might have been the reason that brought me to the street, he knew it was not mere looseness or love of excitement. 'But thousands of girls are driven by economic necessity,' I blurted out. He looked at me in surprise. 'Where did you get that stuff?' I wanted to tell him all about the social question, about my ideas, who and what I was, but I checked myself. I must not disclose my identity: it would be too dreadful if he should learn that Emma Goldman, the anarchist, had been found soliciting on Fourteenth Street. What a juicy story it would make for the press!

He said he was not interested in economic problems and did not care what the reason was for my actions. He only wanted to tell me that there was nothing in prostitution unless one had the knack for it. 'You haven't got it, and that's all there is to it,' he assured me. He took out a ten-dollar bill and put it down before me. 'Take this and go home,' he said. 'But why should you give me money if you don't want me to go with you?' I asked. 'Well, just to cover the expenses you must have had to rig yourself out like that,' he replied; 'your dress is awfully nice, even if it does not go with those cheap shoes and stockings.' I was too astounded for speech.

I had met two categories of men: vulgarians and idealists. The former would never have let an opportunity pass to possess a woman and they would give her no other thought save sexual desire. The idealists stoutly defended the equality of the sexes, at least in theory, but the only men among them who practised what they preached were the Russian and Jewish radicals. This man, who had picked me up on the street and who was now with me in the back of a saloon, seemed an entirely new type. He interested me. He must be rich. But would a rich man give something for nothing? The manufacturer Garson came to my mind; he would not even give me a small rise in wages.

Perhaps this man was one of those soul-savers I had read about, people who were always cleansing New York City of vice. I asked him. He laughed and said he was not a professional busybody. If he had thought that I really wanted to be on the street, he would not have cared. 'Of course, I may be entirely mistaken,' he added, 'but I don't mind. Just now I am convinced that you are not intended to be a street-walker, and that even if you do succeed, you will hate it afterwards.' If he were not convinced of it, he would take me for his mistress. 'For always?' I cried. 'There you are!' he replied; 'you are scared by the mere suggestion and yet you hope to succeed on the street. You're an awfully nice kid, but you're silly, inexperienced, childish.' 'I was twenty-three last month,' I protested, resentful of being treated like a child. 'You are an old lady,' he said with a grin, 'but even old folks can be babes in the woods. Look at me; I'm sixty-one and I often do foolish things.' 'Like believing in my innocence, for instance,' I retorted. The simplicity of his manner pleased me. I asked for his name and address so as to be able to return his ten dollars some day. But he refused to give them to me. He loved mysteries, he said. On the street he held my hand for a moment, and then we turned in opposite directions.

Lady Theodora Guest (1895)

Lady Theodora Guest was the ninth daughter of the second Marquess of Westminster. In this extract from A Round Trip in North America *she is intriguing as an aristocrat enjoying a Grand Tour of the beguilingly sordid demi-monde of San Francisco.*

San Francisco is a very hilly town: some of the streets are almost per-pendicular, and one wonders how vehicles can get up them without slipping backwards all the time. They have electric and cable cars, as everywhere; but the streets are so wide they are not as objectionable as in many towns. We caught sight of a horse rearing and bounding so uncontrollably in a cart I am sure he must have come to a bad end, but we got out of sight too soon to see what happened. They have very handsome high-spirited horses in most of their conveyances, and a bad or worn-out one is a rare sight. They breed such quantities, and they are so cheap, there is probably no inducement to use inferior ones. They always leave their tails untrimmed, and as soon as the eye gets accustomed to it, these long sweeping tails look rather well.

We took our Rocky Mountain stones to be set at Shreve's the jeweller's, and then came in to dine at six, as there was an evening before us; and a strange one it proved!

At eight o'clock we set out under the guidance, not only of Mr. S., but also of a detective, or at any rate of a man conversant with the Chinese tongue, to explore China-town, the oldest part of the city being now given over entirely to that celestial race. A few minutes in an electric car took us to the district, whence on foot we walked up a street amongst Chinese shops, seeing and meeting only Chinese – chiefly men, but a few women also here and there. The shops were principally barbers, as they are, as a race, all the world knows, very particular about their pigtails. What struck me most was what very good artists they must be as a nation, for every Chinese we met I felt sure I knew; he was so exactly like his counterpart on the screens and fans I had seen all my life – his attitudes, his dress, his hair, his eyes, were identical; and as they are not at all noisy, there was not even any striking novelty in sound. The guide took us first down a dark gangway, which seemed to lead some way under ground, to a house which was only a little square room, not much over six feet square; with one small recess where a sort of shelf acted as a bed; and here lived five people. A little girl of ten, with jade bracelets to avert misfortune, and gold bangles to ensure health, and otherwise covered with a kind of cotton coat and beads, was requested to sing; when, rather to my horror I own, she squirmed out a verse of a hymn, 'Jesus loves me'. I don't believe she had an idea of the meaning, but had been taught the words, by rote, by a missionary. She sang a Chinese song next, with much more *verve*, and was very sharp about the value of her bracelets, which she put at ten dollars each.

We were next taken to a terrible place; an opium den; down a long underground dark passage to a place that looked like a wine-cellar, or still more a mushroom house, all shelves, with a passage between them. They were in three rows, I think, one over the other, and in these shelves lay creatures huddled up, smoking opium. Each had a long pipe, and a little lamp; and, with perfect indifference to us, heated and rolled up his little balls of opium, which were put into the pipe, and, after two or three ecstatic whiffs, had to be renewed. Our guide said a few words, which were merely to ask if it was good, and Johnny languidly agreed. It certainly was rather horrible; but in no way as degrading a sight as that of the ordinary European drunkard. The smell of the opium was too nasty, so that we were glad to get out, and into the street again: but we were not in fresh air for long, for soon on the other side, we plunged into another dark and very narrow passage, to a den where resided another uninviting family group; and then to the theatre. To reach the latter we had to climb up one or two step-ladders, only about fifteen inches wide, and then found ourselves on the stage. Chairs were put for us by the scene-shifter at the side, and we sat down to watch the performance; or rather part of it, as one piece occupies about a month, from five o'clock to midnight every evening. They have long historical plays, chiefly in dumb show, though occasionally the actors indulge in a howl or two.

They are robed in richly embroidered dresses, and the chief art of their best actor, a young man acting the Queen, seemed to lay in the handling of two Argus pheasants' tail feathers, which, starting like horns from the head, bent round in a graceful curl, to the waist. She indulged in a fine frenzy at times, whirling round and round, and cutting her rival's head off; the latter went head over heels, and promptly came to life again. Horrible, deafening, music was going on all the time; the back of the stage being occupied by the orchestra, who made frightful noises with the banging of cymbals and gongs, and no other instruments. The curious part lay in the rapt attention of the large audience; all dressed in dark blue linen, and all staring fixedly at the stage; the men below, the women above in galleries. They say they attend night after night regularly, and delight in it. So true it is that one man's meat is another man's poison. However, it was still possible to meet on common ground, and that we found at a restaurant opposite, when tea à la Chinoise was served to us in egg-shell covered cups. Holding cup and cover tight, you pour out what tea you want into the saucer, and, creamless, drink it from that; but you may add powdered sugar to taste, and with chopsticks, eat almonds and litchis. The latter were very nice, and not so dry as those we get in England. As we looked at the kitchen, the guide put his fingers in a little box, and pulled out a pinch of thread-like gelatine, which he gave me. This was the bird's nest material, for the much prized birds' nest soup. Hardly enough, I fear, for my next dinner-party at home.

We then asked for the bill, and, leaving the hall, hung with coloured lamps and Chinese draperies and paintings, we went downstairs to pay it; an ancient Celestial was making it out, with knitted brows, and a paint brush, held perpendicularly, and Indian ink. He signed it, and I kept it, more in the light of a curiosity than of a receipt. At a shop hard by I secured a jade bangle, and trust its magic influence for good, in which the Chinese so firmly believe, and which gives it such great value in their eyes, may have a beneficial effect on my luggage; and also a netzuki, to add to my collection at far-off home, some embroidered handkerchiefs, and several tiny little China plates (nearly all of which were broken ere they got to England – so the jade forgot to look after them). Next we were led to a joss-house, where, in a temple richly decorated with gold and colour, divers gods were worshipped, and a little offering to any one whose special attribute appears likely to be of use in a dire emergency, and a turn of the prayer-wheel will probably ensure relief if not success. A lamp of sandalwood oil was burning before each of the images of these strange deities.

We bought a sweet smelling box of sandalwood chips, and departed for a druggist's store, where 'the doctor' in attendance was requested to make up and give us a prescription. He did so, the object being to make us waterproof and fireproof as a total result. But the individual ingredients had separate virtues besides. There was saffron for consumption, dried locusts for sore eyes (this we thought might be of service to H. N., who has had a weak one), bark for strength; and, as he flung these on a sheet of paper on the counter, he said that if he added a sea-horse it would be fifteen cents more; but as it was for dyspepsia, we considered it indispensable. There were a few more ingredients, but all were wrapped up together, and when we propose to make ourselves fireproof and so on, we are to boil all slowly and drink the result. The witches of Macbeth will be nothing to it! We brought the packet and the bill, which he wrote very fast, safe home for future use. We were not sorry to leave this opium-smelling district of the Heathen Chinese behind us, and get home to our Christian rooms and profound repose, feeling, thankfully, that, should it not prove convenient in the future that we should visit Hong Kong, Pekin, or Canton, we really know quite enough about them now for all practical purposes.

All the washing or 'laundry' all over America is done by the Chinese, and in all the large towns are shop signs of 'Ching Fou' or 'Sing Chou,' taking in washing. They are quite busy people as a rule, harmless, very industrious, and living on very little.

Bertrand Russell (1896)

After a glittering undergraduate career at Cambridge, Bertrand Russell was attached for a time at the British Embassy at Paris. In December 1894 he married Alys Pearsall Smith (sister of writer Logan), who came from a family of rich Philadelphia Quakers. His 1896 trip, recalled here in his Autobiography, *was the first of numerous visits.*

In the autumn of 1896, Alys and I went to America for three months, largely in order that I might make the acquaintance of her relations. The first thing we did was to visit Walt Whitman's house in Camden, N. J. From there we went to a small manufacturing town called Millville, where a cousin of hers, named Bond Thomas, was the manager of a glass factory which had, for a long time, been the family business. His wife, Edith, was a great friend of Alys's. According to the Census, the town had 10,002 inhabitants, and they used to say that they were the two. He was a simple soul, but she had literary aspirations. She wrote bad plays in the style of Scribe, and imagined that if only she could get away from Millville and establish contact with the literary lights of Europe, her talent would be recognized. He was humbly devoted to her, but she had various flirtations with men whom she imagined to be of finer clay.

In those days the country round about consisted of empty woodland, and she used to take me long drives over dirt tracks in a buggy. She always carried a revolver, saying one could never know when it would come in handy. Subsequent events led me to suspect that she had been reading Hedda Gabler. Two years later, they both came to stay with us in a palace in Venice, and we introduced her to various writers. It turned out that the work she had produced with such labour during the ten years' isolation in Millville was completely worthless. She went back to America profoundly discouraged, and the next we heard was that, after placing her husband's love letters over her heart, she had shot herself through them with the revolver. He subsequently married another woman who was said to be exactly like her.

We went next to Bryn Mawr to stay with the President, Carey Thomas, sister of Bond Thomas. She was a lady who was treated almost with awe by all the family. She had immense energy, a belief in culture which she carried out with a business man's efficiency, and a profound contempt for the male sex. The first time I met her, which was at Friday's Hill, Logan said to me before her arrival: 'Prepare to meet thy Carey.' This expressed the family attitude. I was never able myself, however, to take her quite seriously, because she was so easily shocked. She had the wholly admirable view that a person who intends to write on an academic subject should first read up the literature, so I gravely informed her that all the advances in non-Euclidean geometry had been made in ignorance of the previous litera- ture, and even because of that ignorance. This caused her ever afterwards to regard me as a mere farceur. Various incidents, however, confirmed me in my view of her. For instance, once in Paris we took her to see 'L'Aiglon', and I found from her remarks that she did not know there had been a Revolution in France in 1830. I gave her a little sketch of French history, and a few days later she told me that her secretary desired a handbook of French history, and asked me to recommend one. However, at Bryn Mawr she was Zeus, and everybody trembled before her.

She lived with a friend, Miss Gwinn, who was in most respects the opposite of her. Miss Gwinn had very little will-power, was soft and lazy, but had a genuine though narrow feeling for literature. They had been friends from early youth, and had gone together to Germany to get the Ph.D. degree, which, however, only Carey had succeeded in getting. At the time that we stayed with them, their friendship had become a little ragged. Miss Gwinn used to go home to her family for three days in every fortnight, and at the exact moment of her departure each fortnight, another lady, named Miss Garrett, used to arrive, to depart again at the exact moment of Miss Gwinn's return. Miss Gwinn, meantime, had fallen in love with a very brilliant young man, named Hodder, who was teaching at Bryn Mawr.

This roused Carey to fury, and every night, as we were going to bed, we used to hear her angry voice scolding Miss Gwinn in the next room for hours together. Hodder had a wife and child, and was said to have affairs with the girls at the College. In spite of all these obstacles, however, Miss Gwinn finally married him. She insisted upon getting a very High Church clergyman to perform the ceremony, thereby making it clear that the wife whom he had had at Bryn Mawr was not his legal wife, since the clergyman in question refused to marry divorced persons. Hodder had given out that there had been a divorce, but Miss Gwinn's action showed that this had not been the case. He died soon after their marriage, worn out with riotous living. He had a very brilliant mind, and in the absence of women could talk very interestingly.

While at Bryn Mawr, I gave lectures on non-Euclidean geometry, and Alys gave addresses in favour of endowment of motherhood, combined with private talks to women in favour of free love. This caused a scandal, and we were practically hounded out of the college. From there we went to Baltimore, where I lectured on the same subject at the Johns Hopkins

University. There we stayed with her uncle, Dr Thomas, the father of Carey. The Thomases were a curious family. There was a son at Johns Hopkins who was very brilliant in brain surgery; there was a daughter, Helen, at Bryn Mawr, who had the misfortune to be deaf. She was gentle and kind, and had very lovely red hair. I was very fond of her for a number of years, culminating in 1900. Once or twice I asked her to kiss me, but she refused. Ultimately she married Simon Flexner, the Head of the Rockefeller Institute of Preventive Medicine. I remained very good friends with her, although in the last years of her life I saw her seldom. There was another daughter who had remained a pious and very orthodox Quaker. She always alluded to those who were not Quakers as 'the world's people'.

They all of them used 'thee' in conversation, and so did Alys and I when we talked to each other. Some of the Quaker doctrines seemed a little curious to those not accustomed to them. I remember my mother-in-law explaining that she was taught to consider the Lord's Prayer 'gay'. At first this remark caused bewilderment, but she explained that everything done by non-Quakers but not by Quakers was called 'gay', and this included the use of all fixed formulas, since prayer ought to be inspired by the Holy Spirit. The Lord's Prayer, being a fixed formula, and therefore 'gay'. On another occasion she informed the dinner-table that she had been brought up to have no respect for the Ten Commandments. They also were 'gay'. I do not know whether any Quakers remain who take the doctrine of the guidance of the Spirit so seriously as to have no respect for the Ten Commandments. Certainly I have not met any in recent years. It must not, of course, be supposed that the virtuous people who had this attitude ever, in fact, infringed any of the Commandments; the Holy Spirit saw to it that this should not occur. Outside the ranks of the Quakers, similar doctrines sometimes have more questionable consequences. I remember an account written by my mother-in-law of various cranks that she had known, in which there was one chapter entitled 'Divine Guidance'. On reading the chapter one discovered that this was a synonym for fornication.

My impression of the old families of Philadelphia Quakers was that they had all the effeteness of a small aristocracy. Old misers of ninety would sit brooding over their hoard while their children of sixty or seventy waited for their death with what patience they could command. Various forms of mental disorder appeared common. Those who must be accounted sane were apt to be very stupid. Alys had a maiden aunt in Philadelphia, a sister of her father, who was very rich and very absurd. She liked me well enough, but had a dark suspicion that I thought it was not literally the blood of Jesus that brought salvation. I do not know how she got this notion, as I never said anything to encourage it. We dined with her on Thanksgiving Day. She was a very greedy old lady, and had supplied a feast which required a gargantuan stomach. Just as we were about to eat the first mouthful, she said: 'Let us pause and think of the poor.' Apparently she found this thought an appetizer. She had two nephews who lived in her neighbourhood and came to see her every evening. They felt it would be unfair if the nephew and nieces in Europe got an equal share at her death. She, however, liked to boast about them, and respected them more than those whom she could bully as she chose. Consequently they lost nothing by their absence.

America in those days was a curiously innocent country. Numbers of men asked me to explain what it was that Oscar Wilde had done. In Boston we stayed in a boarding-house kept by two old Quaker ladies, and one of them at breakfast said to me in a loud voice across the table: 'Oscar Wilde has not been much before the public lately. What has he been doing?' 'He is in prison,' I replied. Fortunately on this occasion I was not asked what he had done. I viewed America in those days with the conceited superiority of the insular Briton. Nevertheless, contact with academic Americans, especially mathematicians, led me to realize the superiority of Germany to England in almost all academic matters. Against my will, in the course of my travels, the belief that everything worth knowing was known at Cambridge gradually wore off. In this respect my travels were very useful to me. . . .

W. H. Davies (1890s)

After serving as an apprentice to a picture-frame maker, Davies spent his early manhood tramping through America, crossing the Atlantic many times on cattle-boats. He wrote up his adventures as The Autobiography of a Super-Tramp, *which was first published in 1908.*

Brum informed me of a freight train that was to leave the yards at midnight, on which we could beat our way to a small town on the borders of the hop country. Not knowing what to do with ourselves until that time arrived, we continued to drink until we were not in a fit condition for this hazardous undertaking – except we were fortunate to get an empty car, so as to lie down and sleep upon the journey. At last we made our way towards the yards, where we saw the men making up the train. We kept out of sight until that was done and then in the darkness Brum inspected one side of the train and I the other, in quest of an empty car. In vain we sought for that comfort. There was nothing to do but to ride the bumpers or the top of the car, exposed to the cold night air. We jumped the bumpers, the engine whistled twice, toot! and we felt ourselves slowly moving out of the yards. Brum was on one car and I was on the next facing him. Never shall I forget the horrors of that ride. He had taken fast hold on the handle bar of his car, and I had done likewise with mine. We had been riding some fifteen minutes, and the train was going at its full speed when, to my horror, I saw Brum lurch forward, and then quickly pull himself straight and erect. Several times he did this, and I shouted to him. It was no use, for the man was drunk and fighting against the over-powering effects, and it was a mystery to me how he kept his hold. At last he became motionless for so long that I knew the next time he lurched forward his weight of body must break his hold, and he would fall under the wheels and be cut to pieces. I worked myself carefully towards him and woke him. Although I had great difficulty in waking him, he swore that he was not asleep.

I had scarcely done this when a lantern was shown from the top of the car, and a brakesman's voice hailed us. 'Hallo, where are you two going?' 'To the hop fields,' I answered. 'Well,' he sneered, 'I guess you won't get to them on this train, so jump off, at once. Jump! d'ye hear?' he cried, using a great oath, as he saw we were little inclined to obey. Brum was now wide awake. 'If you don't jump at once,' shouted this irate brakesman, 'you will be thrown off.' 'To jump,' said Brum quietly. 'will be sure death, and to be thrown off will mean no more.' 'Wait until I come back,' cried the brakesman, 'and we will see whether you ride this train or not,' on which he left us, making his way towards the caboose.

'Now,' said Brum, 'when he returns we must be on the top of the car, for he will probably bring with him a coupling pin to strike us off the bumpers, making us fall under the wheels.' We quickly clambered on top and in a few minutes could see a light approaching us, moving along the top of the cars. We were now lying flat, so that he might not see us until he stood on the same car. He was very near to us, when we sprang to our feet, and unexpectedly gripped him, one on each side, and before he could recover from his first astonishment. In all my life I have never seen so much fear on a human face. He must have seen our half drunken condition and at once gave up all hopes of mercy from such men, for he stood helpless, not knowing what to do. If he struggled it would mean the fall and death of the three, and did he remain helpless in our hands, it might mean being thrown from that height from a car going at the rate of thirty miles an hour.

'Now,' said Brum to him, 'what is it to be? Shall we ride this train without interference, or shall we have a wrestling bout up here, when the first fall must be our last? Speak!' 'Boys,' said he, affecting a short laugh, 'you have the drop on me; you can ride.' We watched him making his way back to the caboose, which he entered, but every moment I expected to see him reappear assisted by others. It might have been that there was some friction among them, and that they would not ask assistance from one another. For instance, an engineer has to take orders from the conductor, but the former is as well paid, if not better, than the latter, and the most responsibility is on his shoulders, and this often makes ill blood between them. At any rate, American tramps know well that neither the engineer nor the fireman, his faithful attendant, will inform the conductor or brakesman of their presence on a train. Perhaps the man was ashamed of his ill-success, and did not care to own his defeat to the conductor and his fellow brakesmen; but whatever was the matter, we rode that train to its destination and without any more interference.

Maxim Gorki (1906)

The Russian playwright Maxim Gorki (1868–1936) arrived in New York after he was exiled from Czarist Russia for his participation in the failed Revolution of 1905. He subsequently wrote a damning account of New York in The City of the Yellow Devil *(1906). This was one of a series of bitter articles on the United States, which culminated in the striking conclusion: 'I could write a million words about America and not one good among them.'*

... Over earth and ocean hangs a fog well mixed with smoke, and a fine slow rain is falling over the dark buildings of the city and the muddy waters of the roadstead.

The immigrants gather at the ship's side and gaze silently about them with the curious eyes of hope and apprehension, fear and joy.

'Who's that?' a Polish girl asks softly, staring in wonder at the Statue of Liberty.

'The American god,' someone replies.

The massive figure of the bronze woman is covered from head to foot with verdigris. The cold face stares blindly through the fog, out to the wastes of ocean, as though the bronze is waiting for the sun to bring sight to its sightless eyes. There is very little ground under Liberty's feet, she appears to rise from the ocean on a pedestal of petrified waves. Her arm, raised aloft over the ocean and the masts of the ships, gives a proud majesty and beauty to her pose. The torch so tightly gripped in her hand seems about to burst into a bright flame, driving away the grey smoke and bathing all around in fierce and joyous light.

And around that insignificant strip of land on which she stands, huge iron vessels glide over the waters like prehistoric monsters, and tiny launches dart about like hungry beasts of prey. Sirens wail, angry whistles shrill, anchor chains clang, and the ocean waves grimly slap against the shore.

Everything is running, hurrying, vibrating tensely. The screws and paddles of the steamers rapidly thresh the water which is covered with a yellow foam and seamed with wrinkles.

And everything – iron, stone, water and wood – seems to be protesting against a life without sunlight, without songs and happiness, in captivity to exhausting toil. Everything is groaning, howling, grating, in reluctant obedience to some mysterious force inimical to man. All over the bosom of the waters, ploughed and rent by iron, dirtied by greasy spots of oil, littered with chips and shavings, straw and remains of food, a cold and evil force labours unseen. Grimly and monotonously it operates this stupendous machine, in which ships and docks are only small parts, and man an insignificant screw, an invisible dot amid the unsightly, dirty tangle of iron and wood, the chaos of steamers, boats and barges loaded with cars.

Dazed, deafened by the noise, unnerved by this mad dance of inanimate matter, a two-legged creature, all sooty and oily, with his hands thrust deep in his pockets, stares curiously at me. There is a layer of greasy dirt on the face, relieved not by the gleam of human eyes but by the ivory of white teeth.

Slowly the steamer makes her way through the throng of vessels. The faces of the immigrants look strangely grey and dull, with something of a sheeplike sameness about the eyes. Gathered at the ship's side, they stare in silence at the fog.

In this fog something incomprehensibly vast, emitting a hollow murmur, is born; it grows, its heavy odorous breath is carried to the people and its voice has a threatening and avid note.

This is a city. This is New York. Twenty-storeyed houses, dark soundless skyscrapers, stand on the shore. Square, lacking in any desire to be beautiful, the bulky, ponderous buildings tower gloomily and drearily. A haughty pride in its height, and its ugliness is felt in each house. There are no flowers at the windows and no children to be seen . . .

From this distance the city seems like a vast jaw, with uneven black teeth. It breathes clouds of black smoke into the sky and puffs like a glutton suffering from his obesity.

Entering the city is like getting into a stomach of stone and iron, a stomach that has swallowed several million people and is grinding and digesting them.

The street is a slippery, greedy throat, in the depths of which float dark bits of the city's food – living people. Everywhere – overhead, underfoot, alongside, there is a clang of iron, exulting in its victory. Awakened to the life and animated by the power of Gold, it casts its web about man, strangles him, sucks his blood and brain, devours his muscles and nerves, and grows and grows, resting upon voiceless stone, and spreading the links of its chain ever more widely.

Locomotives like enormous worms wriggle along, dragging cars behind them; the horns of the automobiles quack like fat ducks, electric wires hum drearily, the stifling air throbs with the thousands of strident sounds it has absorbed as a sponge absorbs moisture. Pressing down upon this grimy city, soiled with the smoke of factories, it hangs motionless among the high, soot-covered walls.

Alma Mahler (1909)

By birth a Jew, Gustav Mahler (1860–1911) became a Catholic in his thirties. Between 1908 and 1911 he was conductor of the New York Philharmonic Society. On first seeing Niagara Falls he is said to have exclaimed: 'Fortissimo at last!' This account of his stay in San Francisco is by his widow, Alma.

We were invited by the music publisher, Schirmer, and his wife to dine with them one day and drive with them afterwards 'down town', into Chinatown. The indispensable detective sat beside the chauffeur. We turned out of the busy streets into narrower ones which became by degrees quieter, narrower, darker and more uncanny. We got out, accompanied by the detective with a loaded revolver in his pocket, and went into an opium den. A creature with a sickeningly womanish face received us in an ante-room, where we had to put down a sum of money. He began at once to give us a long account of his successes with white ladies, and told us he acted female parts in the Chinese Theatre. A Chinese woman, of course, may not either act or look on a theatre. He showed it in his face – it was the most degenerate man-woman face you could imagine. He showed us numerous photographs of American women he had – and he said the rest by gestures. Then he conducted us into several small but high rooms, empty in the middle but furnished with bunks along the sides, each of which contained a stretcher; and on each stretcher lay a doped Chinese with his head lolling into the room. Some of them raised their heads heavily as we approached, but at once let them sink again. It was a gruesomely horrible sight. They were simply dumped there to sleep off their intoxication. They might be robbed or murdered while they were in this state and know nothing about it. The whole scene resembled a baker's shop with human loaves.

On now to a house of cards higher and higher, up into a room luxuriously furnished for strangers, cushions everywhere, and beside each cushion an opium pipe. And a Chinese, for payment, was ready to smoke a pipe on the spot while we watched him slowly succumb, rolling his eyes and twisting his limbs about. We were exhorted to smoke too but declined with horror. Next the theatre. Charming, but no play was being given. If it had been, no European would have been allowed among the audience. On again. Rats with long pigtails slunk nimbly and rapidly along the walls of the stinking street. Mahler said: 'I can hardly believe that these are my brothers.'

On again. Small shops, small hotels, but all silent. Finally, on the outskirts of this district we came on the habitat of a religious sect. There was a large hall at the far end of which sat a man with the face of a fanatic playing hymns on a harmonium in a pronouncedly whining style. The benches were occupied by a starving congregation. We were given the explanation. For listening to the hymns and joining in – a cup of coffee and a roll. What wretchedness in those faces! We pushed our way out, followed by hostile eyes, and for long afterwards we could still hear the flat notes of the hungry singers.

On again, and now the Jewish quarter. It was dark by this time. But here all was life and bustle, chaffering and shouting. The racial difference was staggering, but it was because the Jews worked day and night shifts to lose no time. The whole street was full from end to end of old clothes and rags. The air was heavy with the smell of food. I asked Mahler softly in his own words, 'Are *these* our brothers?' He shook his head in despair.

With a sigh of relief we at last turned a corner and found ourselves in a well-lighted street among our own sort of people. Can it be that there are only class and not race distinctions?

We went a lot to the opera, and the theatre too. Boxes and seats were, naturally, always at Mahler's disposal. Once we went to a play by a young and unknown playwright named MacKay. This play – *The Scarecrow* – was based on a symbolical use of fairy-tales; it was extremely talented and marvellously produced. We saw it three times and would have seen it ten times, but as we were the whole audience it was taken off.

Arnold Bennett (1912)

In Those United States the English novelist Arnold Bennett describes his first encounter with the traffic of New York.

At the centre of the first cross-roads, I saw a splendid and erect individual, flashing forth authority, gaiety, and utter smartness in the gloom. Impossible not to believe that he was the owner of all the adjacent ground, disguised as a cavalry officer on foot.

'What is that archduke?' I inquired.

'He's just a cop.'

I knew then that I was in a great city.

Charles Chaplin (1915)

Chaplin went to Hollywood in 1914 as part of the Fred Karno stage company. His early films were directed by Mack Sennett. As his autobiography recalls, the tramp that made him famous was the inspiration of a moment.

Each day my peace of mind depended on Sennett. If perchance he saw me and smiled, my hopes would rise. The rest of the company had a wait-and-see attitude but some, I felt, considered me a doubtful substitute for Ford Sterling.

When Saturday came Sennett was most amiable. Said he: 'Go to the front office and get your cheque.' I told him I was more anxious to get to work. I wanted to talk about imitating Ford Sterling, but he dismissed me with the remark: 'Don't worry, we'll get round to that.'

Nine days of inactivity had passed and the tension was excruciating. Ford, however, would console me and after work he would occasionally give me a lift down-town, where we would stop in at the Alexandria Bar for a drink and meet several of his friends. One of them, a Mr. Elmer Ellsworth, whom I disliked at first and thought rather crass, would jokingly taunt me: 'I understand you're taking Ford's place. Well, are you funny?'

'Modesty forbids,' I said squirmishly. This sort of ribbing was most embarrassing, especially in the presence of Ford. But he graciously took me off the hook with a remark. 'Didn't you catch him at the Empress playing the drunk? Very funny.'

'Well, he hasn't made me laugh yet,' said Ellsworth.

He was a big, cumbersome man, and looked glandular, with a melancholy, hangdog expression, hairless face, sad eyes, a loose mouth and a smile that showed two missing front teeth. Ford whispered impressively that he was a great authority on literature, finance and politics, one of the best-informed men in the country, and that he had a great sense of humour. However I did not appreciate it and would try to avoid him. But one night at the Alexandria bar, he said: 'Hasn't this limey got started yet?'

'Not yet,' I laughed uncomfortably.

'Well, you'd better be funny.'

Having taken a great deal from the gentleman, I gave him back some of his own medicine: 'Well, if I'm half as funny as you look, I'll do all right.'

'Blimey! A sarcastic wit, eh? I'll buy him a drink after that.'

At last the moment came. Sennett was away on location with Mabel Normand as well as the Ford Sterling Company, so there was hardly anyone left in the studio. Mr. Henry Lehrman, Keystone's top director after Sennett, was to start a new picture and wanted me to play a newspaper reporter. Lehrman was a vain man and very conscious of the fact that he had made some successful comedies of a mechanical nature; he used to say that he didn't need personalities, that he got all his laughs from mechanical effects and film-cutting.

We had no story. It was to be a documentary about the printing press done with a few comedy touches. I wore a light frock-coat, a top hat and a handlebar moustache. When we started I could see that Lehrman was groping for ideas. And of course being a newcomer at Keystone, I was anxious to make suggestions. This was where I created antagonism with Lehrman. In a scene in which I had an interview with an editor of a newspaper I crammed in every conceivable gag I could think of, even to suggesting business for others in the cast. Although the picture was completed in three days, I thought we contrived some very funny gags. But when I saw the finished film it broke my heart, for the cutter had butchered it beyond recognition, cutting into the middle of all my funny business. I was bewildered and wondered why they had done this. Henry Lehrman confessed years later that he had deliberately done it, because, as he put it, he thought I knew too much.

The day after I finished with Lehrman, Sennett returned from location. Ford Sterling was on one set, Arbuckle on another; the whole stage was crowded with three companies at work. I was in my street clothes and had nothing to do, so I stood where Sennett could see me. He was standing with Mabel, looking into a hotel lobby set, biting the end of a cigar. 'We need some gags here,' he said, then turned to me. 'Put on a comedy make-up. Anything will do.'

I had no idea what make-up to put on. I did not like my get-up as the press reporter. However, on the way to the wardrobe I thought I would dress in baggy pants, big shoes, a cane and a derby hat. I wanted everything a contradiction: the pants baggy, the coat tight, the hat small and the shoes large. I was undecided whether to look old or young, but remembering

Sennett had expected me to be a much older man, I added a small moustache, which, I reasoned, would add age without hiding my expression.

I had no idea of the character. But the moment I was dressed, the clothes and the make-up made me feel the person he was. I began to know him, and by the time I walked on to the stage he was fully born. When I confronted Sennett I assumed the character and strutted about, swinging my cane and parading before him. Gags and comedy ideas went racing through my mind.

The secret of Mack Sennett's success was his enthusiasm. He was a great audience and laughed genuinely at what he thought funny. He stood and giggled until his body began to shake. This encouraged me and I began to explain the character: 'You know this fellow is many-sided, a tramp, a gentleman, a poet, a dreamer, a lonely fellow, always hopeful of romance and adventure. He would have you believe he is a scientist, a musician, a duke, a polo-player. However, he is not above picking up cigarette-butts or robbing a baby of its candy. And, of course, if the occasion warrants it, he will kick a lady in the rear – but only in extreme anger!'

I carried on this way for ten minutes or more, keeping Sennett in continuous chuckles. 'All right,' said he, 'get on the set and see what you can do there.' As with the Lehrman film, I knew little of what the story was about, other than that Mabel Normand gets involved with her husband and a lover.

In all comedy business an attitude is most important, but it is not always easy to find an attitude. However, in the hotel lobby I felt I was an imposter posing as one of the guests, but in reality I was a tramp just wanting a little shelter. I entered and stumbled over the foot of a lady. I turned and raised my hat apologetically, then turned and stumbled over a cuspidor, then turned and raised my hat to the cuspidor. Behind the camera they began to laugh.

Quite a crowd had gathered there, not only the players of the other companies who left their sets to watch us, but also the stage-hands, the carpenters and the wardrobe department. That indeed was a compliment. And by the time we had finished rehearsing we had quite a large audience laughing. Very soon I saw Ford Sterling peering over the shoulders of others. When it was over I knew I had made good.

At the end of the day when I went to the dressing-room, Ford Sterling and Roscoe Arbuckle were taking off their make-up. Very little was said, but the atmosphere was charged with cross-currents. Both Ford and Roscoe liked me, but I frankly felt they were undergoing some inner conflict.

It was a long scene that ran seventy-five feet. Later Mr. Sennett and Mr. Lehrman debated whether to let it run its full length, as the average comedy scene rarely ran over ten. 'If it's funny,' I said, 'does length really matter?' They decided to let the scene run its full seventy-five feet. As the clothes had imbued me with the character, I then and there decided I would keep to this costume whatever happened.

That evening I went home on the street-car with one of the small-bit players. Said he: 'Boy, you've started something; nobody ever got those kind of laughs on the set before, not even Ford Sterling – and you should have seen his face watching you, it was a study!'

'Let's hope they'll laugh the same way in the theatre,' I said, by way of suppressing my elation.

A few days later, at the Alexandria Bar, I overheard Ford giving his description of my character to our mutual friend Elmer Ellsworth: 'The guy has baggy pants, flat feet, the most miserable, bedraggled-looking little bastard you ever saw; makes itchy gestures as though he's got crabs under his arms – but he's funny'.

My character was different and unfamiliar to the American, and even unfamiliar to myself. But with the clothes on I felt he was a reality, a living person. In fact he ignited all sorts of crazy ideas that I would never have dreamt of until I was dressed and made up as the Tramp.

G. K. Chesterton (1922)

G. K. Chesterton (1874–1936), English novelist, creator of Father Brown, poet, social critic, Catholic apologist, visited the United States in 1922. He recorded his thoughts in his book, What I Saw in America.

When I had looked at the lights of Broadway by night, I made to my American friends an innocent remark that seemed for some reason to amuse them. I had looked, not without joy, at that long kaleidoscope of coloured lights arranged in large letters and sprawling trade-marks, advertising everything, from pork to pianos, through the agency of the two most vivid and most mystical of the gifts of God; colour and fire. I said to them, in my simplicity, 'What a glorious garden of wonder this would be, to any one who was lucky enough to be unable to read.'

New York is a cosmopolitan city; but not a city of cosmopolitans. Most of the masses in New York have a nation, whether or not it be the nation to which New York belongs. Those who are Americanised are American, and very patriotically American. Those who are not thus nationalised are not in the least internationalised. They simply continue to be themselves; the Irish are Irish; the Jews are Jewish; and all sorts of other tribes carry on the traditions of remote European valleys almost untouched. In short, there is a sort of slender bridge between their old country and their new, which they either cross or do not cross, but which they seldom simply occupy. They are exiles or they are citizens; there is no moment when they are cosmopolitans. But very often the exiles bring with them not only rooted traditions, but rooted truths.

Indeed it is to a great extent the thought of these strange souls in crude American garb that gives a meaning to the masquerade of New York. In the hotel where I stayed the head waiter in one room was a Bohemian; and I am glad to say that he called himself a Bohemian. I have already protested sufficiently, before American audiences, against the pedantry of perpetually talking about Czecho-Slovakia. I suggested to my American friends that the abandonment of the word Bohemian in its historical sense might well extend to its literary and figurative sense. We might be expected to say, 'I'm afraid Henry has got into very Czecho-Slovakian habits lately,' or 'Don't bother to dress; it's quite a Czecho-Slovakian affair.' Anyhow my Bohemian would have nothing to do with such nonsense; he called himself a son of Bohemia, and spoke as such in his criticisms of America, which were both favourable and unfavourable. He was a squat man, with a sturdy figure and a steady smile; and his eyes were like dark pools in the depth of a darker forest; but I do not think he had ever been deceived by the lights of Broadway.

But I found something like my real innocent abroad, my real peasant among the sky-signs, in another part of the same establishment. He was a much leaner man, equally dark, with a hook nose, hungry face, and fierce black moustaches. He was also a waiter, and was in the costume of a waiter, which is a smarter edition of the costume of a lecturer. As he was serving me with clam chowder or some such thing, I fell into speech with him and he told me he was a Bulgar. I said something like, 'I'm afraid I don't know as much as I ought to about Bulgaria. I suppose most of your people are agricultural, aren't they?' He did not stir an inch from his regular attitude, but he slightly lowered his low voice and said, 'Yes. From the earth we come and to the earth we return; when people get away from that they are lost.'

To hear such a thing said by the waiter was alone an epoch in the life of an unfortunate writer of fantastic novels. To see him clear away the clam chowder like an automaton, and bring me more iced water like an automaton or like nothing on earth except an American waiter (for piling up ice is the cold passion of their lives), and all this after having uttered something so dark and deep, so starkly incongruous and so startlingly true, was an indescribable thing, but very like the picture of the peasant admiring Broadway. So he passed, with his artificial clothes and manners, lit up with all the ghastly artificial light of the hotel, and all the ghastly artificial life of the city; and his heart was like his own remote and rocky valley, where those unchanging words were carved as on a rock.

D. H. Lawrence (1924)

D. H. Lawrence's essay 'The Spirit of Place' deals not so much with his personal impressions of the United States, but with his theories as to why people have chosen to emigrate there.

Let us look at this American artist first. How did he ever get to America, to start with? Why isn't he a European still, like his father before him?

Now listen to me, don't listen to him. He'll tell you the lie you expect. Which is partly your fault for expecting it.

He didn't come in search of freedom of worship. England had more freedom of worship in the year 1700 than America had. Won by Englishmen who wanted freedom, and so stopped at home and fought for it. And got it. Freedom of worship? Read the history of New England during the first century of its existence.

Freedom anyhow? The land of the free! This is the land of the free! Why, if I say anything that displeases them, the free mob will lynch me, and that's my freedom. Free? Why I have never been in any country where the individual has such an abject fear of his fellow-countrymen. Because, as I say, they are free to lynch him the moment he shows he is not one of them.

No, no, if you're so fond of the truth about Queen Victoria, try a little about yourself.

Those Pilgrim Fathers and their successors never came here for freedom of worship. What did they set up when they got here? Freedom, would you call it?

They didn't come for freedom. Or if they did, they sadly went back on themselves.

All right then, what did they come for? For lots of reasons. Perhaps least of all in search of freedom of any sort: positive freedom, that is.

They came largely to get *away* – that most simple of motives. To get away. Away from what? In the long run, away from themselves. Away from everything. That's why most people have come to America, and still do come. To get away from everything they are and have been.

'Henceforth be masterless.'

Which is all very well, but it isn't freedom. Rather the reverse. A hopeless sort of constraint. It is never freedom till you find something you really *positively want to be*. And people in America have always been shouting about the things they are *not*. Unless, of course, they are millionaires, made or in the making.

And after all there is a positive side to the movement. All that vast flood of human life that has flowed over the Atlantic in ships from Europe to America had not flowed over simply on a tide of revulsion from Europe and from the confinements of the European ways of life. This revulsion was, and still is, I believe, the prime motive in emigration. But there was some cause, even for the revulsion.

It seems as if at times man had a frenzy for getting away from any control of any sort. In Europe the old Christianity was the real master. The Church and the true aristocracy bore the responsibility for the working out of the Christian ideals: a little irregularly, maybe, but responsible nevertheless.

Mastery, kingship, fatherhood had their power destroyed at the time of the Renaissance.

And it was precisely at this moment that the great drift over the Atlantic started. What were men drifting away from? The old authority of Europe? Were they breaking the bonds of authority, and escaping to a new more absolute unrestrainedness? Maybe. But there was more to it.

Liberty is all very well, but men cannot live without masters. There is always a master. And men either live in glad obedience to the master they believe in, or they live in frictional oppostion to the master they wish to undermine. In America this frictional opposition has been the vital factor. It has given the Yankee his kick. Only the continual influx of more servile

Europeans has provided America with an obedient labouring class. The true obedience never outlasting the first generation.

But there sits the old master, over in Europe. Like a parent. Somewhere deep in every American heart lies a rebellion against the old parenthood of Europe. Yet no American feels he has completely escaped its mastery. Hence the slow, smouldering patience of American opposition. The slow, smouldering, corrosive obedience to the old master Europe, the unwilling subject, the unremitting opposition.

Whatever else you are, be masterless.

> Ca Ca Caliban
> Get a new master, be a new man.

Escaped slaves, we might say, people the republics of Liberia or Haiti. Liberia enough! Are we to look at America in the same way? A vast republic of escaped slaves. When you consider the hordes from eastern Europe, you might well say it: a vast republic of escaped slaves. But one dare not say this of the Pilgrim Fathers, and the great old body of idealist Americans, the modern Americans tortured with thought. A vast republic of escaped slaves. Look out, America! And a minority of earnest, self-tortured people.

The masterless.

> Ca Ca Caliban
> Get a new master, be a new man.

What did the Pilgrim Fathers come for, then, when they came so gruesomely over the black sea? Oh, it was in a black spirit. A black revulsion from Europe, from the old authority of Europe, from kings and bishops and popes. And more. When you look into it, more. They were black, masterful men, they wanted something else. No kings, no bishops maybe. Even no God Almighty. But also, no more of this new 'humanity' which followed the Renaissance. None of this new liberty which was to be so pretty in Europe. Something grimmer, by no means free-and-easy.

America has never been easy, and is not easy to-day. Americans have always been at a certain tension. Their liberty is a thing of sheer will, sheer tension: a liberty of THOU SHALT NOT. And it has been so from the first. The land of THOU SHALT NOT. Only the first commandment is: THOU SHALT NOT PRESUME TO BE A MASTER. Hence democracy.

'We are the masterless.' That is what the American Eagle shrieks. It's a Hen-Eagle.

The Spaniards refused the post-Renaissance liberty of Europe. And the Spaniards filled most of America. The Yankees, too, refused, refused the post-Renaissance humanism of Europe. First and foremost, they hated masters. But under that, they hated the flowing ease of humour in Europe. At the bottom of the American soul was always a dark suspense, at the bottom of the Spanish-American soul the same. And this dark suspense hated and hates the old European spontaneity, watches it collapse with satisfaction.

Every continent has its own great spirit of place. Every people is polarised in some particular locality, which is home, the homeland. Different places on the face of the earth have different vital effluence, different vibration, different chemical exhaltion, different polarity with different stars: call it what you like. But the spirit of place is a great reality. The Nile valley produced not only the corn, but the terrific religions of Egypt. China produces the Chinese, and will go on doing so. The Chinese in San Francisco will in time cease to be Chinese, for America is a great melting-pot.

There was a tremendous polarity in Italy, in the city of Rome. And this seems to have died. For even places die. The Island of Great Britain had a wonderful terrestrial magnetism or polarity of its own, which made the British people. For the moment, this polarity seems to be breaking. Can England die? And what if England dies?

Men are less free than they imagine; ah, far less free. The freest are perhaps least free.

Men are free when they are in a living homeland, not when they are straying and breaking away. Men are free when they are obeying some deep, inward voice of religious belief. Obeying from within. Men are free when they belong to a living, organic, *believing* community, active in fulfilling some unfulfilled, perhaps unrealised purpose. Not when they are escaping to some wild west. The most unfree souls go west, and shout of freedom. Men are freest when they are most unconscious of freedom. The shout is a rattling of chains, always was.

Men are not free when they are doing just what they like. The moment you can do just what you like, there is nothing you care about doing. Men are only free when they are doing what the deepest self likes.

And there is getting down to the deepest self! It takes some diving.

Because the deepest self is way down, and the conscious self is an obstinate monkey. But of one thing we may be sure. If one wants to be free, one has to give up the illusion of doing what one likes, and seek what IT wishes done.

But before you can do what IT likes, you must first break the spell of the old mastery, the old IT.

Perhaps at the Renaissance, when kingship and fatherhood fell, Europe drifted into a very dangerous half-truth: of liberty and equality. Perhaps the men who went to America felt this, and so repudiated the old world together. Went one better than Europe. Liberty in America has meant so far the breaking away from *all* dominion. The true liberty will only begin when Americans discover IT, and proceed possibly to fulfil IT. It being the deepest *whole* self of man, the self in its wholeness, not idealistic halfness.

That's why the Pilgrim Fathers came to America, then; and that's why we come. Driven by IT. We cannot see that invisible winds carry us, as they carry swarms of locusts, that invisible magnetism brings us as it brings the migrating birds to their unforeknown goal. But it is so. We are not the marvellous choosers and deciders we think we are. IT chooses for us, and decides for us. Unless, of course, we are just escaped slaves, vulgarly cocksure of our ready-made destiny. But if we are living people, in touch with the source, IT drives us and decides us. We are free only so long as we obey. When we run counter, and think we will do as we like, we just flee around like Orestes pursued by the Eumenides.

And still, when the great day begins, when Americans have at last discovered America and their own wholeness, still there will be the vast number of escaped slaves to reckon with, those who have no cocksure, ready-made destinies.

Which will win in America, the escaped slaves, or the new whole men?

The real American day hasn't begun yet. Or at least, not yet sunrise. So far it has been the false dawn. That is, in the progressive American consciousness there has been the one dominant desire, to do away with the old thing. Do away with masters, exalt the will of the people. The will of the people being nothing but a figment, the exalting doesn't count for much. So, in the name of the will of the people, get rid of masters. When you have got rid of masters, you are left with this mere phrase of the will of the people. Then you pause and bethink yourself, and try to recover your own wholeness.

So much for the conscious American motive, and for democracy over here. Democracy in America is just the tool with which the old master of Europe, the European spirit, is undermined. Europe destroyed, potentially, American democracy will evaporate. America will begin.

American consciousness has so far been a false dawn. The negative ideal of democracy. But underneath, and contrary to this open ideal, the first hints and revelations of IT. IT, the American whole soul.

You have got to pull the democratic and idealistic clothes off American utterance, and see what you can of the dusky body of IT underneath.

'Henceforth be masterless.'

Henceforth be mastered.

Federico Garcia Lorca (1929)

The Spanish dramatist, Federico García Lorca (1896–1936), visited New York in the late twenties. Here, in an excerpt from a lecture he gave while reading some of the poems, he describes his impressions of the city.

I will not tell you what New York is like *from the outside*, because New York, like Moscow, those two antagonistic cities, is already the subject of countless descriptive books. Nor will I narrate a trip. But will give my lyrical reaction with all sincerity and simplicity, two qualities that come with difficulty to intellectuals, but easily to the poet. So much for modesty!

The two elements the traveller first captures in the big city are extra-human architecture and furious rhythm. Geometry and anguish. At first glance, the rhythm can seem to be gaiety, but when you look more closely at the mechanism of social life and the painful slavery of both men and machines you understand it as a typical, empty anguish that makes even crime and banditry forgivable means of evasion.

Willing neither clouds nor glory, the edges of the buildings rise to the sky. While Gothic edges rise from the hearts of the dead and buried, these ones climb coldly skyward with beauty that has no roots and no yearning, stupidly sure of themselves and utterly unable to conquer or transcend, as does spiritual architecture, the always inferior intentions of the architect. There is nothing more poetic and terrible than the skyscrapers' battle with the heavens that cover them. Snow, rain, and mist set off, wet, and hide the vast towers, but those towers, hostile to mystery, blind to any sort of play, shear off the rain's tresses and shine their three thousand swords through the soft swan of the mist.

It only takes a few days before you get the impression that that immense world has no roots, and you understand why the seer Edgar Poe had to hug mystery so close to him and let friendly intoxication boil in his veins.

The Great Black City

What I had before my eyes was neither an aesthetic norm nor a blue paradise. What I looked at, strolled through, dreamed about, was the great black city of Harlem, the most important black city in the world, where lewdness has an innocent accent that makes it disturbing and religious. A neighbourhood of rosy houses, full of pianolas and radios and cinemas, but with the *mistrust* that characterizes the race. Doors left ajar, jasper children afraid of the rich people from Park Avenue, phonographs that suddenly stop singing, the wait for the enemies who can arrive by the East River and show just where the idols are sleeping. I wanted to make the poem of the black race in North America and to emphasize the pain that the blacks feel to be black in a contrary world. They are slaves of all the white man's inventions and machines, perpetually afraid that some day they will forget how to light the gas stove or steer the automobile or fasten the starched collar, afraid of sticking a fork in their eyes. I mean that these inventions do not belong to them. The blacks live on credit, and the fathers have to maintain strict discipline at home lest their women and children adore the phonograph record or eat flat tyres.

And yet, as any visitor can see, for all their ebullience, they yearn to be a nation, and even though they occasionally make theatre out of themselves, their spiritual depths are unbribable. In one cabaret – Small's Paradise – whose dancing audience was as black, wet and grumous as a tin of caviar, I saw a naked dancer shaking convulsively under an invisible rain of fire. But while everyone shouted as though believing her possessed by the rhythm, I was able, for a second, to catch remoteness in her eyes – remoteness, reserve, the conviction that she was far away from that admiring audience of foreigners and Americans. All Harlem was like her.

Another time I saw a little black girl riding a bicycle. Nothing could have been more touching: smokey legs, teeth frozen in the moribund rose of her lips, the balled-up sheep's hair of her head. I stared at her and she stared right back. But my look was saying, 'Child, why are you riding a bicycle? Can a little black girl really ride such an apparatus? Is it yours? Where did you steal it? Do you think you can steer it?' and sure enough, she did a somersault and fell – all legs and wheels – down a gentle slope.

But every day I protested. I protested to see little black children guillotined by hard collars, suits, and violent boots as they emptied the spittoons of cold men who talk like ducks.

I protested to see so much flesh robbed from paradise and managed by Jews with gelid noses and blotting-paper souls, and I protested the saddest thing of all, that the blacks do not want to be black, that they invent pomades to take away the delicious curl of their hair and powders that turn their faces grey and syrups that fill out their waists and wither the succulent persimmon of their lips.

I protested, and the proof of it is this 'Ode to the King of Harlem,' spirit of the black race, a cry of encouragement to those who tremble and doubt and sluggishly, shamefully search for the flesh of the white woman.

And yet, the truly savage, phrenetic part of New York is not Harlem. In Harlem there is human steam and the noise of children and hearths and weeds, and pain that finds comfort and the wound that finds its sweet bandage.

The Crash

The terrible, cold, cruel part is Wall Street. Rivers of gold flow there from all over the earth, and death comes with it. There as nowhere else you feel a total absence of the spirit: herds of men who cannot count past three, herds more who cannot get past six, scorn for pure science, and demoniacal respect for the present. And the terrible thing is that the crowd who fills the street believes that the world will always be the same, and that it is their duty to move the huge machine day and night forever. The perfect result of a Protestant morality that I, as a (thank God) typical Spaniard, found unnerving. I was lucky enough to see with my own eyes the recent crash, where they lost various billions of dollars, a rabble of dead money that slid off into the sea, and never as then, amid suicides, hysteria, and groups of fainters, have I felt the sensation of real death, death without hope, death that is nothing but rottenness, for the spectacle was terrifying but devoid of greatness. And I, who come from a country where, as the great poet Unamuno said, 'at night the earth climbs to the sky,' I felt something like a divine urge to bombard that whole shadowy defile where ambulances collected suicides whose hands were full of rings.

That is why I included this dance of death. The typical African mask, death which is truly dead, without angels of 'resurrexit'; death as far removed from the spirit, as barbarous and primitive as the United States, which had never fought, and never will fight for heaven.

Claud Cockburn (1929)

The journalist Claud Cockburn was a correspondent for The Times *at the time of the Wall Street Crash. In his autobiography,* In Time of Trouble, *he recalls meeting Al Capone.*

In Chicago the director of the Illinois Central Bank, to whom I had been putting solemn questions on the subject of car loadings, commodity prices and the like, said moodily, 'Hell, boy, the capitalist system's on the skids anyway, let's go and get a drink.' I was glad of this attitude on his part because I had not really come to Chicago to discuss commodity prices in the Middle West, but to report the background to a murder. A couple of days before, we in New York had read the news of the killing in broad daylight of Jake Lingle, then crime reporter of the *Chicago Tribune* and – as emerged later – an important liaison officer between the Capone gang and the police department. It was one of the most spectacular and, for many reasons, looked like being one of the most revealing Chicago killings of the period when Al Capone was at approximately the height of his power. From a friend in New York who knew Chicago I learned enough of the background of the crime to make me very eager to go to Chicago myself. Hinrichs, who thought it would be a splendid story, was nevertheless hesitant. He explained to me that whenever *The Times* published a crime story from the United States somebody from the American Embassy or the English-Speaking Union or some other agency for promoting Anglo-American relations would ring up or would attack the editor at dinner, saying how much he had always previously admired *TheTimes's* treatment of American affairs, and could there not be at least one British newspaper which did not represent the United States as a land dominated by gunmen and hoodlums? Hinrichs thought we had better cable London asking whether they wished me to go to Chicago.

As an assignment to report a murder the reply from *The Times* was probably a classic. 'By all means,' it said, 'Cockburn Chicagowards. Welcome stories ex-Chicago not unduly emphasising crime.'

By the time I was in the air over Cleveland the difficulty of carrying out this directive successfully had notably increased. Ex-Ambassador Charlie Gates Dawes had impetuously been 'drafted' or had drafted himself to act as 'strong man' of the situation, to put himself, it was stated, at the head of 'the better element' and to 'clean up' Chicago. Before I touched down at Chicago Airport he had arrested nearly six hundred people and a number of others had been wounded in indiscriminate gunplay. I drove to the Criminal Courts Building and sought the advice of the dean of Chicago crime reporters, the original, I believe, of one of the central characters in Ben Hecht's play *The Front Page*. I showed him my cable. His deep laughter shook the desk. What, he asked, did I want to do? I said I supposed the first thing to do was to interview Mr Capone. He suggested that I listen in on an extension while he telephoned Mr Capone at the Lexington Hotel where he then had his offices. Presently I heard Capone's voice on the wire asking what went on. The crime reporter explained that there was a Limey from the London *Times* who wanted to talk with him. They fixed up an appointment for the following afternoon and just before he rang off the crime reporter said, 'Listen, Al, there's just one thing. You know this bird's assignment says he's to cover all this "not unduly emphasising crime".' Bewilderment exploded at the other end of the line. 'Not what?' Capone said. 'You heard me,' said the crime reporter. 'Not unduly emphasising crime.'

The Lexington Hotel had once, I think, been a rather grand family hotel, but now its large and gloomy lobby was deserted except for a couple of bulging Sicilians and a reception clerk who looked at once across the counter with the expression of a speakeasy proprietor looking through the grille at a potential detective. He checked on my appointment with some superior upstairs, and as I stepped into the elevator I felt my hips and sides being gently frisked by the tapping hands of one of the lounging civilians. There were a couple of ante-rooms to be passed before you got to Capone's office and in the first of them I had to wait for a quarter of an hour or so, drinking whisky poured by a man who used his left hand for the bottle and kept the other in his pocket.

Except that there was a sub-machine gun, operated by a man called MacGurn – whom I later got to know and somewhat esteem – poking through the transom of a door behind the big desk, Capone's own room was nearly indistinguishable from that of – say a 'newly arrived' Texan oil millionaire. Apart from the jowly young murderer on the far side of the desk, what took the eye were a number of large, flattish, solid silver bowls upon the desk, each filled with roses. They were nice to look at, and they had another purpose too, for Capone when agitated stood up and dipped the tips of his fingers in the water in which floated the roses.

I had been a little embarrassed as to how the interview was to be launched. Naturally the nub of all such interviews is somehow to get around to the question 'What makes you tick?' but in the case of this millionaire killer the approach to this central question seemed mined with dangerous impediments. However, on the way down to the Lexington Hotel I had had the good fortune to see, in I think the *Chicago Daily News*, some statistics offered by an insurance company which dealt with the average expectation of life of gangsters in Chicago. I forgot exactly what the average expectation was, and also what was the exact age of Capone at that time – I think he was in his very early thirties. The point was, however, that in any case he was four years older than the upper limit considered by the insurance company to be the proper average expectation of life for a Chicago gangster. This seemed to offer a more or less neutral and academic line of approach, and after the ordinary greetings I asked Capone whether he had read this piece of statistics in the paper. He said that he had. I asked him whether he considered the estimate reasonably accurate. He said that he thought that the insurance companies and the newspaper boys probably knew their stuff. 'In that case,' I asked him, 'how does it feel to be, say, four years over the age?'

He took the question quite seriously and spoke of the matter with neither more nor less excitement or agitation than a man would who, let us say, had been asked whether he, as the rear machine-gunner of a bomber, was aware of the average incidence of casualties in that occupation. He apparently assumed that sooner or later he would be shot despite the elaborate precautions which he regularly took. The idea that – as afterwards turned out to be the case – he would be arrested by the Federal authorities for income-tax evasion had not, I think, at that time so much as crossed his mind. And, after all, he said with a little bit of corn-and-ham somewhere at the back of his throat, supposing he had not gone into this racket? What would he have been doing? He would, he said, 'have been selling newspapers barefoot on the street in Brooklyn'.

He stood up as he spoke, cooling his finger-tips in the rose bowl in front of him. He sat down again, brooding and sighing. Despite the ham-and-corn, what he said was quite probably true and I said so, sympathetically.

A little bit too sympathetically, as immediately emerged, for as I spoke I saw him looking at me suspiciously, not to say censoriously. My remarks about the harsh way the world treats barefoot boys in Brooklyn were interrupted by an urgent angry waggle of his podgy hand.

'Listen,' he said, 'don't you get the idea I'm one of these goddam radicals. Don't get the idea I'm knocking the American system. The American system . . .' As though an invisible chairman had called upon him for a few words, he broke into an oration upon the theme. He praised freedom, enterprise and the pioneers. He spoke of 'our heritage'. He referred with contemptuous disgust to Socialism and Anarchism. 'My rackets,' he repeated several times, 'are run on strictly American lines and they're going to stay that way.' This turned out to be a reference to the fact that he had recently been elected the President of the Unione Siciliano, a slightly mysterious, partially criminal society which certainly had its roots in the Mafia. Its power and importance varied sharply from year to year. Sometimes there did seem to be evidence that it was a secret society of real power, and at other times it seemed more in the nature of a mutual benefit association not essentially much more menacing than, say, the Elks. Capone's complaint just now was that the Unione was what he called 'lousy with black-hand stuff'. 'Can you imagine,' he said, 'people going in for what they call these blood feuds – some guy's grandfather was killed by some other guy's grandfather, and this guy thinks that's good enough reason to kill the other.' It was, he said, entirely unbusinesslike. His vision of the American system began to excite him profoundly and now he was on his feet again, leaning across the desk like chairman of a board meeting, his fingers plunged in the rose bowls.

'This American system of ours,' he shouted, 'call it Americanism, call it Capitalism, call it what you like, gives to each and every one of us a great opportunity if we only seize it with both hands and make the most of it.' He held out his hands towards me, the fingers dripping a little, and stared at me sternly for a few seconds before reseating himself.

A month later in New York I was telling this story to Mr John Walter, minority owner of *The Times*. He asked me why I had not written the Capone interview for the paper. I explained that when I had come to put my notes together I saw that most of what Capone had said was in essence identical with what was being said in the leading articles of *The Times* itself, and I doubted whether the paper would be best pleased to find itself seeing eye to eye with the most notorious gangster in Chicago. Mr Walter, after a moment's wry reflection, admitted that probably my idea had been correct.

Even so, when I did start writing my thesis from Chicago – not unduly emphasising crime – I became aware, really for the first time, that about fifty per cent of what seemed to me to be the truth about the situation in Chicago would certainly be unpalatable and perhaps in parts unintelligible to *The Times*. I struggled with the article, produced a couple of readable pieces, and *The Times* wired me quite a large and much-needed bonus on the strength of it.

P. G. Wodehouse (1930)

In 1930 P. G. Wodehouse went to California to work in the film industry. This is a letter to his friend, the novelist Denis Mackail.

Hollywood, 2 June 1930.
Frightfully sorry I haven't written before. I have been in a whirl of work. After three months absolute deadness my brain began to whirr like a dynamo. So you see one does recover from these blank periods. I hope yours has gone. I have written three short stories, an act of a play, and the dialogue for a picture in three weeks, and have got six brand new plots for short stories!!! I believe our rotten brains have to go through these ghastly periods of inertness before getting a second wind. Susan is dead. Did Ethel tell you? Apparently she just toppled over quite quietly in the Park, and it was all over in a minute. She had no pain, thank goodness. It's just like losing part of oneself. The only thing is that everything is so unreal out here and I feel so removed from ordinary life that I haven't yet quite realised it. . . .

This is the weirdest place. We have taken Elsie Janis's house. It has a small but very pretty garden, with a big pool. I have arranged with the studio to work at home, so I sometimes don't get out of the garden for three or four days on end. If you asked me, I would say I loved Hollywood. Then I would reflect and have to admit that Hollywood is about the most loathsome place on the map but that, never going near it, I enjoy being out here.

My days follow each other in a regular procession. I get up, swim, breakfast, work till two, swim again, work till seven, swim for the third time, then dinner and the day is over. When I get a summons from the studio, I motor over there, stay for a couple of hours and come back. Add incessant sunshine and it's really rather jolly. It is only occasionally that one feels one is serving a term on Devil's Island. We go out very little. Just an occasional dinner at the house of some other exile e.g. some New York theatrical friend. Except for one party at Marion Davies's place, I've not met any movie stars.

By dinner time I was dying on my feet. Poor old Snorky had to talk to the same man from 7.15 till 9.30 and then found she was sitting next to him at dinner. Luckily it was such a big party that we were able to slip off without saying good-bye directly dinner was over.

The actual work is negligible. I altered all the characters to earls and butlers with such success that they called a conference and changed the entire plot, starring the earl and butler. So I'm still working on it. So far I've had eight collaborators. The system is that A gets the original idea, B comes in to work with him on it, C makes the scenario, D does preliminary dialogue, and then they send for me to insert class and what not, then E and F, scenario writers, alter the plot and off we go again. I could have done all my part of it in a morning but they took it for granted that I should need six weeks.

The latest news is that they are going to start shooting quite soon. In fact there are ugly rumours that I'm to be set to work soon on something else. I resent this as it will cut into my short story writing. It is odd how soon one comes to look upon every minute as wasted that is given to earning one's salary. (Now don't go making a comic article out of this and queering me with the bosses.)

C. G. Jung (1930)

Carl Gustav Jung (1875–1961) was the second father of psychoanalysis after Freud, with whom he quarrelled. It is to him that we owe the concepts of the libido, synchronicity, extraversion, and introversion. His open-mindedness sometimes strays into credulity, for instance towards astrology and numerology, but it has to be said that Jungian theory is a lot more fun than Freud's.

The most amazing feature of American life is its boundless publicity. Everybody has to meet everybody, and they even seem to enjoy this enormity. To a central European such as I am, this American publicity of life, the lack of distance between people, the absence of hedges or fences round the gardens, the belief in popularity, the gossip columns of the newspapers, the open doors in the houses (one can look from the street right through the sitting-room and the adjoining bedroom into the backyard and beyond), the defencelessness of the individual against the onslaught of the press, all this is more than disgusting, it is positively terrifying. You are immediately swallowed by a hot and all-engulfing wave of desirousness and emotional incontinence. You are simply reduced to a particle in the mass, with no other hope or expectation than the illusory goals of an eager and excited collectivity. You just swim for life, that's all. You feel free – that's the queerest thing – yet the collective movement grips you faster than any old gnarled roots in European soil would have done. Even your head gets immersed. There is a peculiar lack of restraint about the emotions of an American collectivity. You see it in the eagerness and in the bustle of everyday life, in all sorts of enthusiasm, in orgiastic sectarian outbursts, in the violence of public admiration and opprobrium. The overwhelming influence of collective emotions spreads into everything. If it were possible, everything would be done collectively, because there seems to be an astonishingly feeble resistance to collective influences.

Elsa Lanchester (1935)

Charles Laughton and Elsa Lanchester lived in Los Angeles while he was working on a three-year contract for M.G.M. The last film was to be Ruggles of Red Gap. *While it was being scripted, Laughton fell ill and had to go into hospital. It left his wife time to explore what other entertainment the place had beside the film industry.*

Although I used to go and see him three times every day while he was in hospital I naturally had a lot of time to myself, and so I really was forced to find out how the inhabitants of Los Angeles entertained themselves.

The theatre is not very well served. Sometimes an odd star turns up for a revival, and usually there is a touring company or some kind of variety show. The 'burlesques' with risky sketches and strip-tease acts have an old-world appeal for a few visits. Stage stars from the New York theatres do tour America in their successes, and they occasionally land in Hollywood, but on the whole shows are poor.

However, there are compensations. There is no better place than Hollywood for seeing the current films. For entertainment at parties there is often a private showing of a picture which has not yet been seen by the public. We saw *The Barretts of Wimpole Street* in this way before it was previewed, at the Thalbergs' house. They also have a very good system of trying films out 'on the dog', which means they take a newly finished film and show it unexpectedly in a suburban cinema. The idea is to get outside criticism. It is added to the programme at short notice, so that the studio technicians and personnel do not get to know; but if you are a good sleuth you can get wind of one of these secret showings almost any night. The audience, consisting of ordinary folk, are given post cards on which to write their opinions. An audience's reaction is invariably so unexpected that final cuts are then made to the film.

In Hollywood, football matches, all-in wrestling and boxing are terrifically popular. A football match will empty factories, homes and film studios. Saturday afternoons in the studios – although work should go on – see the burials of many grandmothers.

All-in wrestling is equally popular. At the matches you hear the audience screamng and shouting, and getting very savage. I once heard an elderly spinster scream: 'Gouge his eyes out.' An old man countered: 'Go on, break his arm.' In fact, the wrestlers work the audience up into a frenzy deliberately, and the audience loves it. I have often suspected from the frightful faces the wrestlers pull and the general ham performances that they put on, that as well as their trainers they might have dramatic coaches. They open their mouths wide, screw up their eyes in agony and groan and pant so much that obviously there is not a body in the world that could stand it all.

Every week there is, so to speak, a new cast, so that you never get too many Adonises or too many beasts at once. There is Man-Mountain Deane, of course, known as 'The Henry VIII of the Mat', who weighs 315 pounds. I saw him thrown three rows out into the audience by Londos, who is about half his weight. This is a typical example of type-casting; the small man who is very strong and the big man who is very foolish. Sometimes wrestlers wear peculiar clothes, and they can be exceedingly funny. One, called 'The Scorpion', used to come on with a yellow mask over his head. I think the mask was made out of a stocking or something with slits in it for the features. The 'face' got worked round to the back of the head during the wrestling, and the opponent attacked the face at the back though everybody knew it was not the real face. It all reminded me of the Crazy Gang at the Palladium.

There is a man called Jumping Joe Savoldi who generally wins. He jumps off the ground with both feet up, knocks his partner out by a blow on the chin from both feet, and then lands on the floor *on his feet* – all in one movement. There is also an Indian wrestler who wears a little row of beads, and has bare feet and long black hair. He is a great favourite and I have never seen him lose. His speciality is to catch his partner's leg between his own from a curious Buddha-like position and painfully lever his partner's shoulders to the floor. After his triumph he does a little simple dance like a child dancing to a barrel-organ: he goes round waving his pointing fingers from side to side and doing a little hop and skip.

When wrestlers are thrown into the audience, I noticed that they were usually thrown into two rather surprisingly empty seats – although people have had wrestlers in their laps.

I prefer to sit up in the circle from which it is possible to look down on the thousands of people. It is an enormous place and the whole picture is marvellous. I like to hear the sound rising up, a chaotic symphony of yells and screams. Some of the film people who go to wrestling matches, the 'toughies', sit in the front row and lean under the ropes to get a close-up. Blood is occasionally drawn. Once after a match I spoke to a blue-eyed box-office attraction who was frightfully thrilled and excited because she had got a spot of blood on her dress from one of the fighters. She did not get a wrestler in her lap while I was there, but she may have at some other time. *Bonne chance, ma petite.*

Laurence Olivier (1938–9)

Though the affair of Laurence Olivier and Vivien Leigh was known to many in Hollywood in the late thirties, they had, as Lord Olivier recalls in his autobiography, Confessions of an Actor, *to behave as if it were secret. Marriage was to come during the war, which temporarily brought to a close their Hollywood careers. Their last parts before the war were to be their most glamorous: he played Heathcliff in* Wuthering Heights *and Maxim de Winter in* Rebecca; *while she overcame extraordinary competition to get the most sought-after role of all, that of Scarlett O'Hara in* Gone with the Wind.

I got my dearest old friend on the phone one day and asked him, 'Ralphie, be an angel and think a minute for me, there's a friend. Should I go to

Hollywood and play Heathcliff in *Wuthering Heights?*' Ralph obligingly thought for a moment and then said, 'Yes. Bit of fame. Good.' For some reason I had the greatest misgivings about the offer; but after that mini-colloquy I didn't have them any more. William Wyler, the most prestigious of Hollywood film directors, had, of course, come over to goose me into it. And when I got to Hollywood my apprehensions returned. I had done one film with Merle Oberon (now Mrs Alex Korda) and liked her reasonably well; but now, as I tried to establish some relationship with both my director and my co-star, I found that my feelings were obstinately lukewarm towards both of them. I was blind with misery at being parted from Vivien, who would have been the perfect Cathy, and I was sure that Merle was lacking in the essential passionate qualities.

Vivien, in company with a myriad of other actresses, had an almost demoniac determination to play Scarlett in *Gone With The Wind*. It should be appreciated, though it isn't easy in retrospect, that the odds against her getting the part would create a whole new scale of betting at Ladbrokes today; but I too nursed the secret ambition for her. This provided a secondary reason for her to sail across and then fly from New York to Clover Field airport; the first was pure, driving, uncontainable, passionate love, which to my joy she shared strongly enough to make the journey as speedily as possible. In the meantime I had a few quiet words with Myron Selznick, indicating to him that there was someone coming over to visit me who might quite possibly be of extraordinary interest to him. He looked knowingly at me and we said no more.

I waited for her crouched in the back of a car a few feet beyond the airport entrance.

The Beverly Hills Hotel in those days was not at all what it is now – it had rather shabby basket furniture, only dismally achieving a colonial style. As in the general run of hotels the world over, if you invested in a suite nobody asked any questions. I took Vivien along to Myron, who studied her, looking from her to me and back with growing interest. I said innocently, '*I* think we ought to take her along to meet David, don't you, Myron?' He nodded slowly, realization beginning to dawn; his brother, about to launch into production with *GWTW*, had become badly stuck over the casting of Scarlett.

He had put Rhett Butler straight out to the American public for them to cast. The public had responded with several million votes, almost everyone citing Clark Gable. Leslie Howard was an obviously popular choice for Ashley Dukes, as indeed was Olivia de Havilland for Melanie. Only Scarlett remained. David had boiled it down to a final choice between three – Bette Davis, Paulette Goddard and Jean Arthur; this provoked endless arguments and much ill-feeling. Davis was universally regarded as exceptional, in fact the best actress, but did not approximate to Margaret Mitchell's description; Goddard was much the closest in looks, but her acting accomplishment was in doubt; Arthur had the advantage of being the darkest horse of the three. I never believed that David had serious intentions towards Joan Crawford. He liked to boost the competitive element.

Myron picked us up in a car that evening and we headed due south down to Culver City where on the old Pathé lot David was burning forty acres of ancient exterior sets for the fire in Atlanta. Three times we saw the horse and buggy drive through the flaming archway of the barn, with the same double for Gable each time but three different types for Scarlett; after the last passage through, a wire was pulled and the roof of the barn fell in a flaming crash. (Flames are obligingly easy things to cut on, so the three Scarletts were readily interchangeable.) The shooting over, no attempt was made to extinguish the fire; and by its light I could just make out the figures of George Cukor, the original director and devoted friend, and David, whom I also knew well from our business differences in 1932.

I looked back at Vivien, her hair giving the perfect impression of Scarlett's, her cheeks prettily flushed, her lips adorably parted, her green eyes dancing and shining with excitement in the firelight; I said to myself, 'David won't be able to resist that.' I retreated, leaving the field to Myron; David and George were approaching and Myron stepped towards them. He indicated Vivien and said, 'David, meet Scarlett O'Hara.'

David peered very intently at Vivien; Myron made a vague gesture towards me. David threw a 'Hello, Larry' into the air, roughly in my direction. Myron and I were left together, eye to eye and ho to hum. David had drawn Vivien a little way apart from the crowd and was fixing up an immediate test with her, promising to make every allowance for what would naturally be a very imperfect Southern accent. George was with them and was clearly interested too. I could hardly believe what was happening; but there it was.

David took every advantage possible in her contractual negotiations, insisting on a one-way option contract for seven years – seven years is the most that is legally allowed in any American contract on account of an old anti-slavery law. The film was envisaged to take at least six months and he would not move higher than $20,000; this for the movie part of the century was hardly generous, and I said as much to him a bit later. David defended himself stoutly, saying I was unreasonable, and 'I'd be the laughing-stock of all my friends if I paid her any more, an unknown, a discovery, for such an opportunity.'

Wuthering Heights was well finished and I had to think about getting back to some work. It was better not to smudge the career image by hanging around, hoping for a job. *Wuthering Heights* wouldn't make its effect yet awhile, and I was against just continuing to dance attendance, 'announcing her guests and walking the pekingese'; the best thing career-wise would be to get myself a good appearance in the New York theatre, and this was most felicitously provided for me by Miss Katharine Cornell (the top people had a 'Miss' or 'Mr' in front of their names; it was the American equivalent of a knighthood – always 'Mr George Arliss'). The play this time was *No Time for Comedy* by Sam Behrman, another friend. It was a wild success and I 'besported myself at the organ with more than my usual success' (Handel, on his *Messiah* opening in Dublin).

As rehearsals drew to an end, worrisome news was coming from Hollywood; exhaustion coupled with hysteria due to our harshly testing separation was producing dangerous symptoms, and David got me on the phone and implored me to get out there somehow to use my influence to calm things down, 'if only for a *day*'. How fortunate I was to have such warmly understanding managers as Kit Cornell and Guthrie McClintic; they actually let me off the dress rehearsal in Indianapolis to give me one day to fly there, one day to soothe as much as I possibly could, and the next day to fly direct

to Indianapolis and open that night. It was short shrift; very. We opened to
'golden opinions from all sorts of people'; Alexander Woollcott was one of
them, and all in all the success was richly rewarding.

Vivien was allowed, while still due for a series of retakes, to leave Hollywood for a few weeks' respite. She was a bit too quick off the mark for me,
as I had not finished my engagement by a couple of weeks or so. I was
sharing a house with Kit Cornell, Guthrie McClintic, darling Margalo
Gillmore, her husband Robert Ross and equally loved John Williams, firmly
tried friends in the play with me, as was Robert Flemyng, a constantly
welcome visitor. Vivien had perforce to stay and be made most welcome by
this precious group. In due course we were on the ss *Majestic* going home.
It was sweet, it is always sweet, to be home; we took a fortnight in our
adored France. We stopped off at home again to pick up her mama, 'and
her mother came too', a sweet, pretty woman, a highly successful beautician
named Gertrude Hartley.

Then back to Hollywood where Vivien was quickly involved in her *GWTW*
retakes and I, happy with Hitchcock, in *Rebecca*. It seemed no time at all
before the unbelievable shock of the war was upon us.

Dougie Fairbanks Jr happened to have taken a yacht for that day and we
were part of a delightful party on it. We were just off Catalina, when
Chamberlain came on the radio and said what he had to say. Many of us
burst into tears at once. Along with most other inhabitants of the earth, we
felt blighted right through: careers, lives, hopes. Shortly reaction set in.
Doug knew what drink existed for and a consequent hysteria began; my
own manifestation of this was a show of frank vulgarity, careering around
in a speedboat in and out between the other yachts berthed off the island,
declaiming: 'You are finished, all of you; you are relics . . . that's what you
are . . . relics!' It was often said at this time that I bore some resemblance
to Ronald Colman, with my slight moustache and dark hair. Unfortunately
the rumour went round that it was Ronnie himself who had taken this
extraordinary turn; it was a shame, for nothing could have been less typical
of his habitual dignity or exquisite manners.

There was a general directive to all our countrymen abroad who did not
already have a commission or were not within the required age-group to
stay put; did we not appreciate that if every Englishman living abroad were
to come gallantly dashing home, the public services would have to face an
additional population of anything up to half a million extra mouths to feed
and extra hands to find employment for? It was a painful situation, and
wretchedly embarrassing with the Americans who for once were not very
enthusiastic hosts. Many of them seemed far from certain whose side they
were on. There was an enthusiastically pro-German feeling in those areas of
the United States containing extensive proportions of German immigrants.
Milwaukee, for instance, was largely German-speaking. Whether it would
be useful or not, I soon began to feel it would be better for us to go home
and take whatever came.

And so the 1930s went limping out, on a note as baleful and grim as a
fog-horn on a dark night.

Christopher Isherwood (1939)

The writer Christopher Isherwood (1904–80) apprehensive of the coming war in Europe, emigrated to the United States in January 1939, along with his one-time collaborator W. H. Auden. Both men adopted American citizenship and became convinced pacifists. The following passage, although written in the third person, is from Isherwood's autobiography Christopher and His Kind *and describes his feelings on arrival in New York.*

The voyage was stormy. The *Champlain* seemed very small, slithering down the long grey Atlantic slopes, under a burdened sky. On this voyage, Wystan and Christopher had no literary collaboration to occupy them. Wrapped in rugs, they lay sipping bouillon, or they paced the deck, or drank at the bar, or watched movies in the saloon, where French tapestries flapped out from the creaking, straining walls as the ship rolled. They amused themselves by taking over the puppet-show in the children's playroom and improvising Franco-English dialogue full of private jokes and double meanings. Their audience of children didn't care what the puppets said, as long as they kept jumping about. Off the coast of Newfoundland, the ship ran into a blizzard. She entered New York harbour looking like a wedding-cake.

At the end of Christopher's brief visit in 1938, he had felt absolutely confident of one thing, at least. If he did decide to settle in America – and, by America, he meant New York – he would be able to make himself at home there. This, he said to himself, was a setting in which his public personality would function more freely, more successfully than it could ever have functioned in London. Oh, he'd talk faster and louder than any of the natives. He'd pick up their slang and their accent. He'd learn all their tricks. Someone had repeated to him a saying about the city: 'Here, you'll find sympathy in the dictionary and everything else at the nearest drugstore.' This delighted him. He had accepted it as a challenge to be tough.

But now New York, on that bitter winter morning, appeared totally, shockingly transformed from the place he had waved goodbye to the previous July. Christopher experienced a sudden panicky loss of confidence.

There they stood in the driving snow – the made-in-France Giantess with her liberty torch, which now seemed to threaten, not welcome, the newcomer; and the Red Indian island with its appalling towers. There was the Citadel – stark, vertical, gigantic, crammed with the millions who had already managed to struggle ashore and find a foothold. You would have to fight your way inland from your very first step on to the pier. Already, it was threatening you with its tooting tugboats, daring you to combat.

God, what a terrifying place this suddenly seemed! You could feel it vibrating with the tension of the nervous New World, aggressively flaunting its rude steel nudity. We're Americans here - and we keep at it, twenty-four hours a day, *being* Americans. We scream, we grab, we jostle. We've no time for what's slow, what's gracious, what's nice, quiet, modest. Don't you come snooting us with your European traditions – we know the mess they've got you into. Do things our way or take the next boat back – back to your Europe that's falling apart at the seams. Well, make up your mind. Are you quitting or staying? It's no skin off *our* nose. We promise nothing. Here, you'll be on your own.

Christopher, trying hard to think positive thoughts, declared that he was staying. But the Giantess wasn't impressed. The towers didn't care. Okay, Buster, suit yourself.

Now, however, the quarantine launch arrived. On it were Erika and Klaus Mann, come out to welcome them. They were full of liveliness and gossip. And, at once, the Giantess stopped threatening, the towers no longer appalled. Christopher felt himself among friends, cared for, safe. And Vernon would be waiting for him on shore; Christopher had cabled to him from the *Champlain*. A couple of hours from now, somewhere within the grimness of that icebound Citadel, in a place of warmth and joy, the two of them would be in each other's arms.

This is where I leave Christopher, at the rail, looking eagerly, nervously, hopefully towards the land where he will spend more than half of his life. At present, he can see almost nothing of what lies ahead. In the absence of the fortune-telling lady from Brussels, I will allow him and Wystan to ask one question – I can already guess what it is – and I will answer it:

Yes, my dears, each of you will find the person you came here to look for – the ideal companion to whom you can reveal yourself totally and yet be loved for what you are, not what you pretend to be. You, Wystan, will find him very soon, within three months. You, Christopher, will have to wait much longer for yours. He is already living in the city where you will settle. He will be near you for many years without your meeting. But it would be no good if you did meet him now. At present, he is only four years old.

Jessica Mitford (1939)

One of the six daughters of Lord Redesdale, Jessica Mitford eloped with her cousin Esmond Romilly to fight in the Republican cause in the Spanish Civil War. They only got as far as Bayonne, from where Lady Redesdale eventually managed to retrieve them. In February 1939 they sailed for New York. Her autobiography, Hons and Rebels, *tells how they set about job-hunting.*

Those first days in New York were filled with opportunities to check our prior conceptions of America against reality. The Times Square-Broadway–42nd Street area lived up to all expectations, with its bright, movie-like quality and the added musical comedy touch provided by pickets for ever circling in front of the Brass Rail restaurant delivering in unison their eternal message: 'Brass Rail's on Strike. Please Pass By.'

Of course we were told that New York is 'not typical' of America - how untypical we were not then in a position to judge – but we did get the impression there was a distinct New York personality. The unique feature of this personality seemed the bright spark of momentary interest lit in New Yorkers by the most casual of contacts.

A stranger asked for directions would, for the brief second spent talking on the street, throw himself vigorously into one's problem, questioning the very wisdom of one's plan, often suggesting a completely different course of action:

'Could you direct me to the Museum of Modern Art?'

'It's two blocks over, but the Picasso show closed last Wednesday. If you wait till next week, there'll be a Van Gogh exhibit. How long are you folks planning on staying in town? Tell you what, why don't you take in the Museum of Natural History today?'

A lady shopper, stopped in full flight for directions to Macy's, might elaborate her answer: '. . . but, honey, their sale don't start till Friday. Try Bloomingdale's; it's closer, anyway.' Often they would add: 'You're from England, aren't you? How long are you staying? How do you like it here?'

Roaming the streets of New York, we encountered many examples of this delightful quality of New Yorkers, for ever on their toes, violently, restlessly involving themselves in the slightest situation brought to their attention, always posing alternatives, always ready with an answer or an argument.

The letters of introduction brought a flood of invitations to the greatest variety of social functions we'd ever known, and for a while we basked and wallowed in the fabled American hospitality.

Having lost the carefully compiled descriptive list of the people to whom we had written we had no way of knowing whether the person we were about to meet was a dear old friend of Cousin Dorothy's, a business acquaintance of Esmond's boss in the London advertising agency or a dashing young friend of Peter Nevile's. In some ways this made it more exciting: 'Like hunters not knowing if they're stalking a deer or a rabbit,' Esmond said.

In contrast to the predicament we should have been in had a similar situation arisen in England, our ignorance about the 'contacts', as Esmond now insisted on calling them, hardly mattered at all. Even the old and rich treated us with surprising warmth and informality; they were devoid of the familiar quality of 'disapproving auntism', really a form of automatic rude- ness to the young, so ready to pop out bleakly at one from their English counterparts.

The lack of bleakness we noted in the natives of this fascinating terrain extended to their dwellings, uniformly as cosy and sheltered as greenhouses. The lovely blasts of heat which greeted one on entering seemed to go with the quick friendliness of the occupants, a welcome change from England, where it was a too-common experience to find the mid-winter temperature in someone's drawing-room the same, degree for degree, as that outside.

We felt like explorers in a territory that encompassed apartments and offices throughout Manhattan, with occasional excursions on the terrifying parkways to outlying suburbs.

The 'contacts' fell into roughly three groups, into which Esmond, with his incongruous mania for classification, began to list them. There were the Grant's Tombers, those inclined to take us to see monuments of interest rather than suggesting cocktails or dinner; Possible Job-getters; and – since we had not been in America long enough to discover how few of its inhabitants really spoke in the accents of Peter's enthusiastic rendering – the Genoowinely Innaresting People.

The one thing common to contacts of all three categories was the inevitable question: 'Do you like America?' This always stumped us a bit at first.

'It would never occur to us to ask a foreigner if he liked England,' Esmond pointed out, 'because, if he did, so what? And if he didn't there would be nothing one could do about it.'

We often wondered what the contact would say if one answered, 'Loathe it.' However, this was fortunately far from the case, and we were able to answer truthfully, 'Oh, very good – wonderful. . . .'

Esmond wrote to Peter: 'There's one little fly I notice. People here – I mean even the intelligent ones – are so damned nationalistic. They keep bringing up points of history and the American War of Independence – whereas you must admit one's own mind is completely blank on that subject.' Esmond's schooling, though considerably more thorough than mine, had left him also vaguely under the impression that America had had to be kicked out of the British Empire for causing trouble, but we were quickly disabused of this theory by the Grant's Tombers.

By the end of the first few weeks in New York we felt we knew almost as many people as we did in London. Our acquaintance, while it hardly constituted a cross-section – for it was heavily weighted with publishers, advertising people, editors – was kaleidoscopic in its variety. It ranged from radical to conservative, from Park Avenue millionaires to young wage-earners, with a sprinkling of dancers, artists and writers thrown in.

Among the dozens of new places, faces and experiences, a few still stand out sharply in memory: the lavatory at Random House, fixed up like a miniature library, lined from floor to ceiling with such appropriate titles as *Gone with the Wind, Mein Kampf, King John;* the fascinating Graham and Meyer families; the *Time-Lifers;* the English tailoring fanciers; the Park Avenue snobs. . . .

One invitation from a Possible Job-getter bore the ominous words: 'Black Tie.'

'That's good. I happen to have a black tie,' Esmond said. I quickly disabused him.

'I think it means a dinner jacket, only they call it a tuxedo here,' I said. 'If we're going, you'll have to get hold of one somehow. It would have been a violation of all our rules to turn down an invitation. Esmond consulted the head waiter at the Shelton Hotel, and returned with a gloomy report.

'He says a tuxedo would cost at least forty dollars at the only places he knows of. He says you can rent them, but even that costs about fifteen dollars. So that's out. . . . I think I'll go and see what I can find in a cheaper part of New York.'

He arrived back very late, but victorious.

'Look!' he exulted. 'Only six dollars, waistcoat and all. I got it at a little place on a street called Third Avenue. It's a wonderful place for shopping. The salesman let me have it extra cheap, because the last person who had it had been shot in it, and that's supposed to bring bad luck, so no one else would buy it.'

The tuxedo fitted all right. I looked carefully for the bullet hole, but couldn't find it. The worst part about the suit was the satin lapels, which gleamed and shone like mirrors. I rubbed face powder in them, dimming the lustre somewhat. We debated whether or not to take out the enormous pads in the shoulders, which gave Esmond the appearance of a prize-fighter, but decided against it, for fear it might bring about a total collapse of the coat.

'After all, they'll probably never see you again, so they'll go on thinking those are your normal shoulders,' I said.

Thanks to the power of suggestion Esmond's tuxedo was a great success. I carefully avoided catching his eye when our host was heard to say, 'There's nothing like English tailoring; they sure know their stuff. Say, that tux is sure a beaut; where did you get it, Savile Row?'

There had been a small flurry of publicity shortly after we arrived, when the New York papers briefly revived the story of our running away to Spain. We were pleased to find the news accounts on the whole sympathetic, and more accurate than we had been accustomed to in our experiences with the English press. *Time* magazine quoted Esmond as saying: 'We came here to get away from a terrible, deathlike atmosphere of depression and hopelessness. England is one of the saddest places in the world.'

As a result of all this we met two people about our age who worked for *Life* magazine: Liz Kelly, a *Life* researcher, and Dave Scherman, a cub photographer, who had been assigned to interview us. We were fascinated by them, for they seemed so typically American – Liz, fresh from Nebraska, Small-Town-Girl-Makes-Good-in-Big-City written all over her; Dave, with his quicksilver repartee – and soon we were great friends. Dave came out quite naturally with expressions we'd only heard in the movies: 'That guy's a low-down, good-for-nothing heel', or 'Can you beat it?' They often came to see us, and we regaled them with accounts of the Grant's Tombers and our excursions into Park Avenue life.

We inadvertently got poor Dave into serious trouble with his superiors at *Life*. Esmond casually remarked to a *Daily Mirror* reporter, 'The most hard-boiled American I've met so far is a photographer on *Life*.' The next day the *Mirror* carried the quote in one of its columns. Dave came rushing over.

'Listen, you crazy people, don't go around telling other newspaper guys I'm hard-boiled. My boss didn't like that crack *one bit*. He bawled me out but good about your quote in the *Mirror*. He said *Life* men don't talk tough. We're not *supposed* to be hard-boiled in our racket. Get it?'

We apologized profusely, but couldn't help roaring slightly because Dave's speech of protest was one we could just imagine being delivered by Humphrey Bogart himself, cigarette butt casually hanging from one corner of his mouth.

The Possible Job-getters were taking up most of our days. Esmond had a sheaf of introductions to various advertising people, and this list was frequently added to by suggestions from the Genoowinely Innaresting People or even by the Grant's Tombers.

Our cash reserve was getting depressingly low. Life at the Shelton was making fierce ravages on what was left of the hundred pounds. 'The trouble is,' Esmond told me disconsolately, 'I seem to make a great hit with the secretaries and people in the outside office. But then when I get down to the interview they tell me that my English advertising experience won't help much, as England is twenty years behind America in advertising. I suppose they mean this sort of thing.' He showed me an ad in an old copy of the London *Evening Standard:* 'Seller's Bouillon Cubes. . . . As Good as Beef Tea.' 'In America they never just say something's *as good as* something else. Specially if it's only as good as something so depressing-sounding as beef tea. . . .'

One firm suggested that he should submit a sample of 'soap opera'. 'I wonder what on earth that is,' Esmond said. 'I told him I'm not a bit musical, but he said that didn't matter.'

We made some discreet inquiries and found out that a soap opera is a dramatized serial story, usually about a small town druggist and his family. Esmond worked on one, but his druggist sounded more like a mixture of a British Army Officer and a north of England character actor, with a few 'I guesses', 'swells' and 'lousys' thrown in. When he submitted it the cruel suggestion was made that he should seek a job as an office boy somewhere where he could 'start at the bottom and work up'.

In the end I was the first one to land a job. Having shamelessly invented a long background in the fashion industry in London and Paris, I was hired as a salesgirl at Jane Engels Dress Shop on Madison Avenue, at twenty dollars a week.

'You should have seen me, starting at the bottoms and working up,' I told Esmond after my first day. 'Getting the customers' clothes on and off, I mean. Really, it's frightfully difficult; I had no idea. Either the dress gets caught half way, and the poor thing stands there struggling and protesting with muffled screams, or else *everything* comes off and she's all bare and shivering. I suppose I'll get on to it after a while.'

Most of the other salesgirls were young, uniformly pretty, friendly and uncomplicated. They had none of the aura of warped and embittered selfishness which had been such a distressing feature of some of the market researchers. Free and easy and above-board, they were full of curiosity about me.

'What does your old man do?'

'*Do?* Well, he listens to the wireless most of the time. There's a mag called the *Radio Times* which is his favourite thing. It only comes out once a week, but he's an awfully slow reader so he's generally still poring over it when the next issue comes.'

'No, but I mean what does he do, like my old man's a shoe salesman?'

'Goodness, what a terrifying thought! No, I shouldn't think anyone would want him selling their shoes. I'm afraid he's rather a subhuman.'

I could see I was rapidly being classified as an odd one, and sought to make recovery.

'Actually he has done a lot of things in his time. He has a dear little gold-mine in Canada, staked a claim to it when he was very young, with a person called Harry Oakes, who staked the next-door one. There isn't actually any gold in my father's, but he and my mother often used to go there for months at a time to dig about hopefully. Then he's frightfully interested in new inventions.' I told them about Reno's tank, and about one of the few investments Farve had passed up. Early in the century an inventor approached him with a machine that could make little squares of ice in the home. 'Never heard such damned foolishness in my life,' Farve had roared. 'Feller must be loony. Little squares of ice, indeed!'

The girls were full of sympathy, and assured me that in America who a person's folks are doesn't matter a bit, here I would be judged strictly on my own merits without regard for unfortunate heredity.

Another problem was solved about this time; we managed to find a rented furnished apartment. 'Charming one-room walk-up' (this is American for a flat without a lift) 'in picturesque old-world Greenwich Village – quaint, unhaunted quarter full of the breath of old New York,' Esmond wrote to Peter in best Grant's Tomber's style.

The apartment was a dear little place, more like a bed-sitter really, but efficient and comfortable in spite of its tiny size. It was furnished *en écossais* with cheerful plaid covers and curtains. Everything in it was geared for space-conservation; the Murphy bed (and, Esmond claimed, even a Murphy kitchen and Murphy bath, both were so tiny and self-effacing), the neat dining-nook into which chairs fitted as in a doll's house.

It would do nicely until we found the gold that lay just beneath the pavement in New York.

Noël Coward (1941)

During the war Noël Coward worked for the intelligence services. He was stationed in Paris until the fall of France. He was also sent to the United States to view American isolationism at close hand. While in Washington, he was invited to dinner by President Roosevelt. Coward's description is from his book of war memoirs, Future Indefinite.

The next day a note arrived from Mrs Roosevelt inviting me to dine that night. This flung me into a slight dilemma, for I had already arranged to dine with Walter and Helen Lippmann, but I rang them up and explained truthfully how anxious I was to meet the President and Mrs Roosevelt and that probably such an opportunity would not occur again, whereupon they gracefully forgave me and I promised to join them at eleven-thirty.

Upon arrival at the White House I was led, much to my surprise, directly to the President's study, where he received me alone and we talked, uninterrupted, for quite a while. So much has been written about Franklin D. Roosevelt, so much love, hate, praise, blame, vilification, prejudice, abuse and hero worship have been poured over his memory, that one more personal impression of him cannot matter either way. I never knew him well although we met subsequently on two occasions. I knew nothing of his alleged perfidies, his political treacheries, his reckless expenditures, his double-faced diplomatic betrayals and his unscrupulous egomania. I know nothing of them now. All I knew of him then and later was that he had kindness, courage and humour. Even discounting his personal charm, which was impressive, these qualities seemed to me to be perfectly clear in him. Perhaps his immediate friendliness to me, his utter lack of pomposity, his apparently effortless manner of putting me at my ease, blinded and flattered me to such an extent that my critical perceptions atrophied. Perhaps it was all a professional trick; perhaps such facile conquests were second nature to him and the whole performance was a habitual façade behind which he was regarding me with cynical contempt. If this were so I can only say that he went to a lot of trouble to deceive me, and for motives which must remain for ever unexplained.

His study was typical of him, I think. It was furnished unpretentiously and in quiet taste: there were a number of personal knick-knacks and books and models of ships; his desk was solid and business-like, although at the moment it had banished affairs of state for the day and given itself up to frivolity, for it was littered with an elaborate paraphernalia of cocktail implements. There were bottles, glasses of different sizes for short and long drinks, dishes of olives and nuts and cheese straws, also an ice bucket, a plate of lemons with a squeezer, a bowl of brown sugar, two kinds of Bitters and an imposing silver shaker. Among all these the President's hands moved swiftly and surely; they were flexible hands and never erred, whether he happened to be looking at what he was doing or not. He was evidently proud of his prowess as a barman, as indeed he had every reason to be, for the whisky-sour he finally handed me was perfect.

Throughout the whole operation he talked incessantly. He commented guardedly on Neville Chamberlain, glowingly on Winston Churchill and casually on international affairs. He jumped lightly from subject to subject, occasionally firing a question at me and suspending cocktail-mixing for a moment while he waited for my reply. He even told me a few funny stories, at which my heart sank, for as a rule I resent and despise funny stories, but he told them briefly and well.

Presently Mrs Roosevelt came in with Miss le Hand and Mr and Mrs Henry Morgenthau. The President proceeded to mix a fresh brew of whisky-sours and the conversation became general. The first thing that struck me about Mrs Roosevelt was her grace of movement; the second, that she was as warm and approachable as her husband. Never having seen her before I was surprised to observe how discourteous cameras had always been to her: they had shown merely a heavy face with a too large mouth; their inaccurate lenses had transformed her wide friendly smile into a grin and ignored the expression of her eyes, which was gentle and slyly humorous; they had also ignored her quality of distinction, which, in its essence, was curiously Victorian; I could imagine her driving through the nineteenth-century English countryside to take tea with Mrs Gaskell.

When dinner was announced she ushered us all out of the room first and the President remained behind. When we were settled in the dining-room he was wheeled in by his valet, who transferred him from his invalid chair to his ordinary chair at the head of the table. This operation was effected smoothly, without fuss, and without the faintest suggestion of spurious gallantry. This good-looking man, bursting with energy and vitality, bearing so lightly the heavy responsibilities of his position, just happened to be paralysed from the waist down and that was that; it seemed to be the most natural thing in the world and cried for no pity.

It is an established rule that no liquor may be served in the White House and so, fortified by the illicit Presidential whisky-sours, we settled down to pleasant food and delicious iced water.

After dinner I obliged with a few songs at the piano, and noted with a pang of dismay the President's marked partiality for 'Mad Dogs and Englishmen', which he made me sing twice. It could now only be a matter of time, I thought, before I received an official request from him to go to Norfolk, Virginia, and sing it to the naval cadets. Happily, however, this idea didn't occur to him, and after a little while the party broke up and he asked me back to his study for a night-cap. This time he talked specifically about the war and America's, as yet, confused attitude towards it. He explained, candidly and without prejudice, the point of view of the Isolationists and the various political, emotional and religious elements underlying it. He had, I felt, a personal admiration and affection for England, but he, rightly, seemed to consider that it was unnecessary to stress this and spoke of our problems and policies and statesmanship realistically rather than sentimentally. When finally I rose to go he asked me to come and see him again before I returned to Europe, and I left the White House with the conviction that it was fortunate, not only for Great Britain, but for all the democratic peoples of the world, that the man in command of the vast resources, potentialities and power of the United States of America possessed both vision and common sense.

Robin Maugham (1944)

After the fall of France in 1940 Somerset Maugham fled to the United States, where he lived for the duration of the war. In 1944 his lover, Gerald Haxton, died. As his nephew, Robin Maugham, records in this extract from his book, Conversations with Willie, *he was heartbroken.*

In November 1944, Gerald died in Doctors' Hospital in New York. Willie, stricken with grief, travelled down to South Carolina, buried himself in his remote little house in the wilds of Yemassee, and went – I can think of no other phrase to describe his condition – into a decline. He refused to leave Parker's Ferry and he refused to meet anyone – even his closest friends. It was then that Ellen and Nelson Doubleday suggested that I should come out to stay with him. I was ill and jittery as a result of a head wound received in the Western Desert. The calm of Yemassee might restore my nerves; my presence might help to drag Willie from his decline. I was keen to go. And thanks to the kindness of Brendan Bracken in the Ministry of Information and Victor Weybright, his American opposite number in London, I managed to get a passage on a ship to Halifax, Nova Scotia. When I arrived at Yemassee, I found Willie overwhelmed with misery.

'With the pills they've given me, I sometimes manage to sleep or doze for as much as six hours a night,' he told me. 'But I think of Gerald every single minute that I'm awake. I try to forget him all the eighteen hours of the day. You can't imagine what it was like – hour after hour – listening to that terrible cough that seemed to tear him to pieces.'

Suddenly Willie lowered himself on to the sofa and buried his face in his hands. He began to cry with long racking sobs. 'You'll never know how great this grief has been to me,' he said when he had controlled himself and could speak again. 'The best years of my life – those we spent wandering about the world – are inextricably connected with him. And in one way or another – however indirectly – all I've written during the last twenty years has something to do with him, if only that he typed my manuscripts for me.' Suddenly Willie was again shaken with sobs. 'I try to forget,' he moaned, 'but a dozen times a day something I come across, something I read, a stray word reminds me of him and I am overcome with grief.' Willie became a little calmer. 'They tell me time will help, but time flows dreadfully slowly. For thirty years he had been my chief care, my pleasure and my anxiety. Without him I am lost and lonely and hopeless. He was nearly twenty years younger than I was, and I had every right to think that he would have survived me. He would have been terribly upset at my death, but he would have got drunk for a week or two and then reconciled himself to it, for he had a naturally happy temper, but I am too old to endure so much grief. I have lived too long.'

Willie seemed inconsolable. But at least my arrival forced him to make a slight effort to recover. He took me to dine with Ellen and Nelson Doubleday and their family in what we both called 'the big house', and their friendliness and splendid if erratic hospitality did much to restore both of us. As the sunlit days passed by, Willie began to look less forlorn, and soon he began to manage a shaky smile. But it was not until New Year's Eve that I realised that Willie had managed to steer himself round the corner towards recovery.

There was a large party up at the big house on New Year's Eve. Willie and I were invited. A minute or so before midnight someone gaily suggested that we should all sing 'Auld Lang Syne'. Immediately Willie's face froze with dismay – not because he was afraid that the hackneyed tune would remind him of Gerald: by now he could cope with that misery. I could see from his hectic glances to right and to left that the reason for his consternation was more superficial and immediate. From childhood Willie had had a morbid dread of physical contact with strangers, and he was now suddenly confronted with the prospect of his hands being crossed and then clasped in the sticky palms of two unknown females who had come in late and who were now standing on either side of him. Into his eyes came the look of a frantic hunted animal. I was wondering how Willie would get out of his predicament, when he spoke:

'When on New Year's Eve,' Willie said, 'I hear people singing that song in which they ask themselves the question "should old acquaintance be forgot?" I can only ter-tell you that my own answer is in the affirmative.'

That did the trick. Hands that had been crossed and outstretched to clasp Willie's fell down in limp despondency. Mouths that had been open to chant merrily closed with a snap. And Willie had saved himself. At that instant he caught me looking at him and gave me a broad wink, and I knew that for a while at least he was back to his old form again.

Later that night, when we had returned to Willie's little house, we sat before the dying embers of the fire, having one last drink before going to bed. We had been sitting in silence for some moments, sipping our drinks, enjoying our cigarettes. Then Willie spoke:

'Gerald always insisted on us having a nightcap before we went to bed . . .' he said. 'You know, if I believed in God, I'd pray that I could join him soon. But I'm nearly seventy, so I haven't long to wait . . . As Epicurus said – there's nothing terrible in not living . . . I'm a millionaire, and they tell me that I'm the most famous writer alive. But I don't really care . . . I shall go back to the Mauresque eventually. I suppose I might as well live there as anywhere . . .'

Herbert Hodge (1945)

The London taxi-driver Herbert Hodge was sponsored by the Workers' Education Association to give a lecture-tour in the United States shortly after the Second World War. In his account of the journey, A Cockney in Main Street, *he expresses his reservations about one-man buses, then being introduced in the United States.*

I was invited by the president of the Detroit Bus and Street-Car Workers to try driving one of their buses – the Detroit Street Railway Company's latest model: a single-decker, built to carry twenty-seven passengers seated and as many more as could be squeezed in standing. It was like an oblong box in shape, with hardly any difference in looks between back and front. The engine, a petrol-driven Ford V.8, was at the back. The driver sat some three feet ahead of the front axle (there was a considerable body overhang, both back and front). His windscreen extended to the full width of the bus. To ensure his clear view there were four large sliding wipers with blades about two feet long; and, on the inside, a rubber-bladed fan to dry off condensation. There were two outside mirrors, off and near; and, inside the bus, a mirror just above the windscreen, to show the driver what the passengers were up to behind him; and another mirror higher up, and over to his right (the driver sits on the left-hand side in America, of course) to show him when the passengers were waiting to get off by the rear door. There were two doors; one for entry, at the front, level with the driver's seat, and one for exit, about threequarters of the way back. Both were automatic sliding doors, controlled by levers near the driver's left hand. On the dashboard was a red light which glowed when a passenger was standing on the rear step. This, of course, was to help quick starting. The moment the last alighting passenger lifted his last foot off the step, down went the driver's foot on the accelerator. There was no conductor.

There was a flat-rate fare of ten cents. As the passengers entered, they dropped their dimes into a box under the driver's eye. He also carried a change machine, slung from his shoulder, consisting of a set of metal tubes which issued the required small change complete on pressing a button. On a ledge at his left, alongside the door levers, was a wad of transfer tickets, covering other routes included in the flat-rate fare; and on his right, hung from a hook on the dashboard, was a ticket punch with which he indicated the transfer passenger's destination. In his spare time he also drove the bus.

There is no doubt in my mind that driving and conducting a bus on a busy town route is altogether too much for one man. Bus schedules are too tight to allow of fares being taken, change given, and transfers issued, while the bus is at rest. The result, as I saw on one-man buses all over the States, is that the driver starts away immediately the last passenger is on; then tries to steer, change gear, give change, put the dollar bills in his pocket, and issue and punch transfer tickets, at one and the same time. Yet with all the much publicized American road-safety campaigns, I never once came across an instance of any of the safety-orators having the guts to fight the big road transport interests on this issue – though several American busdrivers I spoke to about it confirmed my own impression that it was extremely dangerous.

All I had to do on this occasion, however, was to drive. My passengers were union and company officials. I found the bus much easier to handle than the average English bus of the same size. The steering was as light as that of a baby car, without the baby car's tendency to bounce. The gears were synchro-mesh, and the footbrake, an airbrake, was as light in operation as the accelerator. I once touched it with the tip of my toe (by mistake) and nearly shot myself through the windscreen. The acceleration was all the heart could desire.

Mechanically, these buses are the driver's dream. But the snag of this beautiful tool, under its American method of operation, is that every advantage it offers is pushed to the utmost in the interests of profit making – or what the owners, of course, would call public service. The easy steering and the ultra-rapid starting and stopping, make possible schedules that don't allow a man time to spit. The Detroit busdriver earns every cent of his $1.20 (approximately 5/6) an hour. Owing to the wartime shortage of labour, many of these driver-conductors were putting in a hundred hours a week. Detroit is no place for the middle-aged.

Ian Fleming (1946–8)

Ian Fleming (1908–64) was the inventor of James Bond. Ann Rothermere (1913–81) was the wife of the proprietor of the Daily Mail. *At the time of their affair Fleming was foreign manager of the* Sunday Times. *Later Ann divorced and they married.*

From Ian Fleming to Ann Rothermere

New York

[Early January 1946]

sweetheart,
i shall have to write this like james joyce because the machinery for making capitals has broken on the typewriter and i shall also not be able to make question-marks or any of the exciting things which happen on the top half of a typewriter. you will also observe a certain rainbow effect which is all to do with the same trouble. i am afraid it will affect my style but i know you wont mind.

everybody here talks about their health and about the russians and how long are you staying and what part of england do you come from and thats absolutely all, except the most intelligent ones talk about soandsos quote machine unquote and about shadowy figures called marsh and prendergast etc who are supposed to be running the president – much that i care. i keep on explaining to these intelligent people that i am not interested in english politics let alone american. this is not to say that i dont enjoy the orange juice and fried eggs and so on but i am submerged beneath a deep gloomth at the fabulous limitations of these people and their total unpreparedness to rule the world which is now theirs with the exception of you and peter and cyril and ed and a few more prickly ones – on a list of whom you and i would disagree ... so i am sitting here sloshing down three roses like in the advertisements and writing to you as if i were one of your other and better lovers in the burma jungle or otherwise engaged with an enemy. i think it will be all right when i get to jamaica because i shall sweat it out of me and dig a hole in the ground and be away. i have spoilt myself for too long to stand the fencing in which goes on here and which god knows is worse than the very worst i have ever suffered at your dear hands.

however, there has been plenty of work to do during the day and the mighty kemsley foreign service is thrusting our deep and enduring roots into the lush soil. i took iddon and alastair cook out to lunch at toots shaws, and told him you all love him [Iddon] which worries him all the time. he has much ambition but i explained with that blunt camaraderie which a. forbes appreciates so much that all columnists like all great editors reached a point where they thought they were making the chancelries tremble but that since northcliffe this had been a pipedream and that he would be wise to stick to his last and relax. i did suggest to him that any question of an iddon london diary was littlehampton madness and that the most promising alternative was an iddon world diary. this sunk in, so if the idea comes home you will know that i never cease to cosset my competitors particularly when i love their wives. he is a very good lad with the highest regard for you and reverence for es [Lord Rothermere] and he will do the mail very well till he dies. if he doesnt it will be your fault – but dont make him do serious stuff because he doesnt understand what its all about, though he wishes he did. cook is strictly third rate, though i must say i have always enjoyed his column in the standard. i much admire your overseas edition which is very well done. all this is in the best traditions of journalism, namely that one says how wonderful everyone elses stuff is – waiting for them to say how wonderful they think you are. you neednt say it to me because i should only ever work for gomer – not even for the times – and you wouldnt understand that and i am the only person in the world who knows whether what i do is good or not. bracket im afraid the four roses is beginning to work and that it is nearly time for me to go to bed bracket.

i wish you were here as i would like to walk out with you very much and go to 123 which is a late night club where nothing happens except that a man plays the piano when he feels like it. its always the wrong time and place with us but never mind.

there should be an awful lot of interesting gossip for me to tell you but i have been in the wrong hands all the time. someone cut the cards wrong at the beginning and its been like that all along. i havent fought for a redeal because i havent and thats why my last letter and this sound so awry. frinstance i spent last weekend with the morgans on long island which really was quelquechose as you would say. rather like glenborrodaile castle where i spent some of the unhappiest years of my youth and there have been several other bits like that which have all added up – to the point where i had to take to the four roses and write to you. so far as women are concerned i am sorry to say i have been corralled and that it all couldnt be wronger or more confused and my face is getting out of hand and its time i was away before i carve a chip out of anglo-american relations. and its not what you might imagine any kind of affair to be like but just something out of juan in america where everything starts wrong and goes on wrong and getting wronger – and god knows what she thinks its all about and it really isnt all one persons fault but just that both our sets of rules are wrong – like baseball and rounders, which is really what happens between most english and american people. but i find it very galling and very uninteresting and very difficult to straighten out and altogether unsatisfactory. one day i will tell you all the affairs i have ever got into and you will tell me what i have done wrong and why they have been such mazes. but you will have to be very wise and concentrate and sit quiet or i shall get impatient because i have thought over all the obvious answers and none of them quite fit.

well my darling it has been nice writing to you and you are a fine girl and one day i shall write you my first love letter since i was 22.

ian

Cecil Beaton (1946)

An account by the English photographer Cecil Beaton (1904–80) of his courtship
of the Swedish film-actress Greta Garbo (1905–) in New York in 1946.

April, 1946

Several days elapsed without her calling. I was not permitted to telephone her, so nothing to do but wait in patience and hope. I was beginning to think she would never make the initial move. One afternoon, when least expected, she inquired without explaining who it was on the telephone: 'What are you doing?' I gulped: 'Not a thing in the world.' Of course anything I was doing, or should have been doing, was shelved forthwith – for a miracle was about to happen and she was coming to see me right away.

She arrived, somewhat out of breath, dressed entirely in darkest blue, looking pale but even more incandescent than before. A crowd of bobbysox autograph-hunters had run after her on her way to my hotel, and they were cruel and ruthless and they upset her so much. But now she would enjoy a cigarette – calmly. We sat side by side on a long red sofa. She had not telephoned before because she had been ill: she had caught cold – doubtless by going onto that roof-top. I felt great guilt. But she explained she is an easy victim of colds, and it was foolish of her to be tempted out into the icy night winds. 'But if you had not come out on the roof with me you wouldn't be here this afternoon.' She smoked more Old Golds and drank a cup of tea remarking that cows' milk tastes so much better if it is not pasteurized, and when she pronounced a biscuit to be '*deliciosa*' I remarked: 'Then this is a festival', to which she chirped: 'Is zat so?' She talked with the excited vivacity of a child just home for the holidays, and did not look around her at my room, or show surprise or curiosity at what might be considered its somewhat startling decoration. But she did compliment me on keeping the rooms at a reasonable temperature: in fact, the steam heat was never turned on. 'Ah, fresh air!' then saluting, she cried: 'British Empire!' This was funny and somehow made sense, and I suppose I was flattered by, even in fantasy, personifying the Empire. Garbo employed many 'service' terms and, in reply to my question as to where she lived most of the year, said: 'Oh, I follow the Fleet.' She elaborated: 'I don't quite know what that means, but I often say things like that, that only signify if you scratch beneath the surface.' But I discovered quickly that it displeased her to be asked any direct questions, and she would invariably answer with some evasion.

We continued with a game of badinage that made little sense and yet was light and fantastic and to me, her abject victim, devastatingly entertaining. 'Are you a cobbler?' she suddenly asked apropos of nothing, 'or are you a cutter?' 'No, I don't think I am,' I answered lamely, not yet on to the game. She certainly did not consider herself as an actress. 'Being stared at by all those people is a pretty shabby business,' she said, and went on to tell how once in Sweden she had gone to a theatre alone. The audience was well-dressed and they were watching an actor play 'a well-dressed part', but he had a tear in his coat. 'That was so poignant! But then things can so often be so dismal, uncongenial and obnoxious.' About a man with a goitre: 'How can you laugh at a human being who is having trouble with his glands!' Albinos: 'They have such uneasiness with their eyes – they can hardly see. They are so pained and humiliated! Poor creatures of the world! Poor human beings!'

The whole conversation had a rather wacky, inconsequential quality, but because the creature sitting by my side was so ineffably strange and beautiful one automatically and willingly accepted the idiom imposed by her. This wackiness took the place of wit and would change erratically from gay to sad. 'A doctor once looked at me very carefully and asked: "Why are you unhappy? Is it because you imagine you're ill?" Another doctor asked: "Are you bored?" I don't know why he used so violent a word!' . . .

Apropos I know not what, she said: 'My bed is very small and chaste. I hate it. I've never thought of any particular person in connection with marriage; but, just lately, I have been thinking that as age advances we all become more lonely, and perhaps I have made rather a mistake – been on the wrong lines – and should settle down to some permanent companionship.'

This gave me the opportunity for which, subconsciously, I had been waiting. During the last few minutes I had known that – as the phrase has it – we were made for each other. Of this I was now quite certain. Not as a pleasantry, but to be taken very seriously, I asked: 'Why don't you marry me?'

I had never before asked anyone to marry me, and yet to make this proposal now seemed the most natural and easy thing to do. I was not even surprised at myself. But Garbo looked completely astounded. 'Good heavens, but this is so sudden!' She went on to soften her reaction. 'I once said to a friend of mine who invited me out to lunch: "Why, this is so sudden!" and he looked so hurt. But really, this is very frivolous of you. I don't think you should speak slightingly of marriage.'

'But I mean it. I've never been more serious.'

'But you hardly know me.'

'I know all about you, and I want to tame you and teach you to be much happier.'

'But we would never be able to get along together and, besides, you wouldn't like to see me in the morning in an old man's pyjamas.'

'I would be wearing an old man's pyjamas, too. And I think we *would* get along well together – unless my whistling in the bathroom got on your nerves?'

'You're being very superficial: one doesn't plan one's life on other people's bathroom habits. Besides, you'd worry about my being so gloomy and sad.'

'Oh no – you'd have to worry about why I was so happy, and you'd be the reason.'

'It's a funny thing, but I don't let anyone except you touch my vertebrae
– they so easily get out of place.'

When it was time for her to leave, I took her down to the street. Returning
to my room I wondered had she really been here? Or had I, by some
extraordinary wish-fulfilment, dreamt into actuality the scene that had
passed?

I looked around to see the proof that my imagination had not played a
trick on me. Here was the reality: the tea cup with the lipstick, the ash-tray
with the Old Gold cigarette stubs and the used matches – and the cushions
against which she had leant. I would have liked to ask the hotel maid not
to 'tidy' the room; I did not want her to puff out the cushions, but to
preserve them just as they were now, or to cast them in bronze for always.

Next day was a typically busy working one with my delightful and tactful
secretary, Miss Cleghorn, helping me to answer the succession of telephone
calls which consisted mainly of appointments being re-arranged or switched.
Suddenly I was impatient for all this activity to close down and for nice
Miss Cleghorn to leave, for an appointment had been made that was not
to be rearranged or switched: Greta was to come in to see me at 5.30. I
put a 'Do not disturb' signal on the telephone, and a few minutes later
there was an impatient woodpecker knocking at the door.

Greta's mood was as inconsequential as yesterday's. She had no information to impart, made no reference to my outburst of a proposal, and gave
a spontaneous performance of sheer gaiety and nonsense. With no apparent
context she recited little pieces of Goethe in an excellent German accent,
used a few French words as if to the manner born, then came down to
earth with American slang: 'By heck!' – 'Shucks!' – 'Darn it!' etc. She told
me of any little oddment that had amused her: a woman wrote her a fan
letter saying: 'You have the character of a man, but the body of a woman
– blast it!' She could not help being amused at the brutal finality of the
disbelieving New York cop who interrupted a long-winded bum by telling
him to 'beat it'. Her friend Molnar, the Hungarian playwright, tells comic
stories wonderfully well, and has one in particular that amuses her, but it
contains the use of a very crude word without which this story would not
be funny. Therefore, although she objects to the use of coarse language in
her presence, Greta excuses the word and whenever she sees Molnar she
begs him to repeat the story; each time he does so, Greta turns her face
away and laughs.

Greta jumped from one conversational orbit to another and we talked
about ourselves only in oblique terms. I tried, somewhat tentatively, to bind
her down to plans that would necessitate our meeting one another continually in the near future. Would she not like to see a certain play, or go to
see the Grecos in the Hispanic Museum, or to eat soft-shell crabs in a
downtown restaurant? But her answers were deliciously vague, as if she
never went to theatres, picture shows, or restaurants. I must be satisfied
with the present and not bank upon any further dividends.

When she came to take her leave, she gathered her belongings together
saying: 'I never wear white gloves. I simplify life like mad!' I notice that
when she puts on a hat she never looks to see how it is placed on her head.
She is completely without feminine vanity though at times she is interested

in clothes – the sort that she likes: she peers a lot at shoes in shop windows, and at leather coats and sweaters. Suddenly she turned and said: 'I don't know you from Adam [pronounced '*Ardhumme*'] and yet I was quite willing to stay here until breakfast time. That is, if you had remained with your head on the pillow beside me like a brother.' Then very sweetly and humbly she asked: 'May I be permitted to make a telephone call?' and, when she lifted the receiver, doubtless to call 'the little man', the operator asked: 'Are you now taking your calls, Mr Beaton?' 'Yes,' Garbo replied. As G. was leaving the telephone rang. 'Ah, there's life!' she said, but for me life was leaving.

We have started going out for walks together in Central Park. We 'steppe outte' for miles very fast – round the reservoir then all the way home from Ninety-Sixth Street to Fifty-Ninth. During these walks over the grass, under the early springtime trees, her mood becomes euphoric. To be part of nature gives her the same elation as champagne to a novice. She strides, leaps, laughs, becomes as lithe as a gazelle. She takes deep quaffs of water at the public fountains.

Sometimes photographs are more like people than they are themselves. Occasionally, when I am walking along with Greta, I suddenly see her as she appeared in a prized photograph cut out from an old movie magazine. Today there were many such flashes; and once, when she stopped to turn and look at the new moon, I could see something that I knew intimately before I had ever met her. I watched her face in the varying lights of afternoon, and I could not help revealing to her that I had seen that particular effect before in *Queen Christina*. This sort of observation she considers unnecessary; she does not relish allusion to her film career, and I must try to avoid the subject. It was typically humble and unassuming that she remarked: 'Once in Hollywood – to mention such a distant place . . .'

This afternoon the park air was so cold, but bracing, that we had almost to gallop in order to stay warm. On the spur of the moment we ran up the steps of the Metropolitan Museum to thaw and to look at the Apocalypse tapestries. Greta became so carried away that she was completely unselfconscious, as she whistled and sighed in admiration, while other visitors stared at her. She made birdlike noises of delight at the rabbits and butterflies and other small animals and insects woven into the needlework ground of wild flowers in the 'Unicorn' tapestries. Pointing to some draperies done in reds and rose and dull pink: 'Those are now my most beloved colours. It's incredible that human-beings can do such things!' she said. 'Think of it – it's of an overwhelming elegance!' '*Quelle flamboyance!*' was her reaction to more formal Louis XIV designs. Although she may not speak any tongue grammatically, she has such an appreciation for words and sounds of words that she picks them from many different countries to use on the spur of a moment. '*Ah, le petit chien!*' she said of a little white tapestry dog that was much more a *chien* than a 'dog'. She often uses archaic words and, for example, talks about somebody's 'dwelling', and she describes her own looks as 'poor and beggarly'.

On seeing a down-trodden bum, she would remark he was a '*verflucht mensch*'.

Her voice possesses a remarkable range of expressiveness: its warmth and sympathy is one of the major elements in this towering personality. She imagines she now has very little Swedish accent; it is only when people do imitations of her to her face that she understands she may be wrong. When I asked her to repeat a word that began with a 'j' ('jolly' she pronounces '*yolly*') she said: 'No, won't do it! You're trying to find out if I have a Swedish accent.'

I was impressed by her spontaneous appreciation of the best. Perhaps it is that, being of such a fine quality herself, she has an affinity with works of art. She does not seem even to notice the second-rate.

Soon we wandered among the plaster casts of the Michelangelo sculpture. Greta remembered from a sonnet that Michelangelo had said he liked only the things that would destroy lesser people. From this, and other scraps of odd information, she built up in vivid imagination a picture of an ugly little man, remote from sex and the ordinary contacts of life, who became to her as real as if she had known him. Her imagination is highly inflammable: given one spark she ignites into wild dreams and imaginings which can consume her completely. She often used to come to this sculpture room and stand for hours in front of these heads, which, if she stared long enough, became absolutely alive until she was almost mesmerized.

When we looked at huge, over-life-size nudes, I realized how little the human body means to me in comparison to her. She was positively ravenous in admiration of the physical perfection of some of these figures which she judged as if they were fruit or succulent sweets. She flicked out her tongue as if to taste them.

On the way back she quoted snatches of poetry, professing not to know the authors of the poems she recites in many languages: 'It's something I picked up years ago, and I've always been impressed by.' In fact it is by Heine, or Michelangelo, or Sappho. Modestly she claimed that nowadays she seldom reads even newspapers – though she keeps them 'for future use'. 'I always have a pile of three-months-old papers. I don't read them, but I collect them.' However, she did admit that for a short while in the mornings now she is absorbed by the biography of a Swedish poet. 'A young woman who died of tuberculosis, who wrote such adorable poetry, and whenever she referred to herself, or drew pictures of herself, she saw herself as a man. Her name was Harriet.' This is no doubt the reason why, when Greta travels 'incognito', she uses the name Harriet Brown.

Today she tried to quote a paragraph from Conrad, but she had forgotten most of it; it came, she said, from the story called *Youth*. I later found the quotation and read it over the telephone: 'The strength of it! And the faith of it! And the imagination of it!' But no – that was not it. I gave her several other quotes. 'No.' she said: 'It's the feeling that youth dies before you know it.' Later I found the passage: 'The glow in the heart that with every year grows dim, grows cold, grows small and expires too soon – too soon before life itself.'

Evelyn Waugh (1947)

After the huge success of Brideshead Revisited *in 1945, M.G.M. wanted to buy the film rights. In 1947 Waugh travelled to Hollywood to negotiate terms eventually turning down an offer of $125,000. Much of Waugh's time in California was spent in the Forest Lawn cemetery, which was the inspiration for his novel* The Loved One. *On returning to England he wrote an article on Hollywood for the* Daily Telegraph *and an essay on 'Californian Burial Customs' for* Life *magazine.*

Why Hollywood is a Term of Disparagement.

It may seem both presumptuous and unkind to return from six weeks' generous entertainment abroad and at once to sit down and criticize one's hosts. In the case of Hollywood it is neither.

Not presumptuous: first, because a fortnight is ample time in which to appreciate the character of that remote community; there are no secrets under those unflickering floodlights; no undertones to which the stranger must attune his ear. All is loud, obvious and prosaic. Secondly, because Hollywood has made its business the business of half the world. Morally, intellectually, aesthetically, financially, Hollywood's entries are written huge in the household books of every nation outside the USSR; largest of all in those of America but, because of our common language, second only to them in our own.

Nor is it unkind, for one may say what one likes in perfect confidence that one is powerless to wound. No game licences are issued in the reserve where the great pachyderms of the film trade bask and browse complacently. They have no suspicion that in most of America and in the whole of Europe the word 'Hollywood' is pejorative.

Even in southern California the film community are a people apart. They are like monks in a desert oasis, their lives revolving about a few shrines – half a dozen immense studios, two hotels, one restaurant; their sacred texts are their own publicity and the local gossip columns. The only strangers they ever meet have come to seek their fortunes; refugees from central Europe for whom the ease and plenty and affability of the place, seen against the background of the concentration camp, appear as supreme goods, and astute renegades from the civilizations of the East who know that flattery is the first step to preferment. None of these will hold a mirror up to Caliban; all feel their own security threatened by a whisper of criticism. Artists and public men elsewhere live under a fusillade of detraction and derision; they accept it as a condition of their calling. Not so in Hollywood, where all is a continuous psalm of self-praise.

Place and people have the aspect of Philo's Alexandria; such, one thinks in one's first few days, must have been the life there in the great days of the Mouseion; some such withdrawal of the arts is necessary everywhere if culture is to survive the present century. But this is a whimsy. Things are not really like that. The seclusion of these hermits is purely one-sided. They live for and by the outer world of which they know nothing at first hand and whose needs they judge by gross quantitative standards. 'No film of ours is ever a failure,' an executive said to me. 'Some are greater successes than others, but we reckon to get our money back on everything we produce.'

There is the impasse, the insurmountable barrier of financial prosperity. Behold the endless succession of Hollywood films, the slick second-rateness of the best of them, the blank fatuity of the worst – and none of them failures! What goes on there?

Three groups are responsible for making a film, the technicians, the players and the writers. (Producers-directors bear the guilt of all three.)

Of these the least culpable are the technicians. It is they who make the studio the vast, enchanted toyshop which delights the visitors. In only two respects are the technicians guilty. It is their fault that the studios are there, 3,000 miles from the world's theatrical centre in New York, 6,000 miles from the intellectual centres of London and Paris. They came there because in the early days they needed the sun. Now almost all photography is done by artificial light. The sun serves only to enervate and stultify. But by now the thing has become too heavy to move. And the technicians are too enterprising. Their itch for invention keeps them always a move ahead of the producers.

Twenty years ago the silent film was just beginning to develop into a fine art; then talking apparatus set it back to its infancy. Technicolor is the present retarding revolution. Soon no doubt we shall have some trick of third-dimensional projection. Mr Charles Chaplin, abused everywhere as a 'progressive', is the one genuine conservative, artistically, in Hollywood. The others allow themselves no time to get at ease with their materials.

The technicians are almost anonymous. All the devices of publicity are employed to give exclusive prominence to a few leading players. They possess the popular imagination and excite the visitor's curiosity. What of them? Dramatic critics often ask why the cinema has produced no actors comparable with the great figures of the stage, and point to the fact that in many 'documentaries' and continental films the best performances are given by unknown and untrained players. Even in Hollywood this year the highest Academy honours have gone to a man who was chosen simply because he had been maimed in the war. The wonder should be that so many stars are able to give as much as they do, for the conditions of their work are hostile to dramatic tradition. Certain disabilities seem to be inherent in the film; others are peculiar to Hollywood; all are exaggerated there.

There is an essential inhumanity about a film star's life. Compare it with that of a leading actress of fifty years ago. The latter worked in the capitals of the world; once her play was running smoothly her days were her own; she lived a life of leisure and fashion in an infinitely various society of her own choosing. The company formed a corporate unit with its own inti-macies, scandals and jokes; each performance was a separate artistic achieve-ment; the play was conceived as an artistic whole which was nightly brought into existence in a sustained and cumulative emotional mood which is the essence of acting. The players were in direct contact with their audience. Each audience was different; the manager would nightly visit the dressing-rooms with news of who was 'in front'. Above all, acting was recognized as an art which it took a lifetime to learn. Almost all great plays were written for mature players; the 'juvenile lead' and the '*ingénue*' were for youngsters learning their trade.

The Hollywood star lives in a remote suburb. She sees no one from one year's end to another except a handful of people all in the same trade as herself. She remains in purdah in the studio, inhabiting a tiny bathing-machine, surrounded by satellites who groom her and feed her until the technicians have finished with the 'stand-in' and require her presence on the set. When her work begins it consists of isolated fragments, chosen at the convenience of the technicians. It is rehearsal, hour after hour, for a few minutes of finished acting. At last in a Trilby-like trance she achieves the expression the director requires. She is 'shot', and they proceed to another, often unrelated fragment. And finally she has produced only the raw material for the 'cutter', who may nonchalantly discard the work of weeks or dovetail it into an entirely different situation.

And she must be young. Her life is as brief as a prize fighter's. By the time that she has become a finished actress she is relegated to 'supporting' roles. The work is physically exhausting and intellectually stultifying and there are no very great material rewards. A myth survives from past years that film stars live in Petronian luxury. The salary figures seem dazzling, and, indeed, she does often live in a degree of comfort very enviable by contemporary European measure. But it is no more than that. In fact her standard of life is precisely that of a moderately successful professional Englishman of fifty years ago. That is to say, she lives in a neat little villa with half an acre of garden; she has three servants, seldom more, very often fewer. Her antique furniture, collected at vast expense, would be commonplace in an English rectory. Her main time of entertainment is Sunday luncheon when she asks half a dozen professional friends to share her joint of beef. She has more clothes than her counterpart, but her menfolk are infinitely worse dressed. In only one substantial particular does she differ. She has a swimming pool which can be lit up at night. That is the mark of respectability, like the aspidistra in the cottage parlour.

And unlike her counterpart it is almost impossible for her to save money. If she attempted to live in simpler style she would lose 'face' and be rebuked by her studio. She cannot live more elaborately, for taxation intervenes. She can make this maximum in one film. After that for the rest of the time she is working for nothing. Consequently it is becoming increasingly hard to persuade her to do any work. Vanity is the sole inducement. She will therefore take no part in which she, and her male colleague, are anything less than the whole film. She must be on the stage all the time in a continuously alluring fashion. A play which depends on a team of various characters has no interest for her. A film must be her personal romantic adventures and nothing else. It is a short-sighted preference, for it means that when she is 50 there will be no adequate parts for her. But no one in Hollywood considers the possibility of growing up.

Half in Love with Easeful Death
An examination of Californian burial customs.

In a thousand years or so, when the first archaeologists from beyond the
date-line unload their boat on the sands of southern California, they will
find much the same scene as confronted the Franciscan missionaries. A dry
landscape will extend from the ocean to the mountains. Bel Air and Beverly
Hills will lie naked save for scrub and cactus, all their flimsy multitude of
architectural styles turned long ago to dust, while the horned toad and the
turkey buzzard leave their faint imprint on the dunes that will drift on
Sunset Boulevard.

For Los Angeles, when its brief history comes to an end, will fall swiftly
and silently. Too far dispersed for effective bombardment, too unimportant
strategically for the use of expensive atomic devices, it will be destroyed by
drought. Its water comes 250 miles from the Colorado River. A handful of
parachutists or partisans anywhere along that vital aqueduct can make the
coastal strip uninhabitable. Bones will whiten along the Santa Fé trail as
the great recession struggles eastwards. Nature will reassert herself and the
seasons gently obliterate the vast, deserted suburb. Its history will pass
from memory to legend until, centuries later, as we have supposed, the
archaeologists prick their ears at the cryptic references in the texts of the
twentieth century to a cult which once flourished on this forgotten strand;
of the idol Oscar – sexless image of infertility – of the great Star Goddesses
who were once noisily worshipped there in a Holy Wood.

Without the testimony of tombs the science of archaeology could barely
exist, and it will be a commonplace among the scholars of 2947 that the
great cultural decline of the twentieth century was first evident in the
graveyard. The wish to furnish the dead with magnificent habitations, to
make an enduring record of their virtues and victories, to honour them and
edify their descendants, raised all the great monuments of antiquity, the
pyramids, the Taj Mahal, St Peter's at Rome, and was the mainspring of
all the visual arts. It died, mysteriously and suddenly, at the end of the
nineteenth century. England, once very rich in sepulchral statuary, comme-
morated her fallen soldiers of the First World War by a simple inscription
in the floor of an abbey built nine centuries earlier to shelter the remains
of a Saxon king. Rich patrons of art who, in an earlier century, would have
spent the last decade of their lives in planning their own elaborate obsequies,
deposed that their ashes should be broadcast from aeroplanes. The more
practical Germans sent their corpses to the soap boiler. Only the primitive
heathens of Russia observed a once-universal tradition in their shrine to
Lenin.

All this will be a commonplace in the schools of 2947. The discoveries,
therefore, of the Holy Wood Archaeological Expedition will be revolutionary, for when they have excavated and catalogued, and speculated
hopelessly about the meaning of, a temple designed in the shape of a Derby
hat and a concrete pavement covered with diverse monopedic prints, and
have surveyed the featureless ruins of the great film studios, their steps will
inevitably tend northward to what was once Glendale, and there will
encounter, on a gentle slope among embosoming hills, mellowed but still
firm-rooted as the rocks, something to confound all the accepted generali-

zations, a necropolis of the age of the pharaohs, created in the middle of the impious twentieth century, the vast structure of Forest Lawn Memorial Park.

We can touch hands across the millennium with these discoveries, for it is in the same mood of incredulous awe that the visitor of our own age must approach this stupendous property. Visitors, indeed, flock there – in twice the numbers that frequent the Metropolitan Museum in New York – and with good reason, for there are many splendid collections of art elsewhere but Forest Lawn is entirely unique. Behind the largest wrought-iron gates in the world lie 300 acres of park-land, judiciously planted with evergreen (for no plant which sheds its leaf has a place there). The lawns, watered and drained by eighty miles of pipe, do not at first betray their solemn purpose. Even the names given to their various sections – Eventide, Babyland, Graceland, Inspiration Slope, Slumberland, Sweet Memories, Vesperland, Dawn of Tomorrow - are none of them specifically suggestive of the graveyard. The visitor is soothed by countless radios concealed about the vegetation, which ceaselessly discourse the 'Hindu Lovesong' and other popular melodies, and the amplified twittering of caged birds. It is only when he leaves the seven and a half miles of paved roadway that he becomes aware of the thousands of little bronze plates which lie in the grass. Commenting on this peculiarity in the *Art Guide of Forest Lawn with Interpretations* Mr Bruce Barton, author of *What can a man believe?*, says: 'The cemeteries of the world cry out man's utter hopelessness in the face of death. Their symbols are pagan and pessimistic ... Here sorrow sees no ghastly monuments, but only life and hope.' The Christian visitor might here remark that by far the commonest feature of other graveyards is still the Cross, a symbol in which previous generations have found more Life and Hope than in the most elaborately watered evergreen shrub. This reproach will soon be removed in Forest Lawn's own grand way by a new acquisition, a prodigious canvas of the Crucifixion which took thirty years of the Polish painter, Jan Styka's life to complete; it will require a vast new building to house it. A miniature, 1/49th of the area of the original, now occupies one whole side of the largest hall in Forest Lawn and an explanatory speech has been recorded for the gramophone, identifying the hundreds of figures which in the original abound in life size. The canvas has had an unhappy history. Shipped to the USA in 1904 for the St Louis Exhibition, it was impounded for excise dues and sold, without profit to the artist, to its importer, who was, however, unable to find a pavilion large enough to house it. Since then it has lain about in warehouses, a prey to 'silver fish', and has been shown only once, in the Chicago Opera House, where it filled the entire stage and extended far into the auditorium. Soon it will form a suitable addition to the wonders of Forest Lawn.

These can be only briefly indicated in an essay of this length. There is the largest assembly of marble statuary in the United States, mostly secular in character, animals, children and even sculptured toys predominating; some of it erotic, and some of it enigmatically allegorical. There is also what is claimed to be the finest collection of stained glass in America, the glory of which is 'The Last Supper' in the Court of Honour; the original by Leonardo da Vinci has here, in the words of *Pictorial Forest Lawn*, been 'recreated in vibrant, glowing and indestructible colours'.

There are gardens and terraces, and a huge range of buildings, the most prominent of which is the rather Italian Mausoleum. There in marble-fronted tiers lie the coffins, gallery after gallery of them, surrounded by statuary and stained glass. Each niche bears a bronze plaque with the inmate's name, sometimes in magnified counterfeit of his signature. Each has a pair of bronze vases which a modest investment can keep perpetually replenished with fresh flowers. Adjacent lies the Columbarium, where stand urns of ashes from the Crematory. There is the Tudor-style Administration Building, the Mortuary (Tudor exterior, Georgian interior) and the more functional Crematory. All are designed to defy the operations of time; they are in 'Class A steel and concrete', proof against fire and earthquake. The Mausoleum alone, we are told, contains enough steel and concrete for a sixty-storey office building, and its foundations penetrate thirty-three feet into solid rock.

The Memorial Court of Honour is the crowning achievement of this group. 'Beneath the rare marbles of its floor are crypts which money cannot purchase, reserved as gifts of honoured interment for Americans whose lives shall have been crowned with genius.' There have so far been two recipients of this gift, Gutzon Borglum, the first sculptor in history to employ dynamite instead of the chisel, and Mrs Carrie Jacobs-Bond, author and composer of 'The End of a Perfect Day', at whose funeral last year, which cost $25,000, Dr Eaton, the Chairman of Forest Lawn, pronounced the solemn words: 'By the authority vested in me by the Council of Regents, I do herewith pronounce Carrie Jacobs-Bond an immortal of the Memorial Court of Honour.' Then G. K. Chesterton, in a masterly book, sadly neglected in Europe but honoured in the USA – *The Everlasting Man* – gently exposed their fatuity. But they will flourish again, for it is a brand of scholarship well suited to dreamy natures who are not troubled by the itch of precise thought. What will the professors of the future make of Forest Lawn? What do we make of it ourselves? Here is the thing, under our noses, a first-class anthropological puzzle of our own period and neighbour-hood. What does it mean?

First, of course, it is self-evidently a successful commercial undertaking. The works of sculpture enhance the value of the grave sites; the unification in a single business of all the allied crafts of undertaking is practical and, I believe, unique. But all this is the least interesting feature.

Secondly, the Park is a monument to local tradition. Europeans, whose traditions are measured in centuries, are wrong to suppose that American traditions, because they are a matter of decades, are the less powerful. They are a recent, swift and wiry growth. Southern California has developed a local character which is unique in the United States. The territory was won by military conquest less than a century ago. In the generations that followed the Spanish culture was obliterated, and survives today only in reconstruc-tions. The main immigrations took place in living memory, and still continue. In 1930 it was calculated that of the million and a quarter inhabitants of Los Angeles half had arrived in the previous five years; only one tenth could claim longer than fifteen years' standing. In the last seventeen years the balance has changed still more in the newcomers' favour. Of this vast influx the rich came first. There was no pioneer period in which hungry young people won a living from the land. Elderly people from the East and Middle

West brought their money with them to enjoy it in the sunshine, and they set up a tradition of leisure which is apparent today in the pathological sloth of the hotel servants and the aimless, genial coffee-house chatter which the film executives call 'conferences'.

It is not the leisure of Palm Beach and Monte Carlo where busy men go for a holiday. It is the leisure of those whose work is done. Here on the ultimate, sunset-shore they warm their old bodies and believe themselves alive, opening their scaly eyes two or three times a day to browse on salads and fruits. They have long forgotten the lands that gave them birth and the arts and trades they once practised. Here you find, forgetful and forgotten, men and women you supposed to be long dead, editors of defunct newspapers, playwrights and artists who were once the glory of long-demolished theatres, and round them congregate the priests of countless preposterous cults to soothe them into the cocoon-state in which they will slough their own bodies. The ideal is to shade off, so finely that it becomes imperceptible, the moment of transition, and it is to this process that Forest Lawn is the most conspicuous monument.

Dr Eaton has set up his Credo at the entrance. 'I believe in a happy Eternal Life,' he says. 'I believe those of us left behind should be glad in the certain belief that those gone before have entered into that happier Life.' This theme is repeated on Coleus Terrace: 'Be happy because they for whom you mourn are happy – far happier than ever before.' And again in Vesperland: '. . . Happy because Forest Lawn has eradicated the old customs of Death and depicts Life not Death.'

The implication of these texts is clear. Forest Lawn had consciously turned its back on the 'old customs of death', the grim traditional alternatives of Heaven and Hell, and promises immediate eternal happiness for all its inmates. Similar claims are made for other holy places – the Ganges, Debra Lebanos in Abyssinia, and so on. Some of the simpler crusaders probably believed that they would go straight to Heaven if they died in the Holy Land. But there is a catch in most of these dispensations, a sincere repentance, sometimes an arduous pilgrimage, sometimes a monastic rule in the closing years. Dr Eaton is the first man to offer eternal salvation at an inclusive charge as part of his undertaking service.

There is a vital theological point on which Dr Eaton gives no *ex cathedra* definition. Does burial in Forest Lawn itself sanctify, or is sanctity the necessary qualification for admission? Discrimination is exercised. There is no room for the Negro or the Chinaman, however devout; avowed atheists are welcome, but notorious ill-doers are not. Al Capone, for example, had he applied, would have been excluded, although he died fortified by the last rites of his Church. 'Fatty' Arbuckle was refused burial, because, although acquitted by three juries of the crime imputed to him by rumour, he had been found guilty, twenty years or so earlier, of giving a rowdy party. Suicides, on the other hand, who, in 'the old customs of death' would lie at a crossroads, impaled, come in considerable numbers and, often, particularly in cases of hanging, present peculiar problems to the embalmer.

Embalming is so widely practised in California that many believe it to be a legal obligation. At Forest Lawn the bodies lie in state, sometimes on sofas, sometimes in open coffins, in apartments furnished like those of a luxurious hotel, and named 'Slumber Rooms'. Here the bereaved see them for the last time, fresh from the final beauty parlour, looking rather smaller than in life and much more dandified. There is a hint of the bassinet about these coffins, with their linings of quilted and padded satin and their frilled silk pillows. There is more than a hint, indeed, throughout Forest Lawn that death is a form of infancy, a Wordsworthian return to innocence. 'I am the Spirit of Forest Lawn,' wrote K. C. Beaton, in less than Wordsworthian phrase: 'I speak in the language of the Duck Baby, happy childhood at play.' We are very far here from the traditional conception of an adult soul naked at the judgment seat and a body turning to corruption. There is usually a marble skeleton lurking somewhere among the marble draperies and quartered escutcheons of the tombs of the high Renaissance; often you find, gruesomely portrayed, the corpse half decayed with marble worms writhing in the marble adipocere. These macabre achievements were done with a simple moral purpose – to remind a highly civilized people that beauty was skin deep and pomp was mortal. In those realistic times Hell waited for the wicked and a long purgation for all but the saints, but Heaven, if at last attained, was a place of perfect knowledge. In Forest Lawn, as the builder claims, these old values are reversed. The body does not decay; it lives on, more chic in death than ever before, in its indestructible class A steel and concrete shelf; the soul goes straight from the Slumber Room to Paradise, where it enjoys an endless infancy – one of a great Caucasian nursery-party where Knights of Pythias toddle on chubby unsteady legs beside a Borglum whose baby-fingers could never direct a pneumatic drill and a Carrie Jacobs-Bond whose artless ditties are for the Duck Baby alone.

That, I think, is the message. To those of us too old-fashioned to listen respectfully, there is the hope that we may find ourselves, one day beyond time, standing at the balustrade of Heaven among the unrecognizably grown-up denizens of Forest Lawn, and, leaning there beside them, amicably gaze down on southern California, and share with them the huge joke of what the professors of anthropology will make of it all.

There is at the highest point a water-tower named 'The Tower of Legends', where at the dawn of Easter Sunday a number of white doves are liberated in the presence of a huge concourse whose singing is broadcast 'from coast to coast'. Of this building 'a noted art authority' has remarked: 'It depicts, more truly than any structure I have ever seen, real American architecture. It deserves the attention of the world' (*Art Guide*). But this precious edifice, alas, is due for demolition and will soon give place to the non-sectarian, Bishopless 'Cathedral' which is to house Jan Styka's masterpiece and provide in its shade fresh galleries of urns and coffins.

There are already three non-sectarian churches, 'The Little Church of the Flowers', 'The Wee Kirk o' the Heather' and 'The Church of the Recessional'. The first is, with modifications, a replica of Stoke Poges Church where Gray wrote his 'Elegy'; the second a reconstruction of the ruins of a chapel at Glencairn, Dumfriesshire where Annie Laurie worshipped; the third, again with modifications, is a replica of the parish church of Rottingdean in Sussex where Rudyard Kipling is claimed by Dr Eaton to have been inspired – by heaven knows what aberration of oratory from the pulpit so artlessly reproduced – to write *Kim*. The American visitor may well be surprised at the overwhelmingly British character of these places of worship in a state which has never enjoyed the blessings of British rule and is now inhabited by the most cosmopolitan people in the United States. The British visitor is surprised also at the modifications.

It is odd to find a church dedicated to Kipling, whose religion was highly idiosyncratic. The building is used not only for funerals but for weddings and christenings. Its courtyard is used for betrothals; there is a stone ring, named by Dr Eaton the Ring of Aldyth, through which the young lover is invited to clasp hands and swear fidelity to what Kipling described as 'a rag and a bone and hank of hair'. Round the courtyard are incised the texts of 'Recessional', 'If' and 'When earth's last picture is painted'. The interior of St Margaret's, Rottingdean, is not particularly remarkable among the many ancient parish churches of England, but the architects of Forest Lawn have used their ingenuity to enliven it. One aisle has been constructed of glass instead of stone, and filled with pot-plants and caged canaries; a chapel, hidden in what is no doubt thought to be devotional half-darkness, is illuminated by a spotlit painting of Bougereau's entitled *Song of the Angels*; in a kind of sacristry relics of the patron saint are exposed to veneration. They are not what ecclesiastics call 'major relics'; some photographs by the Topical Press, a rifle scoresheet signed by the poet, the photostatic copy of a letter to Sir Roderick Jones expressing Kipling's hope of attending a christening, a copy of Lady Jones's popular novel, *National Velvet*, an oleograph text from a nearby cottage; and so forth.

What will the archaeologists of 2947 make of all this and of the countless other rareties of the place? What webs of conjecture will be spun by the professors of comparative religion? We know with what confidence they define the intimate beliefs of remote ages. They flourished in the nineteenth century.

Graham Greene (1947)

In the late 1930s Graham Greene was film critic for the magazine Night and Day. *Later he was commissioned to write film-scripts. Perhaps the most famous of them was the film* The Third Man, *directed by Carol Reed. At first the American producer David Selznick was not sympathetic to the story-line.*

If I had remained a film critic, the brief comic experience which I had then of Hollywood might have been of value to me, for I learned at first hand what a director may have to endure at the hands of a producer. (One of the difficult tasks of a critic is to assign his praise or blame to the right quarter.)

Mr David Selznick, famous for having produced the world's best-selling film, *Gone With The Wind*, held the American rights in *The Third Man* and, by the terms of the contract with Korda, the director was bound to consult him about the script sixty days before shooting began. So Carol Reed and I journeyed west. Our first meeting with Mr Selznick at La Jolla in California promised badly, and the dialogue remains as fresh in my mind as the day when it was spoken. After a brief greeting he got down to serious discussion. He said, 'I don't like the title.'

'No? We thought . . .'

'Listen, boys, who the hell is going to a film called *The Third Man?*'

'Well,' I said, 'it's a simple title. It's easily remembered.'

Mr Selznick shook his head reproachfully. 'You can do better than that, Graham,' he said, using my Christian name with a readiness I was not prepared for. 'You are a writer. A good writer. I'm no writer, but you are. Now what we want – it's not right, mind you, of course it's not right, I'm not saying it's right, but then I'm no writer and you are, what we want is something like *Night in Vienna*, a title which will bring them in.'

'Graham and I will think about it,' Carol Reed interrupted with haste. It was a phrase I was to hear Reed frequently repeat, for the Korda contract had omitted to state that the director was under obligation to accept Mr Selznick's advice. Reed during the days that followed, like an admirable stonewaller, blocked every ball.

We passed on to Mr Selznick's view of the story.

'It won't do, boys,' he said, 'it won't do. It's sheer buggery.'

'Buggery?'

'It's what you learn in your English schools.'

'I don't understand.'

'This guy comes to Vienna looking for his friend. He finds his friend's dead. Right? Why doesn't he go home then?'

After all the months of writing his destructive view of the whole venture left me speechless. He shook his grey head at me. 'It's just buggery, boy.'

I began weakly to argue. I said, 'But this character – he has a motive of revenge. He has been beaten up by a military policeman.' I played a last card. 'Within twenty-four hours he's in love with Harry Lime's girl.'

Mr Selznick shook his head sadly. 'Why didn't he go home before that?'

That, I think, was the end of the first day's conference. Mr Selznick removed to Hollywood and we followed him – to a luxurious suite in Santa Monica, once the home of Hearst's film-star mistress. During the conferences which followed I remember there were times when there seemed to be a kind of grim reason in Mr Selznick's criticisms – surely here perhaps there *was* a fault in 'continuity', I hadn't properly 'established' this or that. I would forget momentarily the lesson which I had learned as a film critic – that to 'establish' something is almost invariably wrong and that 'continuity' is often the enemy of life. A secretary sat by Mr Selznick's side with her pencil poised. When I was on the point of agreement Carol Reed would quickly interrupt – 'Graham and I will think about it.'

There was one conference which I remember in particular because it was the last before we were due to return to England. The secretary had made forty pages of notes by this time, but she had been unable to record one definite concession on our side. The conference began as usual about 10.30 p.m. and finished after 4 a.m. Always by the time we reached Santa Monica dawn would be touching the Pacific.

'There's something I don't understand in this script, Graham. Why the hell does Harry Lime . . . ?' He described some extraordinary action on Lime's part.

'But he doesn't,' I said.

Mr Selznick looked at me for a moment in silent amazement.

'Christ, boys,' he said. 'I'm thinking of a different script.'

He lay down on his sofa and crunched a Benzedrine. In ten minutes he was as fresh as ever, unlike ourselves.

I look back on David Selznick now with affection. The forty pages of notes remained unopened on Reed's files, and since the film proved a success, I suspect Selznick forgot that the criticisms had ever been made. Indeed, when next I was in New York he invited me to lunch to discuss a project. He said, 'Graham. I've got a great idea for a film. It's just made for you.'

I had been careful on this occasion not to take a third Martini.

'The Life of St Mary Magdalene,' he said.

'I'm sorry,' I said, 'no. It's not really in my line.'

He didn't try to argue. 'I have another idea,' he said. 'It will appeal to you as a Catholic. You know how next year they have what's called the Holy Year in Rome. Well. I want to make a picture called The Unholy Year. It will show all the commercial rackets that go on, the crooks . . .'

'An interesting notion,' I said.

'We'll shoot it in the Vatican.'

'I doubt if they will give you permission for that.'

'Oh sure they will,' he said. 'You see we'll write in one Good Character.'

Dmitri Shostakovich (1949)

Shostakovich made his first trip to the United States in March 1949 for the Cultural and Scientific Conference for World Peace, which took place at the Waldorf-Astoria Hotel in New York.

Naturally, Stalin didn't give a damn about the West, and the Western intelligentsia in particular. He used to say, 'Don't worry, they'll swallow it.' But the West did exist and he had to do something with it. They had started a peace movement, and they needed people for it. And Stalin thought of me. That was his style completely. Stalin liked to put a man face to face with death and then make him dance to his own tune.

I was given the order to get ready for a trip to America. I had to go to the Cultural and Scientific Congress for World Peace in New York. A worthy cause. It's obvious that peace is better than war and therefore struggling for peace is a noble effort. But I refused, it was humiliating for me to take part in a spectacle like that. I was a formalist, a representative of an antinational direction in music. My music was banned, and now I was supposed to go and say that everything was fine.

'No,' I said. 'I won't go. I'm ill, I can't fly, I get airsick.' Molotov talked to me, but I still refused.

Then Stalin called. And in his nagging way, the leader and teacher asked me why I didn't want to go to America. I answered that I couldn't. My comrades' music wasn't played, and neither was mine. They would ask about it in America. What could I say?

Stalin pretended to be surprised. 'What do you mean, it isn't played? Why aren't they playing it?'

I told him that there was a decree by the censors, that there was a blacklist. Stalin said, 'Who gave the orders?' Naturally, I replied, 'It must have been one of the leading comrades.'

Now came the interesting part. Stalin announced, 'No, we didn't give that order.' He always referred to himself in the royal plural – 'We, Nicholas II.' And he began rehashing the thought that the censors had overreacted, had taken an incorrect initiative: We didn't give an order like that, we'll have to straighten out the comrades from the censorship, and so on.

This was another matter, this was a real concession. And I thought that maybe it would make sense to go to America, if as a result they would play the music of Prokofiev, Shebalin, Miaskovsky, Khachaturian, Popov, and Shostakovich again.

And just then, Stalin stopped going on about the question of the order and said, 'We'll take care of that problem, Comrade Shostakovich. What about your health?'

And I told Stalin the pure truth: 'I'm nauseated.'

Stalin was taken aback and then started mulling over this unexpected bulletin. 'Why are you nauseated? From what? We'll send you a physician, he'll see why you are nauseated.' And so on.

So finally I agreed, I made the trip to America. It cost me a great deal, that trip, I had to answer stupid questions and keep from saying too much. They made a sensation out of that too. And all I thought about was: How much longer do I have to live?

Thirty thousand people were jammed into Madison Square Garden when I played the scherzo from my Fifth Symphony on the piano, and I thought, This is it, this is the last time I'll ever play before an audience this size.

I still recall with horror my first trip to the U.S.A. I wouldn't have gone at all if it hadn't been for intense pressure from administrative figures of all ranks and colours, from Stalin down. People sometimes say that it must have been an interesting trip, look at the way I'm smiling in the photographs. That was the smile of a condemned man. I felt like a dead man. I answered all the idiotic questions in a daze, and thought, When I get back it's over for me.

Stalin liked leading Americans by the nose that way. He would show them a man – here he is, alive and well – and then kill him. Well, why say lead by the nose? That's too strongly put. He only fooled those who wanted to be fooled. The Americans don't give a damn about us, and in order to live and sleep soundly, they'll believe anything.

Just then, in 1949, the Jewish poet Itsik Fefer was arrested on Stalin's orders. Paul Robeson was in Moscow and in the midst of all the banquets and balls, he remembered that he had a friend called Itsik. Where's Itsik? 'You'll have your Itsik,' Stalin decided, and pulled his usual base trick.

Itsik Fefer invited Paul Robeson to dine with him in Moscow's most chic restaurant. Robeson arrived and was led to a private chamber in the restaurant, where the table was set with drinks and lavish *zakuski*. Fefer was really sitting at the table, with several unknown men. Fefer was thin and pale and said little. But Robeson ate and drank well and saw his old friend.

After their friendly dinner, the men Robeson didn't know returned Fefer to prison, where he soon died. Robeson went back to America, where he told everyone that the rumors about Fefer's arrest and death were nonsense and slander. He had been drinking with Fefer personally.

GI Brides (1940s)

The United States entered the Second World War in 1941. The first GIs arrived in Britain the year after, bringing with them chewing-gum and nylons. Many British girls were unable to resist these blandishments. Those who married GIs were eligible to join their husbands in the United States after the war. Sentimental Journey, *from which the following extract is taken, was compiled from interviews with many of the women themselves.*

The brides began to settle into being home bodies, US style. No longer did they flinch and think in terms of air-raids when they heard a siren. 'At first, the hairs on the back of my neck would prickle, then I discovered it was the Fire Brigade testing their equipment.'

Pampered ladies learned to live without their maids and became adept at baking brownies [nutty chocolate cakes] and replacing winter storm windows [double glazing] with summer screens (to keep out those ever-present insects).

So what if you did have to beat a 'funny little orange gelatine bead' into margarine – which came white – to make it yellow. [The strong dairy lobby in Washington at that time prevented margarine being sold resembling butter.] It was all part of the fun of being in the States. And, if real butter came in 'sticks' instead of quarter-pound packets, at least it was unrationed.

Even though jelly was jam it came in such pretty flowered glasses they could be used again for Seven-Up Floats, while the matching smaller ones which held unusual taste treats like pimento-flavoured cream-cheese were also handy for breakfast. By now the brides were all hooked on freshly-squeezed orange juice – it was a far cry from carrot-flavoured 'orange' squash or that wartime vitamin C booster, rose-hip syrup.

If you pretended hard enough, a hot-dog bun could resemble an oversized bridge roll and it was soon easy to differentiate between an oil mop to polish the floor and a dry mop for the dust. Once, that is, they figured out neither bore any relationship to a roll mop herring! If lunch was at 11.30 and high tea was called supper, it still gave you time to ride out to the Dairy Queen for a pineapple marshmallow sundae in the evening. 'They were delicious,' enthused Pamela, 'I used to have three a day until I go so fat I had to go on a diet.'

'Using a recipe that called for ten egg-whites was difficult. We'd been so conditioned by food rationing since childhood, it seemed wrong –

wasteful. It was a long time before I made an Angel Food cake.' Was an Angel Food cake really a cake? Yes! A high, white, light, frothy sponge cut into gigantic slices that melted in the mouth.

Sandwiches, on the other hand, could be jaw-breakers. 'Putting all that stuff like two slices of meat and cheese in a sandwich seemed gross at first and as far as all that tomato and lettuce was concerned – why it was more than my Mum used for a salad.'

The United States certainly was a whole new world.

Girls who had grown up playing with skipping ropes on grimy pavements in mill towns now became self-assured, elegant women, sweeping into their country clubs with panache. 'It's not where you start but how you finish.' This song truly exemplifies the American scene.

'Being English in America opened many doors to me that would have remained shut.'

'The class situation in America, from my point of view,' records Marie, 'is worse than in England. Supposedly it doesn't exist, but *it is there* – and it is the worse kind – it is based strictly on money and has nothing to do with breeding. If you have money you're in and people just have to put up with you, because you have what seems to count.'

So, in the American democracy, presentation of the person was what counted. Cockney, country and county accents were beginning to merge into the American drawl, even though, 'I always felt different. I would always be to some, "that foreigner he's married".'

The children became instant Americans, 'though it did seem a shame for them to miss out on the other set of grandparents pining for them in England. Exchanged photographs were a poor substitute.'

Brenda B had even sent back a set of baby's footprints which were re-printed in the *Manchester Evening News*. 'Aren't they cute?' She asked of the readers and explained this American method of registering a baby's birth. In a baby these are just as unique as finger prints, and the procedure for taking them is the same.

There was some confusion among the children as they began to go to school. 'My son David thought all mothers spoke with an English accent and all fathers American,' remembers Pamela.

Another girl reports how her son was asked at school if his father had brought back any souvenirs of the war. 'Yes, my mother,' he said proudly.

'Baseball looked very much like rounders,' said one mother whose son joined the Little League – a very American institution. 'But, I went along to the matches and cheered like any other dutiful mother.'

Other types of Americanisation were resisted for the children. 'He came home from school one day insisting he was going to sell magazines to the neighbours. "Then I can earn points for a toy fire engine." A man at the school gates had been encouraging these six- and seven-year-old children to sign up for this project. I telephoned the company and complained. "It's the American way of business," I was told. "Well, I'm English," I told them, "So go away".'

For how much longer could that situation continue? Immigrants – which of course, the GI brides were – could, after a five-year residence, become eligible to pursue citizenship.

One day, a man said to Eunice, 'Have you got your civilisation papers yet?' Was that the logical thing to do? The general opinion among the GI brides was 'Yes'. While the majority of them were already acting in a civilised manner, the time had come for them to be naturalised.

'I felt if my husband was and my son was – why when he came on leave to England to see his new baby, the first thing my husband did was march us up to the US Embassy, 'to make an American of this little Limey.' [All children of American servicemen born overseas automatically became Americans, if the parents were married] – I felt the time had come for me to do the same' – Pamela.

Marie was horrified, however, when one of her friends became a citizen. 'She said she didn't mean it – the Pledge – she was just going to say the words – that was wrong.'

Another woman who has resolutely remained British to this day and prefers to be quoted anonymously, put it this way. 'I love my homeland and to be an American would be taking everything away from me. I don't see how a person can become a citizen when their heart is forever in England.'

The many who resisted naturalisation were more than outnumbered by those, like Pamela, who studied American history and passed their exams, although the question, 'If the United States and England went to war, how would you side?' was a difficult one. 'I reasoned, in that unlikely event, if my son was fighting for the United States, then that was where my loyalty would be – and I meant it.'

Olive's reason for becoming an American harkened to the War of Independence – perhaps because her husband could trace his ancestors that far back, so she felt strongly, 'No taxation without representation.'

The GI brides stood in court, hand over heart, 'To Pledge Allegiance to the Flag of the United States of America'.

'She's changed her nationality.' Major hysteria in Liverpool from my mother and calm acceptance from my father when he heard the news, reports Brenda H.

There were excuses and explanations. 'I became a citizen on account of the kids and also non-citizens had to register every year.'

'I refer to myself as Anglo-American and am delighted to have dual nationality.'

GI brides could have the best of both worlds, unless they renounced their British nationality in writing. As one of them put it. 'I will forever feel a-straddle the Atlantic.'

Hilda has refused to be an American to this day. 'My allegiance is to the UK as I am very proud of my country. I live in America, not by choice, but because my heart ruled my mind. I happened to fall in love with a person from America. I will always respect this country because it is my husband's but my heart will always be over there.'

So here they were, new Americans with new houses; by dint of hard work and a variety of part-time jobs they eased their financial burdens. 'I did some part-time tea-room modelling for a department store in St Louis,' said Brenda B, who was fortunate to live only seventeen miles from a fair-sized city. 'Plus I worked part-time in the French salon millinery department of the same store when the children were in school. I also worked part-time at the Post Office during the Christmas rush.' Here was another GI bride, who had been trained to be a secretary, trying out various other jobs to help them, as a family, 'get ahead'.

They began to have the kind of homes with some of the shiny appliances they had previously only seen in the movies or magazines. Quite a lot was bought on credit.

'In England.' This was a phrase repeated *ad nauseum*.

'In England' in our house, you saved up for what you wanted – it was considered common to use the 'never-never'.

'In America' credit was a way of life and the brides gave in.

'I, of course, had to continue working now we were buying the house,' said Marie. 'It seemed as if we were always buying something – never managed to save.' This was a British habit discarded reluctantly, they had all been taught to save 'something for a rainy day'.

'I remember when I first went shopping with Ricky he insisted that I buy two dresses at the same time – I almost had a fit – it seemed so extravagant. He continued in the same fashion all our married life – always spending more than he made – it seemed to be the American way of life with that type of family that he came from. The house brought a succession of salesmen – storm windows, garden tools, kitchen equipment, drapes [curtains] and so on. We did buy combination storm windows and screen. They cost three hundred and fifty dollars which we, of course, put on a budget plan. I have never before or since had so many little books to make monthly payments on.'

There was also 'layaway'. This method of purchase could be applied in several directions, the bigger the item on 'layaway' the more dollars had to be forked out weekly and the length of time to pay off was not so extensive as if one bought on credit. 'An American friend showed me how I could pick out a dress and pay a dollar down and a dollar a week until eventually it was paid off and mine to wear,' said Brenda H. It must be remembered this was all before the days of credit cards.

Whichever way they began to furnish their homes or clothe themselves, loaded down with payments and hospital bills for all those babies, many plans for visits back 'home' were put in storage. The women compensated with little touches of England they'd brought with them – those wedding presents they could finally unpack, and the mementoes they had squirrelled away.

'Just before I left home, I sneaked the clock off the mantelpiece. It wasn't anything special, but I just wanted a touch of "home" with me.'

There were also house-warming presents that arrived: hanging horse brasses, tea caddies, tea cosies, teapots and then, a picture of the Queen. The pretty young Princess they had left behind had succeeded her father to the throne. 'Our family room is decorated like a British pub, tartan carpet, beams, etc.' As their financial situation improved and the husband gained promotion, they enlarged their new houses. 'Above the fireplace (artificial unfortunately) I have a coat of arms, Union Jack, and US flag'.

None of this overcame the fact that, for most girls, Mum just wasn't close enough to pop round for a cup of tea.

Dylan Thomas (1950)

The first of Dylan Thomas's four visits to America was made in the spring of 1950. Poetry-readings on the lecture-circuit were undertaken 'to make some money' – always badly needed. From these tours he was able to send cash home to his wife Caitlin at their cottage at Laugharne in Wales.

Letter to Caitlin Thomas
New York

Saturday, 25 February 1950

My darling far-away love, my precious Caitlin, my wife dear, I love you as I have never loved you, oh please remember me all day and every day as I remember you here in this terrible, beautiful, dream and nightmare city which would only be any good at all if we were together in it, if every night we clung together in it. I love you, Cat, my Cat, your body, heart, soul, everything, and I am always and entirely yours.

How are you, my dear? When did you go with Ivy back to Laugharne? I hope you didn't racket about too much because that makes you as ill as racketing makes me. And how is my beloved Colum and sweet fiend Aeron? Give them my love, please. I will myself write to Llewelyn over this weekend when I temporarily leave New York and go to stay with John Brinnin – a terribly nice man – in his house in the country an hour or so away. And how are the old ones? I'll write to them, too. I love you, I can see you, now this minute, your face and body, your beautiful hair, I can hear your lovely, un-understandable voice. I love you, and I love our children, and I love our house. Here, each night I have to take things to sleep. I am staying right in the middle of Manhattan, surrounded by skyscrapers infinitely taller and stranger than one has ever known from the pictures. I am staying in a room, an hotel room for the promised flat did not come off, on the 30th floor: and the noise all day and night: without some drug, I couldn't sleep at all. The hugest, heaviest lorries, police-cars, fire brigades, ambulances, all with their banshee sirens wailing and screaming, seem never to stop; Manhattan is built on rock, a lot of demolition work is going on to take up yet another super Skyscraper, and so there is almost continuous dynamite blasting. Aeroplanes just skim the tips of the great glimmering skyscrapers, some beautiful, some hellish. And I have no idea what on earth I am doing here in the very loud, mad middle of the last mad Empire on earth: – except to think of you, and love you, and to work for us. I have done two readings this week, to the Poetry Center of New York: each time there was an audience of about a thousand. I felt a very lonely, foreign midget orating up there, in a huge hall, before all those faces, but the readings went well. After this country weekend, where I arrange with Brinnin some of the rest of my appallingly extensive programme, I go to Harvard University, Cambridge, Boston, for about 2 days, then to Washington, then back to

New York, then, God knows, I daren't think, but I know it includes Yale, Princeton, Vassar – 3 big universities, as you know, old know-all - and Salt Lake City, where the Mormons live, and Notre Dame, the Jesuit College, and the middle West, Iowa, Ohio, Chicago – and Florida, the kind of exotic resort, and after that the mere thought makes my head roar like New York. To the places near to New York, Brinnin is driving me by car; to others I go by myself by train; to the more distant places, I fly. But whatever happens, by God I don't fly back. Including landing at Dublin, Canada, and Boston, for very short times, I was in the air, cooped up in the stratosphere, for 17 hours with 20 of the nastiest people in the sky. I had an awful hangover from our London do as well; the terrible height makes one's ears hurt like hell, one's lips chap, one's belly turn; and it went on forever. I'm coming back by boat.

I've been to a few parties, met lots of American poets, writers, critics, hangers-on, some very pleasant, all furiously polite and hospitable. But, apart from on one occasion, I've stuck nearly all the time to American beer, which, though thin, I like a lot and is ice-cold. I arrived, by the way, on the coldest day New York had had for years and years: it was 4 above zero. You'd have loved it. I never thought anything could be so cold, my ears nearly fell off: the wind just whipped through that monstrous duffle. But, as soon as I got into a room, the steamed (heat?) was worse: I think I can stand zero better than that, and, to the astonishment of natives, I keep all windows open to the top. I've been, too, to lots of famous places: up the top of the Empire State Building, the tallest there is, which terrified me so much, I had to come down at once; to Greenwich Village a feebler Soho but with stronger drinks; and this morning John Brinnin is driving us to Harlem. I say 'us', you see: in the same hotel as me is staying our old New Zealander, Allen Curnow, and I see quite a bit of him. I've met Auden, and Oscar Williams, a very odd, but kind, little man.

And now it must look to you, my Cat, as though I am enjoying myself here. I'm not. It's a nightmare, night and day; there never was such a place; I would never get used to the speed, the noise, the utter indifference of the crowds, the frightening politeness of the intellectuals, and, most of all, these huge phallic towers, up and up and up, hundreds of floors, into the imposs-ible sky. I feel so terrified of this place, I hardly dare to leave my hotel room – luxurious – until Brinnin or someone calls for me. Everybody uses the telephone all the time: it is like breathing: it is now nine o'clock in the morning, and I've had six calls: all from people whose names I did not catch to invite me to a little party at an address I had no idea of. And most of all most of all most of all, though, God, there's no need to say this to you who understand everything, I want to be with you. If we could be here together, everything would be all right. Never again would I come here, or to any far place, without you; but especially never to here. The rest of America may be all right, and perhaps I can understand it, but that is the last monument there is to the insane desire for power that shoots its buildings up to the stars and roars its engines louder and faster than they have ever been roared before and makes everything cost the earth and where the imminence of death is reflected in every last powerstroke and grab of the great money bosses, the big shots, the multis, one never sees. This morning we go down to see the other side beyond the skyscrapers:

black Harlem, starving Jewish East Side. A family of four in New York is very very poor on £14 a week. I'll buy some nylons all the same next week, and some tinned stuff. Anything else?

Last-minute practicalities: How does the money go? Have any new bills arrived. If so, send them, when you write (and write soon my dear love, my sweetheart, that is all I wait for except to come home to you) to the address on the kitchen wall. I enclose a cheque to Phil Raymond, and an open cheque to Gleed; pay that bill when you can.

Remember me. I love you. Write to me.

Your loving, loving Dylan

My dear Mother and Dad,

How are you both? How are you keeping, Dad? Get stronger every day, please, so that when I come home to Laugharne, you'll be up and about and able to join me for one at Phil's. And Mother, too, by that time, must be spry enough to be able to run, like a goat, down the Boat House path. I was very sad to leave you at such a moment, with Dad so weak and with Mother not fit to do all the little things for him that must be done. I was very sad, driving away that morning, leaving you and Laugharne, but it had, God help me, to be done.

Caitlin's told you, I suppose, about our London visit and Margaret's house and party at which such a lot of old – and some new – friends turned up, so I won't add anything to that. Helen and Bill, by the way, send their fondest regards to you both. The plane trip was ghastly. It seemed to go on for ever, and all my 20 fellow passengers seemed either actively unpleasant or moronic. The plane was stiflingly hot, and there wasn't any of the usual slight plane ventilation because of the height we travelled: in the stratosphere. We couldn't put down at the airport in Newfoundland because of icy weather conditions, so had to land somewhere in Canada. We got out for an hour: the cold was unbelievable, all the airport ground crew dressed up like Hudson Bay trappers and beating their great grizzly-bear-gloved hands together and stamping on the snow. And when we did, after several stifling eternities spent high as the moon, arrive in New York, it was to find it one of the coldest days there for years: when we got off the plane, it was four above zero. Luckily I'd rather the cold than the heat, and my old duffle coat was very helpful. John Brinnin, my agent, a terribly nice man, met me at the airport – about an hour from the centre of the city – and drove me to my hotel: right in Manhattan, among the unreal, shooting skyscrapers, and my room was on the thirtieth floor. Then we drove around the city, me gawping, like the country cousin I am, at this titanic dream world, soaring Babylon, everything monstrously rich and strange. That evening, I went to a party, given in my honour by the Professor of English at Columbia University: pack full of American dons, critics, writers, poets, all of the older and more respectable kind. Then home to the 30th floor, to hear, all night, the roaring of heavy lorries, the hooting of ships from the East River – I could see the Queen Mary, or Elizabeth from my window – and the banshee-screaming of police and ambulance sirens, just as on the films. There seems, at first sight, to be no reality at all in the life here: it is all an enormous façade of speed and efficiency and power behind which millions of little individuals are wrestling, in vain, with their own anxieties. The next day, Brinnin took me touring over half of this mad city: Broadway, Harlem, the Wall Street area, the East Side (where the Dead End Kids come from). I drank huge icy milkshakes in the drug-stores, and iced lager beer in the Third Avenue saloons almost every one of which is kept by an Irishman; I ate fried shrimps, fried chickens, and T-bone steak the size of a month's ration for an English family. I went to the top of the Empire State Building, the tallest skyscraper in the world, had one look at the nightmare city, and came down quickly. That night I went to a party given to me by some of the younger writers. The next day Brinnin and I did little but prepare my itinerary, which seems to take me to every state in the U.S.A., and that evening I made my first public appearance before an audience of 800 people. The reading seemed to go very well. After that, a reception, so-called, in the flat of a young man whose name I didn't catch: flats are called apartments here, but this one had 20 rooms. The next day all over the city again, meeting many people, mostly, again, writers, painters, or actors. And yesterday, Saturday, my second appearance in the same hall as the first: 800 again, the full seating capacity. Today, Sunday, I go to the country, with Brinnin, until Tuesday when I make my way to Yale University and from there to Harvard, Boston. After that, I've got about 10 readings in 20 days. Don't you worry about me, now. I'm feeling tiptop. By the way, the first people to come along to the stage-door after my first reading were three people from Llanelly, utter strangers, now living in N. York. I'll write again next week. Tell me everything. And Get Stronger. My forwarding address is c/o John Brinnin, Valley Road, West-port, Connecticut. All my love to you both. I think of you. Give my regards to Billy and Mrs Thomas.

Caitlin. Just to write down your name like that, Caitlin. I don't have to say My dear, My darling, my sweetheart, though I do say those words, to you in myself, all day and night. Caitlin. And all the words are in that one word. Caitlin, Caitlin, and I can see your blue eyes and your golden hair and your slow smile and your faraway voice. Your faraway voice is saying, now, at my ear, the words you said in your last letter, and thank you, dear, for the love you said and sent. I love you. Never forget that, for one single moment of the long, slow, sad Laugharne day, never forget it in your mazed trances, in your womb and your bones, in our bed at night. I love you. Over this continent I take your love inside me, your love goes with me up in the aeroplaned air, into all the hotel bedrooms where momentarily I open my bag – half full, as ever, of dirty shirts – and lay down my head and do not sleep until dawn because I can hear your heart beat beside me, your voice saying my name and our love above the noise of the night-traffic, above the neon flashing, deep in my loneliness, my love.

Today is Good Friday. I am writing this in an hotel bedroom in Vancouver, British Columbia, Canada, where yesterday I gave two readings, one in the University, one in the ballroom of the Vancouver Hotel, and made one broadcast. Vancouver is on the sea, and gigantic mountains doom above it. Behind the mountains lie other mountains, lies an unknown place, 30,000 miles of mountainous wilderness, the lost land of Columbia where cougars live and black bears. But the city of Vancouver is a quite handsome hellhole. It is, of course, being Canadian, more British than Cheltenham. I spoke last night – or read, I never lecture, how could I? – in front of two huge union jacks. The pubs – they are called beer-parlours – serve only beer, are not allowed to have whiskey or wine or any spirits at all – and are open only for a few hours a day. There are, in this monstrous hotel, two bars, one for Men, one for Women. They do not mix. Today, Good Friday, nothing is open nor will be open all day long. Everybody is pious and patriotic, apart from a few people in the university and my old friend Malcolm Lowry – do you remember Under the Volcano – who lives in a hut in the mountains and who came down to see me last night. Do you remember his wife Margery? We met her with Bill and Helen in Richmond, and, later, I think, in Oxford. She, anyway, remembers you well and sends you her love.

This afternoon I pick up my bag of soiled clothes and take a plane to Seattle. And thank God to be out of British Canada and back in the terrible United States of America. I read poems to the University there tonight. And then I have one day's rest in Seattle, and then on Sunday I fly to Montana, where the cowboys are, thousands of them, tell Ebie, and then on Monday I fly – it takes about 8 hours – to Los Angeles and Hollywood: the nightmare zenith of my mad, lonely tour.

But O, San Francisco! It is and has everything. Here in Canada, five hours away by plane, you wouldn't think that such a place as San Francisco could exist. The wonderful sunlight there, the hills, the great bridges, the Pacific at your shoes. Beautiful Chinatown. Every race in the world. The sardine fleets sailing out. The little cable-cars whizzing down the city hills. The lobsters, clams, and crabs. Oh, Cat, what food for you. Every kind of seafood there is. And all the people are open and friendly. And next year we both come to live there, you and me and Colum and maybe Aeron. This is sure, I am offered a job in two Universities. When I return to San Francisco next week, after Los Angeles, for another two readings, I shall know definitely which of the jobs to take. The pay will be enough to keep us comfortably, though no more. Everyone connected with the Universities is hard-up. But that doesn't matter. Seafood is cheap. Chinese food is cheaper, and lovely. Californian wine is good. The iced bock beer is good. What more? And the city is built on hills; it dances in the sun for nine months of the year, and the Pacific Ocean never runs dry.

Last week I went to Big Sur, a mountainous region by the sea, and stayed the night with Henry Miller. Tell Ivy that; she who hid his books in the oven. He lives about 6,000 feet up in the hills, over the blinding blue Pacific, in a hut of his own making. He has married a pretty young Polish girl, and they have two small children. He is gentle and mellow and gay.

I love you, Caitlin.

You asked my about the shops. I only know that the shops in the big cities, in New York, Chicago, San Francisco, are full of everything you have ever heard of and also full of everything one has never heard of or seen. The foodshops knock you down. All the women are smart, as in magazines – I mean, the women in the main streets; behind, lie the eternal poor, beaten, robbed, humiliated, spat upon, done to death – and slick and groomed. But they are not as beautiful as you. And when you and me are in San Francisco, you will be smarter and slicker than them, and the sea and sun will make you jump over the roofs and the trees, and you will never be tired again. Oh, my lovely dear, how I love you. I love you for ever and ever. I see you every moment of the day and night. I see you in our little house, tending the pomegranate of your eye. I love you. Kiss Colum, kiss Aeron and Llewelyn. Is Elizabeth with you? Remember me to her. I love you. Write, write, write, write, my sweetheart Caitlin. Write to me still c/o Brinnin; though the letters come late that way, I am sure of them. Do not despair. Do not be too tired. Be always good to me. I shall one day be in your arms, my own, however shy we shall be. Be good to me, as I am always to you. I love you. Think of us together in the San Franciscan sun, which we shall be. I love you. I want you. Oh, darling, when I was with you all the time, how did I ever shout at you? I love you. Think of me.

Your Dylan

I enclose a cheque for £15
I will write from Hollywood in three days.
I will send some more money.
I love you.

Edith Sitwell (1951)

When Edith Sitwell went on a reading-tour of America with her Osbert, she chose the part of Lady Macbeth. When asked why she said: 'Because she amuses me. Because the part suits my voice. And because she was one of my ancestresses.'

To John Lehmann

17 January 1951
Fairmont Hotel,
San Fransisco

My dear John,
   I was so delighted to get your letter. (I never got the previous one). A very happy new year to you, if such a thing is possible at this awful time.
   I am very distressed to hear about the proofs and expense of the American anthology. Now look here. I have for a very long time wanted to make a present to the firm of Messrs Lehmann. Please allow me to make a present of the book. In fact I won't take one. All I shall want will be Higham's fee paying.
   I've been awfully ill. I got amoebic dysentery in Mexico, and really thought

I was dying. However I didn't die. As soon as I was up again, long before I was fit to travel, I had to spend three days and three nights (and fourteen hours extra because the Mexican train was late) in the train, because of the infernal fussing of the man who had engaged us to speak in Los Angeles.

As a result of fatigue, I got bronchitis, for the second time in three months. I had to give three readings here, coughing my head off. However, the reading in Hollywood was a great success, I do think. Lots of film stars, including Harpo Marx, came. And during my reading of the *Macbeth* sleep walking scene, I was just announcing that Hell is murky, when a poor gentleman in the audience uttered the most piercing shrieks, and was carried out by four men, foaming at the mouth. As one of the spectators said to me, 'You ought to be awfully pleased. It was one of the most flattering things I have ever seen.'

I've made records of that scene, the pillow scene from *Othello*, Cleopatra's death scene, etc., for the Columbia records. There will be *rough* copies ready by the time we return, and I'll bring them with me.

In Hollwood I got into a Laocoon entanglement with Miss Mary Pickford, that lasted for ¾ of an hour. Miss P . . . discoursed to me of her role as Little Fauntleroy, and said she always regarded herself as a Spiritual Beacon. We also met Miss Ethel Barrymore, who was delightful, although Osbert ascribes my bronchitis to her, as she was breathing heavily. – I must say I couldn't have enjoyed Hollywood more. We think all the waiters at the Hotel were suffering from the effects of marijuana, their conduct was so strange. They would shriek with laughter suddenly, join in the conversations, and lean on the sofa on which we sat for our meals, putting their heads between ours. . . .

John Gielgud (1952)

By the time he played Cassius in Julius Caesar *in 1952, John Gielgud had secured a reputation as one of the greatest Shakespearean actors of the century and a director of considerable talent. As he recalls, in* An Actor and his Time, *he was rather embarrassed by the awe in which he was held, particularly by Marlon Brando.*

Joseph Mankiewicz's *Julius Caesar*, made in 1952, was the first film I really enjoyed making. The producers wanted to emphasize the political side of the play and Caesar was played as a Tammany boss, so it was said, though I did not see much sign of it. One or two effective scenes in the play were left out, such as the 'Cinna the poet' scene and the scene when Portia sends the boy to the Senate House, but the film was made with sincerity and was quite well mounted, except for the battle scenes, which were done in a great hurry in the Hollywood Bowl on the last day of shooting, when I was nearly killed by a horse leaping on top of me. The set for Caesar's house appeared to be so full of gongs and statues and elephants' tusks that you could hardly move, so I plucked up my courage and said to Mankiewicz: 'I don't think Roman rooms were quite so full of clutter as this,' and he had a lot of it taken away. The big set for the opening scene had been built for *Ben Hur* in Italy and then transferred to Hollywood and re-erected. But when I took a very erudite friend to see the Forum set one day he remarked: 'This is quite good, but all the statues are of Emperors who haven't been born yet.'

Brutus was played by James Mason and I very much enjoyed working with him and thought his performance under-rated by the critics, since Brutus is certainly the most difficult part in the play. He was extremely kind and generous to me. I was the only Englishman out there (of course Mason was English too, but he had not been in England for a long time) and I was afraid the Americans would think I was the star actor from London who had come over to teach them how to play Shakespeare. So I kept my mouth shut as much as possible and we all got on very well together. I got the part of Cassius almost by accident. Mankiewicz had come to London to get Paul Scofield to play Mark Antony. He saw me as Benedick (Paul was playing Don Pedro in my production) and engaged me for Cassius. But when Brando's tests for Antony arrived they were so successful that he was engaged and Scofield never even made the test.

I was amused to find that the huge crowd of extras were all paid different salaries. The ones in the front row who had the most striking faces were the highest paid, next came those who were only vaguely seen, and the ones at the back of the crowd who were not seen at all were the lowest paid but were able to keep their trousers on under their togas. One of my favourite moments was when a whole menagerie of animals, sheep, dogs and pigeons, was brought in to make the streets of Rome look more lively. The pigeons were put on the statues and plinths and I could not understand why they did not fly away. I was told later that their wings were clipped. Next day, I was waiting to go on the set when one of the pigeons, which had been perched on a pillar, jumped off and began walking about on the floor of the studio. A hefty cowboy, who evidently looked after all the animals, dashed up and yelled at the bird, 'Get back, get back, don't you want to work tomorrow?' I was told by a friend who acted in a film with Lassie, the star dog, that every day they used to bring an entire wagonful of Lassies to the studio: the smiling Lassie, the scowling Lassie, the gloomy Lassie and so on, and there was a great argument when she won an Academy prize as to which Lassie should appear at the dinner to collect the coveted award.

I was surprised to find that I did not have to alter my stage performance for the film to any great extent, and my knowledge of the play was a great help. Marlon Brando, on the other hand, was greatly hampered by the fact that he did not know how the scenes were placed by Shakespeare or how they progressed from one climax to another. They would photograph him for a couple of days in the taxing speeches of the Forum scene, and then he would lose his voice and be unable to work. They would fill in time by filming the extras, taking a lot of shots of faces in the crowd responding, then Brando would recover and come down to the studio to do another speech. I imagine that the director hoped he could put it all together in the cutting-room, but Shakespeare is too big for that.

Brando was very self-conscious and modest, it seemed to me. He would ·

come on to the set in his fine, tomato-coloured toga, his hair cropped in a straight fringe, and would look around nervously, expecting to find someone making fun of his appearance. Then he would take out a cigarette and stick it behind his ear. He told me that he was so well-off that he sent all his money home to his father and that he really had no need to work at all. I begged him to play Hamlet, and said that I would like to direct him if he did, but he said he never wanted to go back to the theatre.

I had only one scene with him in the film. We went through the speeches in the morning and he asked me: 'What did you think of the way I did those speeches?' So I went through them with him and made some suggestions. He thanked me very politely and went away. The next morning, when we shot the scene, I found that he had taken note of everything I had said and spoke the lines exactly as I had suggested.

The next time I came down to shoot, Mankiewicz said: 'Oh Marlon's done the great speech over the body absolutely marvellously,' and asked me to see the rushes, which I did not like very much. I thought he was giving a bad imitation of Olivier, but it was hardly my place to say so. I never met Brando again, which was a pity because I felt that he was enormously responsive. The very first day I was introduced to him he said, 'You must come and do a speech for me – one of my Antony speeches. I've got a tape-recorder in my dressing-room.' He had tapes of Maurice Evans and John Barrymore and three or four other actors and listened to them every day to improve his diction. I thought he would have made a wonderful Oedipus.

After *Caesar*, I had no film offers until I did Clarence for Olivier in *Richard III*, which involved only a few short scenes. Then Tony Richardson asked me to go to Hollywood to play in *The Loved One* from the Evelyn Waugh novel. We became good friends at once, and in 1967 he asked me to play Lord Raglan in *The Charge of the Light Brigade*, a most amusingly written part.

Alec Guinness (1955)

Before his Oscar-winning performance in Bridge on the River Kwai *Alec Guinness's most famous film-parts were comic, as Fagin in* Oliver Twist *and the entire Gascoyne family in* Kind Hearts and Coronets. *His first Hollywood film coincided with a deepening interest in religion and a number of mysterious psychic experiences; one of which he related in this extract from* Blessings in Disguise.

In the autumn of 1955 I went to Los Angeles to make my first Hollywood film, *The Swan*, with Grace Kelly and Louis Jourdan. I arrived, tired and crumpled after a sixteen-hour flight from Copenhagen. Thelma Moss, who had written the film script of *Father Brown* (*The Detective* in the USA), had said she wished to take me out to dinner my first night in town. We arrived at three restaurants of repute at each of which we were refused admission because she was wearing slacks (ah, far-off days), and finally settled for a delightful little Italian bistro, where she was confident of a welcome. When we got there – Los Angeles is an endless city to drive through – there was no table available. As we walked disconsolately away I said, 'I don't care where we eat or what. Just something, somewhere.' I became aware of running, sneakered feet behind us and turned to face a fair young man in sweat-shirt and blue-jeans. 'You want a table?' he asked. 'Join me. My name is James Dean.' We followed him gratefully, but on the way back to the restaurant he turned into a car-park, saying, 'I'd like to show you something.' Among the other cars there was what looked like a large, shiny, silver parcel wrapped in cellophane and tied with ribbon. 'It's just been delivered,' he said, with bursting pride. 'I haven't even driven it yet.' The sports-car looked sinister to me, although it had a large bunch of red carnations resting on the bonnet. 'How fast is it?' I asked. 'She'll do a hundred and fifty,' he replied. Exhausted, hungry, feeling a little ill-tempered in spite of Dean's kindness, I heard myself saying in a voice I could hardly recognise as my own, 'Please, never get in it.' I looked at my watch. 'It is now ten o'clock, Friday the 23rd of September, 1955. If you get in that car you will be found dead in it by this time next week.' He laughed. 'Oh, shucks! Don't be so mean!' I apologised for what I had said, explaining it was lack of sleep and food. Thelma Moss and I joined him at his table and he proved an agreeable, generous host, and was very funny about Lee Strasberg, the Actors' Studio and the Method. We parted an hour later, full of smiles. No further reference was made to the wrapped-up car. Thelma was relieved by the outcome of the evening and rather impressed. In my heart I was uneasy – with myself. At four o'clock in the afternoon of the following Friday James Dean was dead, killed while driving the car.

David Niven (1956)

David Niven wrote arguably the most amusing view of Hollywood in his memoirs, The Moon's a Balloon.

One Sunday afternoon, the phone rang in the Pink House.

'This is Mike Todd. I'm over at Joe Schenck's. I wanna see you. Get your ass over here.'

I was halfway through a polite excuse before I realised that he had long since hung up. I had never met Todd but I had heard a hundred stories about the legendary master showman, gambler, promoter or con man – everyone saw him from a different angle.

We had a houseful of friends that afternoon and the consensus of opinion was that, whatever else, Todd was always interesting and I should indeed get my ass over to Joe Schenck's.

When I arrived, Todd was by the pool. Of medium height and perfect proportions, he was tanned dark mahogany. He wore the briefest of swimming slips. On his head was a white ten-gallon hat, in his mouth was a cigar of grotesque proportions.

He had no time for preliminaries.

'Ever heard of Jules Verne?'

'Yes, of course.'

'Ever read *Around the World in 80 Days?*'

'I was weaned on it.'

'I've never made a picture before but I'm gonna make this one . . . How'd you like to play Phileas Fogg?'

My heart bounded. 'I'd do it for nothing.'

Todd tossed aside his hat and cigar.

'You gotta deal,' he said and disappeared beneath the surface of the pool.

From that moment till the time, six months later, that the picture was finished, I lived in an atmosphere of pure fantasy. Nobody knows where Todd raised the necessary seven million dollars and he certainly didn't raise it all at once because several times production ground to a halt while strange, swarthy gentlemen arrived from Chicago for urgent consultations. For weeks on end we went unpaid. Todd induced S. J. Perelman to write the screen play and employed John Farrow to direct it.

The Mexican bullfighter comedian, Cantinflas, arrived to play my valet, Passepartout, and Shirley MacLaine was signed to play Princess Aouda.

'But who the hell do we got to play Mr. Fix the Detective?' said Todd, chomping on the inevitable cigar.

'How about Robert Newton?' I suggested.

Todd was enchanted with the idea and immediately put in a call.

'But I warn you, Mike,' I said, feeling every kind of heel, 'Bobbie is a great friend of mine but he does drink a lot these days and you must protect yourself. Lots of people are scared to employ him – he disappears.'

'I want to see Newton,' said Todd firmly, 'and when he comes in, I want you here in the office.'

'For Christ's sake, don't tell him I said anything,' I begged, 'he'll never forgive me.'

A little later, Bobbie Newton shuffled in. I hadn't seen him for some weeks and it was obvious that he had been on a bender of heroic proportions.

Todd went into his routine.

'Ever heard of Jules Verne?'

'Ah, dear fellow,' said Newton, 'what a scribe!'

'*80 Days Around the World?*'

'A glorious piece, old cock.'

'How'd you like to play Mr. Fix?'

'A splendid role,' said Bobbie, rolling his eyes. 'Do I understand you are offering it to me, dear boy?'

'I might,' said Todd and I felt like the slimiest worm when he continued, 'But your pal, Niven here, says you're a lush.'

'Aah!' said Newton, 'my pal, Niven, is a master of the understatement.'

He was hired immediately and gave his word of honour to Todd that he would go on the wagon for the duration of the picture. He stuck manfully to his promise.

On location at Durango, Colorado, Bobbie and I went off every evening after shooting to catch big, fighting rainbow trout in the mountain lakes. One cold autumn sunset with streaks of blue wood-smoke clinging to the surface of the water and the last rays of the sun falling on the glorious colours of the aspens and beeches, Bobbie confessed to me that his promise to Todd had not really been all that difficult because that very morning his doctor had warned him that one more session with the bottle would almost certainly be fatal. Two weeks after we finished the picture, Todd called some of us back for an added scene on a ship. Bobbie Newton was only required for one day but when he arrived for work, a roaring delivery of 'Once more unto the breach . . .' announced alarming news. 'Oh, Bobbie,' I said, 'what have you done to yourself.'

He put his arm around my neck and tears rolled down his swollen cheeks. 'Don't chide me, dear fellow, please don't chide me,' he said.

Within a very few days, the doctor's warnings to that warm-hearted, talented and wonderful soul proved tragically correct.

If Todd had difficulty in raising money for his epic, he seemed to have none persuading the biggest names in show business to play small 'cameos' for fun. We started shooting in Spain with Louis Miguel Dominguin playing himself in the bullring, and there, after a falling out, Todd replaced the director, John Farrow, by the young Englishman, Michael Anderson.

With gorgeous Elizabeth [Taylor] by his side, Todd remained undefeated to the end even when the sheriff of Los Angeles locked up the finished footage of his picture, thereby immobilising his only asset with the State of California till various local creditors had been mollified.

Todd was allowed to assemble and score the film during the day under the watchful eye of a sheriff's deputy but at night, back it went into the vault.

Somehow, Todd staved off the enemy and, at last, the picture was ready for presentation. The sheriff was persuaded to allow the film to travel to New York for its big gala opening at the Rivoli Theatre.

'You gotta get your ass back East,' Todd told me. 'You gotta be there at the pay-out window.'

Todd sent air tickets and installed us in the most expensive apartment in the St. Regis Hotel. There was a present for Hjördis when we arrived and the rooms were full of flowers; champagne and caviar were waiting for us.

The opening was a Todd bonanza; mounted police held back the screaming crowds as the audience of a thousand famous people in evening dress filed into the theatre. Every member of the audience received a beautifully bound and illustrated programme embossed in gold on the cover with the name of each recipient. After the showing, Todd gave a champagne supper for fifteen hundred at the Astor Hotel.

Where did he get the money for all this? The answer, according to Bennett Cerf of Random House, who produced the programme, was that he didn't. The morning after the opening, his cheque made out to the publishers – bounced.

No matter, Gambler Todd had got right to the wire with his last penny and when the audience had finished cheering and the ecstatic reviews were being read, there he was standing happily at the pay-out window.

The picture won the Academy Award as the Best Picture of the Year and became one of the biggest money spinners of all time.

Todd married Elizabeth and gave her a diamond the size of a skating rink. He bought himself a twin-engined plane.

Hjördis and I, with peculiar logic, decided that with a lot of good pictures now being offered to me, it was the ideal moment to go away from Hollywood for a few months so we flew off around the world.

Nikita Khruschev (1959)

From 1953 to 1964 Nikita Khruschev (1894–1971) was first secretary of the Russian Communist Party. This is an extract from a speech he gave in the studios of Twentieth Century Fox in Hollywood on September 21st 1959.

In conclusion, I want to express once more my heartfelt thanks for the invitation to visit your country, and to say that my companions and I are pleased with our stay in America. But, on the other hand, I cannot help voicing my disappointment, voicing some surprise, at a certain circumstance.

We have always regarded the United States as a strong, well-organized state whose people have a highly-developed culture. Here we are now, in your city, where you have the cream of the artistic world – film stars, as you say in your country. Also living here are industrial workers, ordinary Americans, people of a vast variety of trades. We should have liked to meet them, to see how they live, and how they work and rest. Now just think of it, I, a Soviet man, the Prime Minister of the Soviet Union, have come to you as a guest; when I was on my way here, an itinerary was drawn up for me and a programme of what I could see here and what places I could visit. It was planned, among other things, that I would visit Disneyland. But I have just been told that I cannot go to Disneyland. (*Laughter.*) Why not? I asked. Is it by any chance because you now have rocket-launching pads there? (*Laughter.*) 'No,' they tell me,'you can't go there because' – just listen to this! – 'the American authorities cannot guarantee your safety if you go there.'

What is it? Has cholera or plague broken out there that I might catch? (*Laughter.*) Or has Disneyland been seized by bandits who might destroy me? But your policemen are such strong men, they could lift a bull by the horns. Surely they could deal effectively with the bandits! Then I said I should like to go to Disneyland just the same and see how Americans spend their leisure. (*Applause.*) 'Do as you like,' they answered me, 'but in that case we cannot guarantee your safety.' What was I to do – go and commit suicide? (*Laughter.*) This is the situation I, your guest, find myself in! It is more than I can understand. I won't know how to explain it to my people. Come to our country if you like, we will go with anyone, you may walk in our streets and parks, and I guarantee that a foreign guest will hear nothing from Soviet people but words of respect and welcome. What am I to say to the organizers of my U.S. tour? I thought you had a well-organized household. Putting me in a closed car and stewing me in the sun is not the right way to guarantee my safety. I thought I could walk freely in your country and meet Americans. But I am told it's impossible. This development causes me bitter regret and I cannot but express my disappointment.

You might say, 'What a restless guest.' But I keep to the Russian maxim, 'Break bread with me, but speak your mind.' And that should in no way affect our friendly relations.

Please forgive me for speaking somewhat vehemently or heatedly. But the temperature here is to blame for it, to some extent. (*Laughter.*) Besides, Mr. Skouras had warmed me up to it. (*Laughter, applause.*) Please forgive me if I have said anything not quite pleasing to your ear, if I have let slip anything that has jarred you a little. The sentiment that guided me in speaking here before you was one of friendship and respect for you, for your people and for your President, Mr. Eisenhower.

Thank you for your attention. Thank you, dear friends, thank you, Mr. Johnston. (*Stormy, prolonged applause.*)

Malcolm Muggeridge (1962)

Originally a journalist – he was editor of Punch *in the fifties – Muggeridge was one of the first of the new breed of television personalities, making frequent appearances on both sides of the Atlantic. He was also in much demand for lectures, and this is one of several tours he made to the United States.*

September 27, 1962
Coming over Triboro Bridge, as always, the lift to one's spirits. Thought of the car-load in *The Great Gatsby* making for New York. A misty evening; huge cars bumper to bumper, hugely powered, and crawling along. America.

At about three in the morning I looked out of my hotel window; drizzling, some lights still on, a few cars, steam rising from the pavement as though the city were on fire. Perhaps it is. Sleepless, I watched the awakening; garbage men noisily at work, more lights coming on, traffic gradually increasing. In the grey light, it was like being in a prison; walls everywhere, no escape.

Clark, my dear old friend, a Negro chauffeur, met me at the airport. He laughs and laughs with abandon. This unrestrained laughter of American Negroes may in the end subdue the wry-faced whites. They begin to look a little furtive even here.

N.B. Great distinction of Americans in menial employment, like lift men and waiters. They have none of the dejected resentfulness of their European equivalent. They might be professors or diplomats. A lift man said to me that he liked his work. It brought him into contact with a lot of people. Happiness can be pursued as well in one job as in another. I never feel with Americans (outside teachers, non-best-selling writers, etc.) that they're eaten up with a sense of missing things.

October 2, 1962
New sort of isolationism – inward, of the spirit. Americans retreating into America and Americanism despite treaties and commitments. In some ways, out of the *Zeitgeist*. The Kennedy set-up somehow malodorous. He's an IBM equipped to speak and gesticulate, particularly to move his forearm up and down with mechanical dead emphasis.

The sweetness of Americans – 'You're welcome!' 'May I shake your hand?' Later, in Cincinnati, feeling full of distaste for America and Americans, a waiter brought tea and cookies to my hotel room. 'It's a double portion today,' he said, 'because it's pay day.' He showed me his cheque. We both began to laugh uproariously.

Beaver – an American girls' college near Philadelphia. The college is a preposterous castle, built at a cost of $2m. by some Philadelphia tycoon at the turn of the century; dark, massive, unspeakable. Talking about this abomination aware, just in time, that it was taken seriously. The girls preferred the dormitory in it to the modern ones. They found it romantic, almost hallowed. Walked round the campus reflecting on the perfection of this false castle as a symbol of the American dream, of the American attitude to Europe. A folly; a joke in its sham, ponderous antiquity – massive, expensive, preposterous, phoney. Yet, to them, an authentic castle. Thus are Americans involved in Europe's decay, but unaware of the perils of their involvement because they had vested it with a seeming solidity. Everything reconstructed, down to the smallest and most abject details. The Europe the Americans imagine themselves to be defending is, in fact, a nineteenth-century, transatlantic model.

One of those dry, agreeable Americans, head of the English Faculty at Beaver, and the only other male besides myself around the place, told me how the Ford Foundation had decided to entrust the design of their pavilion at the 1964 World Fair jointly to a talented Japanese architect, Minoui Yamasaki, and Walt Disney, thereby, as they hoped, combining good taste and popularity. A pity Yamasaki wouldn't accept the collaboration. As my informant said, like breeding from Arthur Miller and Marilyn Monroe with the idea of producing some combination of their talents – a literate sex symbol, a third force. 150 million Americans can't be wrong, Disney has said. But they can.

October 3, 1962 – Potsdam near Messena
Exquisite autumn day, flying low up the Hudson Valley, leaves gloriously autumnal. This part of America, towards the Canadian frontier, once much more prosperous than now (wood-pulp industry now derelict); has an air of decay. The affluent society is not really affluent at all; only flushed in places, with the blood draining away in others.

The inconceivable boredom that can overwhelm one in these American towns. 'Miss K has done a lot for America – culture – elegant turn-out.' I downed my fifteenth cup of coffee, and said that I wished Miss K wouldn't smile so much but spent just half an hour a day scowling.

The town waking up. Noisy gear changes, the crowing of the cock; soon a roar of passing automobiles. The St Lawrence River seen out of my window, with the mist dissolving in the morning sunshine. Students variously attired going willingly to school. Education a mighty endeavour, a booming industry; the Gross National Mind ever soaring upwards.

October 14, 1962 – Indianapolis
Another metropolis of lights, shimmering, moving, changing. Neon lighted faces somehow look very weary. Only the cars glisten with new life. Driving them, American faces fall into repose and serenity. They are not only the index of American prosperity; they are that prosperity.

October 15, 1962 – Chicago
The business Americans are constantly seen in hotels, and travelling about; in a black alpaca-type suit, trim white shirt with starched cuffs and collar; hair fairly close cut, well-shaved and well groomed. They're quite indistinguishable from one another, like Guards Officers.

Chicago Lakeside Drive a solid throng of motor cars coming into town in the morning, and returning in the evening. By the lake's edge practically no one. I stood there for quite a while, feeling detached from the town looming up in front of me, and the roar of the cars going by.

October 16, 1962 – Oshkosh
Tiny churches and chapels in lonely places, strangely named – Chapel of the Birthright; rather touching, a tiny, bizarre gesture of faith.

At Oshkosh, as at Beaver College, large Elizabethan style residence constructed by pulp tycoon; new art gallery, mostly dedicated to nineteenth-century American painter, Innes. Ghastly edifice. Shown round by curator, in authentic Harris Tweed deep brown jacket, who pointed out with pride the various styles in the house's architecture, and in interior decoration. The death-watch beetle is at work here, too. Not by Communism, or its own internal violence and nationalism, will America die, but through a mania to participate in our dry rot. The immigrants were cheated. They did not escape from Europe, but took Europe with them.

October 22, 1962 – Colorado Springs
The lush motel, carpeted, full of sounds, sweet airs. A blue, warmed pool, with wreaths of steam rising from it. All under steam heat, all neon-lighted; all hermetically sealed against the elements, against life.

President Kennedy on the screen, perhaps announcing the end of the world; pudding-faced, and reading from a paper like a child, knowing the words, but not always making sense out of the sentences. His appearance was preceded by an ad for some sort of jet-toy – a little boy firing, and triumphantly saying: 'Got it!' (Which was the ad and which the Presidential broadcast?)

October 26, 1962 – Salt Lake City
Met at airport by Mormon youth with gentle eyes who'd been missionary in England. 'We can at least be perfect in abstinence and in talking.' In other respects – like living up to the Gospel, perfection is unattainable. Took a walk towards the mountains, reflecting (Cuban crisis still going)

that perhaps one might get cut off in Salt Lake City and spend one's remaining days among the Mormons. If this happened, they'd claim, plausibly enough, that Brigham Young foresaw it all, the nuclear holocaust, also he said 'This is the place!' A prophecy fulfilled. No support among Mormons, however, when I hopefully suggest signs and portents presaging the world's end. No more than usual, they insist. 'Life is too marvellous,' I say in my lecture, 'to be taken seriously, and truth too stupendous and luminous to be solemnly propounded,' and mean it, too.

October 29, 1962 – San Francisco, California
Everyone says San Francisco nicest town in US. I often say it, but doubt if it's true. In most moods, secretly, prefer the straight American product. Walked up and down the hills. Heard that Khruschev had seemingly climbed down over Cuba.

Lunched at the Pacific Club with Scottish business man and two of his cronies. All very rich. English-style club. Americans of English origin like sahibs, but the others coming up – coloured, Puerto Ricans, Mexicans, etc. Will they ultimately, perhaps, get self-government, like the Indians and Africans? Anti-semitism prevalent, but rarely admitted.

October 30, 1962 – Modesto, California
Caught Greyhound bus – cheapest form of travel. Queuing for my bus with poor people, coloured, etc., felt a mounting blissful sense of relief at being with them. Great truth in saying that the poor are blessed. All the manifestations of riches contain misery, implicit if not explicit. Joyousness comes from below. In bus, all windows sealed, glass blue-tinted. Once again the governing American passion to exclude the world – air, sound, light, food, sensuality. Everything wrapped, packaged.

After my lecture sat with several Faculty figures and listened to record of Canadian radio satire on McCarthy hearings. Quite a conspiratorial air. We were like an underground company daring to listen to clandestine broadcast, glancing anxiously over our shoulders to make certain we were unobserved. Actually, the satire was harmless enough, and in some respects distorted. Milton and Cromwell appeared as champions of freedom. Tried to explain that they had been on the other side. Liberalism, I reflected, always wrong whichever way it's played.

October 31, 1962 – Los Angeles, California
Los Angeles probably most horrible town in the world, enveloped in hurtful smog, all roads; a truly corrupted distorted place. One feels it at once on arrival. My hotel room at Pasadena had a balcony on which I could breathe, and from which see nearby mountains. I looked out with delight, and enjoyed the soft warm night.

At UCLA great gathering, good lecture, uproarious laughter and applause. Afterwards, taken off by weird disorderly woman who said she wanted to take my photograph. Drove back with her and her son to what was obviously rather affluent house at Santa Monica, which should have been overlooking the sea, but actually only overlooked smog.

November 6, 1962 – San Diego, Rancho Santa Fe

San Diego naval base. Place full of sailors who all fell asleep with that touching, rather exquisite abandon of the very tired and the very young. Lady (Mrs Ames) met me and showed me the sights of San Diego before leaving for Rancho Santa Fe. The 300 affluent housing area, etc. A doubt seized her. 'Are you really interested?' I said I was. The Rancho turned out to be an immensely lush little pocket of life; no poor, no Jews, all very elegant. Stayed at the Inn, full of golfers, ageing executives with the faces of boys; weirdly youthful under their grizzled hair and wrinkles. Evening of the Congressional elections. The ladies solid for Nixon.

November 16, 1962 – Cincinnati, Ohio

Journalist telephoned to my hotel room to say: 'Winston Churchill said Cincinnati one of the most beautiful inland cities in the world. Do you agree?' 'No,' I replied. Typical politician's remark, with the qualification 'inland city' to provide a sort of justification for the outrageous lie. Spent the day, as many another, walking about the streets. On the city's outskirts saw small shop with, on the window: 'Eternity, eternity, how will you pass eternity?' These American towns indistinguishable from one another. All one remembers of them is some trivial occurrence; yet I know that whenever I meet an American who comes from Cincinnati I shall say I've been there, and he'll be enthralled.

November 18, 1962 – Chicago

In the evening, sat rather gloomily in a bar. Woman perched next to me mentioned that she was fond of opera, looking forward to *Samson and Delilah*. I bring this out in people. Americans, in their happiness, keep together, excluding outsiders. This is why, alone, we can be so lonely in American cities. Strolling, in such a mood, after the meal, I noticed that Lenny Bruce was appearing at a sort of cabaret place; went in, was recognized by a girl at the ticket place, who arranged for me to see the show, though packed out. Bruce dressed in a kind of swami's suit. Act consisted of a monologue, disconnected in theme; a sort of whimpering, spiteful, petulant complaint against the times and man's lot today. Not particularly funny, but the audience laughed in a nervous sort of way when he used an obscene word ('shit', for instance), or at some sally against nuclear war, etc. Occasionally used Yiddish word, which aroused easier laughter. At my table married couple – mother-in-law, she from New Orleans, wife former air hostess, and her husband. Mother-in-law said she'd been married forty years, wonderful husband, wonderful son-in-law, wonderful home. All wonderful. Somehow, from there, got on to the subject of mistresses. Ex-air hostess said American women liked to be wives and mistresses in one. Large assignment, I said.

November 19, 1962 – Pittsburgh

Met at airport by Monsignor Ryan, large, amiable, talkative man. Confirmed opinion I'd long held that Roman Catholic clergy are having a Reformation of their own now, possibly at the wrong time and in the wrong way. Anyway, they're very evangelical, hearty, anti-ritualist and Italianate. Ryan drove me round the town, talking away. We looked in at Catholic cathedral to see modern statue of St Joan. Reminded me of 1914–18 war memorials; touch of T. E. Lawrence and of Sybil Thorndyke. (I've often wondered what Joan of Arc was really like; probably more in the genre of Edith Summerskill or Sitwell than of Peggy Ashcroft.)

Joined at dinner by characters from the university and art gallery. Talked about education (Pittsburg University's budget $38m). Was it any good? Ryan talked all the way back to his college about how celibacy of clergy now out of date, as Latin Liturgy was.

Always, when I'm with Catholics, I realize I could never join them.[1] All the same, happy day here. Ryan told me rather scornfully how the nuns had set up a shrine to St Philomena, who, he said, probably never existed. 'All the same, it's a pretty name,' I said. He wouldn't have it. 'The shrine has been deactivated,' he said. Even so, I saw a party of nuns visiting it.

November 21, 1962 – Richmond, Virginia
One is less conscious of racial hostility in the south than in the north. All the negroes seem to be smiling. Perhaps the warmer climate suits them better. Or maybe the admission of segregation as distinct from its practice without being admitted, as in Chicago, makes for easier relations.

At Richmond airport got into conversation in cafeteria with substantial citizen who turned out to be some sort of clerical salesman. Americans love selling. It brings out all their ardour. Far from regarding it a demeaning occupation, they glory in it, love to talk about it. Case I heard of – motor car salesman so successful that he became highly paid executive. Used occasionally even then to slip out and sell a car to a difficult customer just for the sheer joy of it.

Everywhere I went, everyone I met, however casually, on this tour for some reason fixed photographically in my memory. Even, in some cases, people I passed along airport corridors. Perceptions heightened.

Plane late in starting, and arrived New York in drenching rain; road into town dense with Thanksgiving Day traffic, lights liquid and wavering in the watery air.

Farewell America
Driving over the Triboro Bridge, on arrival in New York, is always an exhilarating moment. This is especially true if one arrives in the evening. The lighted skyscrapers acquire a particular elegance as darkness descends, like a sluttish woman when she has dressed and got herself up for a dinner party.

Equally, the moment of departure is exhilarating. One loves to leave.

Almost everything that has been said about America is both true and false. It is enormously monotonous, and infinitely varied. Its pace is fast to the point of exhaustion and slow to the point of exasperation. Americans are kind and generous, and, at the same time, hard and demanding. They tell you everything about themselves in the first half hour of a casual acquaintanceship, and retreat behind a wall of impenetrable reserve.

The same man whose husky grace seems to fit him to climb Mount Everest sucks down vitamin pills to keep up his strength, and anxiously weighs himself each morning like a ballerina or jockey fearful of putting on

[1] Muggeridge was received into the Roman Catholic Church in 1982.

weight. No enterprise is too difficult and extensive to be attempted, some of the most trivial remain unattempted. Highways with six lanes a side half unprotected over open railway level-crossings. Huge plates of food fail to nourish, newspapers as big as an encyclopedia fail to inform.

A sense of being the world's arbiter is combined with an agonized need to be reassured about whether the rest of mankind take this pretention seriously. Dr Gallup is a statistical physician whose services are in constant demand. Cuba pulverises America with fright; they can survey, unafraid, Russia's formidable battery of nuclear weapons. They love to get into Burke's *Landed Gentry*, and pride themselves on calling the boss by his Christian name.

Of all countries, America is the one where a stranger may enjoy the most open-handed and affectionate hospitality, and also the one where he can be most lonely. Affluence and dread of penury exist side by side. The millionaire fears that he will soon be penniless; the bum is sure that he will soon be a millionaire.

Virtue is highly regarded, irregular lives are no impediment to public adulation. The Gabors and Mrs Eleanor Roosevelt alike enjoy public esteem. A twelfth marriage is as romantic an occasion as a first one, and college students, in the same breath, ask questions about Chaucer and Jack Paar.

Any gadget which procures leisure is sure of a ready appeal. Yet leisure is abhorrent, and needs to be filled extraneously. On Sundays, as P. G. Wodehouse said, everyone in Jacksonville drives to Johnsonville, and everyone in Johnsonville drives to Jacksonville. Even crossing the Arizona desert car radios are turned on, and the few moments of a lift's ascent or descent requires piped music to be bearable.

Juke boxes play as assiduously in Alaska as in Brooklyn. The fight against silence is assiduously waged. Dentists drill decayed molars to music; and the commuters, as they homeward plod their weary way, are assailed in the terminal stations by pop songs, and, at Christmas time, carols. Afternoon papers appear in the morning, and morning ones in the early evening. Protest processions of unemployed make their way to Washington in a motorcade, and outside one of the largest atomic missile installations appears the notice: 'Our Profession Is Peace' – a slogan which uncannily recalls the Ministry of Peace in Orwell's *1984*.

I decided to make my farewells to a country, not of humans, but of mechanical brains. Though it was a Sunday, several of them were thinking hard, with lights flashing, and bells ringing. As some interesting thought occurred to one or other of them, an attached pointer sprang into sudden activity. Hoping to share its moment of truth, I looked over its shoulder. Alas, they all seemed that day to be wholly preoccupied with figures. There was no divine revelation. I should have liked to ask them about an after-life, and when the end of the world was to be expected, but felt it would be discourteous to intrude upon their cogitations. One of them was ready to play draughts with me, but was, I gather, unbeatable. Another was struggling to translate *Little Red Riding Hood* into English.

It might have been permissible to try a joke on them if only to see whether they could laugh. Unfortunately, I could not think of a suitable one. So I just waved a cheerful good-bye. Afterwards, I asked one of the keepers whether their many accomplishments included laughter. It appeared not, yet.

Brendan Behan (1963)

The Irish dramatist Brendan Behan (1923–1964) spent many of the last years of his life in New York. It has been said that like Dylan Thomas he was 'lionized to death'.

I am not afraid to admit that New York is the greatest city on the face of God's earth. You only have to look at it, from the air, from the river, from Father Duffy's statue. New York is easily recognizable as the greatest city in the world, view it any way and every way – back, belly and sides.

London is a wide flat pie of redbrick suburbs with the West End stuck in the middle like a currant. New York is a huge rich raisin and is the biggest city I can imagine.

A city is a place where Man lives, walks about, talks and eats and drinks in the bright light of day or electricity for twenty-four hours a day. In New York, at three o'clock in the morning, you can walk about, see crowds, read the papers and have a drink – orange juice, coffee, whiskey or anything. It is the greatest show on earth, for everyone. Its fabulous beauty at night, even forty years ago, was the wonder of the world.

When I arrived home from Broadway, where my play *The Hostage* was running, my wife said to me, 'Oh isn't it great to be back. How do you feel coming home?'

'Listen Beatrice,' I said, 'It's very dark!'

And I think anybody returning home after going to New York will find their native spot pretty dark too.

We don't come to a city to be alone, and the test of a city is the ease with which you can see and talk to other people. A city is a place where you are least likely to get a bite from a wild sheep and I'd say that New York is the friendliest city I know. The young Russian poet, Yevtushenko, said that in all honesty he had to admit that New York was the most exciting place that he had ever been to in his entire life.

James Cameron (1966)

The journalist James Cameron reported the Six-Day War and the Vietnam War for The Guardian *in the 1960s.*

Like almost everyone outside the US and not a few in it, I had always been greatly alarmed by the Americans. For many years they had been putting the wind up the world by actions of terrifying charity and menacing goodwill, but especially did they scare me, since the more I alienated myself from everything they did internationally the more I seemed to get mixed up with them personally.

The American nation is unprecedented in history: so rich, so strong, so vulnerable, so generous, so blind, so bountiful, so clumsy, so kind, so perilous, so unmanageable in their simple-minded craftiness, the brutal innocence of their lethal benevolence. Nobody but the Americans could have invented a President who posed as a peasant to conceal the expert ruthlessness that concealed the fact that he was a peasant all the time. Nobody ever knocked people about like the Americans to establish the warmth of their own hearts. (I recalled the genuinely tender consideration with which the army in Viet Nam provided artificial limbs for the children whose legs they had blown off.) The Americans were the people with whose good intentions the road to hell was so painstakingly paved.

Svetlana Alliluyeva (1967)

Stalin's daughter defected from the Soviet Union to the United States in 1967.

New York.

It had been a cold and rainy morning in Zurich. Now the weather had cleared and beneath us lay the blue, sparkling Atlantic, separating two continents – the Old World from the New.

The blue ocean, an eloquent boundary between those two worlds, to me was my own boundary, which we were crossing with amazing swiftness. The hours had to be put back; we were flying west.

This flight was so unlike the one over the Hindu Kush into India! The sparkling surface of the ocean below was not only space, it was also time: my new life into which I was stepping. I wasn't anxious about anything in particular. It was as if I were being reborn, as if I were becoming a different human being, yet remaining myself – this I also knew. I would have liked us to have gone on flying for hours, giving me plenty of time to think about it all. But everything in this modern world moves at such an accelerated pace: no time at all to stop and think.

How very small the world was. One realised this when viewing it from the great height at which our jet was travelling. So helplessly small, all these oceans, continents, the 'Old' world and the 'New' – no land in sight, with only spacious clouds below and overhead the sparkling sky drenched in blinding sunshine, one could clearly perceive how conventional and near-sighted was man's mental outlook.

The luncheon menu was brought. I thought I would try lobster; I had never tasted it before. In Russia, after the Revolution, oysters and lobsters had gone out of circulation. Only my old nurse used to tell me sometimes how 'in St Petersburg one used to serve them in the old days'.

The lunch was abundant. Alan Schwartz had a martini first, then some wine, ending up with a cognac. I drank two glasses of tea with aspirin. I felt a splitting headache in the offing – everything was happening so quickly.

An impending interview with the Press lay in wait for me at the New York airport. I would have to stand behind a microphone and say something. This, like the lobster, was another first experience. How much was there still ahead of me to be done 'for the first time'? The idea of a 'speech at a microphone' made me laugh; in Moscow this was done by all 'arriving V.I.P.s': prime ministers, cabinet ministers, kings, presidents. What did I need with such things? Was it for this that I was coming here?

My day starts with the morning. I never plan ahead. Therefore, I never try to foresee, nor would I know how to go about it. Others are more able in this respect; they try to explain and be helpful, like Kennan, for instance, whose letter I was now rereading:

. . . An unpleasant test awaits you: a meeting with the Press at the airport in New York [sentence written in Russian in the original]. I wish I could spare you this ordeal, I cannot.

. . . There will inevitably be troubles and difficulties in this country; but some of us will do all we can to help you; and I think there will also be pleasures and satisfactions for you in our life here.

. . . Your problem of adjustment to a life outside your native country is a difficult one; for the shadow of your relationship to your father will always tend to follow you wherever you go, and you will have to have greater courage, greater patience, greater faith than most people have [to overcome it] . . .

Later – weeks and months later – I had many occasions to remember those words, but at the time their meaning didn't sink in. It seemed to me that I had cut myself off from my past once and for all, and nothing here could ever remind me of it. Didn't this ocean beneath me, which we had almost crossed by now, confirm that much?

Already I could see the first islands and headlands of America. Alan looked down and said, 'In a moment you'll see a small island - Nantucket – where my family and I go every summer. Next August you must visit us there. Okay? There, look!'

'Okay,' I said.

The ocean with its islands suddenly began to slant – our jet was making a turn.

Of course I shall visit the Schwartzes on Nantucket! My second invitation! The first had been to the Kennan farm in Pennsylvania. I felt happy and light-hearted. Difficulties, did they say? My whole life so far had consisted of difficulties and abnormalities. It couldn't be any worse from now on.

The strip of land below was Long Island. That was where we would land. How splendid that the airport had been named 'Kennedy' – it was nice that America met her newcomers with that name. Alan, meanwhile, was saying that my written statement would be given to the Press, that at present all I needed to say was a few words, mentioning that there would be a press conference soon, at which I would be able to answer all questions.

All right: 'Alan, don't worry, everything will be all right!' I could see that he was nervous. The Press, my statement, difficulties – none of these people seemed to understand how at ease and happy I felt. They had all crossed the Atlantic many times, had travelled over half of the world; nothing could surprise them. They could not grasp what it was like to have always lived under a heavy yoke and suddenly to find oneself able to fly out free, like a bird. They did not value the freedom in which they had been born and bred, for no one values the air he breathes every day. This charming young Schwartz, still almost a boy, how could he have known what it meant to live all one's life in Russia and then be able to leave? Kennan knew, he understood everything; that was why he felt anxious. But I, at that moment, couldn't stop to think of 'difficulties'. I felt so happy and well.

The microphone and the reporters waited for us at the bottom of the ramp. I ran down, stepping as on air.

'Hello! I'm happy to be here!' I said, expressing what was in my heart.

All right, go ahead, take my picture, take notes, write anything you want about me. I know that at present you don't understand me. But someday, maybe, you will know what it's like to be able really to say to the world what one thinks.

From Kennedy Airport we drove to the home of Mr Stuart H Johnson on Long Island. He was the father of Priscilla Johnson, the translator of my book, who had invited me to stay with them upon my arrival.

My first impression of America was of the magnificent Long Island highways. After that tiny, domesticated Switzerland, everything here appeared immense, spacious, vast, reminding one of Russia. This was the strangest thing of all, something I had least expected. The vastness of the flat landscape under a sky which that day was overcast, the litter strewn all over the place (in Switzerland one never saw so much as the minutest scrap of paper). A lot of fat men and women with Slavic features. Maybe this was just my own personal impression – I am forever seeking likenesses, not differences.

No, there was something more than just that here: an informality, a naturalness and simplicity of manner so like ours. In Switzerland I had seen good, unconstrained manners. In India it had been politeness and respect, full of ceremony and manners. But Americans paid no attention to ceremony and manners, just like Russians. Yet how much freer, how unrestrained they were, and how they loved to smile!

The second thing I noticed on our way to Locust Valley was the number of women driving cars. I am a driver from way back, I love good roads and good automobiles; and I noticed at once how many new cars were on the roads. But it was the variety of feminine types at the wheel that struck me: pretty young girls, still almost children; smartly dressed women; many Negroes, young and old; women in furs and extraordinary big hats, like shrubs in bloom – and finally grey-haired women, for whom in the U.S.S.R. the only possible vehicle would have been a wheelchair, driving cars expertly and with a certain dash, smoking a cigarette and chatting with a companion.

'A woman's health is the nation's health.' This was said by some sociologist back in the nineteenth century. These women behind the wheel, apparently the owners of the cars, looked charming, with their hair either cut short or long and flowing, their bright, slightly vulgar ornaments. No uniformity in style here, every woman looking the way she pleased. Many had two or three children with them, and dresses on hangers in the back of the car to avoid damaging them in suitcases. The good health, the freedom and independence of this young nation presented themselves graphically before my eyes during that hour's ride.

In the U.S.S.R. so many men had perished in wars and revolutions that the majority of the population now consisted of women, that's why the majority of doctors, teachers, salespeople were women. Over there women performed some of the heaviest work ordinarily done by men. But then, did they look the least bit like these women here? An unfortunate woman taxicab driver in Moscow, who was forced to work in a cab pool only because she had returned from the war as a driver and there was no other work to be had, cursed her hellish labours, which sooner or later were bound to ruin her health. Apart from a few famous film actresses, no women in the U.S.S.R. owned automobiles.

We came to a stop in front of a white wooden, two-storeyed house with black shutters, and were met at the door by Mr Johnson, rosy-cheeked and blue-eyed, and of course with a broad smile on his face. He looked about sixty, although he was actually seventy-four. It will take me some time to accustom myself to how young Americans look for their age. This, too, is a sign of good health.

As we went up to the second floor, this house amazed me by its old-fashioned appearance. It turned out that Americans love everything that looks to them like an antique. In the U.S.S.R. we thought of all houses in the U.S.A. as being of concrete and glass, either skyscrapers or flat-roofed, one-storeyed, ranch-style houses. And when I saw lively wallpaper every-where, starched, ruffled curtains at small windows. 'Richelieu' runners on the bureau and colourful porcelain figurines, I felt as if I were watching a play by Ostrovsky on the stage of the Maly Theatre in Moscow. Well, it only went to prove that I hadn't studied the United States sufficiently at the university, that I didn't know much. All that day, and again at night lying with closed eyes in a squeaky wooden bed, I couldn't get over my amazement: a Victorian interior was the last thing I had expected to find in the United States of America.

I spent my first month and a half in this house; in the end I grew accustomed to its old-fashioned comfort. I grew attached to my kind-hearted host, too. The library, with its open fireplace, where Mr Johnson always had his evening martinis, where the shelves carried Chekhov, Tolstoy, and Dostoevsky in English, and pictures of Mr Johnson's late wife stood on small rickety tables, was my chosen refuge. It was so very cosy near the fireplace; Mr Johnson would tell stories of the First World War and would show with pride a collection of books and drawings by Winston Churchill. In the dining room, of an evening, we always ate by candlelight – a lovely American custom. The embroideries under glass on the walls and the lace doilies, their angles sticking out in different directions, no longer aroused my curiosity. The house was run according to rules established by its hostess, recently deceased, and the housekeeper, Maria, a neat little German woman, saw to it that they were strictly adhered to. Those dinners, with flowers and candles invariably on the table, were like the performance of a ritual. I found in it a kind of soothing charm, for the world outside was showering me daily with new surprises.

The first ordeal, which awaited me a few days after my arrival, was a press conference at the Plaza Hotel in New York. I must admit, though, that, totally lacking in any idea of what lay in store for me, I treated the whole matter rather offhandly completely forgetting the TV cameras, placed somewhere far away, and concentrating all my attention on finding the proper English words for my answers. That was why, I think, everything passed off successfully; judging by all reports, I had been 'very poised'. Actually, I just didn't realise that I was being watched on TV even in Europe. This sense of unreality had been increased by the difference in time, to which I hadn't quite got adjusted yet, and also by the fact that electric lights were used unrestrainedly throughout the day, so that in the end one lost all sense of day and night.

I felt just as light-hearted and happy as on my first day, I wanted to smile all the time and think of nothing. Everyone congratulated me on my success; that same evening I looked in astonishment at myself on TV, my own voice sounding like that of a stranger.

The reporters and photographers let us go at last, after we got stuck in the same elevator at the Plaza in which Krushchev had got stuck during his first visit here. New York in the evening, under the rain and flooded with lights, reminded me of Moscow in the evening – all large cities are alike at night.

The first ordeal about which Kennan had written was over. Such a pity that the Kennans had gone to Africa, then to Europe, and we wouldn't be seeing each other until August.

Before their departure Mr and Mrs Kennan had come to Locust Valley. It had been a warm spring day, we had walked in the beautiful neglected park; somehow, we hadn't felt like talking business. Anyway, everything was moving along surprisingly successfully. Kennan, however, warned me again of possible future troubles; he was afraid of some unexpected disillusionment. He spoke of his country with great love and pain. He wanted me to understand it:

. . . You simply cannot judge our society as a whole. You must discriminate. It is not really a unified society but a great battlefield, on which are fought out issues that have meaning for all of humanity. The outward aspect of it will often repel you – it repels us. But don't forget the many of us who are struggling, as best we can, against all this ugliness and error. We are in a sense your brothers and sisters; and you must look at us as such – with sympathy for our difficulties.

/

Arnold Schwarzenegger (1968)

Schwarzenegger fulfilled a life-long ambition when he emigrated to the United States at the age of twenty-one in 1968. As he recalls in this talk with the radio folklorist, Studs Terkel, his experience of living in the U.S. has been wholly delightful.

Call me Arnold.

I was born in a little Austrian town, outside Graz. It was a 300-year-old house.

When I was ten years old, I had the dream of being the best in the world in something. When I was fifteen, I had a dream that I wanted to be the best body builder in the world and the most muscular man.

It was not only a dream I dreamed at night. It was also a daydream. It was so much in my mind that I felt it had to become a reality. It took me five years of hard work. Five years later, I turned this dream into reality and became Mr. Universe, the best-built man in the world.

'Winning' is a very important word. There is one that achieves what he wanted to achieve and there are hundreds of thousands that failed. It singles you out: the winner.

I came out second three times, but that is not what I call losing. The bottom line for me was: Arnold has to be the winner. I have to win more often the Mr. Universe title than anybody else. I won it five times consecutively. I hold the record as Mr. Olympia, the top professional body-building championship. I won it six times. That's why I retired. There was nobody even close to me. Everybody gave up competing against me. That's what I call a winner.

When I was a small boy, my dream was not to be big physically, but big in a way that everybody listens to me when I talk, that I'm a very important person, that people recognize me and see me as something special. I had a big need for being singled out.

Also my dream was to end up in America. When I was ten years old, I dreamed of being an American. At the time I didn't know much about America, just that it was a wonderful country. I felt it was where I belonged. I didn't like being in a little country like Austria. I did everything possible to get out. I did so in 1968, when I was twenty-one years old.

If I would believe in life after death, I would say my before-life I was living in America. That's why I feel so good here. It is the country where you can turn your dream into reality. Other countries don't have those things. When I came over here to America, I felt I was in heaven. In America, we don't have an obstacle. Nobody's holding you back.

Number One in America pretty much takes care of the rest of the world. You kind of run through the rest of the world like nothing. I'm trying to make people in America aware that they should appreciate what they have here. You have the best tax advantages here and the best prices here and the best products here.

One of the things I always had was a business mind. When I was in high school, a majority of my classes were business classes. Economics and accounting and mathematics. When I came over here to this country, I really didn't speak English at all. I learned English and then started taking business courses, because that's what America is best known for: business. Turning one dollar into a million dollars in a short period of time. Also when you make money, how do you keep it?

That's one of the most important things when you have money in your hand, how can you keep it? Or make more out of it? Real estate is one of the best ways of doing that. I own apartment buildings, office buildings, and raw land. That's my love, real estate.

I have emotions. But what you do, you keep them cold or you store them away for a time. You must control your emotions, you must have command over yourself. Three, four months before a competition, I could not be interfered by other people's problems. This is sometimes called selfish. It's the only way you can be if you want to achieve something. Any emotional things inside me, I try to keep cold so it doesn't interfere with my training.

Many times things really touched me. I felt them and I felt sensitive about them. But I had to talk myself out of it. I had to suppress those feelings in order to go on. Sport is one of those activities where you really have to concentrate. You must pay attention a hundred percent to the particular thing you're doing. There must be nothing else on your mind. Emotions must not interfere. Otherwise, you're thinking about your girlfriend. You're in love, your positive energies get channelled into another direction rather than going into your weight room or making money.

You have to choose at a very early date what you want: a normal life or to achieve things you want to achieve. I never wanted to win a popularity contest in doing things the way people want me to do it. I went the road I thought was best for me. A few people thought I was cold, selfish. Later they found out that's not the case. After I achieve my goal, I can be Mr. Nice Guy. You know what I mean?

California is to me a dreamland. It is the absolute combination of everything I was always looking for. It has all the money in the world there, show business there, wonderful weather there, beautiful country, ocean is there. Snow skiing in the winter, you can go in the desert the same day. You have beautiful-looking people there. They all have a tan.

I believe very strongly in the philosophy of staying hungry. If you have a dream and it becomes a reality, don't stay satisfied with it too long. Make up a new dream and hunt after that one and turn it into reality. When you have that dream achieved, make up a new dream.

I am a strong believer in Western philosophy, the philosophy of success, of progress, of getting rich. The Eastern philosophy is passive, which I believe in maybe three percent of the time, and the ninety-seven percent is Western, conquering and going on. It's a beautiful philosophy, and America should keep it up.

Stephen Brook (1970)

After graduating from Cambridge (England) in 1969, Stephen Brook (1947–) worked and taught in the United States for seven years. This piece is 'Blood at the Opera' from New York Days, New York Nights.

Seen from Columbus Avenue or Broadway, the Metropolitan Opera at night itself becomes a stage set. Separated from the street by a sizeable plaza, the opera house is glass-fronted and the passer-by looks onto bustling stairways and balconies and bars. To either side of these public areas are the two immense murals which Chagall executed for the Met. Neither the architecture nor, some would say, the colourful murals bear close examination, but on a fine evening it hardly seems to matter. The Met is projecting itself at the outside world, proclaiming its own glamour while keeping it at a safe remove from the Broadway hoipolloi.

Excitement is coshed by disappointment the moment you walk into the place. New Yorkers keep telling each other how beautiful the opera house is but, like the building itself they're putting a brave front on it. It's ostentatious, fussy, tacky, the High Culture equivalent of a Las Vegas casino. The ushers who collect your tickets are decked out in full-length cloaks with red velvet collars, an absurd costume, breaking a cardinal rule: never mimic the audience. The spaces of the auditorium and the lobbies are grand enough, but the detail is as cheap as Hilton Ballroom Rococo: twirly light fittings, distracting wall textures, vulgar chandeliers that have to be raised before the curtain goes up otherwise they would obstruct the view from the galleries. During the intervals you can buy overpriced 'champagne' which is served in shallow plastic 'glasses'.

Indeed, the whole notion of opera and opera-going in New York is essentially vulgar. Singing of the most hectoring kind has always been welcome at the Met. New Yorkers prefer great voices to great singing. They applaud lavish productions rather than good ones. They value display, putting on a show, hitting high C. The stridency and musical insensitivity that characterize the Met at its worst seem to be exactly what the audience most adores. This is not to say that I haven't seen fine productions and heard marvellous performances at the Met, but they often seem to be achieved in spite of the values that prevail there. The badness is not so much a lapse in standards as a built-in consequence of putting value on those elements in opera that are most meretricious.

At least the audiences aren't constrained from expressing their opinion. Peter Hall, a very fine opera producer, came to the Met to mount a new production of Verdi's *Macbeth*. At the first night there was booing and laughter at his brave but misguided attempt to reproduce a 19th-century *mise en scène*; the next morning the *New York Times* declared that this was probably the worst new production to have been mounted at the Met in decades. It wasn't quite that bad, but it came close. The production had its supporters, though, and there was a rousing battle of noise between clappers and booers, one side trying to outdo the other, neither prepared to let the other have the last cheer or snarl. The audience successfully upstaged the performance.

This they failed to do during a performance of *Tannhäuser* a few weeks later. Soon after Maestro (as pretentious New Yorkers call their conductors) James Levine raised his baton, almost the entire audience, myself included, fell into a heavy doze. This reflects no discredit on Levine. It's just that we'd all had a heavy day and were in for a very long evening at the opera, and we simply needed a rest before the protracted musical exertions of the next few hours. A few of us woke briefly to hear Tatiana Troyanos' beautifully sung Venus, but that didn't keep us awake for too long, and we slumbered on for the rest of the act. In the interval, thoroughly refreshed, I wandered down from the Family Circle to the lower parts of the house. Why the gods are called the Family Circle I can't imagine. There were no more families up there than anywhere else. Perhaps Gallery or Upper Circle sound too distant. Americans always like to disguise the least attractive elements as something more acceptable. Family Circle is a neutral term; it doesn't immediately suggest the cheapest and worst seats. It's rather like the American egg. There is no such size as 'small'. On the other hand, the Met, unlike older British opera houses and theatres, does permit the rabble to mingle with the rich and powerful downstairs. The patrons and benefactors disappear into private bars, where they form a mutual admiration society instead of exposing themselves to the public view. I looked instead at the ordinary folks, such as a tall bearded operagoer with a Walkman headset and an elderly man in a Black Watch tartan suit. Tasteful. As were the wonderful groups of tiny old ladies with bleached pinkish blonde hair piled above their anxious lined faces, feminine counterparts to the much-loved Abe Beame doll. They appeared to be swopping bagel recipes. Up in the Family Circle the crowd was practising for Saratoga, since at least half the audience was bent under the weight of huge binoculars strapped round their necks.

At least the Met doesn't go in for the shameless sentimentality of the promotion department of the superlative New York City Ballet. At its home next door at the State Theatre, the lobby shop peddles NYCB jigsaw puzzles and cufflinks as well as more routine T-shirts. Inoffensive enough; but unfortunately the company's distinguished founder, Lincoln Kirstein, has had the preposterous idea of using the sobriquet New York Kitty Ballet, and a whole new line of goods and trinkets has been developed to match, thus appealing simultaneously to balletomanes and cat fanciers. I much preferred a series of witty lapel badges designed by Edward Gorey, portraying ballerinas in a succession of uncomfortable positions. Less tempting were sweaty pairs of ballet shoes, autographed by the dancers who had used them and worn them out. Eight dollars will buy you the tatty pink footwear of a principal, while a mere five bucks will secure the shoes of a promising lesser dancer.

Back at *Tannhäuser*, the next act was enlivened by a blue balloon that belonged to David Hockney's beautiful designs for *Parade*. It came floating across the stage just after *Dich teure Halle* and cheered us up no end. As the act came to a welcome conclusion I reached down under my seat to retrieve my programme and felt a fierce pain. I had jabbed the jagged corner of a light fitting. Withdrawing my hand, I noticed a scarlet streak gathering force as it flowed down my finger. Wrapping the finger in a handkerchief, I asked an attendant to direct me to the dispensary, which is backstage. As I swanned in a door marked No Admission, I was hauled out by a guard, who told me I couldn't go in there.

'I'm looking for the dispensary.'

'Why?'

'Because,' I said grimly, holding up the now bloody rag around my digit, 'my finger is a geyser of blood.'

'Why didn't you say so. Come with me.'

We found the doctor on duty. The dispensary was crowded with his friends who had stopped by for a chat.

'It's not serious,' I said apologetically, as he bathed the wound, which was in fact quite deep. 'I just don't want to get blood everywhere.'

'Oh, I'm used to blood.'

'It's not you I'm worried about. It's your beautiful auditorium.'

There was some mild amusement when no one could find a plaster (Am: Band-Aid), since the appropiate cabinet was locked and the key was missing. Eventually someone rooting about in a drawer found one and my finger was bound up.

'So I went through medical school for this?' murmured the doctor, echoing Dr Vincent. He told me he'd had an eventful day. Earlier, a 12-year-old member of the chorus had come in with a broken arm.

'Bad break?' someone asked.

'Oh, yeh. Pretty serious.' Everyone sighed with relief.

Bellevue's walk-in clinic cost $8 minimum, so for a real bargain next time you need emergency medical care, try the Met dispensary: excellent service and not a penny to pay.

A few days later, my wound healed, I returned to the cultural trail. A famous poet was scheduled to give a reading at an Upper West Side bookshop and I was tempted to attend. Only tempted, since I am bad at being a captive audience. I decided to compromise by turning up towards the end, so I could savour the ambience, hear the poet declaim a final poem, perhaps greet an old friend or two, and then slip away relatively unscathed.

I took the uptown subway at 14th Street. I sat next to a grizzled and dozy black man. I took out a book and read. Somewhere in the Sixties he turned to me, his eyes bloodshot, his jaw slack with weariness.

'Say, we goin' uptown?'

I nodded.

He shook his head ruefully. 'Oh no.'

'Where do you want to get to?'

'Far Rockaway.' In furthest Queens, about 50 stops in the opposite direction.

'Definitely going in the wrong direction.'

'Yeh, sure am.' And he laughed, chuckled to himself for a while, and went back to sleep.

By the time I arrived at the bookshop the reading was over. As I walked in I could see the poet standing in a corner chatting to his publisher. I moved into the shop, and it was at that moment that I spotted Sarah, tall and slim and with an intense smile directed shyly at the floor. As lovely as I remembered her – remarkably unchanged!

But I retreated. She was married now and a relationship that still yielded pleasant memories to me had doubtless been confined to the attic of her remembrance. Feeling oddly disconsolate, I walked off alone down Columbus Avenue. I walked and walked. The incident, trival in itself, suddenly changed my perceptions of the city. A number of places I had come to think of as mere sights were restored as memories. A familiar corner became not just an intersection, but a spot where I had anxiously waited for her all those years ago. Places, bricks and mortar, rang with an emotional resonance they hadn't had before.

The next day I went on a pilgrimage, up to the places near Columbia University which we used to frequent. On the clifftop of Riverside Park bulges Grant's Tomb, a pompous structure modelled on the mausoleum at Halicarnassus. It's now embellished with graffiti, which, in this instance, usefully pull it down a peg or two. Surrounding this grandiose pile are sets of wonderfully garish mosaic benches, with backs that undulate crazily around three sides of the tomb. They're inspired by Gaudi's mosaics in the Parque Guell in Barcelona, but these have a distinct New York quality to them, since they depict the cars and animals and faces of the city. These benches are so different in style and mood from the tomb that they seem barely related to it; they commodiously lounge back from it, as if luxuriating in a knowledge that they reflect, brightly and crudely, the life of the city far more than the lugubrious Grecian sepulchre only a few yards away.

Nearby stands a small urn fenced in on the edge of the small cliff that sheers down to the parkway and the river. The inscription – the more touching for its restraint – reads: *Erected to the memory of an amiable child, St Claire Pollock*, who, in 1797, came to an untimely end when she fell over the edge. I wouldn't have known about the grave had not Sarah made it a frequent stopping point on our walks along the Hudson. Another resting place was the Riverside Church, a huge French Gothic-style edifice, with an immense tower that even dwarfs the bulky church below. Built 1930 with Rockefeller money, it's a Baptist church, though the interior, dimly lit with deep red-and-blue imitation French glass, has a more liturgical feel to it than I associate with peachy Baptists. Riverside is inappropriately comfortable; were the light better, it would be ideal for curling up with a book on a winter's day when the wind whiplashes Riverside Drive. Beautiful in its way, it lacks austerity. Jesus, one suspects, might be turned away at the door if he weren't wearing a jacket and tie. A worshipper would come here for reassurance rather than self-examination, let alone self-improvement.

On the other hand, the Holy Ghost has surely descended on the extraordinary Cathedral of St John the Divine, about a quarter of a mile away on the escarpment that overlooks Morningside Park. Already 600 feet long and 320 feet wide at the transepts, it remains incomplete. The apse and choir and crossing were built at the turn of the century in a Byzantine style, but the nave and aisles and west front were built later, between the world wars, in a lush Gothic revival. Perhaps because of the immense scale of the building, the clash of styles doesn't jar; everything is absorbed into the mightiness of the space. St John's is a disquieting building in a way that Riverside is not: deep aisles hide shadow and darkness that resonate with mystery and emotion. St John's has a nave pyloned with immense, deeply moulded and ribbed piers that bear the great weight and sustain the space. In a side chapel is an awesome monument to some city firemen who were killed in an accident. Its rusty form grasps within it the charred timbers taken, one must assume, from the scene of the fatal fire. Riverside is magisterial but dull; St John's is mighty and moving, a monument to anachronistic ambition.

Absorbed by St John's, I forget about Sarah. I took the subway back down to the Village, getting off at Sheridan Square. Emerging into this unsatisfactory apology for a park, I had another jolt, as I recalled a cool summer morning when, for some reason now entirely forgotten, she and I had sat there. Sheridan Square, scruffy little oasis that it is, was, like those other places in Riverside Park, dragged back from the past and reinstalled as a focus of unjustifiable but inescapable affection, reminding me that places in themselves may be beautiful to us, but that places shown and hence given to us through the mediation of someone we have loved, those places alone become precious.

James Morris (1970)

James Morris visited New York in 1970.

New York.

When I got there, in the fall, an indulgent helicopter pilot flew me to the geographical center of my subject. Helicopters are the familiars of New York, its clanking Ariels. They slide and side-step among the office blocks, they chase their own shadows across the water, they airily alight, as though bringing pearls and bonbons to penthouse paramours, upon the high summits of skyscrapers.

Off the top of a building we fell that day, and sidled across the Hudson River, and in a few moments the helicopter stopped, shook itself, and gingerly descended a couple of hundred feet. Looking out of my side window I found myself hovering, with a disrespectful clatter, close to the nose of the Statue of Liberty. That substantial figure of a lady, to quote one of my favourite guidebook definitions, looked taken aback: and as our aircraft shifted its angle, so her pallid head tilted against its background. Now she was set against a clump of skyscrapers, now against a line of warehouses – one moment grey institutional buildings on an island, the next interminable rows of brown houses marching away to the horizon – a broad river behind her head, as we swung around her coiffure, and a tangle of suspension bridges, chimneys, cranes – until, completing our juddery circumnavigation of the statue, I looked at her in full classical profile, and saw her against the sweep of New York Bay.

We hung there for a minute, and the sunshine reflected off the water shone about her head. A ship was sailing steadily out to sea, and a big orange ferryboat pounded back from Staten Island. There lay the freighters at the quarantine station, dejectedly paraded off-shore, and there sped a Coast Guard cutter back to Governors Island. Beyond Jamaica Bay a jet from Kennedy Airport flung itself into the sky. Fragile as ivory stood the Verrazano Bridge above the Narrows, closing the upper bay as a gate into a lagoon, and beyond it lay the silver void of the sea, beyond Sandy Hook and the Ambrose Light, beyond the Ewash Channel and Flynn's Knoll – out past the Gedney Channel, where the Bay turned into the ocean, and the ocean became the world.

I traced the magical names on my map as we hung there, and all my

fancies of the last few months began their mutation into fact. Then, with a
last curtsey to Liberty, we flew away. 'If we hit her we'd be famous,' I said
to the pilot as we darted off. 'What a way to go,' he answered. 'I'd be the
guy that assaulted the Statue of Liberty, and you'd be instant Shakespeare.'

Seen from up there, in the bright October sunshine, the reasons for New
York looked obvious. Everything below us seemed to be moving – even the
skyscrapers, as they shifted one against the next with our momentum. The
city looked what it was: a landing place and a Bazaar. Every twenty minutes
a ship leaves or enters New York. Every day a multitude equivalent to the
population of Norway enters its business district. Eight railroad lines end
their journeys in the city; expressways circle it, or stalk on stilts across its
tenements. One and a half million passengers pass through Kennedy Airport
in an average month – when I was there, 69,000 in a single day.

New York's qualifications are evident, too, when you see it from the air.
It might have been man-made as a port, so neatly functional is its shape
and situation. On the north-eastern coast of the United States, between
latitudes 40 and 41 North, two large chunks of land stand out from the
coastline like breakwaters. One is the flank of New Jersey, with its long line
of reefs; the other is Long Island in the State of New York, a splendid
boulevard, a hundred miles long, of sand, marsh, and grassland. These two
land masses approach each other at an angle, and very nearly meet: they
are separated by the entrance to New York Bay.

It is a wonderfully sheltered, secretive opening. Long Island protects it
from the northern gales, the arm of sand called Sandy Hook reaches out
from New Jersey to embrace its channel from the south, and the bulk of
Staten Island stands like a cork in the middle. The mariner enters it sailing
almost due west, but a few miles from the open sea he turns abruptly north,
passes through the bottleneck of the Narrows, leaves Staten Island on his
port side, and finds himself in the glorious security of the upper bay - gales
and high seas left behind, even the sea birds domesticated, as he steams
snugly between Brooklyn and Bayonne towards the comforts of the
metropolis.

This is the lordly front door of New York – the carriage sweep. There
is a kitchen entrance too, for between Long Island and the mainland there
lies Long Island Sound, sixty miles of sheltered water linking the port with
the Atlantic by a back route. This will also take a seafarer into the upper
bay, via the tidal strait called the East River, while from the American
interior the noble Hudson River flows into the Bay out of the north, mingling
its icy fresh waters with the salt tide of the Atlantic. Diverse other creeks
and rivers debouch into New York Bay, and all around are little islands,
inlets, and spits, forming a watery sort of filigree upon the large-scale charts.

In the centre of this system of waters stands the island of Manhattan,
the core of the port. With its long flat line of shore it provides safe wharfage
for many ships: surrounded as it is by water, protected by the Narrows from
the open sea, it is a perfect site for a merchant city. It is only just an island,
for while the east River and the Hudson bound it east and west, in the north
only the insignificant winding stream called the Harlem River separates it
from the mainland. But an island it is on the map, an island it looks from
a helicopter, it has water at each end of its cross-town streets, and even at

its broadest part a determined pedestrian can cross from shore to shore in an hour – ninety minutes, say, if she goes halfway by the cross-town bus.

There is a compact elegance of design to this ensemble. The scale is not very large. Manhattan is ten miles long, and is easily sailed around by stertorous pleasure boats in morning excursions. The islands so importantly named upon the maps are sometimes hardly more than river blobs, and privileged visitors boarding an incoming liner at the Narrows barely have time to polish off a Steak Diane, a Camembert, and a bottle of claret before the ship is swinging into the Manhattan pier, and the longshoremen may be seen hunched over their beer and hot dogs in the sidewalk diner.

It is hard to remember, when the ice floes are crunching down the Hudson, and the ships in harbour are filmed in ice, but by literary standards this is a southern port. A geographically ill-educated poet might look for warm beakers here. New York stands well south of Barcelona, not far north of Lisbon, on more or less the same latitude as Valencia, Athens or Catania. No warm ocean current enters the Bay, so that it is much colder in winter than any Mediterranean port, and is hardly the sort of haven better-informed visionaries yearn for, when they hear the nightingale; but the harbour is never frozen solid, winter fogs are rare, and sea traffic does not stop for the cold weather, however snarled up the streets of Manhattan. The climate is officially described as temperate, but with its miserable extremes of heat, blizzard, and humidity, interspersed with glorious intervals of sparkle, it strikes me rather as theatrical.

Dramatic, certainly, almost stagey, are the wide and splendid vistas that extend from the harbourfront of New York. Old prints of this bay show it surrounded by rolling hills, but they must have been elevated for artistic effect, because the highest point for miles is Todt Hill on Staten Island, which is 409 feet high. The physical glories of the place are wide, flat glories. The Bay itself is so superbly spacious and serene that early travellers often likened it to the Venetian lagoon. The Atlantic beaches which flank the port seem to run away for ever to disappear in an apotheosis of sea, sun, and sky. The sunsets of New York are the horizontal sort – not just a ball of surly red, plunging down, but slashing sweeps of pink and crimson, mixed up with the last of the evening blue, and the silver off the sea, and the streaks of the windswept clouds, to lie like a sumptuous edible from end to end of the horizon.

These are goose landscapes, duck skies. Petrels, egrets, herons, grebe haunt the foreshores of the Bay, and along the migratory flyway that passes over New York travel thousands of birds out of the northern wilderness – snow geese sometimes in flights of a hundred birds, ducks of many kinds, now buntings, longspurs from Labrador. Sometimes they are to be seen in haughty formation above the skyscrapers, sweeping south. Before the city was built the Bay and its islands were marvellously rich in wild life. There was venison fat as mutton, wrote a Dutch settler in 1654, pigeons 'as thick as sparrows in Holland,' oysters so big one cut them into slices. Strawberries and blackberries were the weeds of Manhatten. Bears, wolves, and otters frequented the islands then, seals lay on the foreshore, and the landscapes were green with oaks, walnuts, chestnuts, beeches and birches. As for the waters of the Bay, they were 'well furnished,' recorded Daniel Denton in 1670, 'with Fish, as Bosse, Sheepsheads, Place, Perch, Trout, Eels, Turtles and divers others': in 1911, it was reported to the Linnaean Society of New York, 237 species of fish were to be found within fifty miles of the city centre.

Even now, to a visitor from more ancient cities, New York seems thinly laid upon its terrain. From the air especially one may see how much dusty green still stipples the place - the treelessness of New York is much exaggerated – and in unexpected corners of the metropolis one may still find the old-fashioned wild flowers that once covered these harbour shores: meadow violet and John's-wort, Queen Anne's lace, bee balm. There is a primeval air to the weird tidal swamps called the Jersey Meadows, which lie within sight of Manhattan, and are crossed by the New Jersey Turnpike. Brownish, soggy, and sullen they lie there, and they make one think of trolls and will-of-the-wisps. A friend of mine was once driving across this gloomy waste with her dog, on her way home to Manhattan on a dark drizzly night. On both sides other cars were racing up the turnpike towards the city. The rain slanted dismally through her headlights, her windshield wipers sadly swished, before, beside, and behind her the traffic relentlessly hastened, when suddenly her dog, with a muffled bark, leapt out of the half-open window. It was as though he could stand it no longer. She caught a last glimpse of his white body, scrambling and slithering through the cars, and then he was lost over the edge of the road, in the darkness of the Meadows. She never saw him again.

'Say, that's a sad story. Never saw him again, huh? Maybe he's still wandering down there. See where the dredge is working? If they could figure out how to drain those Meadows, they'd be worth millions.'

Jonathan Raban (1982)

An extract from Jonathan Raban's Old Glory, *an account of a journey in a Mississippi steam-boat.*

The Saint James Hotel was more like a waxwork museum than a piece of living history. The desk clerk sat behind an antique cash register with wrought-iron eagles on it, his credit-card stamping machines kept discreetly out of sight. The hallway was lined with polished brass spittoons. I wondered what would happen if I actually expectorated into one of these objects, but decided not to try.

There was no shortage of rooms: I could put up in 'The Natchez', 'The Robert E. Lee', 'The Buckeye State', 'The Ben Franklin', 'The General Pike', 'The A. L. Shotwell', 'The Belle of the West'. I can't remember which of these dead steamboats I finally moved into. Everywhere there were steamboats. Brown photographs of their pilots, in wing collars and top hats, decorated the landings. Livid chromos from the 1880s showed steamboats battling through sloughs of whitecaps with black thunder clouds sitting on their masts. More chromos displayed these famous sternwheelers from a technical draughtsman's point of view; with every portico, every balustrade, every detail of rigging and trelliswork scrupulously etched in, while the boats themselves floated in a ghostly white element, neither air nor water.

The place was a monument to the age of steamboat gothic. It smelled not as one might have hoped, of sweat, beer, oil and coal, but of little china bowls of pot-pourri. In my room there was, as Walter had promised, a miniature four-poster spread with a hand-crocheted quilt. A newspaper had been left for me on the scroll-top escritoire, and I seized it hopefully. The *St James Journal*. Everything in it turned out to be exactly a hundred years out of date.

> This morning a thunder shower of unusual violence came from the west, accompanied by high wind. The lightning struck a chimney of the St James Hotel over the front toward Main Street, knocking the brick into the street and carrying some pieces across Main Street. Mrs Donohue was in Mrs Dodge's room, and was prostrated from her chair upon the floor where she remained a minute insensible. She afterward complained of headache and a slight injury to one foot. She says she did not see any lightning or hear any thunder.

What I wanted, though, was the weather forecast for tomorrow, and this cute facsimile was no use to me at all.

I thought that all American hotel rooms had television; this one apparently refused to acknowledge that the instrument had been invented yet. There was a telephone of sorts, though. I unhooked the trumpet-shaped earpiece from its fluted stand, fearing that all I'd hear would be the cracked recording voice of Rutherford Hayes or Mark Twain. But a girl's voice came through, singing 'Hi, there!', a century out of sync with the apparatus we were using.

'Is there a TV anywhere in the hotel? I want to see the weather forecast.'

'You'll find one in your room, sir.' She made it sound as if this was a cosy game of hide-and-seek that the hotel usually organised for its customers.

'*Where?*'

'You just try that old wardrobe right across from where you're sitting, sir,' She must have been the queen tease of Red Wing High; I imagined her in frilly pants and fishnet tights, swirling a drum-majorette's baton.

I tried the wardrobe, a handsome reproduction piece of pine colonial. The drawers, when I pulled at them, turned out to be doors, and opened on an enormous colour television. I found my weather report. Nothing does so much justice to the gargantuan scale of American life as its national weather maps. In Europe, one is allowed to see the weather only as scraps and fragments: a cake-slice of a depression here; a banded triangle of a ridge of high pressure there. In the United States I was enthralled by the epic sweep of whole weather systems as they rolled across the country from the Pacific to the Atlantic, or coasted down from the Arctic Circle, or swirled up from Mexico and Cuba. The weathermen tapped their maps with sticks. Without betraying the slightest flicker of wonder or concern, they announced that people were being frozen to death in Butte, roasted in Flagstaff and blown off their feet in Tallahassee. Each day they rattled off every conceivable variety of climatic extremity in a blasé drawl. I'd never seen so much weather at once, and was deeply impressed. I shivered vicariously for the Montanans, sweated for the Texans and ran for shelter with the Floridans.

Tonight, though Minnesota was the one place in the nation with really boring weather. Our local man from Minneapolis foretold moderate humidity, low precipitation and winds from the south at ten to twelve miles an hour. By American standards, he might reasonably have asserted that for the next day we would have no weather at all.

I closed the false drawers on the TV. I peered down at Main Street through the dinky white plywood shutters on my bedroom window. There was nothing going on. I tried to distract myself with the *St James Journal:*

> EVEN UP – Last Monday evening, after concluding his day's labor on the bench, Judge Crosby repaired to the basement of the St James hotel for a bath. After concluding his ablutions he enquired of the sable proprietor, Charley Fogg, what the damage was. Said Charley: 'Judge, dis is the first time I has had ob getting eben with you, and guess I'll hab to charge you about seventy-five dollars.' His honor pondered a moment, and then said: 'Do I know you? Have I ever met you before?' 'I tink you hab,' said Charley. 'You sent me up once for three months.' Honors were easy.

I went to the bathroom. The lavatory cover had been fastened to the seat with a paper seal. 'For Your Personal Safety And Convenience'. That, I thought, neatly expressed the general spirit of the Saint James. The era of the Mississippi steamboat had not, on the whole, been notably hygienic. In this expensive piece of 'restoration', American history had been marvellously disinfected. It had been robbed of its vitality and given a smooth patina of fake antiquity. In the Saint James version of things, Ulysses Grant's U.S.A., with its railroad scandals, and Tweed Ring, scallywags and carpet-baggers, had been got up to look as if it was as quaint and remote as the never-never land of Merrie England. With their history so thoroughly sanitised, no-one need fear for their personal safety or convenience as they sat thoughtfully at stool in its purlieus: here, the past had been rendered incapable of passing on any intimate diseases.

Nicholas Coleridge (1984)

Nicholas Coleridge is currently editor of Harpers and Queen. In 1984 he attempted to follow Jules Verne's hero Phileas Fogg and go round the world, across land and sea, within eighty days.

Devastating news caught up with me in San Francisco. The ship I had been hoping to take from the port of New York for the final leg of the journey across the Atlantic to England had been delayed by engine trouble, and would no longer be useful for my itinerary. Furthermore, no ship of any nature – passenger or cargo – was scheduled to sail from New York for the next ten days. Failure loomed sickeningly at the final hurdle.

Up until now I had planned each leg of the route myself. The Atlantic, however, was too far in the future to make a firm booking before leaving England, and too awkward to arrange by telephone from Asia, so I had sought help from Lloyds of London, the international insurance market. It was the cleverness of one of their marine syndicates, who have access to the world's cargo movements, which tracked down the solitary vessel leaving the East Coast that week for Britain. This was a Canadian cargo ship, the *Dart Europe*, which was scheduled to sail not from America but from Montreal at 6 am in four days' time. This was twenty-seven hours earlier than the elusive New York ship and meant covering an additional seven hundred miles as well as a further set of customs and immigration. Did I think I could make Montreal in time? I said 'Of course' and hot-footed it to Amtrak, the Trans American Railroad Company.

Amtrak's Transbay Terminal on 1st Street and Mission, downtown San Francisco, has one of the most efficient computerised ticket routing systems in the world. Press a button and the computer displays the shortest distance between two points, as well as availability and foibles of connections. A Creole woman clerk in the ticket office tapped out a series of digits on her keyboard.

'When did you say you wanted to arrive Montreal?'

'Not later than 8 am on the 17th.'

'I'm sorry, but the earliest we can get you there is 9.30 am on the 18th.'

'That's no good at all. My ship will have sailed. Are you sure there's no quicker way? What if I changed at Chicago for Detroit or Port Huron, crossed the Great Lakes by ferry and headed north via Toronto? Is that possible?'

'No can do.' The Creole clerk consulted her screen. 'The Port Huron train leaves from Chicago every afternoon at 1.40 pm. You don't arrive Chicago until 3.50 pm in two days' time.'

I sat down on a bench and studied the map. There are twelve states between San Francisco and Montreal, including the interminable prairie heartland of Wyoming and Nebraska, and the smallest of them is 270 miles across. I considered hiring a car, but even averaging sixty miles an hour for sixteen hours a day there still didn't seem much prospect of covering the 4,280 miles in time. The train would drive nights as well as during the day, and if that couldn't make it then the position must be hopeless.

On Transbay Central Terminal I sat down and wept, or at any rate cursed my bad luck. Not that one was liable to attract much sympathy on 1st Street and Mission. It is a desolate spot. A drunk was hectoring a lone woman traveller, and bag ladies had made nests out of old newspapers underneath a bench. Several acid-heads were loitering with intent to vandalise a telephone kiosk, and signs everywhere cautioned you that San Francisco is the pickpocket capital of the world.

I hadn't noticed, in my brown study, that the bench I was sitting on was a shoe-shine pew, until a spritely old man began daubing my toe cap with polish. Having your shoes cleaned is one of the most consoling pursuits imaginable, so I kept my best foot forward. Round and round he went, sloughing the heels first with a rag, then a wire brush, before sealing the patina with transparent wax until my walking shoes shone like a pair of conkers. He was completing his seventh and final lap of the sole when the Creole ticket clerk stuck her head out of the window and said, 'If you don't mind a real tight connection in Chicago, I think you might still make it.'

'Heavens, why didn't you say so before?'

'Well we don't recommend it as a rule. If the San Francisco train is late you'll surely miss it and then passengers complain. That's why we route them on the later train to New York Grand Central Station. But if you're prepared to take the risk you can route direct to New York Pennsylvania Station, which is also the terminus for Montreal. That way you could do it.'

'Do I leave tonight?'

'No, the California Zephyr is a morning train. It departs here 10.55 am, arriving Chicago approximately fifty-three hours later at 3.50 pm. Then you take the 4.50 pm Broadway Limited Express to New York arriving late afternoon on the 15th, and connect with the Montrealer later that evening. You arrive Montreal at 9.35 am on the 17th.'

This would allow me a three-hour margin before boarding the *Dart Europe*.

Phileas Fogg and party, as it happens, also gained an additional day in San Franciso for precisely the same reason. Allergic to sightseeing ('He looked without seeing anything'), Fogg wisely decided to take a three-dollar carriage to the International Hotel and there spend the day eating oyster soup and dried beef. On the way, however, he could not help but notice 'the broad streets, low evenly ranged houses, the Anglo-Saxon gothic churches and temples, the immense docks, the palatial warehouses, the numerous vehicles in the streets, and on the crowded sidewalks not only Americans but also Chinese and Indians.'

All these characteristics are still part and parcel of San Francisco, except that the Chinese enjoy full American citizenship, with green cards, and Indiatown has been superseded by Japantown. Today, however, Fogg would also have noticed (or rather not noticed) another, seedier side to San Francisco; the oriental massage parlours on every street corner, the packs of macho homosexuals who roam the city after dark in leather trousers and lumberjack shirts, the dope addicts who crash out in Union Square or against the shop windows of Macey's department store, and the super-annuated hippies jangling tambourines and smelling of joss sticks. The day I arrived in San Francisco the hippies seemed to be suffering a reverse: the Berkeley Psychedelic Cab Rank – for twenty-three years the flower people's own taxi service in East Bay – announced its liquidation. A spokesman for the rank, Buffalo, aka Grateful Dead freak Bill Miller, blamed 'Reaganomics, preppies and the recession.'

'People seem to prefer bow ties and blow drys to our service,' he lamented.

No city in the world distributes more brochures or handbills to its tourists than San Francisco. In the course of the day my pockets were stuffed with them: discount vouchers for crab suppers, invitations to jazz festivals, offers to buy real estate on easy terms, and the magazine *Pleasure*. I did not bother looking at *Pleasure* ('the journal for gentlemen alone on the Bay') until I was soaking in a warm bath at the Bedford Hotel off Union Square.

Only San Francisco could support a magazine for people who prefer sex on their own. *Pleasure* is the contact paper for the city's sixty telephone sex exchanges. The procedure is simple: you dial a switchboard, quote your American Express or Visa credit card number, wait for it to be cleared, than talk dirty. Teams of girls (and men) hang on the line ready to interview your most sinister fantasies out of you. All you need to do is indicate your preference and leave the stimulating probing to them.

'Why risk infection?' asks Linda from a half-page advertisement in which she is wrapped in a passionate embrace with a telephone receiver. 'When you can have me come whisper in your ear?'

'Our service registers on your monthly statement as a cocktail bar,' reassures another. 'Don't worry, Vice-President, your secretary will never know. Confidentiality and satisfaction guaranteed.'

'Special introductory first time offer. Twenty dollars for initial fifteen minutes. Thereafter one dollar per minute or part thereof.'

Since the scare of sexual disease hit San Francisco two years ago, prostitutes have seen their business evaporate. Telephone sex is infection-proof and approved by hotels, who levy a hefty service charge on local calls and are spared the nuisance of whores in the bedrooms.

After bathing I dialled a few of the numbers at random. I do not know whether 6.30 pm – the cocktail hour – is peak rate, but all the sex lines were permanently engaged. From my bedroom window at the top of Post Hill I had a panoramic view of San Francisco, from the brownstones of Sacramento Square to the Trans America Pyramid and back across the tiled pagodas of Chinatown. It was strange to think that, in hundreds of apartments all over the city, people were lolling alone on beds and preening their hang-ups to invisible confessors.

The San Francisco to Chicago Express ('The California Zephyr') leaves not, as you might suppose, from San Francisco but from the West Coast suburb of Oakland. In every other respect, however, the Zephyr is an utterly logical locomotive.

The Amtrak carriages are all double-decker, and short-term passengers travelling in the lower compartment, and lifers billeted upstairs with a high-security observation car of their own. I found my seat, hung up my jacket, took off my walking shoes: there were fifty-three hours until we were scheduled to arrive at Chicago Union Station. The sun beat down onto Oakland goods yard and the rusty Central Pacific cattle trucks and Cotton-Belt box-cars. A steel foundry beyond the perimeter fence looked picturesque in the dancing sunlight. Despite anxiety over my right itinerary, I felt oddly light-headed. I knew by now that I preferred travelling by rail to ship in a crisis: your options remain open, if we ran into a herd of buffalo on the prairie, I could always detrain and dial a minicab.

At 11.25 am the Zephyr rolled out of Oakland and began its journey north along the Pacific coast: Richmond, Martinez, Soisan-Fairfield, Sacramento. There are thirty-five stations between San Francisco and Chicago, and seven of them fall in the first two hours. We started out like a local train, picking up shoppers, and only gradually – somewhere after Colfax, but before Truckee – achieved the gravitas of a Grand Trunk Express. The scenery between the Californian provincial towns was delightful: clapboard

houses with rickety jetties tottering across the mud flats which unite American river with San Pablo Bay; and on the inland side of the track, mustard
fields which stretch like miles of gold teflon carpet into the distance. We
were crawling along so slowly that you could watch people on their verandahs – a man was gutting fish, a woman knitting on a rocking chair – and
when we passed the pink McClennan Airforce base there was time to see
a rookie in a jeep sink a whole can of Coors lager.

'I wonder if we're going to go any faster,' I asked a man with orange
quiffed hair.

'We'll gather a bit of speed in Nevada, but not much. We won't touch
seventy between here and Chicago; these trains can't take it. Or at least the
track can't. The gauge is designed for freight not passenger trains and they
frequently topple over.'

I looked surprised at this.

'Sure they do, I'm not kidding. Almost every month there's an Amtrak
derailment. Then they take you by coach to the nearest station until they
can shunt up a new train. It's nothing like the European system.'

He asked me where I was from and where I had been staying.

'San Francisco? Me also, I've got a girlfriend at college there. Were you
in town last week for the International Hookers Convention? You should
have been, it was incredible: a big parade of hookers from all over the world
followed by a five-day seminar on conditions of work.'

Mike was heading home to Wisconsin. He said he was an abstract
photographer and sold his work to a gallery in Chicago. Chicagoans, he
believed, were just about ready for abstract photography.

'Two years ago they still had a cowhand's mentality: now matters are
improving.' As a measure of his confidence, Mike was refining his style.
Previously he had made fifteen prints of each photograph and asked one
hundred dollars each; from now on he was going to limit the edition to one
print and ask five hundred dollars.

'But won't you lose a thousand dollars on each negative?' I objected.

'Could be,' said Mike. 'I suppose you could look at it that way.'

You can tell you've left California and entered Nevada when the palm trees
stop; they are a much more reliable indication than the state-line which is
half buried under sand. We had reached the lowlands of the Sierra Nevadas
– Carson Valley – and the land was scarred with sandpits like bunkers on
a fantastic overgrown golf course. During the gold rush the population had
exceeded seven thousand; now it is barely a hundred. The prospectors
stripped away the top soil hydraulically, exposing the gold seams and leaving
the earth as barren as a war zone. When the government banned hydraulic
mining, the pits were abandoned as too expensive. Now only the occasional
foundation of a log cabin in the forest marks the site of the boom towns.

From Carson Valley we began to climb. The track followed the gradients,
sometimes circling the same peak three times to gain height, before plunging
into narrow gorges from which there seemed to be no exit. The curves of
the line were so bold and the precipices so extreme, that the engine and
front six carriages often steamed below us in the opposite direction as
though part of a different train.

'Good afternoon ladies and gentlemen, this is your guard speaking.' The intercom crackled through the observation car. 'Well I sure hope you folks are sitting next to someone you like, because we're going through a two-mile tunnel here. After that we will arrive in Reno. Reno in five minutes, ladies and gentlemen, for anyone disembarking at sin city.'

Reno is the Las Vegas of the Sierra Nevadas: a one-tracked casino town said to combine the sleaziest aspects of the Casbah in Tangiers and the Cannebiere in Marseilles. When Phileas Fogg stopped in Reno it was for breakfast. Nowadays breakfast is just about the one thing you can't get in Reno.

You saw the town coming for a mile: the Sunset Motel, the El Taho Motel, Rancho Novalto ('Sleep it off on a waterbed'), the Comstock Casino. It would be hard to invent a place which announced, with the brevity of a few downtown hotels, such a manifesto of frisky sex. The place reeked of brassy blondes who would slit your wallet while they picked your throat; mid-west Jezebels who would love you and leave you, or leave and love you, whichever cut up the roughest; and one-gallon-spivs in ten-gallon-hats who shot from the groin. All the lowlife on the Zephyr disembarked at Reno, wearing slit dresses inappropriate to rail travel. As we gathered steam again, we saw them sloping uptown in twos and three, making for the Golden Nugget Saloon, the Six Gun Motel, the Pink Pussycat Bar or the high kicking cabaret of Frederic Apcar's Top Streak.

A moonfaced man approached me in the bar car. He said he had heard I was English and could I perhaps do him a favour. His thirteen-year-old daughter liked all things English. 'I buy her English shirts, English shorts, I'd buy her English shoes except the sizes are different. Her two favourite people in the world are both English: Princess Diana and Boy George.' The moonfaced man poured me a glass of Napa Valley sherry. 'Now,' he went on, 'I know fathers aren't supposed to interfere, but I *approve* of Kate's taste and I want to encourage her. I mean, Princess Diana makes a great job of being Princess, and Boy George makes a great job of his songs. And neither of them are into drugs that I've heard of; they're neither of them Reds. They're *healthy* heroes. So if I give you Kate's address, could you send her a postcard from England and write it "To Katie. Love Princess Diana." Or "To Katie. Love Boy George."? Could you do that for me?'

(Weeks later, in London, I came across the address tucked inside a book and mailed a card of a British policeman to Trenton, Pennysylvania. I inscribed it 'To Katie. Love Princess Diana. And Boy George.' In two different coloured biros.)

I drank Napa Valley with the moonfaced man as far as Winnemucca. He said he was a chef and was travelling all the way to New York for his eldest daughter's second marriage. The reception was to be a silver service lunch in a fancy hotel. Afterwards, for some reason not connected with the nuptials, the whole party planned to take a limousine to Trump Tower and stare up at Johnny Carson's apartment from the pavement.

Martin Amis (1985)

In this piece from The Moronic Inferno, *Martin Amis describes the impact of AIDS upon America.*

Everywhere you look you see the double bind, the double jeopardy. In America – land of the profit-making casualty ward, home of the taxi-metered ambulance – the bipartite attack assumes its most heartless form. Growing ever weaker, the sick man faces medical bills that average $75,000 and have been known to reach half a million. The medical-insurance system is a shambles of pedantry and expedience. Some policies are soon exhausted; insurance companies often renege, claiming 'prior conditions'; if you lose your job you might lose your cover; and with the two-year waiting period to establish eligibility, 80 per cent of AIDS patients do not survive to draw their first cheque.

'What happens, usually, is a process of *spend-down*,' said Mark Senak of the AIDS Resource Centre.

'Spend-down?' I asked. I sat in Senak's chambers in downtown Manhattan. He is one of many young lawyers active on the AIDS-relief front. AIDS-sufferers need lawyers: to defend themselves against employers and landlords (in America, as in England, you can legally discriminate against homosexuals but not against the disabled); to transfer assets, to wrangle with insurance companies, to formulate declarations of bankruptcy. Lawyers like Senak have drafted wills for young men barely out of college. Wills, bills, audits, lawsuits – all that extra worry, boredom and threat.

Spend-down turns out to be one of those cutely hyphenated nightmares of American life. Briefly, it means that you spend everything you have before qualifying for Medicaid. Until recently there were further complications. One AIDS patient was suffering from a rare opportunistic disease called cryptosporidiosis, normally found only in calves. He applied for social security, and was told that he couldn't have the money. Why? Because he couldn't have the disease.

Duly pauperised by *spend-down*, all spent out, the patient becomes eligible for a bed in one of the city hospitals. Here he will encounter the suspicion and contempt that America traditionally accords to its poor. There is no out-patient care, no intermediate care. He is not legally dischargeable unless he has a home to go to. And AIDS sufferers often do not know if they have a home to go to. You might return to find your remaining possessions stacked outside the door of your apartment. The locks might have been changed – by your landlord, or by your lover.

'What we have,' said Senak, 'are diseased bag-persons living on the street. No one will house them. No one will *feed* them.' Senak's personal project is an accommodation centre for sufferers, on the San Francisco model. But the ruinous cost of real estate is only one of the difficulties. The risk categories for AIDS form a heterogeneous group, colloquially known as 'the 5-H club': haemophiliacs, Haitians, homosexuals, hookers and heroin-addicts (these last two frequently overlapping). How do you house a haemo-philiac stockbroker with a Puerto Rican junkie? One of the reasons why AIDS is seen as a scourge of the homosexual community is that there *is* a homosexual community, however divided.

'I think we've made progress, in changing general attitudes, since the panic began in 1983. Tonight I'm going to see someone in hospital. A year ago I would have had to stop off and buy him some food. The hospital staff wouldn't take in his tray. But they do now.'

That same week in New York a TV crew – battle-scarred *conquistadores*, veterans of wars, revolutions, terrorist sieges – walked off a set rather than affix a microphone to an AIDS-sufferer's clothing. *No one has ever caught* AIDS *through casual contact*. After four years of handling patients' food, laundry, bed-pans, drips and bandages, no health worker has yet succumbed. You cannot say this often enough. But how often will you have to say it? In the end one cannot avoid the conclusion that AIDS unites certain human themes – homosexuality, sexual disease, and death – about which society actively resists enlightenment. These are things that we are unwilling to address or think about. We don't *want* to understand them. We would rather fear them.

In New York, everyone on the public wing refers to AIDS patients as PWAs: persons with AIDS. 'Why?' I asked a young administrator at the AIDS Medical Foundation. 'It's to avoid any suggestion of victim, sufferer, and so on.' 'Why?' I asked again. They are victims; they are sufferers. But the answer is of course 'political', New York being the most politicised city on earth. New York, where even supermarkets and greasy-spoons have their 'policies'; where all action seems to result from pressure, and never from a sane initiative.

Other euphemisms in this sphere include 'sexual preference' ('orientation' being considered 'judgmental'), 'sexually active' (some go further and talk of 'distributive' as opposed to 'focal' sex) and 'intravenous substance-abuser' (as if a junkie is going to feel much cheered or ennobled by this description). Over here, handicapped people are merely 'challenged', and the 'excep-tional' child is the child with brain damage. It is a very American dishonesty – antiseptic spray from the verbal-sanitation department. Having named a painful reality (the belief seems to be), you also dispatch it; you get it off your desk.

In 1983 the total federal budget for the AIDS crisis was $28 million; in 1984 it was $61 million. But this was all grant-hound money, Nobel-race money: not a cent had been allocated to the treatment of patients. During the time of my stay in New York (this was late March 1985), the old tightrope-artist Mayor Koch came across with a $6.5 million package. He was responding to countless protests and petitions; more important (according to many observers), he was responding to the fact that 1985 is election year. The truth is that the New York record on AIDS compares woefully with that of San Francisco, which has long been a coordinated network of treatment and educational services, everything from bereave-ment-counselling to meals-on-wheels. San Francisco has also taken the controversial step of closing the gay bathhouses, by order of the health

authorities. The *Village Voice* claimed that Koch has always been terrified
of any association, pro or anti, with the gay cause. Remember the slogan:
'Vote for Cuomo, Not the Homo'? Koch quickly denounced this 'slander'
as 'vile' and 'outrageous' – also 'irrelevant'. His confusions are plain enough;
but so are those of the gay population, which remains as brittle and frag-
mented as any other stratum in this volatile city, the city of the omni-
partisan.

In New York you will find every permutation of human response to the
AIDS crisis. The bathhouses are still open here, and commercialised gay sex
is still big business. Many gays see any move to limit their activity as an
attack on the civil-rights front, an attempt to isolate, to 'pathologise'. More
extreme are the 'disco dummies' who, even after contracting AIDS themselves, maintain or actually increase their sexual output. You hear talk of
'medical scenarios' in the bathhouses; you hear talk of sado-masochistic
routines featuring AIDS as the ultimate 'sex death'; you hear talk of just about
everything. The heterosexual community has reacted more predictably: the
National Gay Task Force estimates incidents of violent harassment at about
a thousand a month.

Throughout the history of sexual disease, injunctions to enforce celibacy
or monogamy have never had the slightest effect. Then again, the stakes
have never been so high. It is quite clear from statistics on routine complaints
like gonorrhoea (down 50 per cent in some studies) that sexual activity has
drastically decreased. Plainly a lot of thought and lively improvisation, has
already gone into this matter. Strategies include libido-suppressors and
vitamin combinations, stress-reduction seminars, 'jerk-off' circles and
closed groups of 'clear' gays. There are even Orgiasts Anonymous services,
where a sponsor 'talks you down' from an urge to visit the bathhouse. Such
expedients may seem bizarre to the straight world. But that is because the
straight world expects the gay man to follow its own sexual master-mould.
And he doesn't. Homosexuality isn't a *version* of heterosexuality. It is something else again.

The consoling idea of the quietly monogamous gay couple is an indolent
and sentimental myth. With a large number of exceptions, and all sorts of
varieties of degree, it just isn't like that. Friendship, companionship, fellowship – these are paramount; but pairing-and-bonding on the wedlock model
is our own dated fiction. Gay lovers seldom maintain any sexual interest in
each other for more than a year or two. The relationship may remain 'focal',
may well be lifelong, yet the sex soon reverts to the 'distributive'.

Gay men routinely achieve feats of promiscuity that the most fanatical
womaniser could only whistle at. In the heterosexual world you might
encounter the odd champion satyromaniac who – doing nothing else, all his
life – accumulates perhaps a thousand conquests. On some fringes of the
gay world (where a man might average ninety 'contacts' a month) you could
reach this total in less than a year. In the right club or bathhouse, you could
have sex with half a dozen different men without once exchanging a word.

However this may be, the median number of sexual partners for gay
American AIDS patients is over eleven hundred. The exponential leap is
easily explained. Most obviously, both actors in the sexual drama have the
same role; they are both hunters, and can dispense with the usual preliminaries and reassurances (try taking someone to the opera ninety times a

week). Also the gay man, more often than not, is making up for lost time. Throughout his youth he has felt excluded, unstable – illegal; even as an adult much of his daily life is spent incognito, in imitation of a mainstream citizen; but at night he joins an extraverted and hedonistic brotherhood. You could cite genetic factors too. Just as the gay woman seems to exemplify the usual feminine imperatives (monogamy, inconspicuousness, site-tenacity), so the gay man, in equally intense, redoubled form, does as his DNA tells him: he is mobile, aggressive and disseminatory.

There is certainly a political dimension also, as many gay leaders claim. In America, homosexuality is illegal in twenty-three states plus the District of Columbia. In England we have the consenting-adults package: no sex until you are twenty-one, no 'public' sex in clubs and bars, and no group-sex whatever (even troilism is indictable). Despite much harassment and entrapment, those provisos are quite clearly unenforceable. Naturally, then, there is defiance involved, and celebration of the gains already made. Some gay activists even argue that the sexual liberation has worked as an opiate, deflecting the movement from progress of a more tangible kind.

'For fifteen years, we all had a party.' It was a time of dazzling freedoms and self-discoveries. In their new world, the distinctions of class, race, money and privilege were all triumphantly erased. Of course there were the expected perils and boredoms of any long party – the occupational hazard known as feeling 'gayed out'. How many more times (the gay man would wonder) will I wake up to hear myself saying, 'Well, Clint/Skip/Didier/Luigi/Piotr/Basim, what brings you to our fair land?' But the great mix was, on the whole, a vivid and innocuous adventure, one that seemed to redress many past confusions. 'It was so good,' as I was told many times, 'that you couldn't help thinking how it was going to end.'

There has been understandable resistance to the idea that AIDS is 'caused' by promiscuity. 'Life-styles don't kill people – germs do', says the New York pamphlet (perhaps a conscious echo of the National Rifle Association's maxim, 'Guns don't kill people – people do'). One vein of paranoia extends to the view that the epidemic was initiated by the CIA as a form of biological warfare. Certainly the profile of the high-risk groups - the 5-H club – is politically effaced. As Larry Kramer, the author of one of five plays about AIDS recently staged in Manhattan, has pointed out: 'The lowliest of streetsweeper associations has twenty-five lobbyists in Washington, and we [24 million Americans] have one part-timer.' If the AIDS virus had chosen, say, real-estate agents or young mothers for attack, then the medical and social context would now look very different. Yet AIDS has chosen homo-sexual men. The proportion will certainly decrease (and the African epidemic has shown no sexual preference at all), but so far it has remained fairly steady at around 70 per cent.

Throughout the past decade, in New York, gay men were oppressed by an escalating series of health hazards. To begin with, crabs, gonorrhoea and syphilis, the ancient enemies. Then herpes, then cytomegalovirus, then gay-bowel syndrome, then hepatitis B. All venereal diseases compromise the immune system. And so, crucially, does semen. The vagina is evolutionarily designed to deactivate the antigens in semen, the foreign elements which stimulate the production of antibodies. The rectum does the opposite: it is designed to withdraw water from faeces, and so efficiently absorbs antigenic matter through the rectal walls. At each reception the immune system goes on red alert. Ironically, it too becomes paranoid. Repeated reception, repeated infection and repeated trauma prolong the crisis until the cells lose the capacity to correct their own over-corrections. The analogy is as much with cervical cancer as with standard sexual disease. Again, the double bind. It seems that there is a 'natural' – i.e. viciously arbitrary – limit to trauma, to bodily invasion.

There are two lines of thought. One is the single-factor or new-virus theory. This has always been more acceptable to the gay population because it passes no verdict and necessitates no change. The second theory is multi-factorial, the theory of immune-overload, which was immediately perceived in America as 'judgemental', suggesting also that the visitation of AIDS was not a bolt from the blue but a process or a journey. The virus – a retrovirus of a type found only in animals – has been cautiously identified. Yet it seems clear that the two theories are not mutually exclusive; indeed, they go hand in hand.

The secret may lie in an uncertainty principle, in the balance or *potentia* between two factors; the strength of the virus and the weakness of the host. A damaged immune system is susceptible to the AIDS virus, which then destroys that system, so inviting opportunistic infection. Some epidemiologists believe that AIDS is an ancient and world-wide disease of poverty (ineradicable by medicine alone), given passage into society at large through the incubation chambers of the bathhouses. In a sense, perhaps AIDS itself is opportunistic. This is the double jeopardy.

The Gay Men's Health Crisis Centre is just off rugged Eighth Avenue; but the offices are neat, modern, positively *bijou*. Up on the bulletin board is a list of the day's meetings: Volunteer Moral Committee, Care Partner Group One. There are bottle-glass partitions, basketed plants. I asked for the AIDS-information kit and was given a hefty dossier of facts and figures, do's and don'ts, posters and leaflets. The soft-voiced, tiptoeing advisers talk to the worried supplicants, like waiters in a gentle gay restaurant. 'Win With Us', says the slogan on the donation tin. 'We're Winning', says a pamphlet, '... Together. We're winning ... Through Respect'. There are buddy programs, therapy groups, crisis counsellors, PR men. 'Our community keeps on fighting. Keeps on caring. Keeps on loving.' Here they are coping in the American way.

Meanwhile, everything has changed. *Being gay* – which Americans call a life-choice, and which we might perhaps call a destiny – is a different proposition now. But so is the other route, as AIDS becomes a part of the heterosexual experience. The liberation of coitus, the rutting revolution, has probably entered its last phase. When the danger is ultimate, then every risk is ultimate also. It is *over*.

Despite new genetic technologies, any cure or prevention is probably some way ahead. 'We have anti-virals which *seem* to inhibit the retrovirus which *seems* to have a linchpin role,' I was informed at the AIDS Medical Foundation in New York. 'Prospects are uncertain bordering on grim.' The vaccine for hepatitis B took seventeen years.

But some hope can be rescued from the mess, the human disaster of

AIDS. The disease will probably obey Darwinian rules and seek an evolution-arily stable strategy, becoming less virulent, non-fatal. The cure, when and if it comes, will revolutionise medicine. Sexual relations of all kinds will soften, and the emphasis will shift from performance, from sexual muscle. Gay leaders prudently stress the need for trust, for confidentiality in the liaison between the various communities. In the short term, of course, they are absolutely right. But a better situation would clearly be one in which no confidentiality is necessary.

AIDS victims are in the forefront, at the very pinnacle of human suffering. Broadly speaking, they can do you no harm unless you elect to go to bed with them. We are in this together now. An opportunity presents itself. There is no good reason – only a lot of bad ones – why we shouldn't take it.

Derek Cooper (1988)

Derek Cooper is a writer and broadcaster on food. This article was originally published in The Listener.

If I lived in the United States for any length of time I think I might become very large. So overwhelming is the hospitality, so entrenched the virtues of 'more', that eating in moderation begins to seem almost subversive. You can see the results of over-indulgence on every street corner. Men sport paunches which, were they on women, would indicated the imminent arrival of triplets; young girls have the proportions of Donald McGill matrons.

Waiting for a flight in Atlanta recently, I observed a couple who had long since given up the battle of the bulge. They were brought up to Gate 18 on an electric courtesy car, like porkers on a cattle float. He was built like a Sumo wrestler and appeared to be breathing with difficulty. His partner, who must have weighed 25 or 30 stone, could hardly walk. What drew my attention to her was not the ballooning of her buttocks, nor the monstrous deformity of her limbs, but the fact that she was grazing enthusiastically on a Big Whopper ice-cream as large as her fist.

The scale of consumption and the implicit pressures to eat round the clock in America make you feel that your own performance at the trough verges on the anorexic. In Washington I went to a place which for the last eight years has won the Best Pizza in Town award. We settled for the buffet, which turned out to be as much pizza and salad as you could eat for just under four dollars (which represents a potentially paralysing blowout for £2.30). A queue of contented customers were leaving the counter with double portions of pizza the size of Dundee Cakes.

In the South I attended two remarkable barbecues where not piling your plate high would have seemed churlish. The first occurred at the Bronco Rod and Gun Club in a sylvan glade on the banks of a Virginia river. Smoke and sizzling rose from a grill the size of a double bed. 'Is that *all* you want?' said my host when I settled for a slice of tenderloin as big as half a loaf of bread. He looked so unhappy that I promised to return for more at the earliest opportunity.

In Georgia, a friendly peanut farmer cooked a 'pork-roast' for a few neighbours which turned out to be an entire pig the size of a small bear. One of the popular Fall blowouts, in peanut and cotton country, is the annual Shrimp Feast of the Suffolk Ruritan Club which this year was attended by 5,500 hungry Virginians. By shrimp, the Americans do not mean those under-sized brown things from Morecambe Bay but giant prawns. By the time we arrived at 3.30pm, six lines were standing three abreast in wait for these steamed hunks of seafood, fried chicken, carcases, coleslaw, potato salad and various attendant essentials which came under the heading of Bar-B-Que.

Much of the food on offer in America is excessively saccharine. The bread is so sweetened with corn syrup and industrial sugars that one bite is often enough to satisfy the appetite. At most of the alfresco picnics I attended, the proffered drinks were Coca-Cola, which I find unattractively sweet, and iced tea, which I like. But the tea always came pre-sugared.

Sugar is the national vice in the States. Even a 'gourmet meal' can be a disappointment for those who like their food to be savoury rather than sweet.

Could it be this fondness for sugar which has made America a breeding ground for the clinically obese? A question I put to an elegant nutritionist as slim as a spoon. It wasn't just sweet things, she thought, but a national inability to appreciate the causal relationship between excessive eating and overweight. 'You'll get a really fat woman and she'll say, "My, you're so pretty and thin, why am I so fat?"'. And although they've heard of calories and slimming foods, they really haven't made the connection in their own minds that it's the cookies and the candies that are actually making them so obese.'

Could it happen here? Could we become a nation of fatties? My American consultant thought it highly likely. 'If you create a society where continuous eating becomes the norm, then naturally you're going to have problems.' Snacking on rubbish has not yet reached American levels here but the food industry are working on the project with great persistence. There is, unfortunately, a lot of money to be made out of making people overweight.

Paul Johnson (1988)

This piece, 'Reading about Real America' was originally published as an article in The Spectator.

Local newspapers delight me. The more local they are, the more I love them. Unlike the nationals, which are based on strong but arbitrary subeditorial conventions, local papers have the simple news-value of ordinary men and women. They are about people, not personalities. When I go down to the country on Friday I fall eagerly on the *Bridgwater Mercury* and the *Somerset County Gazette*. My current favourite is the *West Somerset Free Press*, with its fascinating survey of all the Women's Institutes and its unselfconscious hunting notes ('The spring staghunting this season was well up to average with 10 stags being accounted for, none of which would have grown into anything useful for the herd'). Even their imperfections are endearing. Last week the *Free Press* published its entire Page 17 upside down and ran a display advertisement for an auction which had taken place the previous Thursday. For me, such peccadilloes add relish.

One of my chief pleasures in visiting the United States is the sheer abundance of local papers. There are many thousands of them; I would not be surprised if there were more local newspapers in America than in the rest of the world put together. Most are fiercely independent and opinionated. Vast numbers of them are published daily, but even the weeklies often report and comment upon national and world events as if no other paper existed. I recently spent a week teaching at a University of California campus, and found that in the inland valleys there are plenty of people who have never in their lives read the *San Francisco Chronicle* or the *Los Angeles Times*, let alone the *New York Times* or the *Washington Post*. For such readers the local paper is *the* paper, the only one they normally see. If possible, I pick up my copy at the place where it is published. In these premises, remarkably unchanged over the past half-century, you can usually see from the front office into the press shop, where grizzled comps are setting up the next issue, or into the newsroom, where the all-purpose sub, often actually wearing a green eye-shade, is thumbing over slips from what is still called the wire-service. In one of those front offices last month I was served by the editor's daughter – the authentic 19th-century touch – and in another the sale was rung up on a massive brass cash register which had been in service since the time of President McKinley.

US local papers, particularly in California, are of every conceivable political complexion. The *Davis Enterprise*, the daily serving the campus town where I stayed, is ultra-progressive, propounding all the sacred causes of donnish dottiness. It gave extensive coverage to a local professor who favours what he called 'bioregional activism', and who wants coyotes, wolves and grizzly bears reintroduced into the region: his message was 'Bring back the predators'. But all these papers, whatever their politics, have a primary commitment to community service. They print all kinds of detailed information. The *Enterprise* publishes photos of animals waiting adoption at the County Animal Shelter. The *St Helena Star*, a weekly, tells you about all the local school lunch menus:

> Monday: hot dog, junior salad bar, veggie dippers and fruit salad. Tuesday: meatball sandwich, salad, buttery corn and raisins. Wednesday: chilli and chips, salad, peanut butter and celery, and iced juice. Thursday: picnic basket, salad, buttery veggies and cherry crisp. Friday: enchilada, salad, fruit salad and peanuts. Bagel dog or spaghetti can be substituted for all entrées.

US locals are particularly good, it seems to me, at covering police activities. If the *St Helena Star* gets a letter from a reader complaining of a police action, it goes to the local policy authority, insists on a blow-by-blow report of what happened, and then prints the reader's account and the police version side by side, without comment, leaving you to judge for yourself.

I found a remonstrance from a visiting San Francisco homosexual (with AIDS) describing how he and his friend were arrested by the St Helena police, and the latter's defence, illuminating about both parties. The *Calistogan*, another weekly I studied, prints the day-by-day, hour-by-hour police incident report, which makes curiously reassuring reading. Thus:

> May 1: 1.03 a.m. A loud party was reported on Lincoln Avenue. On request, the responsibles agreed to quiet down. 2.24 a.m. Alan Johnson of Calistoga was arrested for driving under the influence of alcohol. He was booked into Napa County Jail. 1.32 p.m. A non-injury traffic collision occurred on First Street. 1.46 p.m. A medical aid was reported on Washington Street. The victim was treated at the scene. 6.56 p.m. Two persons were loitering near the elementary school. The subjects left upon the officer's request. 10.00 p.m. An officer assisted in locating a water leak at a business on First Street. The owner was contacted to abate the problem. 1.32 a.m. (May 2): A loud party was reported on Myrtle Street. The responsibles were asked to quiet down. They complied.

Many thousands of words are devoted to detailed 'Community Calendars', which reflect the extraordinary range of activities in which Californians engage. One issue of the *Napa Register* (another weekly) listed 62 events for the week, including the Men's Barbershop Harmony Chorus, Napa Valley Chapter, its female version, the Sweet Adelines Inc., and meetings of the Adolescent Grief Group, the Group for Separated and Divorced Men and Women, the Dead Serious Weight Control Group, the Abused Women's Support Group, Young People's Alcoholics Anonymous and Overeaters Anonymous. Most of the meetings take place in churches and these listings testify to the huge, active power of religion in American life but still more the American obsession with bodily health. Nearly all papers have medical columns, featuring reader's letters and answers. Thus, from the *Davis Enterprise*: 'Dear Dr Donohue: I have been told I have Zollinger-Ellison syndrome. I also have hyperparathyroidism. I also have peptic ulcers. Please comment.' The same paper ran an extensive profile of a woman official described as 'The County's New Aids Coordinator', under the title: 'She Looks for the Human Being Behind All the Needle Marks'. Americans talk and write about medical details with an openness which would make English local papers squirm. Every paper I examined had repeated references to local events, chiefly, 'Open Forums', on the problems of menopause. Another common theme was the growth of 'support groups for relationship addiction', accompanied by fierce arguments about whether such meetings should be single-sex or mixed.

Local papers take you close to the real America in all its touching and neurotic diversity. Despite all the critical fuss about Nancy Reagan's astrologer, I notice that virtually all US papers give space to star-guides. Indeed, every American I questioned on this last trip became shifty on the subject. Reading local newspapers suggests that in this, as in countless other respects, the Reagans are a typical American family.

Acknowledgements

The author and publishers gratefully acknowledge permission to reproduce copyright material in this book.

Svetlana Allileuluyeva (trans. Paul Chavadchadza): from *Svetlana Allileuluyeva* (Century Hutchinson Publishing Group Ltd, 1970). Reprinted by permission of Century Hutchinson Publishing Group Ltd.

Martin Amis: from *The Moronic Inferno* (Jonathan Cape Ltd). Reprinted by permission of the Peters Fraser & Dunlop Group Ltd.

Mark Amory (Ed.): from *The Letters Of Anne Fleming* (Collins Publishers). Reprinted by permission of Collins Publishers.

Cecil Beaton: from *Diaries* (George Weidenfeld & Nicolson Ltd). Reprinted by permission of George Weidenfeld & Nicolson Ltd.

Brendan Behan: from *New York* (Century Hutchinson Publishing Group Ltd). Reprinted by permission of Century Hutchinson Publishing Group Ltd.

Stephen Brook: from *New York Days, New York Nights* (Hamish Hamilton Ltd). Reprinted by permission of Hamish Hamilton Ltd.

James Cameron: from *Point Of Departure* (*The Guardian*). Reprinted by permission of *The Guardian*.

Charles Chaplin: from *My Autobiography* (The Bodley Head). Reprinted by permission of Random House UK Ltd.

Paul H. Chapman: from *The Man Who Led Columbus To America* (Judson Press of Georgia). Reprinted by permission of One Candle Press.

Chateaubriand: from *Voyage To America* (Hamish Hamilton Ltd). Reprinted by permission of Hamish Hamilton Ltd.

Nicholas Coleridge: from *Around The World in 78 Days* (William Heinemann Ltd). Reprinted by permission of William Heinemann Ltd.

Derek Cooper: from an article (*The Listener*). Reprinted by permission of *The Listener*.

Noël Coward: from *Autobiography* (Methuen). Reprinted by permission of Methuen, a division of Octopus Publishing Group.

Emma Goldman: from *Living My Life* (Duckworth). Reprinted by permission of Duckworth.

Graham Greene: from *Ways of Escape* (Jonathan Cape). Reprinted by permission of Lester Opren & Dennys, Canada.

Alec Guinness: from *Blessings In Disguise* (Hamish Hamilton Ltd). Reprinted by permission of Hamish Hamilton Ltd.

Herbert Hodge: from *A Cockney On Main Street* (Michael Joseph Ltd).

Christopher Isherwood: from *Christopher And His Kind* (Candida Donadio & Associates Inc).

Paul Johnson: from *Reading About The Real America* (*The Spectator*, 4 July 1988). Reprinted by permission of *The Spectator*.

Carl Jung (trans. R. F. C. Hull): from *The Collected Works of C. G. Jung*, Bollingen Series 20, Vol. 10; Civilization in Transition (Princeton University Press). Reprinted by permission of Princeton University Press.